A Century in Focus

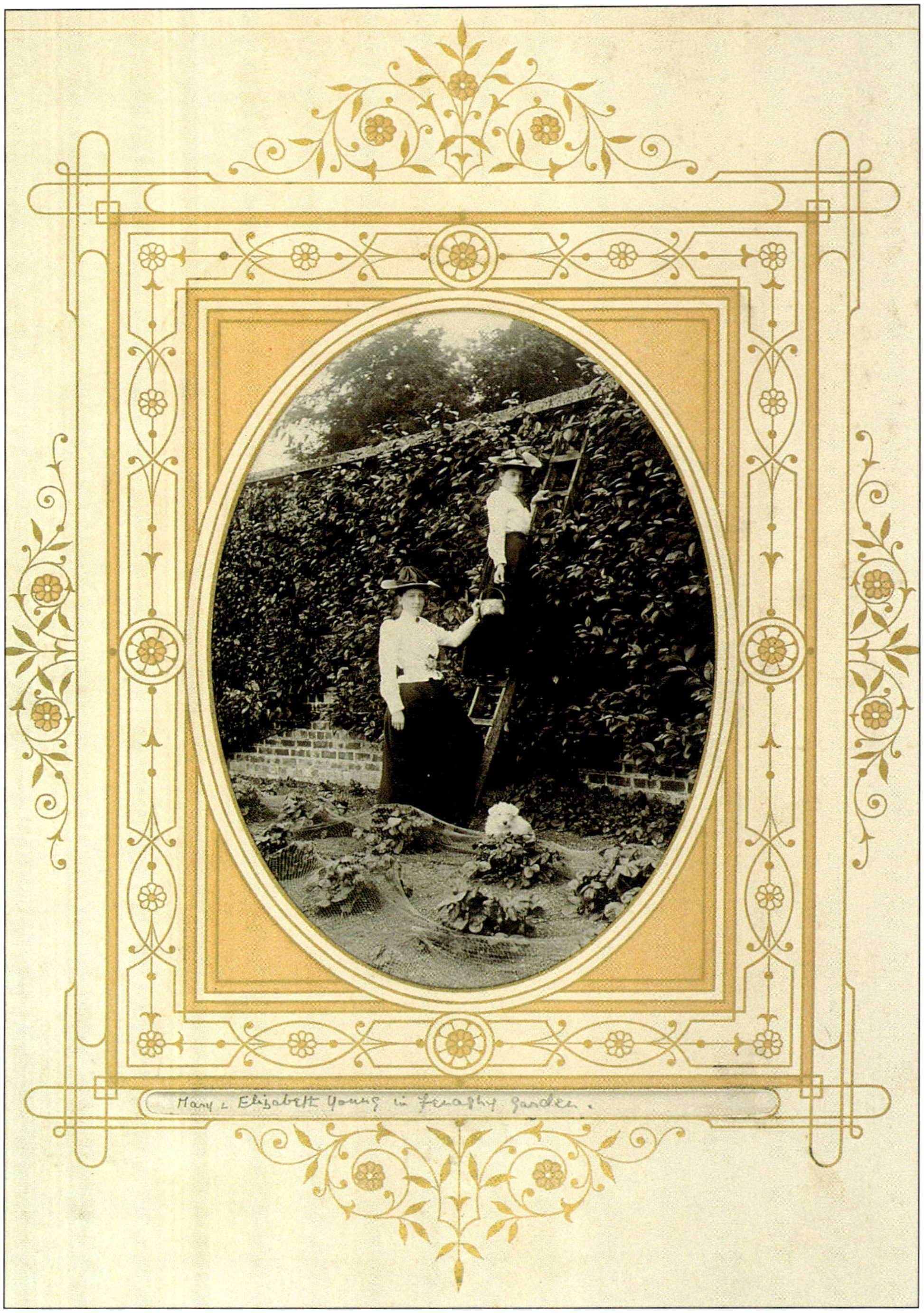

Mary and Elizabeth Young in the garden at Fenaghy House, County Antrim, *c.* 1900, by an unknown amateur photographer.

BY KIND PERMISSION OF MRS ANNA STEWART

A Century in Focus

PHOTOGRAPHY AND PHOTOGRAPHERS
IN THE NORTH OF IRELAND
1839–1939

W.A. MAGUIRE

THE
BLACKSTAFF PRESS
BELFAST

MUSEUMS AND GALLERIES OF NORTHERN IRELAND
(ULSTER MUSEUM)

Note on illustrations

Most of the illustrations used in this book come from the collections of the Museums and Galleries of Northern Ireland (MAGNI), either in the Ulster Museum, Belfast or in the Ulster Folk and Transport Museum, Cultra, Holywood. These have been supplemented by photographs from the collections of the Public Record Office of Northern Ireland, Belfast, and by a small number belonging to private owners who have kindly allowed the Ulster Museum to copy them. Enquiries about the collections should be made as follows: for the R.J. Welch, A.R. Hogg and F.J. Bigger collections, the Ulster Museum; for the W.A. Green, Harland and Wolff, Dundee (McKinney) and Rose Shaw Collections, the Ulster Folk and Transport Museum; for the Allison, Annesley, Cooper and Young Collections, the Public Record Office of Northern Ireland.

Prints of photographs from the Museum collections may be ordered from the two institutions concerned. The Ulster Museum can also supply prints of selected photographs from PRONI's Annesley and Young Collections. Permission to use prints for publication of any kind must be sought from the owners, who hold reproduction rights.

First published in 2000 by
The Blackstaff Press Limited
Wildflower Way, Apollo Road
Belfast BT12 6TA
and the Museums and Galleries of Northern Ireland (Ulster Museum)

Typeset by Techniset Typesetters, Newton-le-Willows, Merseyside

Printed in Ireland by Betaprint

A CIP catalogue record for this book
is available from the British Library

ISBN 0-85640-679-1

www.blackstaffpress.com

In memory of Laura,
who loved photographs

Contents

Acknowledgements

In the course of accumulating material for this book, and more recently in writing it and preparing it for publication, I have drawn heavily on the knowledge and co-operation of many people outside the Ulster Museum. So far as other institutions are concerned, I am particularly indebted to the Deputy Keeper of the Records, Public Record Office of Northern Ireland, and his staff (especially Dr David Lammey); the Royal Photographic Society, Bath (Debbie Ireland and Claire Bertrand); the National Library of Ireland, Dublin (Gráinne MacLochlainn and Bob Monks); the National Museum of Photography, Film and Television, Bradford (Michael Harvey); the Linen Hall Library, Belfast (John Killen); and the Environment and Heritage Service, Department of the Environment for Northern Ireland (Anne Given and Gail Pollock).

Illustrations and/or permission to use them were provided by the following individuals: Dr Eileen Black, William Coleman, Mrs Brenda Collins, Allen Coon, Dr Marjorie Houston, James Kilpatrick, Sir James Langham, Bt., Michael McCaughan, Mrs P. McLean, J.S.D. Madden, A.W. Merrick, J.D. Quail and Mrs Anna Stewart. Valuable source material was provided by John Martin and Dr D.B. McNeill. Dr Peadar Slattery's as yet unpublished thesis, 'The uses of photography in Ireland, 1839–1900', proved to be a mine of information about the first sixty years of the period under review.

In addition to those already mentioned, many others have contributed by answering my queries or taking trouble on my behalf. They include Malcolm Brodie, Mrs Kyleen Clarke, Dr Eull Dunlop, Mrs Gwyneth Evans, Desmond Fitzgerald, Joanna Gault, Hugh Gillespie, Mrs Mary Goodrich, Trevor Green, Dr Rosemary Hughes, Jack Johnston, Roy Lilley, Fred Logan, Dr Charles Ludlow, John McCabe, Judith McCarthy, Eugene Markey, Noel Mitchel, Sean Nolan, Mrs Marguerite Ogilvie, Gerry Quinn, Fred Rankin, Jim Rankin, David Speers, Edward Sterling, Mrs Sally Stevenson, Tom Sullivan, Tom Thompson, Dr B.S. Turner,

Roger Weatherup and Helen Lanigan Wood.

Lastly, it is my pleasure as well as my duty to thank the many colleagues and friends, in what is now the Museums and Galleries of Northern Ireland, who have contributed in various ways to the completion of this book. Deirdre Crone provided the drawings. All the photographes used for the illustrations, except the aerial view of Lyles Hill, were taken and/or printed by the photographic staff of the Ulster Museum (Bill Anderson-Porter, Michael Keown and Bryan Rutledge) or the Ulster Folk and Transport Museum (Ken Anderson and George Wright, with thanks also to Roger Dixon and Sally Skilling). Martin Anglesea, Dr Eileen Black, Kenneth James and Elizabeth McCrum were generous when approached for help and advice. The staff of the History division at the Ulster Museum – Richard Warner, Trevor Parkhill, Robert Heslip, Catherine McCullough, Dr Vivienne Pollock, Tom Wylie and Jane Leonard – all went out of their way to assist; Dr Pollock, curator of photographs, and Robert Heslip, numismatist and polymath, were especially plagued and especially helpful. Finally, as on many previous occasions, my grateful thanks are due to Pauline Dickson, who produced the text with efficiency and good humour. It has been a pleasure to work with all of these people. If the book succeeds, all concerned may claim some of the credit. Any shortcomings are the author's alone.

Preface

The invention of photography was one of the scientific and technological marvels of the Victorian age. Both the French daguerreotype and the English calotype soon ceased to be merely (or only) of scientific interest and became the basis of a lucrative profession on the one hand and a new art-form on the other. From the 1840s to the 1880s, as one of its most respected practitioners pointed out, anyone wanting to succeed as a photographer needed to be an artist, a chemist and a mechanical engineer. As a result, the new medium was for forty years the preserve of people with time and money to invest, namely well-to-do amateurs with artistic aims or 'professionals whose short cuts through the technical difficulties enabled them to produce portraits on what was virtually an assembly line'.[1]

After 1880, the invention of the dry plate and other innovations, such as Kodak cameras and roll film, transformed photography for both amateurs and professionals, making it still more profitable and for the first time truly popular. In England and Wales the number of professional photographers rose from 7,614 to 12,397 between the censuses of 1881 and 1891; and by 1905 it was reckoned that about one-tenth of the population had become occasional users of a camera. The proportion in Ireland was no doubt lower, but the trend was the same. Photography thus became more widely established as an economic fact of life, as well as a leading form of recreation.

The financial profile of a few of the professional photographers mentioned in these pages receives some passing notice, in reference to their estates at the time of death. Often, however, such information is not available (or may not exist, because only those with something substantial to leave went to the trouble and expense of making a will). The virtual anonymity of many photographers, and their restless flitting from one location to another in search of a living, make it difficult to carry out any systematic investigation into the profession's economic and social standing.

Nor has it proved possible to add anything significant to the long-running debate as to whether professional photography could aspire to the status of art or was, rather, essentially an activity for mere technicians and shrewd businessmen. One can only point to some few true (if minor) local examples of 'artist photographers' such as Felix Piccione and Harry H. Douglas, to be distinguished from the many journeymen who claimed that distinction.

The choice of an end date for the period covered by this study is a somewhat arbitrary one. It can be justified, however, on the grounds that the practice of photography was indeed seriously interrupted by the Second World War, while the recent deaths of Robert Welch and Alex Hogg had brought to an end an era in northern photography. The starting date presents no such difficulty: Francis Beatty, that ingenious Belfast engraver, was there at the very outset of the new phenomenon. For that reason alone the story is worth telling. It is all the greater pity that we have none of his original work, and know almost nothing about the man himself apart from the bare facts of his death and pauper funeral.

The main purpose of this book is to supply a context for the study of Irish photographic history at a local level and to provide help of a practical nature to anyone who, for any reason, has to deal with old photographs relating to this part of Ireland and needs to be able to date and place them. Essentially, my excuse for adding to the ever-growing number of photographic publications is that nothing of this kind exists already.

Colin Ford and Brian Harrison, *A Hundred Years Ago: Britain in the 1880s in Words and Photographs* (London, 1983), pp. 9–16.

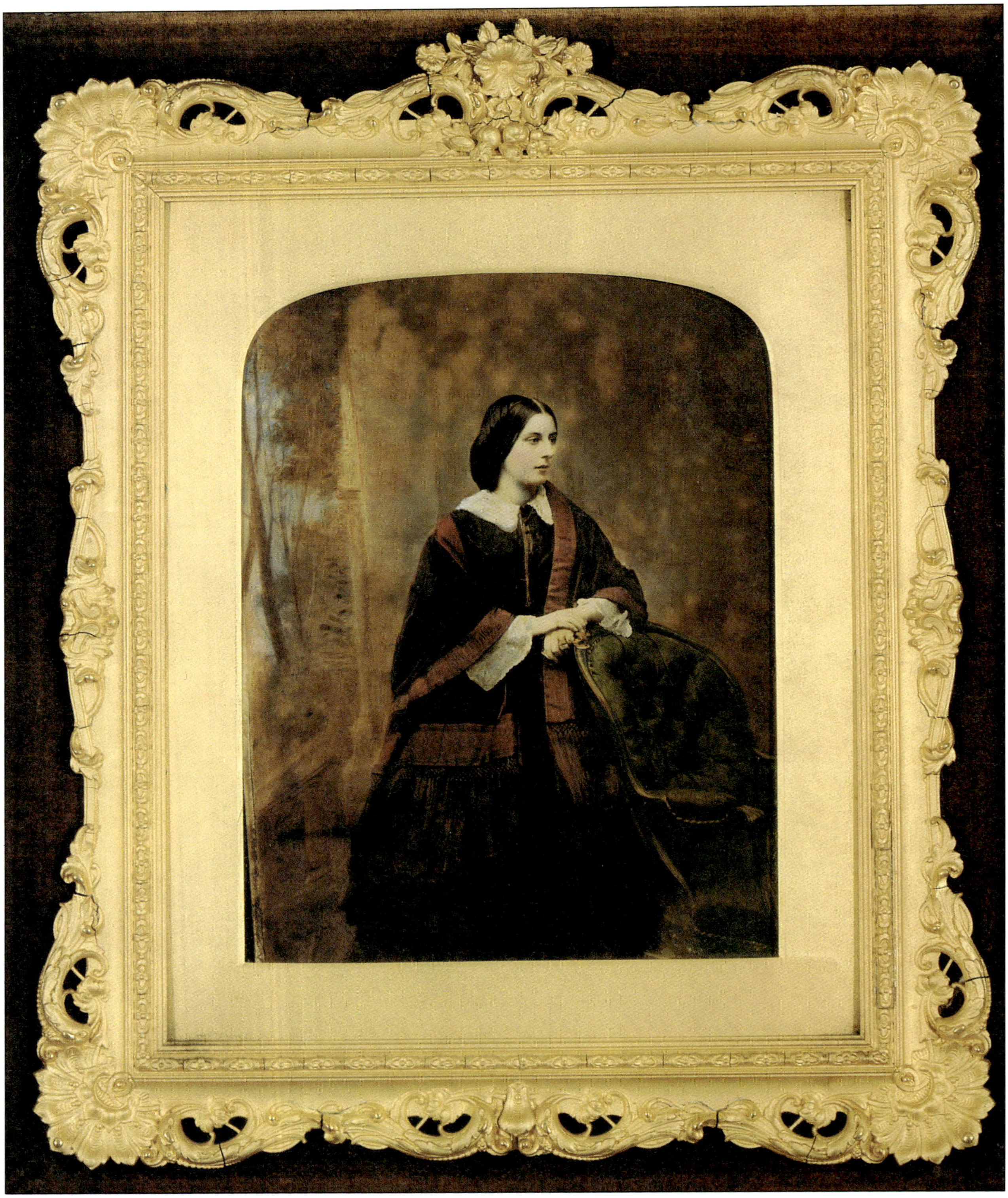

Early days
1839–c. 1860

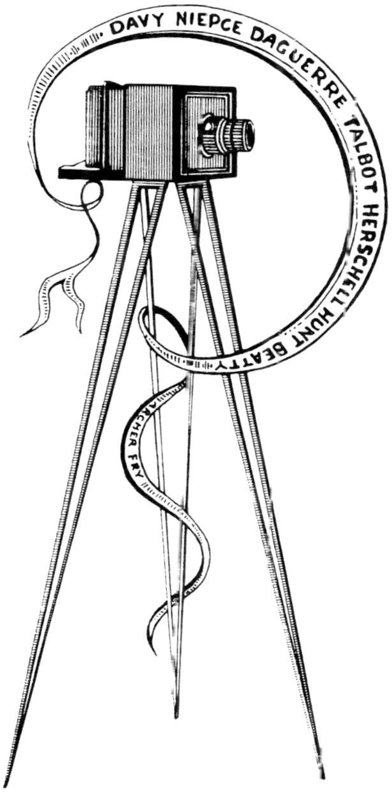

For all practical purposes, photography began in 1839. In January of that year Louis Daguerre, in France, and William Henry Fox Talbot, in England, announced the discovery of two different methods of recording and permanently fixing images seen through the aperture of a camera. The first, called the daguerreotype after its inventor, produced a single, unique image directly onto a sheet of copper plated with silver. The second, which Talbot at first called photogenic drawing but later (when he had improved it) renamed the calotype or Talbotype, produced a negative which was then used to make any number of positive prints on paper. Though the daguerreotype was at first the more successful – because it enabled professional photographers to produce high-quality portraits – the future of photography was to lie with the negative–positive process.[1]

Hand-coloured photograph, one of a pair dated 1857, of Mrs Elizabeth Archdall (née Stewart), wife of Captain Hugh Montgomery Archdall, Drumdravy, County Fermanagh.
BY KIND PERMISSION OF DR MARJORIE HOUSTON

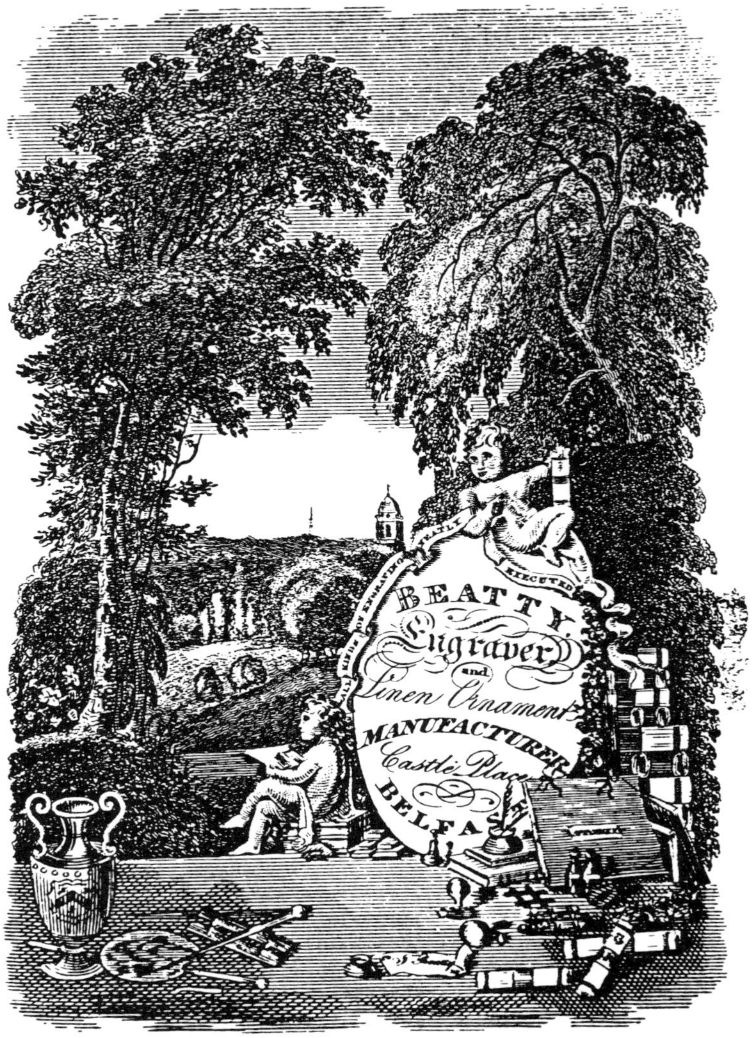

Advertisement for Francis S. Beatty's engraving and printing business, from *Simms and McIntyre's Northern or Belfast Almanack* (Belfast, 1836). Beatty's premises were at 17 Castle Place, 'three doors from the Donegall Arms'. His technical skills, allied to an enquiring mind, made him the pioneer of photography in Ireland three years later.

FRANCIS BEATTY
An Irish pioneer

Belfast, at that time a growing town of seventy thousand people, first heard about these exciting developments on 19 February 1839, when the *Belfast News-Letter* reprinted the *Spectator*'s account of Daguerre's discovery. Daguerre's manual describing the manipulation needed to produce a successful daguerreotype did not appear until 20 August 1839 and its first English edition was not published until 13 September. Yet only a week later, on 20 September, the *Belfast News-Letter* printed a communication entitled 'The Daguerreotype' from Francis S. Beatty,[2] a local engraver and linen ornament manufacturer, which revealed that he had been experimenting with the new medium since its announcement.[3] 'After a number of experiments', he wrote:

> I was somewhat surprised to find that in using silver paper the effect was different from silver plated on copper, although treated in a similar manner. Silver plated on copper gives the true effect of light and shade, while silver on paper gives the opposite, namely, the light parts of the subject are dark, and the dark shades are in a proportionate degree light. In order to convince you of the fact, I send you a specimen; but our days of late having been cloudy, you cannot expect it to be as perfect as I would wish.

What Beatty was describing was in fact a paper negative. Nearly twenty years later, in an anonymous article for the *Dublin Journal*, he said as much: 'In September, 1839, Mr. F.S. Beatty submitted to the public, specimens taken on paper . . . These pictures were negatives, such as are now produced for printing from.'[4]

Beatty's was the first successful permanent image produced in Ireland, he himself the first Irish photographer. He did not say, and we do not know, what his subject was in this first attempt in the exciting new medium. Subsequently, in the autumn of 1839 and in the following year, he produced daguerreotypes of Belfast buildings and of the old Long Bridge spanning the River Lagan. A note published in the local press on 6 August 1840, under the heading 'The Daguerreotype', runs as follows:

> Our ingenious and indefatigable townsman, Mr F.S. Beatty, has produced another photogenic drawing of a portion of the now fast-fading Long Bridge of Belfast [it was taken down in 1841, to be replaced by the Queen's Bridge], taken from the Western bank of the river. It is a beautiful specimen of the art which Mr Beatty is pursuing so successfully, and shows a progress towards perfection, which talent, taste, and close application alone could achieve. As an instructor in the use of the 'pencil of light' (literally), Mr Beatty's productions in this line are sufficient testimonials of his abilities.

The use of the term 'photogenic drawing' indicates that Beatty had been using Talbot's process rather than Daguerre's, despite the heading. The photographs he was advertising for sale in 1840, however, were daguerreotype views of the Long Bridge; he also offered to sell the apparatus used and to instruct purchasers in how to use it. 'The above view may be seen at F. S. Beatty's Engraving Establishment, No. 2 Donegall Street . . .' he added.[5]

Many years later, in an article published in the *Photographic News*, Beatty described his first attempts to master the daguerreotype:

> Ever watchful then, as well as now, to investigate into any new discovery that may be useful and beneficial to the advance of science or art, I resolved at once to exercise what ability I possessed to accomplish what M. Daguerre had

> discovered, and proceeded to work at the problem, being at the time an amateur optician, chemist and careful manipulator (my profession being an engraver). After many failures and up-hill work, I was much surprised when I succeeded in my object to my entire satisfaction, as a letter of mine dated 20th September, 1839, published in the Belfast News-Letter of that date will show . . .[6]

Later still, Beatty recorded his recollections of these early experiments in more detail:

> In 1839, with the object glass of a small telescope 1½ inches diameter, and 16 inches focus, I found it necessary, in order to produce representations of public buildings, to expose fully fifteen minutes, so that the original process was useless for obtaining portraits of the living model. Public buildings, plaster busts, and other stationary objects executed with this object glass of mine were very beautiful and admired by all who saw them. The size of plate was 6 x 8 [inches] being silver plated on copper highly polished; they were manufactured by me, as there was no photographic dealer or manufacturer at that period to supply anything belonging to the infant art.[7]

Beatty's amateur optical efforts enabled him to reduce the exposure time of the daguerreotype by grinding and polishing what he described as 'a concave mirror of

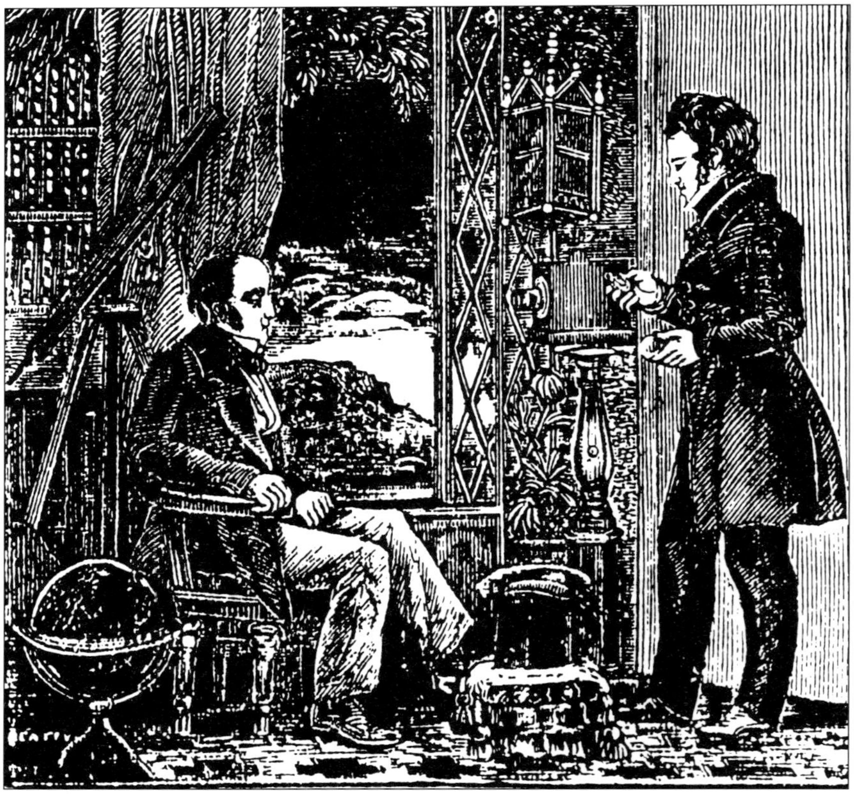

Wood engraving by Francis Beatty, showing a daguerreotype photographer at work. Beatty reversed the image, previously published in the *Illustrated London News* in 1843, and adapted it for use in his article on photography in the *Belfast Penny Journal* (1845) by adding a view of Cave Hill in the background. The original daguerreotype is now in the National Museum of Photography, Film and Television, Bradford.

LINEN HALL LIBRARY, WITH THANKS ALSO TO MICHAEL McCAUGHAN.

short focus in speculum metal'. This was the improvement that Alexander Woolcot of New York patented in May 1840. (In Woolcot's mirror camera, the lens was replaced by a concave mirror which reflected the image onto a 2-by-2-inch plate, greatly increasing the amount of light received and reducing the length of exposure required; daguerreotype portraits thus became possible. The mirror was in due course superseded by the greatly improved lenses used in later cameras.) By way of advertisement, Beatty's efforts enabled him to produce his first portrait in 1841. As a result, he was invited to work in London for Richard Beard, the wealthy coal merchant who had purchased the patent rights of the daguerreotype for England and Wales and had opened in March 1841 in Regent Street the first commercial portrait studio in Europe. Beard subsequently offered Beatty the post of operator in the gallery he proposed to open in Dublin, but they disagreed about terms. Since Beard's patent rights did not in fact extend to Ireland, Beatty decided, instead, to set up a portrait studio of his own. In August 1842 he sold his engraving business and the following October opened his daguerreotype establishment at 22 Castle Street, Belfast. Beatty ingeniously copied an engraving showing a daguerreotypist at work and adapted it for Belfast by adding a background scene featuring Cave Hill overlooking the town. The illustration was subsequently used to introduce an article on the history of photography in the *Belfast Penny Journal* in 1845; in fact the article was the first item in the first issue. Another illustration in the article depicts 'F.S. Beatty's improved Achromatic and Periscopic Camera, for Daguerreotype Portraiture'. These illustrations, and a reference in the text, make it virtually certain that the article, though anonymous, was written by Beatty himself.

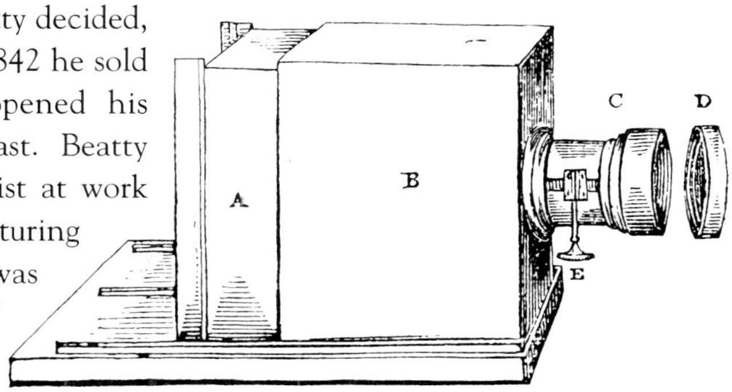

Beatty's improved daguerreotype camera, as described by himself in the *Belfast Penny Journal* in 1845.
LINEN HALL LIBRARY

Incidentally, Beatty employs a local example in the article when extolling the daguerreotype as the best form of portraiture:

> Daguerreotype portraiture is inimitable. It is evident no living artist can produce pencillings so true and faithful; but science has called into action the finger of nature herself . . . who has inscribed upon her productions not the words, 'painted by Hawksett and engraved by Beatty', but 'painted by light and engraved by electricity!'[8]

Daguerreotypes were expensive, however, and Beatty's business did not thrive in what was still a comparatively small town dominated by a sober middle class reluctant to spend money on frivolities – or at any rate to spend more than the cost of the average painted miniature. Even Dublin, which had both a much larger

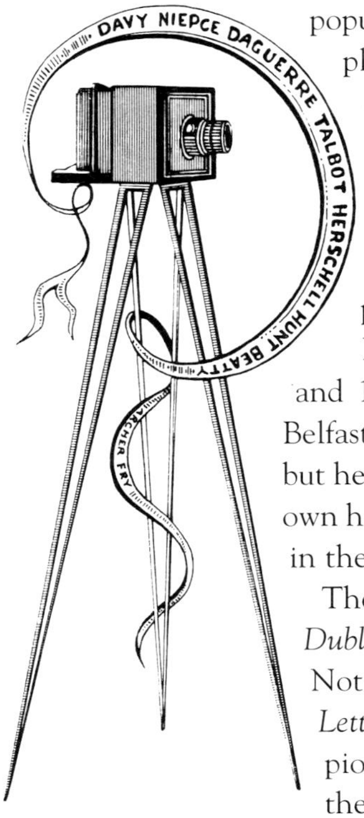

Capital letter P, devised and engraved by Francis Beatty for his article on photography published in the *Dublin Journal* in 1858; redrawn by Deirdre Crone.

MAGNI / UM

No shrinking violet, Beatty included his own name among those of the pioneers listed on the ribbon: English scientists Davy and Herschel; French photographers Niépce and Daguerre; Talbot (inventor of the calotype); Archer (inventor of the collodion process); and Hunt (author of the first English treatise on photography in 1841). The more obscure Fry – small fry indeed in this company – was presumably Peter Wicken Fry (d. 1860), who founded the Photographic Society.

population and a much higher proportion of potential clients, was a difficult place for early photographers. The first studio there, at the Rotunda, established (possibly by Beard) in October 1841, had changed hands by the following February; the new owner, a Frenchman calling himself Le Chevalier Dubreuil, went bankrupt in 1844. A second studio, in Lower Sackville Street, founded by the Scotsman H.W. Treffry, was gone by 1842 – less than a year after it had appeared. If Dublin could scarcely support two photographers, no wonder Belfast could not support even one.

Beatty's name does not appear in the Belfast directories published in 1843 and 1846; he had evidently moved away, possibly to Dublin. He was back in Belfast by 1850 and listed in the directory as living in lodgings at 24 Gordon Street, but he was not employed as either engraver or photographer (or at any rate did not own his own business). Thereafter he disappeared again, surfacing briefly in Dublin in the mid-1850s as proprietor of a studio in St Stephen's Green.

The authoritative article entitled 'The science of photography', published in the *Dublin Journal* in 1858, though anonymous, is almost certainly the work of Beatty. Not only does it quote in full his letter of 20 September 1839 to the *Belfast News-Letter*, but his name appears along with those of Daguerre, Talbot and other pioneers of photography in the design of the engraved capital letter with which the article begins. He was also involved in early experiments in photo-lithography during these years, for in 1860 he and a partner took out a patent for the process. In the 1880s he was listed in the Dublin directories as a patent agent. A bachelor all his life, he died a pauper in the North Dublin workhouse in 1891, aged eighty-four, and was buried in an unmarked grave in Mount Jerome cemetery. His death certificate gave his occupation as 'engraver'.

No original photographs known to be by Beatty survive, so we have no means of judging the quality of his work. One early image has been tentatively identified from circumstantial evidence, however – a portrait said to be that of the 2nd Marquis of Donegall, taken about 1843. This photograph now exists only as an illustration in an article by a local antiquarian, Isaac Ward, published in 1912, where we are told that the original photograph was a calotype which was subsequently copied onto a glass negative; Ward had this copy, which has since vanished. The photograph shows an elderly man seated on a white horse, which is held by a groom, in front of the entrance to a classical house, said to be Ormeau House, Lord Donegall's residence near Belfast. The sitter almost certainly was Donegall. Apart from the resemblance to known portraits, he was living in Belfast at the time, had a lively interest in what went on in the town and might well have co-operated in this novel venture. The place, however, was certainly not Ormeau House, which was in the Elizabethan style. The likely – and much more plausible

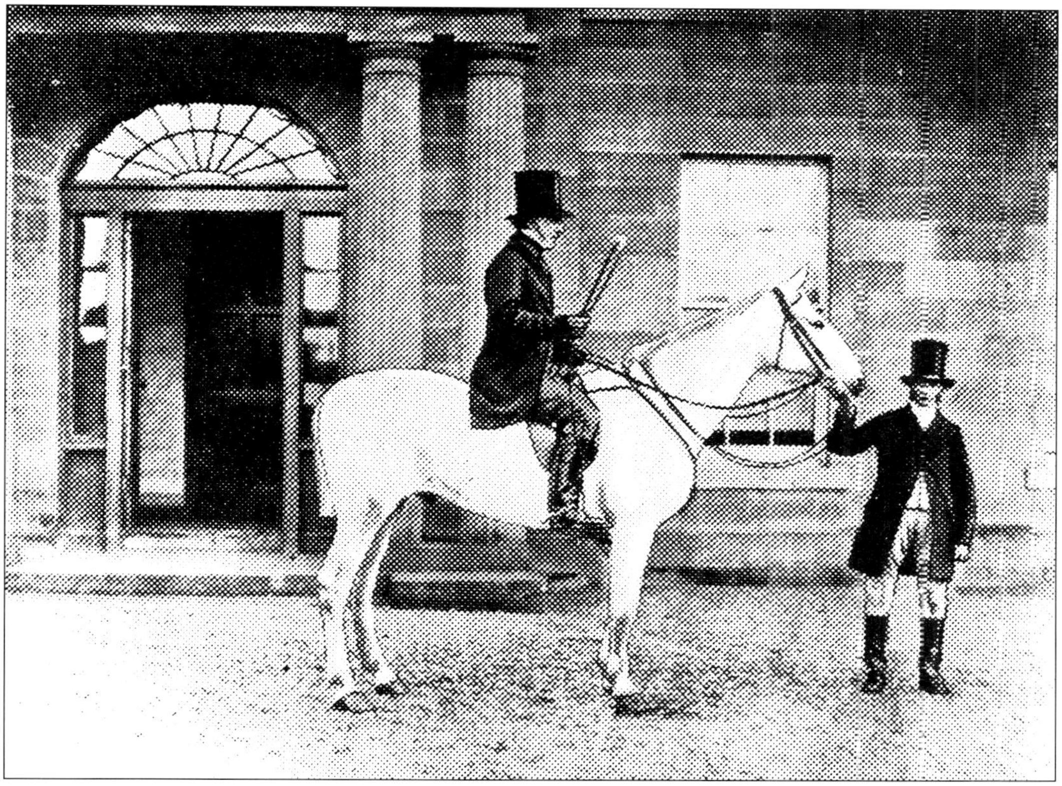

– venue was the house at the corner of Donegall Place and Castle Street, formerly the residence of the Collector of Customs (an appointment held for many years by Donegall's nephew Sir Stephen May). By 1843 the house had become the premises of the Agricultural Bank. Set well back from its frontage on Donegall Place, it still had the space in front which would soon be filled by a two-storey commercial development, the clothing shop of Anderson and McAuley. Just around the corner, in Castle Street, was Beatty's studio. A photograph from the 1860s shows, behind the shop, the upper part of the façade of the old dwelling house and bank. The windows seen are exactly like those in the 1843 calotype.[9]

Despite his undoubted skill and inventiveness, Beatty may have been an awkward character, not well fitted to cajole a fickle public in the only aspect of photographic work that was commercially viable, namely the taking of portraits. However, his place as Ireland's first photographer, and as a pioneer of photography in general, is secure.

So it was that Irish photography began in the north.

George Augustus Chichester (1769–1844), 2nd Marquis of Donegall, with his groom, in front of the Agricultural Bank, Donegall Place, Belfast, in 1843; probably by Beatty.

MAGNI / UM

Though none of Francis Beatty's actual photographs are known to exist, this image was almost certainly his work, for he had recently opened the first studio in Belfast, just around the corner in Castle Street. The original picture, a calotype, was later copied as a glass-plate negative. Both have since disappeared. Fortunately, however, this print from the glass negative was published in an article by a local historian in 1912.

Other early photographers

Beatty's failure in Belfast did not deter other professional photographers from trying their luck in the town. There is no sign of their presence in the directories in the 1840s – they came and went too quickly for that – but there are occasional glimpses of them in the newspapers. One that we know of, named Cherry, arrived in May 1845 and set up his daguerreotype studio on the roof of a building in Donegall Place. He claimed to be able to produce a photograph after a sitting of less than a minute; his advertisements in the *Banner of Ulster* in late May and early June were headed 'Improvements in Daguerreotype'. Each portrait cost the considerable sum of ten shillings, and specimens of his work were displayed at a couple of places in the town as well as at the Portrait Rooms. The article in the *Banner* praised the enhancement, 'by a certain chemical operation', of the complexion of the sitter and the 'exquisite fidelity and delicacy of finish which characterise the likeness'; there was 'nothing in them of the sombre hue which is generally found associated with Daguerreotype drawings, but on the contrary a pleasing effect . . . '[10]

Cherry had gone by 1846, when the next directory was published; there were no photographers or 'photographic artists' listed at that time. The only other daguerreotypist known to have worked in the north of Ireland in the 1840s was Robert McGee in Londonderry, and we know about him only because he was reported insolvent in 1843.[11] There are no photographers listed in the Belfast directories in the early 1850s either, revealing the shortcomings of directories as a source of information about a profession which was at that stage semi-itinerant, for in fact there were several daguerreotypists operating in the town in the summer of 1850 and 1851.

In May 1850 the *Belfast News-Letter* announced the arrival of A. Tulloch, whose studio was at 22 York Street. Tulloch was followed a week later by J.S. Stanton, whose Photographic and Daguerreotype Portrait Gallery was in Castle Street. Emile Orange, who arrived in August, offered coloured daguerrotypes and stayed somewhat longer, first at Castle Buildings, later (from December 1851) at the York Street studio vacated by Tulloch or his successor Steinfeld. None of them appeared in the 1852 directory.

In March 1854 the *Belfast News-Letter* announced the arrival from America of Professors Ransom and Hull, 'who for the last five years have been professionally engaged in this wonderful Art . . . They flatter themselves that they can take, by their process, as good pictures as are made in any part of the world.' They also offered to make copies from oil paintings, ivory miniatures, engravings and daguerreotypes.[12]

Samuel Glyde set up at 12 Bridge Street, next door to the *Belfast News-Letter* office, in 1855 and stayed until February 1859, when the paper announced an auction of his cameras and other equipment. In 1856 James Scott Stewart started in Castle Buildings but his studio apparently did not survive long. In the same year, the Belfast artist Richard Hooke (1820–1908) was offering to make portraits in oils using daguerreotypes and photographs and claiming that the results were 'equal in point of truthfulness to those taken from a living subject'. He even offered a postal service for 'persons living at a distance from town'.[13] The art collections of the Ulster Museum include an example of Hooke's overpainted photography, a portrait of Edward Jones Smith.

By 1858 there were six 'photographic artists' listed (under Artists, of whom there were a dozen in all) in the directory. One of them, a rare instance indeed, was a woman, a Miss Cinnamond; another was Silo and Son. The Silos were a family of Italian carvers and gilders who came to Belfast in the 1850s to find employment, mainly in the new Catholic churches being built at that time, but they also took photographic portraits and coloured and framed them. They first appear in the directories in 1856, but had ceased to be directly involved with photography by the early 1860s. R.J. Welch, when employed in E.T. Church's studio in the early 1880s, produced excellent portraits of Modesto Silo, a second-generation member, and left some notes about the family. Another son, Andrew, was working as a carver and gilder in Londonderry in 1858. There is no record of any photographers who may have practised in Londonderry in the 1850s; at any rate none became established.

The reason for the increasing number of photographers in Belfast in the later 1850s, apart from the ever-increasing size of the town's population (by 1860 it had reached one hundred and twenty thousand), was the invention of the wet collodion process, which superseded the paper negative of the calotype with a glass plate and enabled excellent portraits to be taken more cheaply than by daguerreotype. (Collodion is a colourless or yellowish syrupy liquid, obtained by dissolving pyroxylin – guncotton – in ether and alcohol.) The man who discovered this new process was an English sculptor named Francis Scott Archer, who wanted to use photography to help him in his work. He did not patent the process, thus making it freely available to all. Though far from convenient for outdoor work (the glass plate had to be prepared immediately before taking the photograph and developed immediately after), the wet collodion process was much more sensitive than either the daguerreotype or the calotype; exposure times were therefore greatly reduced.

Emile Orange may have been the first professional user of the new process in the north, only five months after it was made known in March 1851. The portraits he was offering at five shillings each that summer were said to be 'free of dulness and haze' and in a style 'hitherto unattainable out of Paris, with flesh tones clear, rich and warm, as they are in life', suggesting neither daguerreotype nor calotype.[14] A variation of the new process, described by Scott Archer in 1852, was to treat the collodion negative with mercuric bichloride and then give the glass a dark backing (black varnish, paper or cloth) which made the negative image into a positive. This collodion positive or Ambrotype – its tradename in America – soon became very popular for portraits. Being glass it needed a protective cover, like the daguerreotype; and, of course, being a positive it was a one-off. The quality was excellent, however, and since no licence was needed and (unlike the daguerreotype) the process required no great skill and only a modest investment, portraits were comparatively cheap. The protective 'union' cases sometimes carried the photographer's name. The fine portraits of members of the Coates family of Belfast, now in the Ulster Museum, are not named but were probably taken locally in the later 1850s. Tintypes or ferrotypes, another variant, which used black enamelled tinplate instead of glass, also date from this period and became popular from about 1860. They came to be used by itinerant photographers as a cheap way of producing an instant portrait without any need for studio work.

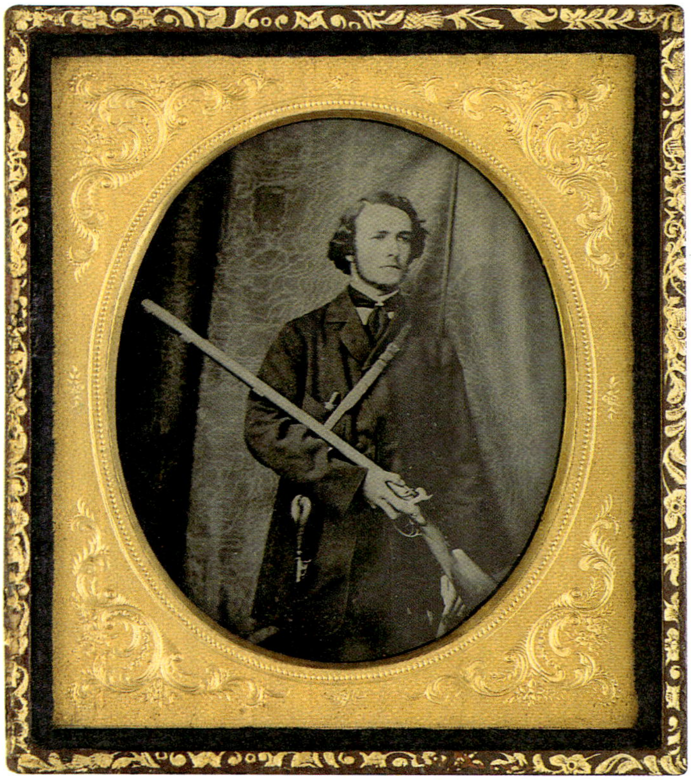

Ambrotype of a member of the Coates family of Belfast in hunting gear, c. 1855, an example of this kind of wet collodion positive in its protective 'union' case.
MAGNI / UM

Beatty was also a pioneer, if not a particularly successful one, of the wet collodion process. His Wet Collodion Field Camera, described in his *Dublin Journal* article of 1858, was an ingenious attempt to overcome the inconvenience of outdoor photography. 'By its construction,' Beatty explained, 'the prepared plate undergoes all the necessary operations within the Camera, no light being admitted but that through the lens to produce the picture.' Since the crucial stages of producing a wet collodion photograph – sensitising the glass plate (already treated with collodion fluid) with a solution of silver nitrate before exposing it to take the picture, then developing the result – had to be carried out in a darkroom of some kind, outdoor photography usually entailed carrying a photographic tent. Beatty's article describes in detail how his apparatus made this unnecessary by a process 'not only elegant but fascinating – which captivates the minds of those engaged in it'.[15] The manipulation involved must have been harder than he made out, or the results not so good – at

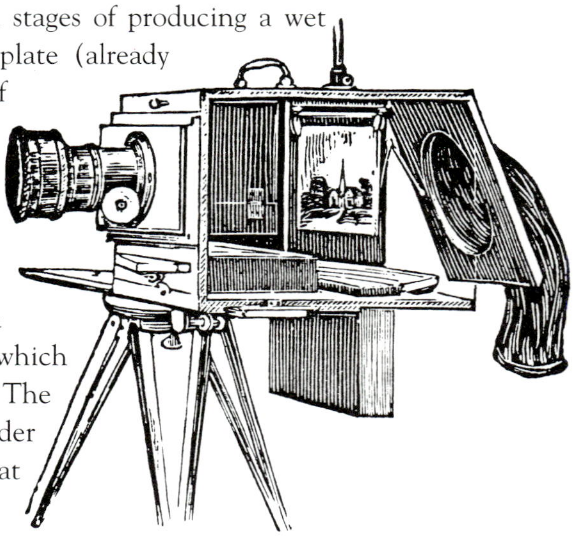

Beatty's Wet Collodion Field Camera, one of his own engravings, used to illustrate an article entitled 'The science of photography' in the *Dublin Journal* in 1858.
LINEN HALL LIBRARY

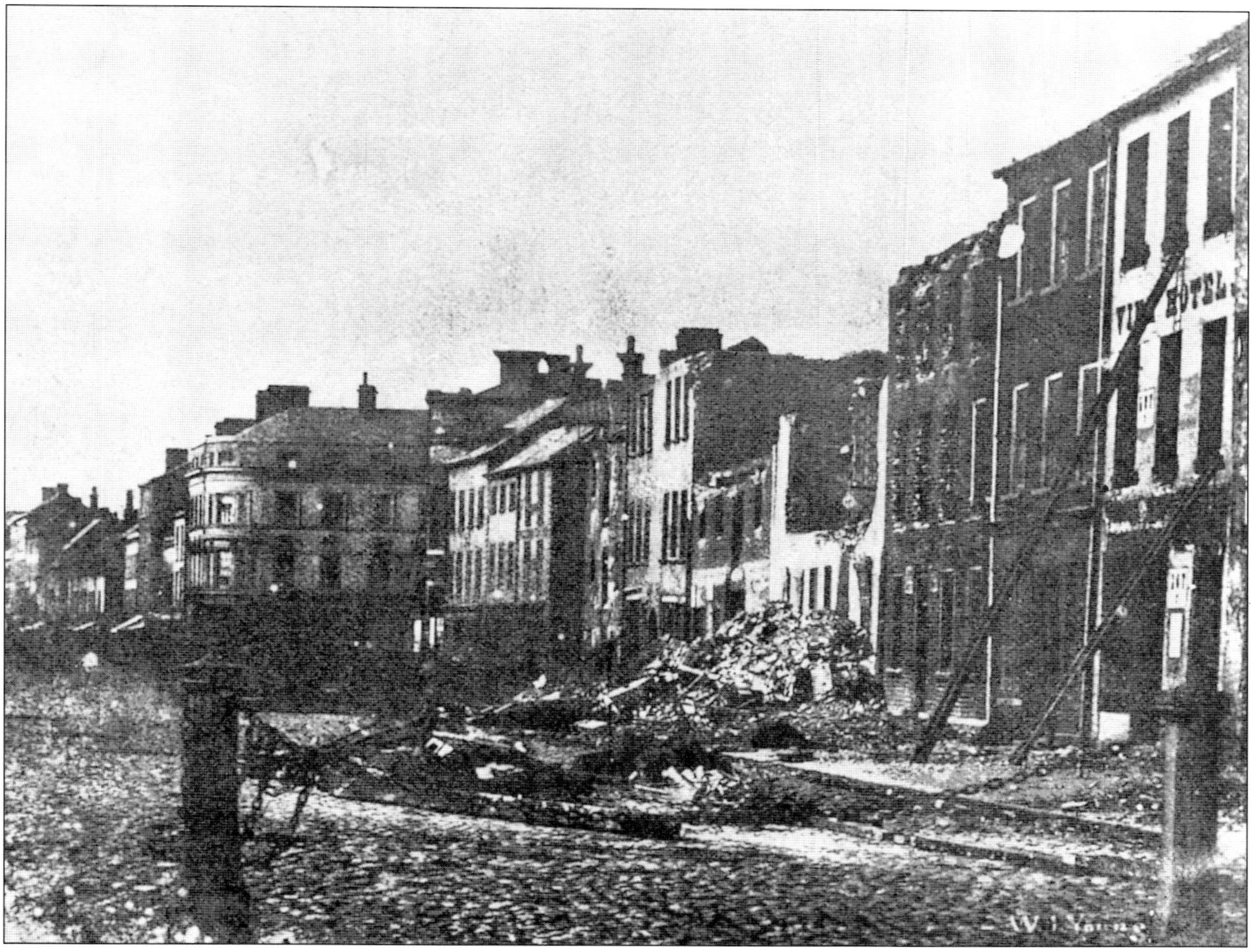

any rate his camera did not catch on. The idea of a camera with a developing attachment was a good one, however, and made the fortune of later inventors.

Old buildings being demolished in Queen's Square, Belfast, in March 1854, from a calotype by W.J. Young, amateur photographer. This is the earliest surviving actual photograph of Belfast.

MAGNI / UM

The houses shown in the foreground were pulled down to make way for the new Custom House (1857). The photographic print, a calotype positive, bears the watermark 'B. Turner Patent Talbotype'. Turner, an artist and a notable early exponent of the calotype or talbotype, is said to have been the last person to use the process – in 1862.

Early amateurs

The wet collodion process gave an important impetus to amateur photography as well as professional. Nevertheless, the earliest surviving photographs taken in the North of Ireland were calotypes. The first, dated March 1854, was taken by W.J. Young, uncle of the noted Belfast antiquarian R.M. Young. It shows houses in Queen's Square, Belfast, which were in the process of being demolished to make way for the new Custom House. The second, taken on 1 November 1855, recorded the scene in College Square East, in front of the Royal Belfast Academical Institution, when the statue of the Earl of Belfast – the town's first public statue – was unveiled by Lord Harcourt, lord lieutenant of Ireland. There is no other photograph of the occasion, though the ceremony itself and accompanying festivities were recorded in minute detail both in a souvenir booklet and in the

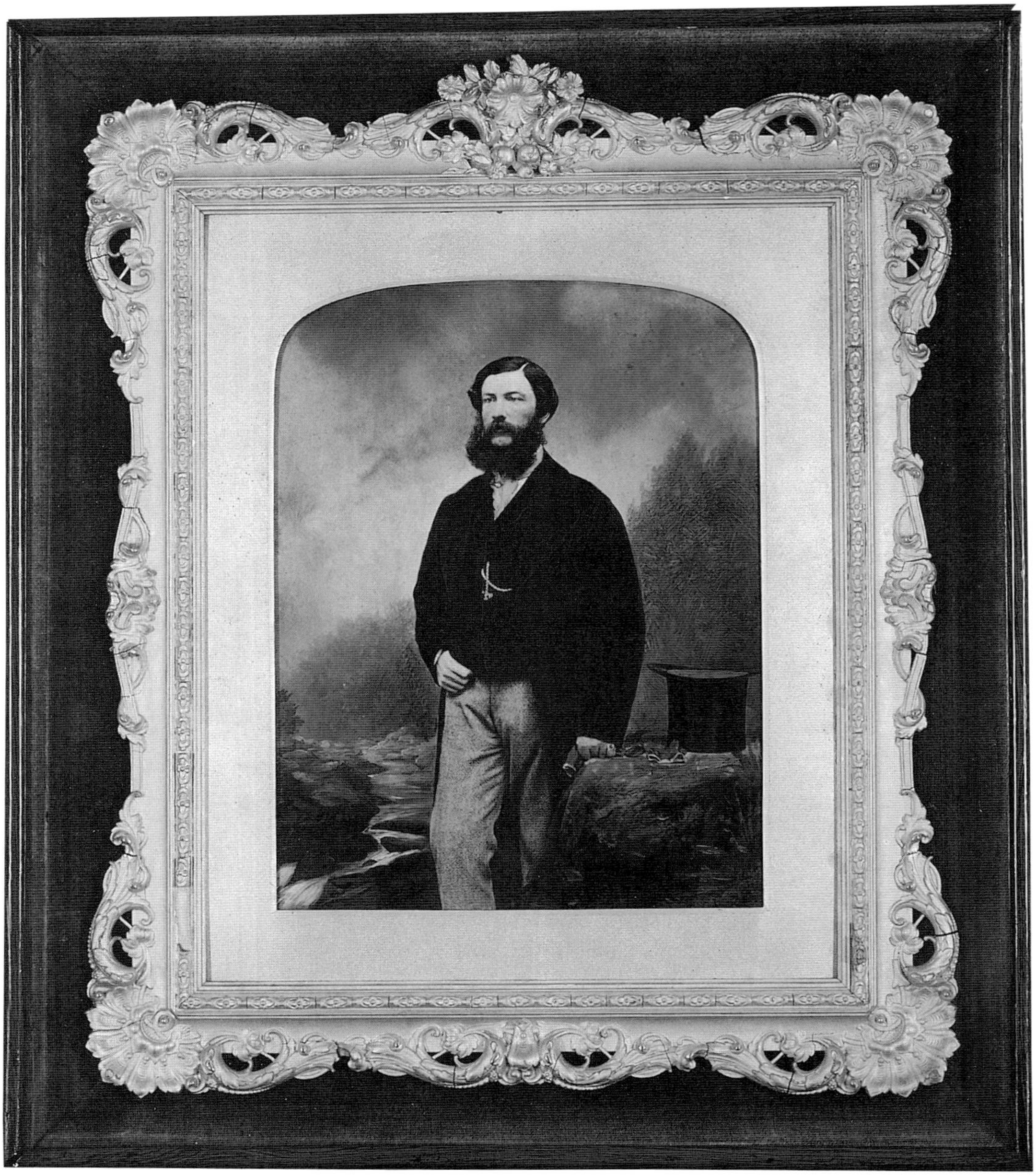

Hand-coloured photograph, one of a pair dated 1857, of Captain Hugh Montgomery Archdall, Drumdravy, County Fermanagh.

BY KIND PERMISSION OF DR MARJORIE HOUSTON

The portraits, though unmarked, were probably taken in Belfast. The gilded mounts and wooden framing were typical of the period. In Belfast such work was done by James Magill of Donegall Place, who was soon to add a high-class photographic studio to his operations.

local press. Either there was no professional photographer on hand or the technical problems of recording such an event at that stage of photography were too daunting for any but an amateur to attempt. Whoever took the picture, now in the Ulster Museum, was clearly prepared to try anything. The result is rather fuzzy, but recognisable. Taken over the heads of the platform party, it shows the canopy on wheels which covered the statue, with the houses of College Square North in the background.

There was a sufficient number of amateur photographers, or would-be photographers, in the town at that time to support a Photographic Society. Public interest had been stimulated by a lecture given in November 1854 to the Belfast Natural History and Philosophical Society by Thomas Andrews, first professor of chemistry at the Queen's College, Belfast; and it was members of this society (which among other things built and ran the Belfast Museum) who in 1857 formed the Belfast Photographic Society. Like many such early bodies throughout the United Kingdom, the Belfast Photographic Society lasted only a few years; its final meeting was held in May 1860.[16]

By the end of the 1850s, photography in the North – or at any rate in and near Belfast – was well established. Progress among amateurs, backed by the scientific interests of staff at the Queen's College and members of the Natural History and Philosophical Society, had created an association of amateurs; and there were half a dozen professional photographers competing for a growing portrait trade.

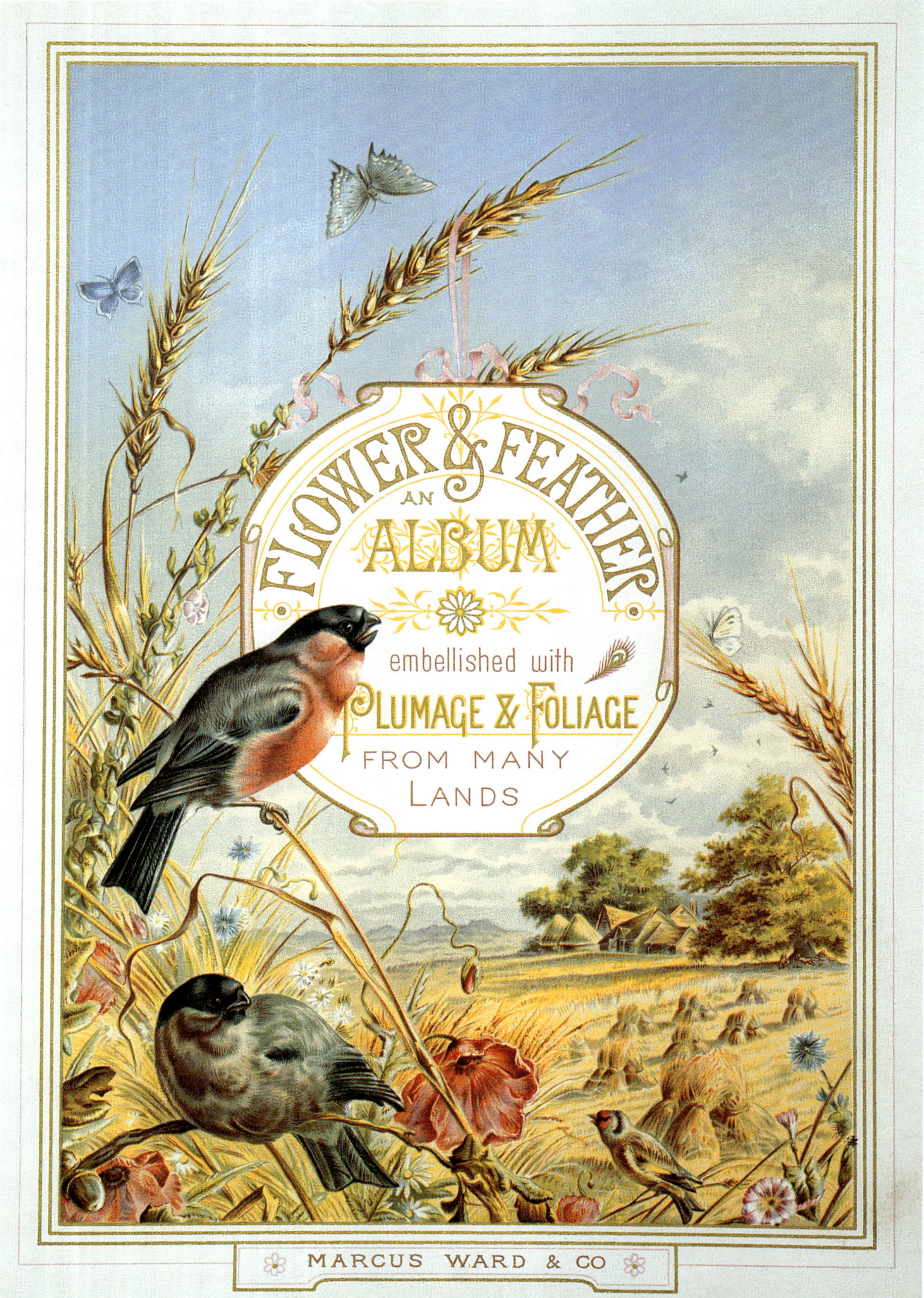
FLOWER & FEATHER
AN
ALBUM
embellished with
PLUMAGE & FOLIAGE
FROM MANY
LANDS
MARCUS WARD & CO

Cartes and wet collodion

c. 1860–*c.* 1880

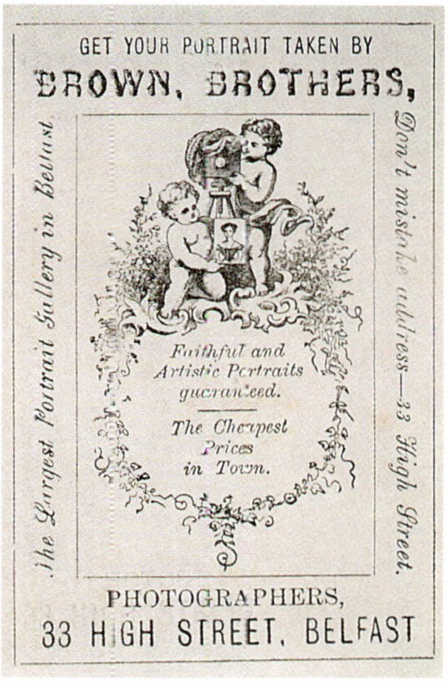

Reverse of carte de visite by Brown Brothers, Belfast, 1868.

MAGNI / UM

From 1860, professional photography in the North of Ireland, as elsewhere, developed to a much greater extent than ever before. The number of studios, both in Belfast and in the smaller towns of Ulster, rose steadily as more and more people became able to afford the comparatively modest cost of having their likeness taken and as the demand for other kinds of photography also grew. The best-established and most successful studios employed a staff of photographers, artists and technicians.

One measure of the growth of business was the number of people who gave their occupation as 'photographer' in the census returns. In 1861 there were only 19 professional photographers in the 9 counties of Ulster (Leinster had 62, most of them in Dublin, Munster 17 and Connaught 3). By 1871 the number in the north had

Opposite
Title page of a 'Flower and Feather' photographic album, c. 1880, by Marcus Ward and Company, Belfast. This superb example belonged to the Young family, of Fenaghy, near Ballymena.

BY KIND PERMISSION OF MRS ANNA STEWART

risen to 68, by 1881 to 83, by 1891 to 176 and by the turn of the century to 234.[1]

This rise in the number of photographers was largely a reflection of urban growth. Belfast's population over the same period shot up from 121,000 to just under 350,000, a phenomenal rate of increase by any comparison. Small towns within easy reach of Belfast, such as Holywood and Bangor in County Down and Lisburn and Larne in County Antrim, also grew substantially: Bangor from 2,500 to 6,000 (seasonally increased by an influx of summer visitors), Lisburn from 7,500 to 11,500 and Larne from 2,800 to 6,800. Slightly farther afield, Ballymena increased from 6,800 to nearly 11,000. Londonderry, the second largest town in the north, almost doubled its population from 21,000 to 40,000. In the more agricultural western areas of the province, towns grew much more slowly, if at all; the populations of Cavan, Monaghan, Clones, Enniskillen and Ballyshannon actually declined, as a result of heavy emigration from their hinterlands.

Centres of population provided opportunities for photographers, as did places with a constantly shifting population: small towns with ports or military garrisons, or with a significant number of tourists. The garrison towns of the north in the mid-nineteenth century were Armagh, Ballymena, Ballyshannon, Belfast, Enniskillen, Londonderry, Monaghan, Newry and Omagh; all of them had at least one studio operating from the 1860s onwards. As ports, Belfast, Londonderry and Newry created work for photographers, particularly for portraits of the emigrants who passed through them. So too did the tourist centres of Belfast (the starting place for many excursions by rail or road), Bangor, Londonderry (the main point of entry for Donegal), Enniskillen (the Fermanagh lakes), Newcastle (the Mourne Mountains), Larne (the Glens of Antrim), Portrush (the Giant's Causeway) – all of which had a considerable summer trade. Clearly Belfast, as a major centre of population, the home of a growing middle class, a major port and a tourist centre, was where most photographers were able to earn their living. For the same reasons, though on a much smaller scale, Londonderry supported a number of successful studios.

The overwhelming majority of photographers in the late nineteenth century were men; women were seldom owners of studios except when widowed, when they usually employed men to carry out the work, or occasionally as daughters who had been trained to help in the family business. Numbers of women were employed by the larger establishments, however, as artists and retouchers. This explains why, though there were only four studios in Belfast run by women between 1850 and 1914, there were fifty-four women listed in the 1901 census of the city as professional photographers.[2] There were only fourteen more in the rest of Ulster, and even that was a comparatively recent development; thirty years earlier there had been only two in the whole province, both of whom worked in Belfast.[3]

It is significant that William Abernethy, who employed upwards of twenty 'experienced assistants' at his printing and finishing works in 1895, claimed that 'the most skilled *men* [my italics] are employed, so that the public may rely on first-class work, and not the hap-hazard results often tolerated by unskilled labour'.[4] It would appear that most women who listed themselves as photographers were engaged in subsidiary work rather than in the taking and developing of photographs.

In areas where there was insufficient custom to support a full-time photographer, the local practitioner was usually either semi-professional or mainly dependent for a living on other activities. Hugh Waide, listed as one of the three photographers working in Cookstown, County Tyrone, in the 1860s and 1870s, was a farmer's son from Cullybackey. After a spell in Maghera he moved to teach – first as an assistant, later as principal – in the National School run by the Seceder sect of Presbyterians in Cookstown (there were no fewer than four National Schools, representing different denominations in the local population). Another man, named Hopper, from the Aughnacloy area of County Tyrone, may have combined photography with farming in the 1860s. He appears in no directory, but is known by a couple of professional-style carte-de-visite portraits of local people. Much later, in the 1920s, a true farmer–photographer features in our list of professionals, in the person of Thomas Gribben, from the Loughinisland area of County Down. Evidence of competence is more substantial in his case: Down Museum has a collection of his work, along with documentation which shows that he subscribed to the *British Journal of Photography* and *Kodak Magazine*.[5] Often people diversified into photography: Andrew Charles in Cookstown and Magherafelt, George Dallas in Kilrea, and Thomas Mercer in Enniskillen, for example, were country watchmakers and jewellers, T. McGurk of Cookstown was a hairdresser and barber, John McKendry in Belturbet a 'sewing agent' (engaged in the distribution and collection of textile products put out by manufacturers for decoration by rural women), Thomas McKey of Newry a tobacconist, Thomas Predy of Limavady a printer, John Fullerton of Ahoghill a druggist and printer, Samuel Corry of Ballyclare a bookbinder, Leo Mulhern of Raphoe a cycle agent and funeral undertaker. James Galway, who ran a successful studio in Clones (carried on after his death by his daughter Kathleen) was also for many years Clerk to the Town Commissioners. In fact, almost anyone with enough business enterprise and sufficiently interested in photography could set up a studio. The high turnover, however, shows that failure was common.

The staple of most photographers, then as now, was portrait work; and the main reason for the growth of professional photography in the 1860s and 1870s was the arrival of the cheap, small photograph known as the *carte de visite* – patented in France in 1854 by the Parisian photographer Disdéri and hugely popular there after

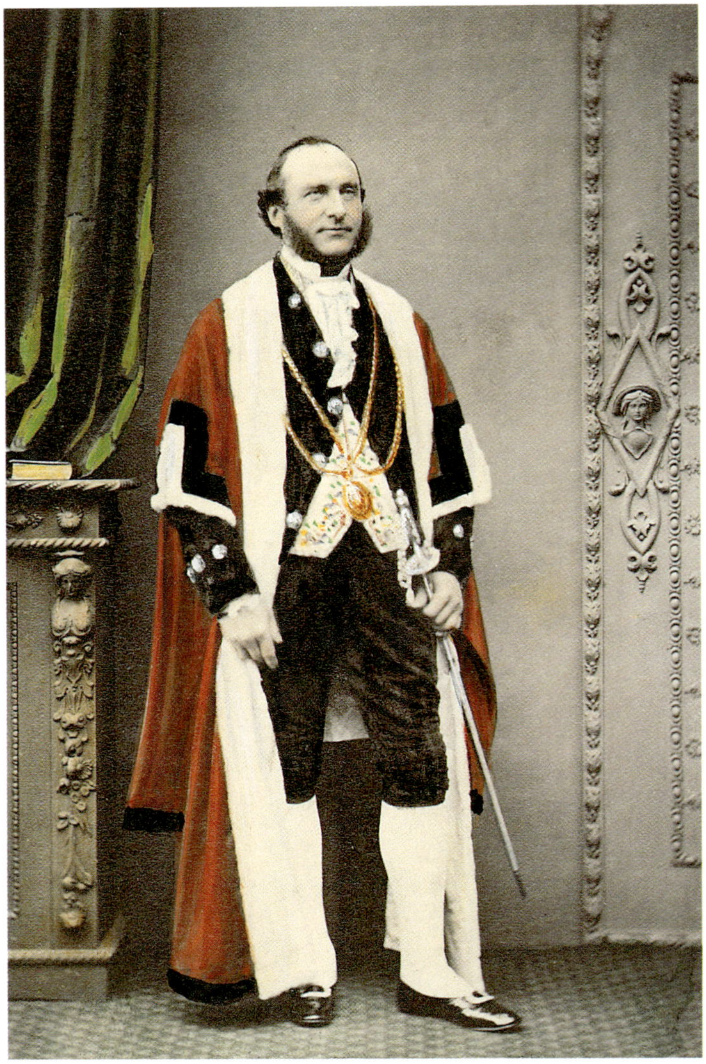

John Lytle, Mayor of Belfast, 1863–6, in his official costume and regalia. This hand-coloured carte-de-visite portrait was taken by the Belfast studio of James Magill around 1865.

MAGNI / UM (COEY ALBUM)

1859, when the Emperor Napoleon III visited Disdéri's studio.[6] The size of the photograph was about the same as that of the visiting cards used in polite circles in western Europe, hence the name. Its comparatively cheap selling price of one shilling to one and sixpence was made possible by taking several small negatives on a single glass plate, which was then developed in one operation. The resulting prints were fixed on stiff card and given a protective varnish.

Among Belfast photographers cartes were usually called 'sticky backs', possibly an American term. One studio, known only from a couple of surviving cartes, even called itself Sticky Backs. The better cartes, if kept in the elaborate albums that were produced at the time, look as fresh now as they did when they left the photographer's studio.

The carte was introduced into England in 1857. 'Cartomania' broke out in 1860, after J.E. Mayall of London published his pictures of the royal family. This seal of approval for photography (the Prince Consort, Albert, was himself keenly interested) ensured the acceptance of the cheap public portrait among the fashionable and famous, who flocked to the studios to be photographed. In the 1860s, no fewer than 300–400 million cartes were sold each year in England alone. For the first time, people were able to see what their rulers and heroes actually looked like, and the collecting of pictures of royalty, aristocracy, clergy, politicians, military leaders, actors and actresses became a favourite pastime in many a household. The same was true all over western Europe and in North America.

The popularity of the carte de visite in fashionable circles began to decline from the later 1860s. The smaller image was increasingly replaced by the larger cabinet format (5½-by-4 inches), which was introduced in England in 1866 and remained popular until the First World War. Cartes continued to be produced in large numbers, however, until the turn of the century and after, particularly in provincial areas. In the north of Ireland there are many surviving examples of it, or of variations on it, from the 1860s to the early 1900s.

Cartes of prominent local figures were popular among collectors. In Ireland, a country dominated by religion, clergy were particularly common as subjects. Controversial politicians were also well aware of the publicity value of circulating icons of themselves among the faithful. A particularly good early example in the north was William Johnston of Ballykilbeg, County Down. Johnston was a leading Orangeman who made himself immensely popular among rank and file members of the Orange Order in 1866–7 by organising processions in defiance of the Party Processions Act (which he was later instrumental in having repealed). In 1868 he was arrested and jailed for organising a Twelfth of July parade. When released he stood for parliament and was elected as one of the two members for Belfast. In his diary he records visiting the studio of a Belfast photographer during his campaign, to look at his likeness, thousands of copies of which were sold. Magill's studio photographed Johnston in 1868 and published the photograph in several sizes, addressing the advertisement for 'a portrait of J of B' to 'the Orangemen and Protestants of Ireland – carte 1 shilling, whole-plate 2 shillings and sixpence, large portrait 10 guineas'.[7] A surviving carte by another Belfast studio, Brown Brothers, depicts him with patriarchal beard and Orange sash orating at the hustings, against a painted backdrop of County Down scenery. This particular one may have been done from a painting rather than from life, as were some local episcopal portraits in carte form, such as one of the Catholic bishop of Down and Connor, Cornelius Denvir. Cartes of evangelical Protestants were being sold in 1865 by Alexander S. Mayne at his Ulster Tract and Bible

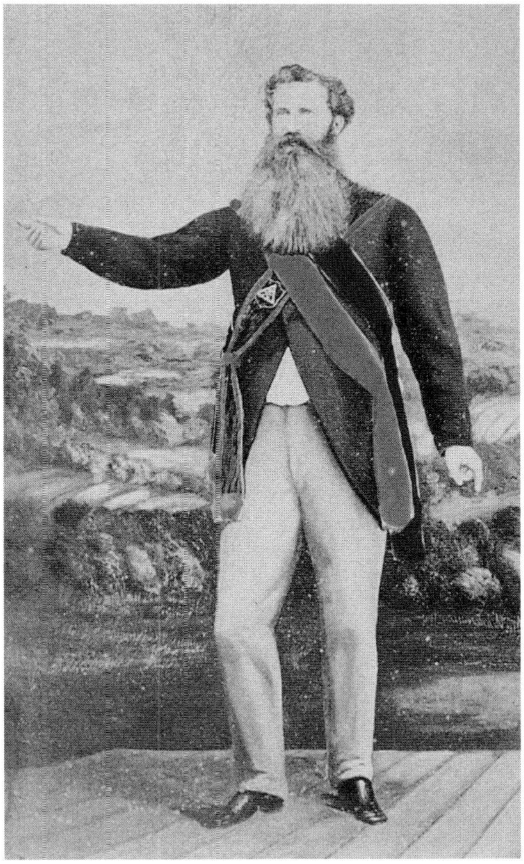

William Johnston of Ballykilbeg, carte de visite by Brown Brothers, Belfast, 1868.

MAGNI / UM

A minor landowner from County Down, Johnston became famous as a radical Orangeman in the 1860s when he defied the Party Processions Act. Imprisoned for organising a Twelfth of July parade, on his release he stood for parliament and was elected for one of the Belfast seats in 1868. This and other photographs of him were produced and circulated during the election campaign.

48 ADVERTISEMENTS.

Kephalolutron,

9, HIGH STREET, BELFAST.

R. GALBRAITH, Proprietor.

THESE Premises are now opened to the Public, and having been built specially for R. G., will be found to be replete with every accommodation. The Shop is Stocked with a Large and Varied Assortment of

ORNAMENTAL HAIR WORK, FRENCH AND ENGLISH TOILET REQUISITES, FANCY GOODS, ARTICLES OF VERTU, CUTLERY, &c., &c.

The Public Hair-Cutting Saloon

on the GROUND FLOOR, (in which the Charge is SIXPENCE), is the most spacious and complete Room for the purpose in the Kingdom.

Ladies' Hair-Cutting Rooms.

On the FIRST FLOOR are a Suite of Rooms for LADIES' HAIR-DRESSING, most handsomely fitted up, and furnished with all the comforts of a boudoir.

Gentlemen's Hair-Cutting Rooms.

By the express desire of many Gentlemen, there is a PRIVATE ROOM for HAIR-CUTTING, in which the Charge will be ONE SHILLING.

In all these Rooms CUMP'S PATENT HAIR-BRUSHING MACHINE, with the recent improvements, is fitted up, and is driven by one of ROBINSON & SON'S (of Rochdale) New Patent Gas Engines.

A Large Staff of First-Class Assistants, from some of the best Houses in London and Paris, are engaged.

Bath Rooms.

The SECOND FLOOR contains two separate Suites of Rooms for Ladies and Gentlemen, for HOT, COLD, and SHOWER BATHS. These Baths have been erected in Marble, at great expense, and the Rooms are most suitably furnished.

Photographic Rooms.

The UPPER PART is laid out for PHOTOGRAPHIC PURPOSES, containing Reception Room, Dressing Rooms, Studio, &c., &c.

This Department is under the Management of Mr. PAYNE JENNINGS (of London), late Principal Operator at the FINE ARTS ESTABLISHMENT of Mr. CRAWFIELD, Dublin.

Advertisement by Robert Galbraith for his 'Kephalolutron' and new photographic studio (where the photographer was Payne Jennings), from the directory for 1868.

MAGNI / UM

Depository in Donegall Square, Belfast, some for as little as sixpence ($2^1/_2$ p) each. In the same year Magill's were advertising cartes of 'the leading clergymen of Belfast and neighbourhood' at a shilling each.

Such was the demand for cartes in the 1860s that photographic studios sprang up in all sorts of premises, some of them pretty unlikely. Hairdressers, butchers, tobacconists, coffee sellers, even dentists set up in the photography business. In most cases this was simply a matter of business entrepreneurship, rather than diversification of skills; typically, the proprietor put up the money and brought in a photographer to do the work. Robert Galbraith, for instance, who ran a hairdressing establishment at 9 High Street, Belfast, which he grandiloquently called his 'Kephalolutron' (from the ancient Greek word meaning head), turned over the top floor of his premises to a studio in 1868. His first photographer was a Londoner who had been principal operator at Cranfield's in Dublin, J. Payne Jennings. Jennings had moved to Belfast a short time earlier and had opened a studio just across the street at No. 6. Galbraith appears as proprietor in the Belfast directories for 1868 and 1870, but for a time at least he and Jennings were in partnership, for there is a surviving carte in the name of Galbraith and Company, 9 High Street, 'late Galbraith Jennings & Co.'.

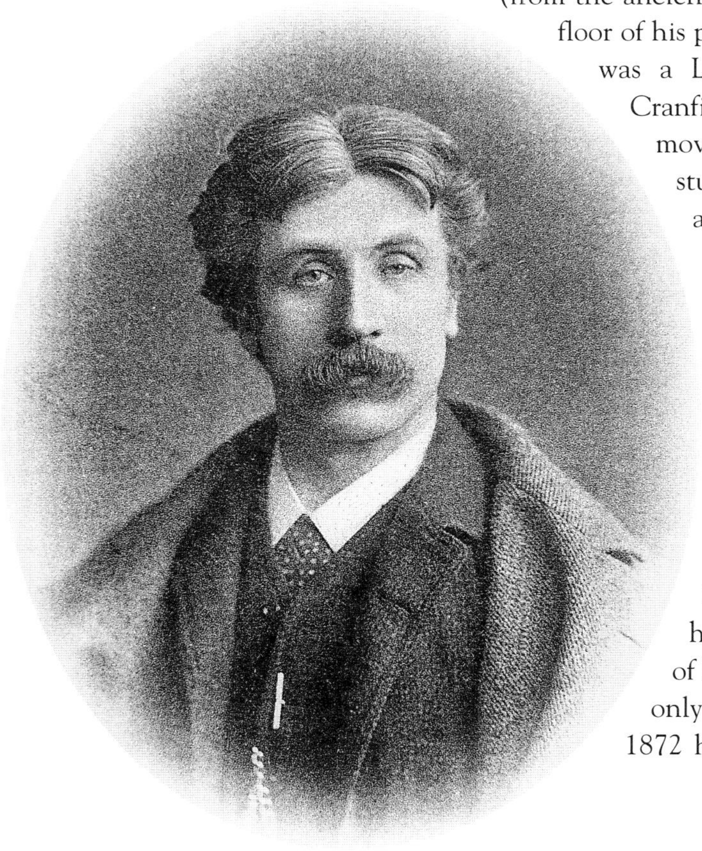

J. Payne Jennings (1843–1926), ink photo by J. Sprague, from *British Journal of Photography*, 18 April 1884.

ROYAL PHOTOGRAPHIC SOCIETY COLLECTION

John Payne Jennings (whose Belfast visit is not generally known in what is otherwise a well-documented career) was to become one of the most successful 'views' photographers of his generation. Jennings returned from Belfast to Rathmines in Dublin around 1870, when he scored his first public success with a series of photographs of Killarney which attracted favourable attention not only in Ireland but also from London reviewers. In 1872 he exhibited a large number of Irish views which

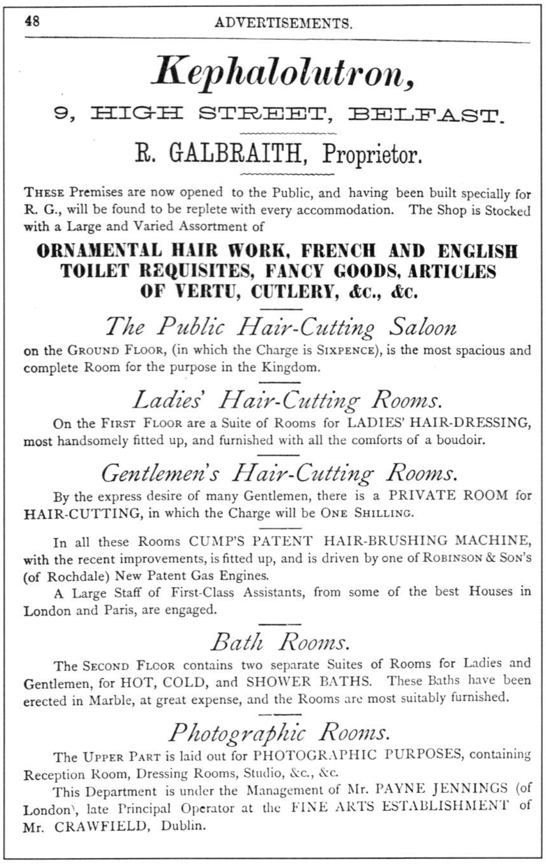

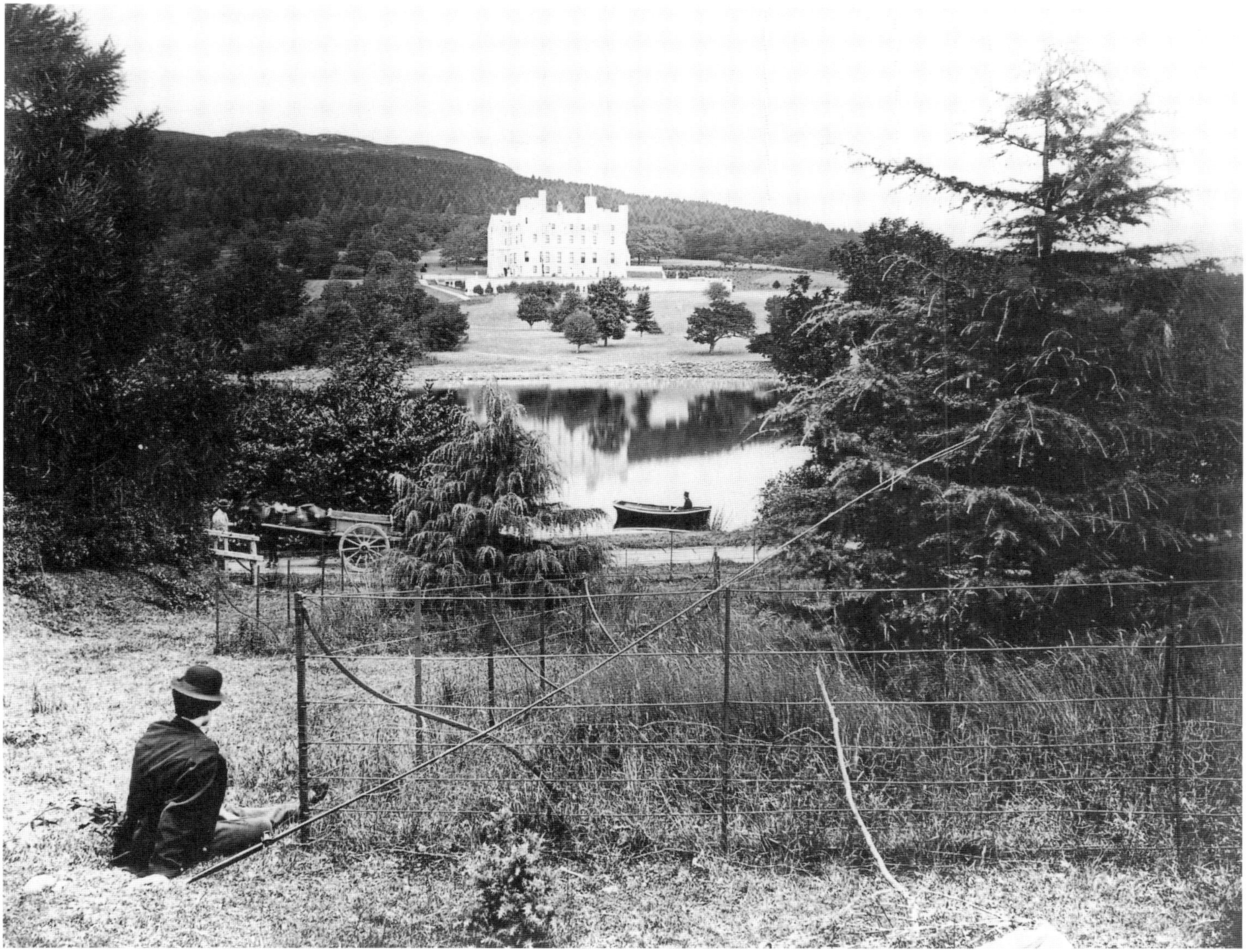

were well received, as were his *Photographic Views of the English Lakes*, published in 1875; these were described as 'uniformly excellent' by the *British Journal of Photography*. In 1876 he exhibited in Philadelphia, where his work was described as 'the wonderful landscapes of Mr Payne Jennings, Dublin'. He moved to London about 1878. His later pictures of the Norfolk Broads, the first of which were taken in the late 1880s, were particularly popular and made him a substantial amount of money. Many of them were displayed in the carriages of the Great Eastern Railway Company, and three selections of his work were published. There is a large collection in Norwich Central Library, and a smaller one at Princeton University in the United States. From the mid-1890s until his death in 1926 he was based at Ashtead in Surrey, where he lived in some style and died wealthy (he left £28,000). Jennings's association with Galbraith's studio and Belfast may have been short because he was not really interested in portrait work: his later reputation was entirely based on his 'views'.

Castlewellan Castle, County Down, c. 1870, by J. Payne Jennings.

MAGNI / UM

Jennings, a notable 'views' photographer, was working in Belfast during the late 1860s. The castle, which had replaced an earlier one-storey lodge as the main residence of the Annesley family, survives, along with its beautiful demense, now a forest park open to the public.

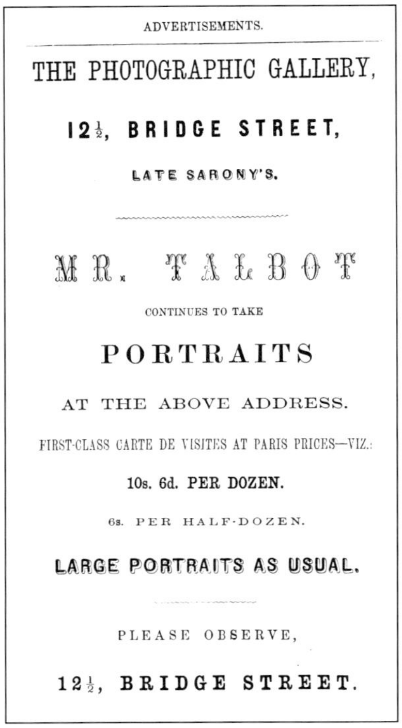
ADVERTISEMENTS.

THE PHOTOGRAPHIC GALLERY,

12½, BRIDGE STREET,

LATE SARONY'S.

MR. TALBOT

CONTINUES TO TAKE

PORTRAITS

AT THE ABOVE ADDRESS.

FIRST-CLASS CARTE DE VISITES AT PARIS PRICES—VIZ.:

10s. 6d. PER DOZEN.

6s. PER HALF-DOZEN.

LARGE PORTRAITS AS USUAL.

PLEASE OBSERVE,

12½, BRIDGE STREET.

Advertisement by Abraham Talbot for the Photographic Gallery (late Sarony's), from a Belfast directory for 1863–4.

MAGNI / UM

The evidence relating to Payne Jennings's stay in Belfast, apart from one or two carte portraits, consists of architectural and landscape work. The Ulster Museum has a bound volume of eleven views of The Moat, Strandtown, *c.* 1869, a house which had been built for the Belfast linen merchant Thomas Valentine. The museum also has two views from County Down, one of which depicts the then recently completed Castlewellan Castle, the other a scene on the Shimna river, taken about 1870. Jennings copyrighted a number of his Irish views, which were published by Cassell's in the late 1890s in *Sights and Scenes in Ireland.* Twenty-four of the one hundred half-tones in this volume were his. Most were of Dublin and southern tourist spots such as Glendalough and Killarney, but there is one of 'The Hermitage, Glenavna' at Whiteabbey, on the outskirts of Belfast, which must date from his northern sojourn.[8]

An earlier brief visitor of some note was Olivier F.X. Sarony, who had come to the British Isles from Quebec in 1843. Sarony announced his imminent arrival in Belfast in the *Belfast News-Letter* in 1859:

> Mr Sarony, of Scarborough, England, and 6 Stephen's Green North, Dublin . . . begs to intimate to the Nobility and Gentry of Belfast and neighbourhood that he will in a few days open at the above address, 12½ Bridge Street, his Gallery of Photographic Portraits, pronounced by the London Press 'as the ultimatum of Photographic and Miniature Art, and excelling in truth and beauty all that has preceded them'.[9]

Sarony may have been the first to offer the new carte-de-visite photographs in Belfast. In January 1861 his portraits 'in the new style' were being advertised at a guinea each – much too expensive. His March offer of ten for a guinea was more like it. By that time, however, he was thinking of giving up the Belfast studio.

In April 1861, an advertisement in the *Ulster Magazine* headed 'Sarony's Last Season will shortly terminate' announced his impending departure; the lease of the premises was advertised in the *Belfast News-Letter* early in July. 'The Photographic Gallery, late Sarony's' was by 1863 being run by A.J. Talbot, who announced in the directory for that year that he continued to take portraits there (presumably he had been the manager). He advertised 'first class carte de visites at Paris prices – viz: 10s. 6d per dozen, 6s. per half-dozen'. At least one successful Belfast photographer, Robert Seggons, learned his trade at Sarony's. The contents of the studio itself were acquired by James Magill, who thus began his own. Olivier Sarony's enormously successful

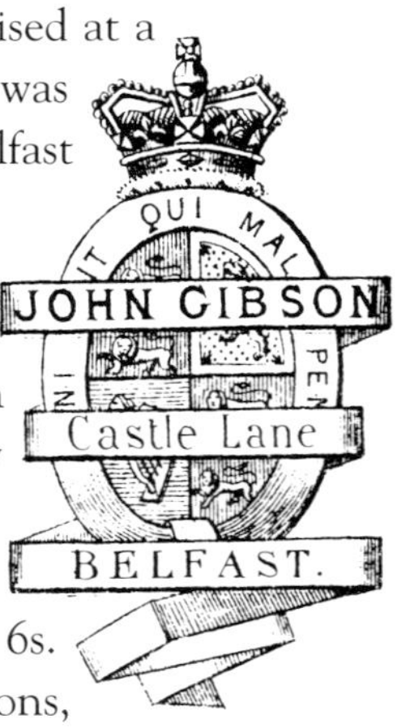

Reverse of a John Gibson carte, c. 1870.

MAGNI / UM

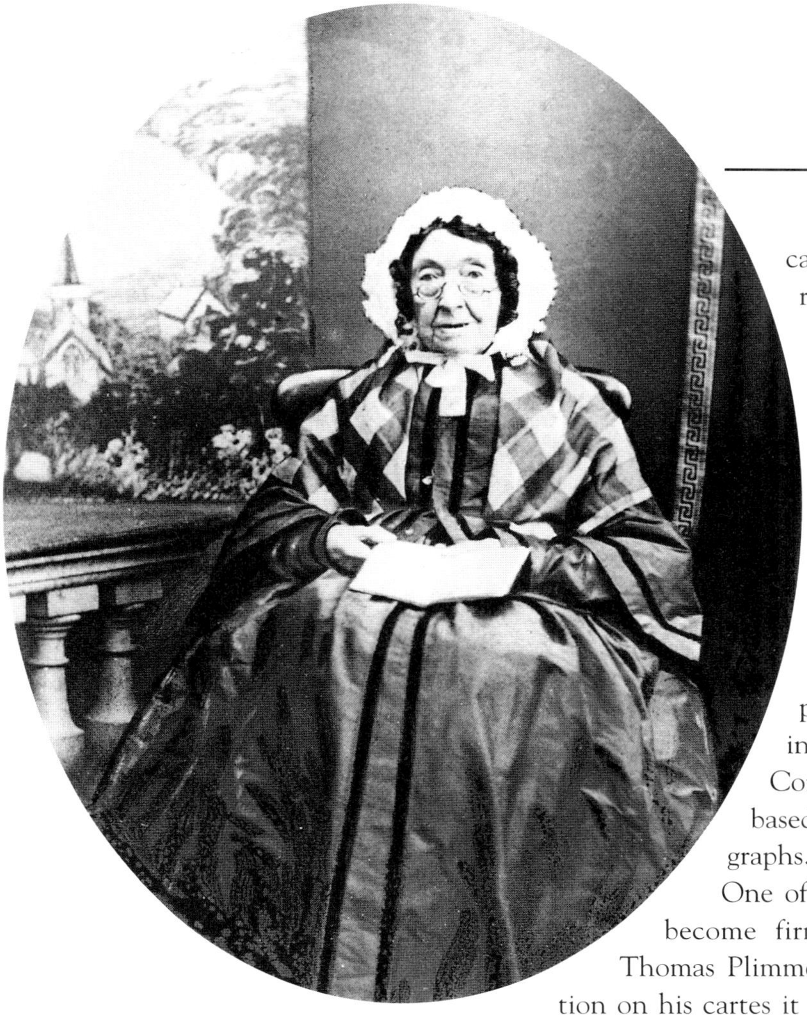

Mary Ann McCracken (1770–1866), from a carte-de-visite portrait by the Belfast photographer John Gibson, c. 1865.

MAGNI / UM

Seen here as an alert nonagenarian, Mary Ann was the sister of Henry Joy McCracken, leader of the northern United Irishmen, who was hanged in 1798. In the course of a long and useful life she devoted herself to charitable and liberal causes.

career in Scarborough, where he reputedly became the richest provincial photographer in the country, was long commemorated by the name Sarony Square. His even more famous brother Napoleon, a lithographer who became a photographer in Birmingham and later in New York, lithographed a view of Belfast c. 1860 which was produced and published by the local printing firm of Marcus Ward and Company; it may well have been based on one of his brother's photographs.

One of the earliest Belfast studios to become firmly established was that of Thomas Plimmer. According to the information on his cartes it opened in 1860, and it is still listed in directories as late as 1898. Initially situated in Bridge Street, by 1865 it had moved to High Street, where it remained. A variation in name between Thomas or Thomas H. in the 1860s and early 1870s, and Thomas or T.S. later (when the studio was called the Ulster Photographic Institute) may indicate two owners,

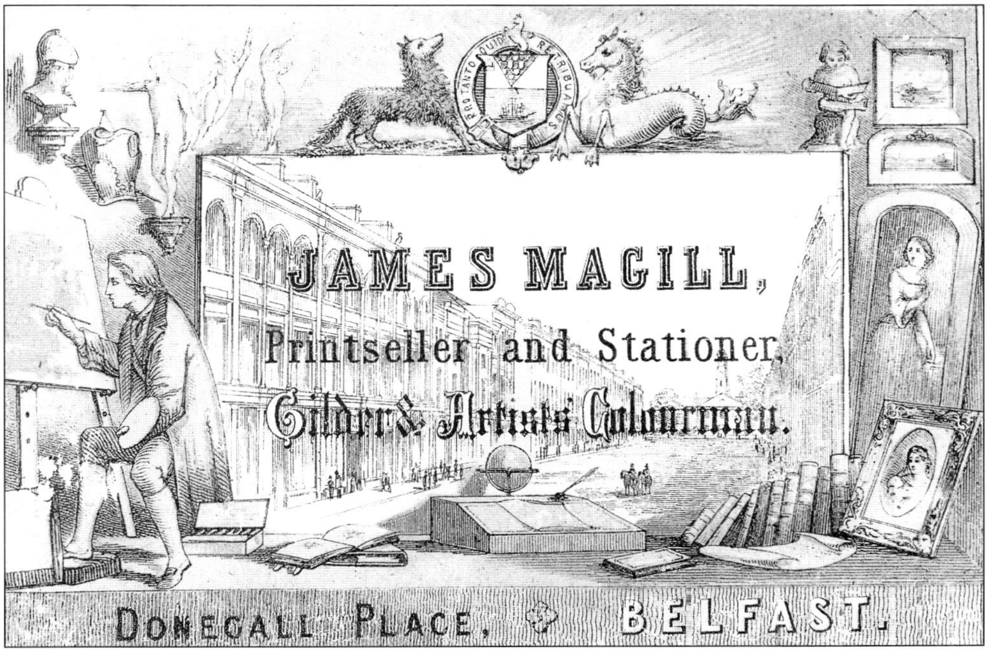

Trade card of James Magill, c. 1860.

MAGNI / UM

Following the closure of Sarony's Belfast branch in 1861, Magill bought the stock and added photography to his other activities. The Magill studio soon became the most fashionable in Belfast, remaining in business for over thirty years.

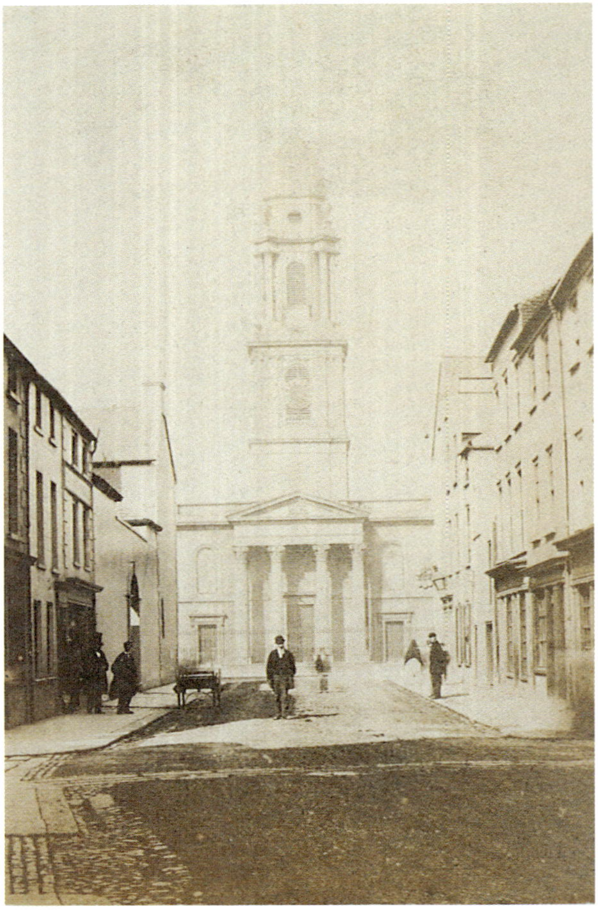

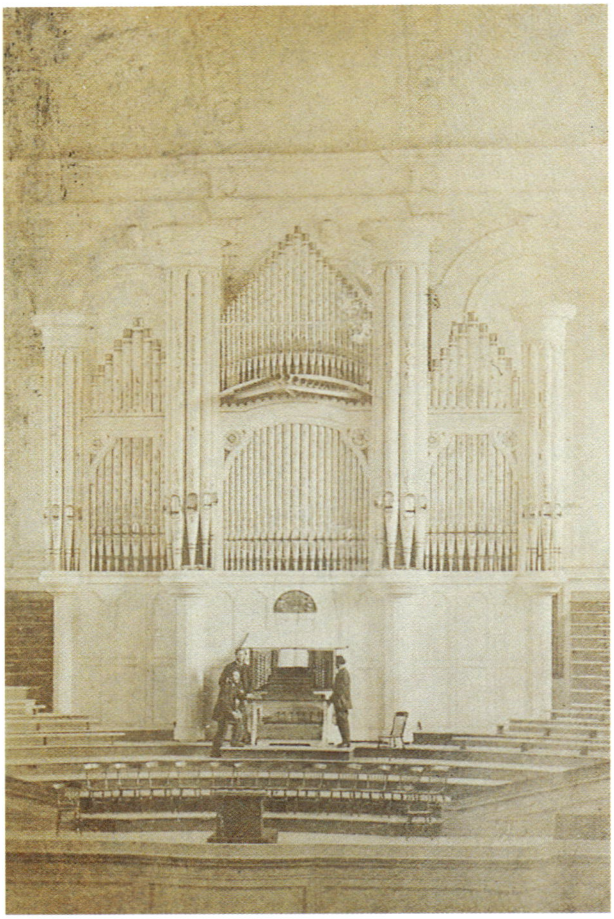

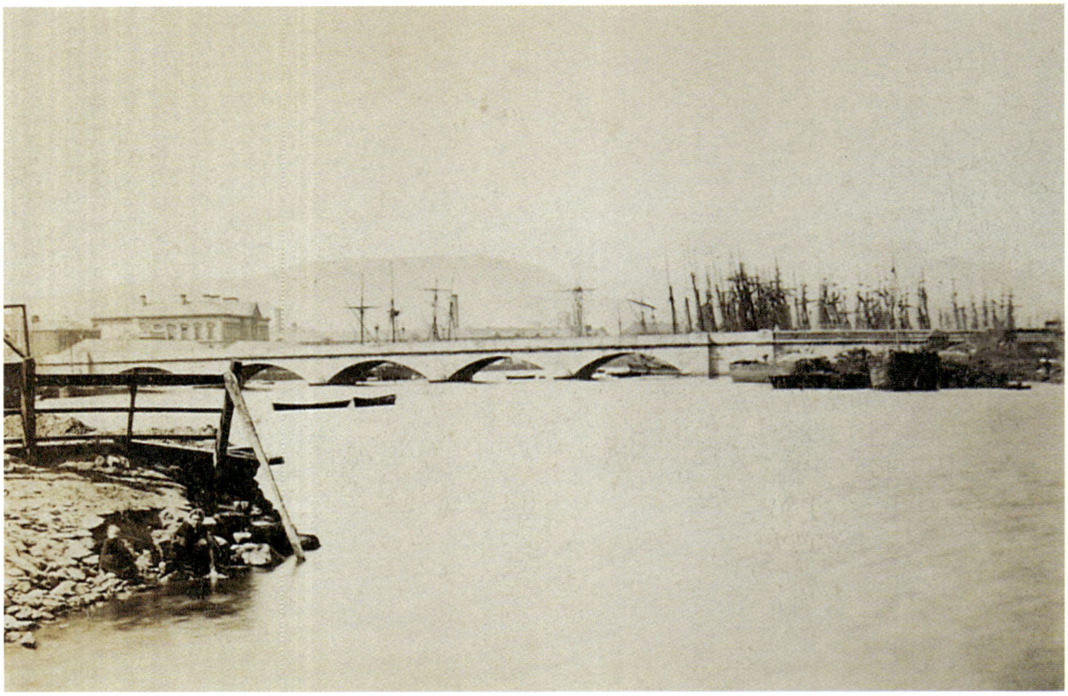

Three carte-de-visite views of Belfast, c. 1865, from the studio of James Magill.
BY KIND PERMISSION OF A.W. MERRICK

Top left
St Anne's Church, from Church Street

Top right
Mulholland organ, Ulster Hall

Right
Queen's Bridge

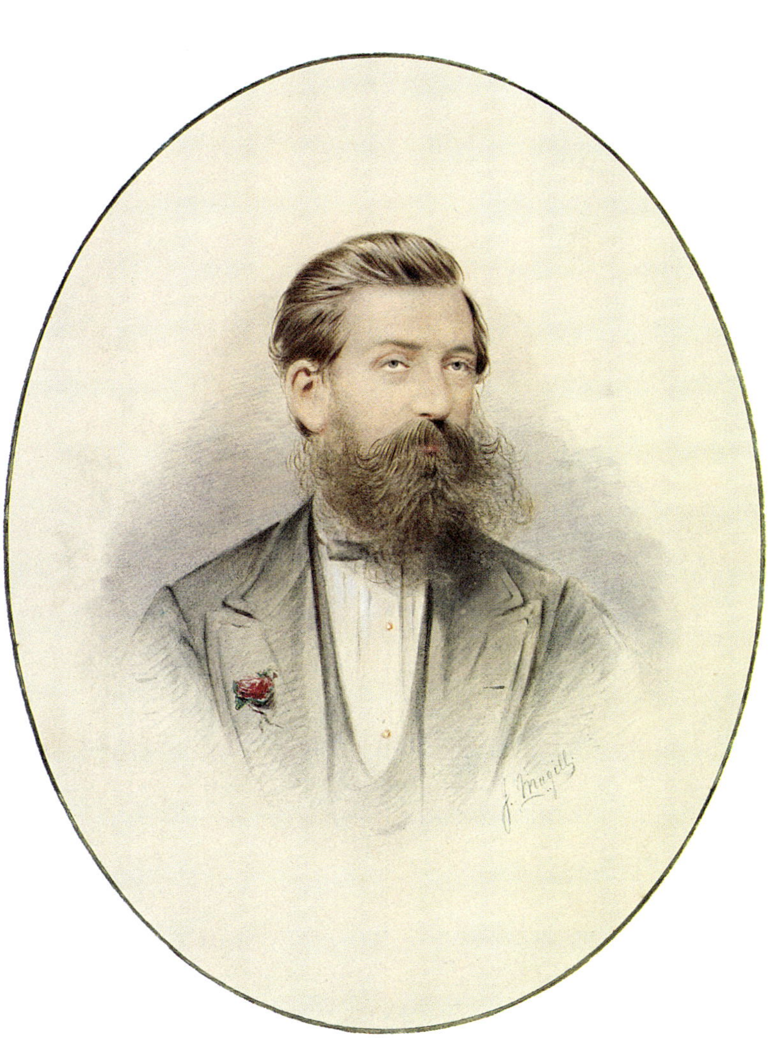

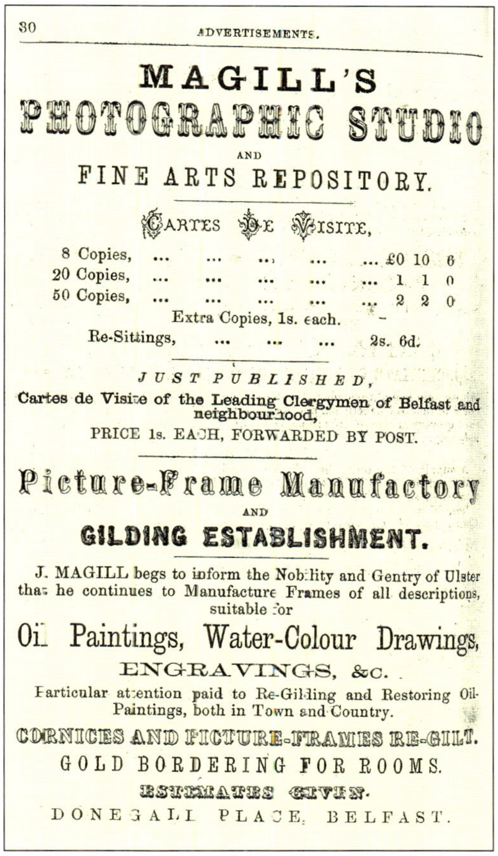

30 ADVERTISEMENTS.

MAGILL'S

PHOTOGRAPHIC STUDIO

AND

FINE ARTS REPOSITORY.

CARTES DE VISITE,

8 Copies, ...	£0 10 6
20 Copies, ...	1 1 0
50 Copies, ...	2 2 0

Extra Copies, 1s. each.

Re-Sittings, ... 2s. 6d.

JUST PUBLISHED,

Cartes de Visite of the Leading Clergymen of Belfast and neighbourhood,

PRICE 1s. EACH, FORWARDED BY POST.

Picture-Frame Manufactory

AND

GILDING ESTABLISHMENT.

J. MAGILL begs to inform the Nobility and Gentry of Ulster that he continues to Manufacture Frames of all descriptions, suitable for

Oil Paintings, Water-Colour Drawings,

ENGRAVINGS, &c.

Particular attention paid to Re-Gilding and Restoring Oil-Paintings, both in Town and Country.

CORNICES AND PICTURE-FRAMES RE-GILT.

GOLD BORDERING FOR ROOMS.

ESTIMATES GIVEN.

DONEGALL PLACE, BELFAST.

Advertisement by James Magill, from a Belfast directory for 1865–6.

MAGNI / UM

William Gray, Hon. Secretary of Belfast Naturalists' Field Club, *c.* 1873.

MAGNI / UM

This delicately coloured portrait forms the frontispiece to an elaborately bound volume of photographs recording club members and their outings, presented to Gray in 1873. The address of thanks includes this note, 'We have . . . thought it right, to ask you to sit specially for a photographic likeness, which now forms a part of the book.' The studio chosen was that of James Magill.

father and son; one carte I have seen gives T. and S. Plimmer, but I suspect this is a printing error for T.S. In any event the earlier Plimmer (if there were two) was a portrait painter who turned to photography. One of Plimmer's surviving cartes is a 'vitretype' with a hard glossy finish. 'This or any other portrait enlarged to order and painted in oil or water colour' runs the legend on the back.

The best known and most successful of the early Belfast studios, however, was Magill's. Like many studio owners of the time, James Magill was a businessman with other interests. He had started as a stationer in 1847.[10] From the early 1850s his shop was at 2 Donegall Place, in what had formerly been the town's most fashionable residential street but was by then largely commercialised. Here, in addition to selling ordnance survey maps and distributing government stamps he sold prints and pictures and carried out cleaning, restoring, framing and gilding work on the premises. In the late 1850s he was also selling 'photographic views of Rome'. Portrait photography, which in its more refined forms entailed retouching and colouring by skilled artists, was a natural extension of Magill's activities.

Magill's photographic studio opened in 1861 as successor to Sarony's, which had closed in that year, and flourished for the next thirty years. The large number of

Magill cartes and other portraits which survive testifies to the studio's popularity among the solid citizens of Belfast. Magill also claimed to produce photographs of 'scenery, mansions, interesting historical ruins &c.'. Fewer of these have survived, but there is a small collection of Belfast views of the 1860s in private hands, in the fashionable carte format. The scenes depicted include St Anne's Church in Donegall Street, the Queen's Bridge, and a rare and very interesting interior view of the Ulster Hall showing the splendid organ presented in 1862 by the linen magnate Thomas Mulholland. It is still there.

Of similar date were the sets of carte-size views of northern places taken by the Dublin photographer F.H. Mares and registered at Stationers' Hall in London in 1863, the first northern views to be registered there. These included six views of St Patrick's Church of Ireland Cathedral in Armagh, six of Belfast (the Ulster and Northern Counties Railway termini, Elmwood Church, the Ulster Hall, Queen's College, and the Deaf and Dumb Asylum) and six places of interest near Belfast (the 'Druid's Altar' at the Giant's Ring, the boathouse at Molly Ward's on the Lagan, Shane's Castle and Carrickfergus Castle, the cave on Cave Hill and McArt's Fort). Registration became more common from the 1870s onwards.

Similar views, some of which were published as *cartes*, were taken from the mid-1860s by the Dublin firm of William Lawrence and Company. Lawrence's stereoscopic views of Belfast, now part of the Lawrence Collection in the National Library of Ireland in Dublin, were taken by an unknown photographer or photographers in Lawrence's employ during the years 1864–80; forty-four of the sixty-six that survive were published.[11] Other views, apparently by amateur photographers and dating from about 1870, include the new, but as yet incomplete, Belfast Castle on the slopes of Cave Hill. For the professional photographer, success has always been as much a matter of seeing opportunities and creating demand as of technical photographic competence. An early example of opportunist publication was a book by the Scottish photographer John McGhie (or Maghie) from Hamilton in Lanarkshire, whose visit to the North of Ireland in 1870 led to the publication of an album entitled *Photography of County Down Scenery* (printed in Belfast in 1870 by Allen and Johnston and reissued the following year) – a volume consisting of a single page of letterpress in florid style followed by thirty-three tipped-in photographs of country mansions and their grounds.

No northern photographers exhibited their work in the Irish Industrial Exhibition of 1853.[12] By 1871, however, when the Belfast Working Men's Exhibition was held in Belfast, Dr James Moore, the surgeon and artist who introduced the show, could claim with some justification that there were 'exhibited specimens of photography which . . . could not be surpassed in any town in the Three Kingdoms . . .'[13] The exhibits included Irish views by Magill and John Mack and portraits, in carte or other form, by Rudolph Mayer and his erstwhile partner E.T. Church. Mayer, who showed several portraits and Mayerotypes, was an Austrian who had been employed, at the substantial salary of five and a half guineas a week, by the printing firm of Marcus Ward and Company, for whom he produced the Mayerotype – an expensive type of finish for coloured photographic portraits. Listed under Artists in the directories, he apparently neither took the photograph nor did the colouring himself. His advertisement in the exhibition catalogue for his Photographic Art Establishment in Castle Place claimed that Mayer and Company were artist photographers to HRH Prince Arthur and Royal Photographers by Letters Patent to the Emperor of Austria. Every branch of portrait photography was undertaken – Mayerotypes, Oleophotographs, composition family groups, the Imperial vignette portrait, portraits finished in carbon, water colour portraits, portraits painted in oil, as well as cartes de visite at prices ranging from six for five shillings to fifty for £1 7s. 6d. (just over sixpence each). The other photographer who advertised in the catalogue was E.T. Church, 'late partner of R. Mayer', who had 'taken all Portraits while in partnership with R. Mayer'. He had just opened his studio in Donegall Place. All his cartes de visite were said to be on enamel and included four positions of the subject; his 'cameo vignette' was a 'new and effective style of Carte-de-Visite, being the nearest approach to a Cameo', selling at 8 shillings for six or 15 shillings for the dozen; 'incaustic portraits' were available from 5 guineas and upwards.

E.T. Church was one of the most successful portrait photographers in the 1870s and 1880s. Before coming to Belfast and joining Mayer he had worked in Henry Hering's studio in Regent Street, London. The entry under his name in a publication of 1891, at the very end of his career, tells us: 'Mr Church undertakes every branch of photography, as cartes de visite, cabinets, enlargements by the new permanent gelatine process, groups, all kinds of out-door photography, and special attention is given to photographing machinery, &c., for trade purposes.' Clearly the phenomenal industrial growth of Belfast had made this last field of photography important even to portrait specialists such as Church. The entry goes on to expatiate on his expertise in portrait work: 'Mr Church has won a special reputation and a great triumph in the new life-sized oil portrait, which is mounted in broad gold frame, thirty by twenty-four inches, complete for £2 2s. . . . Mr Church personally photographs all sitters, and in the colouring department executes all paintings himself.'[14]

In fact Church was by that time an old-fashioned photographer. Even ten years earlier he had been employing techniques that most other photographers had abandoned – but which still gave excellent results. We happen to know this because Robert Welch as a young man worked as Church's assistant, before setting up on his own, and left some detailed notes on a collection of Church's cartes now in the Ulster Museum. The cartes had been printed by Welch in 1881 on collodio-chloride paper – an old soft-surface paper common in the middle years of the century – which was either supplied by Obernetter of Munich (who invented it in 1867) or made on the premises by Church himself. One of Welch's notes reads:

> Printed by R. Welch (with Church) on Church's own Collodio Chloride Paper made with Mawson & Swan's emulsion about 1881 (varnished as usual). Church (& perhaps Bruce of Duns, Scotland) was the only British or Irish photographer who used this collodio process for many years after all the others in the country had given it up. It was always used, however, in Germany (& France?). His gallery was all flat top light and suited the process.

Another note tells us that the soft surface of collodio-chloride papers, especially Obernetter's, required all prints not framed at once to be varnished, because they scratched so easily. Welch added: 'The process is very permanent, especially if varnished, as the hypo is so easily washed out and the collodion does not ferment like the animal albumen in that process.' The varnish Church always used was that produced by Sochnée Frères.[15]

Marcus Ward and Company, the printers for whom Mayer had worked, ran a public photographic studio in the 1860s and early 1870s, probably as an offshoot of the chromolithographic work for which they were becoming famous. Some of their cartes survive, including one of the novelist Anthony Trollope, *c.* 1867, which may have been taken in London, where the firm also had a branch, rather than Belfast. They claimed to be by appointment to the Prince of Wales, and called themselves either 'Portrait Painters and Photographers' or 'Photographers and Portrait Painters'. There is an excellent photograph of the front of their premises at that time, at 13 Donegall Place, which clearly shows the glasshouse studio on the roof of the building and, on the ground floor, a window display of samples of its output. The date is neatly established by a poster in the other window advertising diaries for the year 1868. Marcus Ward and Company in 1867 were advertising for sale photographs of the English and North of Ireland cricket teams, the earliest mention of such photographs in the North.

From quite an early stage in the history of photography, the fierce competition for custom led to the production of novelties. The carte, though retaining the standard 4-by-2½-inch mount which albums were designed to accommodate, might contain a very small 'Gem' portrait. Cheap tintype portraits were sometimes mounted in the same way. Tintypes can be found from any period from the 1850s to the 1940s. A later variation on the carte was the mini-carte, called 'mignon' or

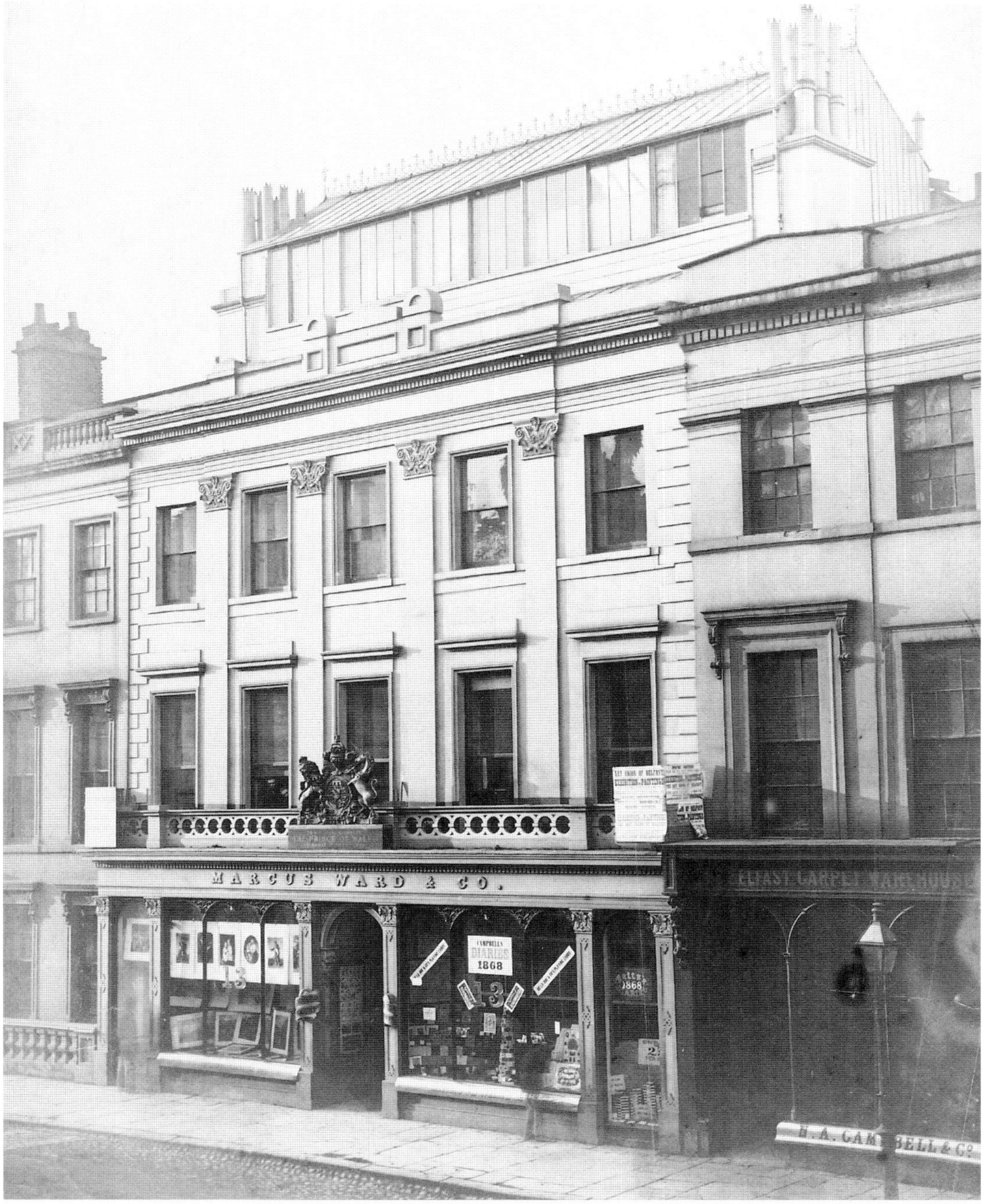

‘victoria’, which measured only $2\frac{1}{2}$-by-$1\frac{1}{4}$ inches. (In fact, this was a revival: the earliest English cartes, introduced by the French photographic firm of Marion and Company, in 1857, had very small portraits, $1\frac{1}{2}$-by-$1\frac{5}{8}$ inches or $1\frac{5}{8}$-by-$2\frac{1}{4}$ inches.) Microphotographs, even smaller, appeared comparatively early, as was the case with a tiny view of the Wesleyan College, Belfast, *c.* 1870, mounted in the pommel of a paper-knife, to be looked at through a magnifying-glass cover measuring only 3mm in diameter.

The earliest reference to the use of photography to illustrate machinery in the

Marcus Ward and Company’s premises in Donegall Place, Belfast, in 1867, showing the rooftop studio.

MAGNI / UM

north of Ireland is an advertisement in the 1865 Belfast directory by Gray and Company, May Street, manufacturers of agricultural implements and machines, whose price lists, 'with Photographic Views of the different Implements', could be had on application. James Massey, who had a studio in High Street from the mid-1860s, advertised himself in the 1865 directory as a 'Professional Landscape Photographer' who would take views of animals or machinery in town or country, as well as 'Noblemen's and Gentlemen's Seats, Public Buildings and Shop Fronts'. Massey's one-time partner, Richard Ward (no known relation of the printers), also described himself as a landscape photographer, and a few excellent specimens of his work from *c.* 1869 survive. He too advertised his willingness to take machinery, as well as works of art and designs; he also offered to give instruction.

The Belfast International Exhibition and Bazaar, held in Belfast in 1876, included displays of views and portraits from Magill's studio and a series of photographic views of Belfast by F.A. Piccione. Magill's entry made reference to the prize medal awarded to James McGreevy (presumably one of their employees); the studio also exhibited a photograph of the part of the Ulster Hall occupied by the Workmen's Exhibition of 1870. Felix Piccione was an Italian artist who settled in Belfast and became well known locally as a painter. Like some other artists he is sometimes listed as 'photographer artist' in the directories, sometimes not. The Linen Hall Library has a photograph by him showing the White Linen Hall in the 1870s, marked with the legend 'F. A. Piccione & Co., artists and photographers (Awarded Prize Medal, London Ex. 1870), 22 Castle Place, Belfast. (Above Cantrell & Co.'s Medical Hall.)'.

Studios outside Belfast 1860–80

Several permanent studios were established in Londonderry during the 1860s, producing both a crop of cartes and the first of many Donegal views for the tourist market. The earliest studio of which we have a record was that of Alexander Ayton, who came to Londonderry from Scotland in the early 1860s. His first studio was in the Crescent. In 1864 he moved to new, purpose-built premises in Kennedy Place, which were described in some detail in the *Londonderry Sentinel* when he opened there in April:

> In order to meet the growing demands of the public, Mr Ayton, whose reputation as a first-class artist is now fully established, has just completed and entered into possession of his new Photographic Gallery . . . Having visited many

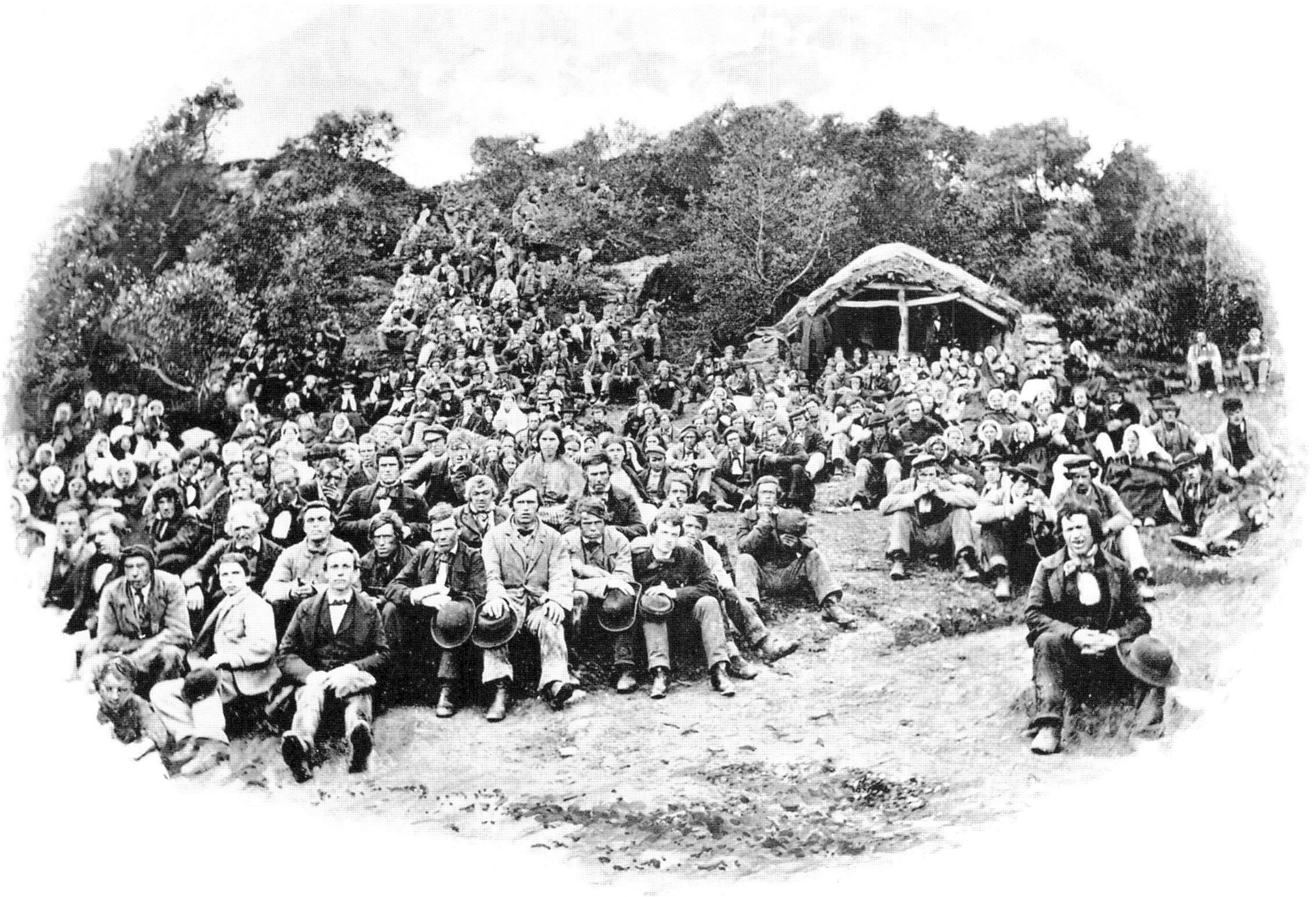

'A Mass in the Mountains of Donegal', 1867, by Alexander Ayton, from *Sights and Scenes in Ireland.*

MAGNI / UM

This extraordinary picture of a congregation assembled for mass in the open air was an early work by Ayton, a Scottish-born Londonderry photographer. The caption in *Sights and Scenes*, a collection of half-tone reproductions published in the late 1890s, gives the date, which might otherwise appear incredible. Many 'Scalans' such as this, relics of penal times, had already been replaced by permanent church buildings.

> studios in London and Dublin, we do not hesitate to say that, for completeness and efficiency in every department, this establishment has not been equalled, certainly not surpassed. The show-room on the ground-floor contains above 1,000 portraits, of various sizes and varieties, besides views of churches, antiquities, and mansions in the North-West district, including our city . . . On the same floor with the show-room is a ladies' dressing-room, elegantly furnished and fitted up with every convenience. The portrait gallery is on the second floor – a fine apartment – measuring 38 feet by 16, and is quite unique of its kind.[16]

With its glass roof and adjustable blinds, hot water heating system and rooms for printing, preparing paper and storage room for negatives, the studio represented a substantial investment. In the event, the outlay was justified. Ayton prospered, moving later to even finer premises in Shipquay Place. Described at his death in 1900 as 'late of Kennedy Place', his will refers to the business 'at present carried on at Shipquay Street and Carlisle Road'. His estate was valued at the substantial sum of £3,283. Under the terms of his will, his son George, who had assisted him in Londonderry, was to have a lease of the business, together with 'negatives, apparatus etc.', for a period of not more than ten years; accordingly his name disappears from the directories after 1909.

Another son, Alexander junior, was also a photographer. Though trained by his father in Londonderry, he made his career in Edinburgh, where he is listed in directories from 1875, first in Hanover Street, later in Bruntsfield Place. The latter studio appears on some of his father's photographs as a branch of the Irish business, but Alexander junior became a leading figure in his own right, being elected president of the Edinburgh Photographic Society in the early 1890s before predeceasing his father in 1894; a Robert Ayton, Edinburgh photographer, mentioned in the old man's will, may have been young Alexander's son. At all events, the Aytons came from Scotland and maintained their links with it – another of Ayton's sons, James, was a prosperous Edinburgh solicitor and one of his sons-in-law was Town Clerk of Ayr.

With a successful career of nearly forty years in one place, Ayton left behind hundreds of portraits, many of which survive. Of more particular interest to historians,

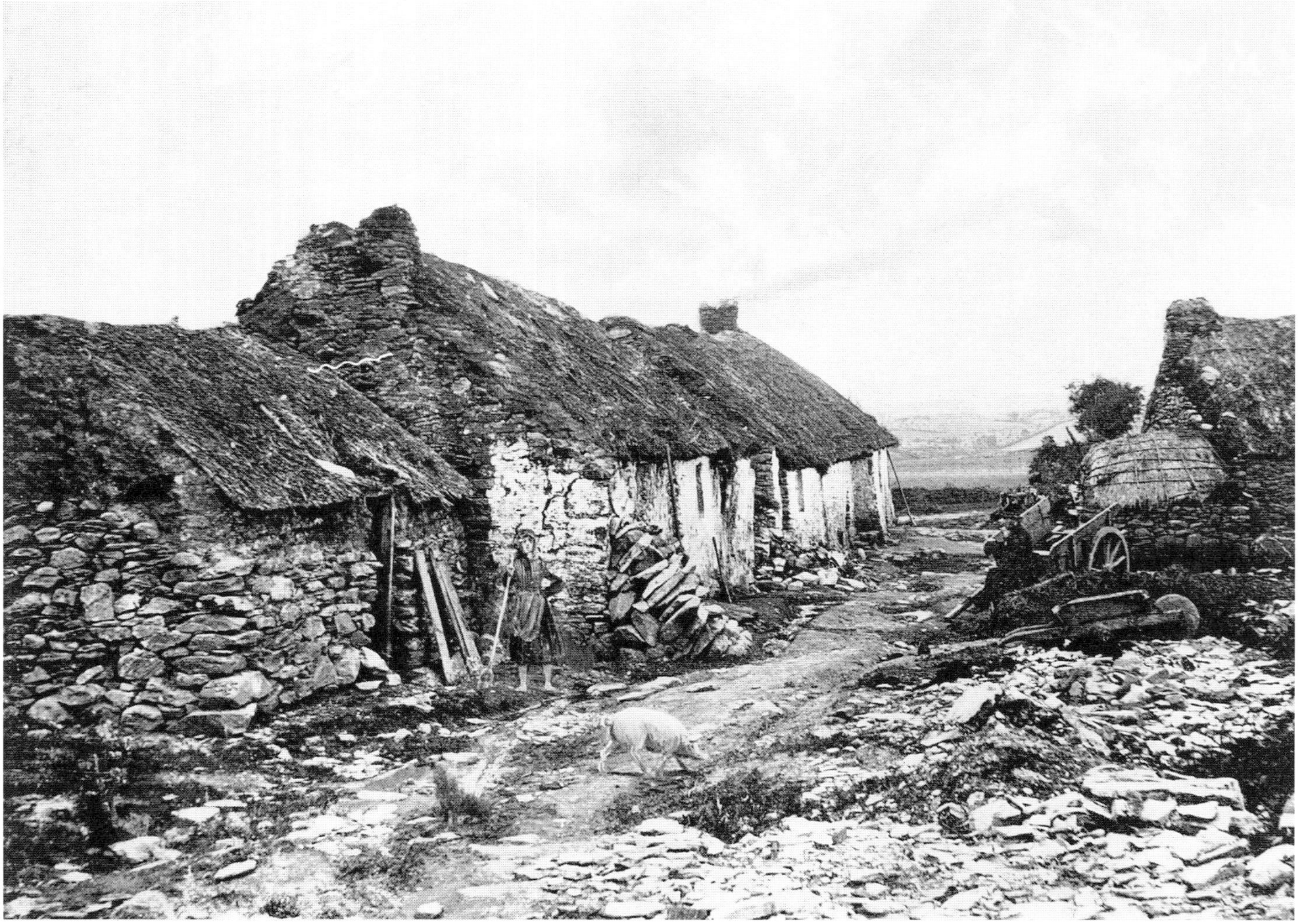

'A Farm-house in Donegal', *c.* 1870, by Alexander Ayton, from *Sights and Scenes in Ireland*. MAGNI / UM

Many photographers, both professional and amateur, were to follow Ayton in recording scenes such as this in the wilder parts of Donegal. Incidentally, the long-snouted pig in the foreground looks like one of the hardy breed known as Old Irish Greyhound – capable, it was said, of clearing a five-bar gate as nimbly as any hunter.

he also took some of the earliest images of peasant life in Donegal. The originals of these do not survive, but some of them were published in the 1890s in *Sights and Scenes in Ireland*. They include 'West Street, Tory Island', pictures of a typical farm-house and an illicit still, and a famous image of worshippers at an open-air 'Mass in the Mountains of Donegal', taken in 1867. Ayton also did photographic work for the police: we know that in 1881 he supplied two sets of prints of the corpse of a man murdered by his wife, to be shown to the jury at her trial.[17]

Incidentally, the prison in Londonderry was one of the earliest local ones (Mountjoy, the convict prison in Dublin, was the first, *c*. 1860) to photograph its inmates on a regular basis, well before it was obliged to do so under the Habitual Criminals Act of 1869. In-house photography was used in Londonderry from 1865, as it was in Enniskillen (Cavan and Lifford began in 1866, Belfast in 1868, Omagh in 1869).[18]

Another successful studio established in Londonderry in the 1860s was that of the Kerr family. Kerr's City Portrait Rooms, which first appeared in 1865 in Market

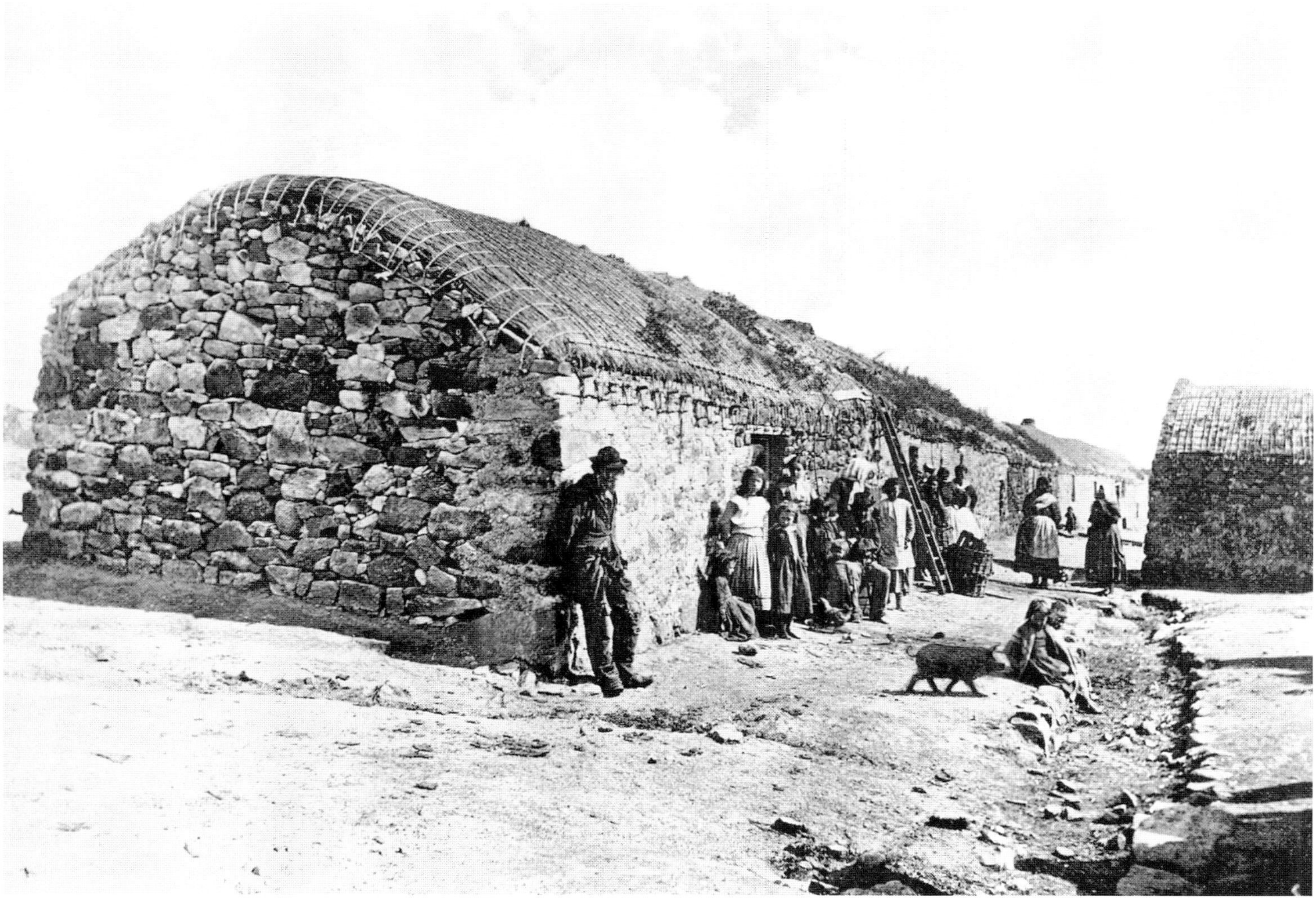

'West Street, Tory Island', by Alexander Ayton, undated, from *Sights and Scenes in Ireland*.
MAGNI / UM

Street, were run at that date by Thomas Kerr, who offered to take portraits of every description in all kinds of weather. Three years later, however, the proprietor was Hugh Kerr. By 1870 he had moved to Carlisle Road, where the studio did good business for the next thirty or forty years. An advertisement of 1899 claimed 'True and Pleasing Photographs, which for Beauty of Tone and Delicacy of Finish cannot be surpassed' and announced that family groups, wedding and excursion parties and cricket or football teams were a speciality. Rural scenes and country mansions (interior and exterior) were also photographed, while cabinet and carte-de-visite enamelled photographs were 'finished in the latest "Parisian Styles"' (surely by 1899 an antique touch). In 1890 Kerr set up a branch studio in the town of Monaghan which was run by his son James until James died in 1907. M. Kerr and Son appear as proprietors of the main studio in Londonderry between 1910 and 1913. A Miss Kerr, presumably a daughter of Hugh, then took it over (1914–24). She also ran the studio in Monaghan, which had continued under a manageress, from 1919 to 1922.

Edmond Huther's Photographic Gallery in Foyle Street, Londonderry, is listed in the 1865 directory, where he also advertised himself as

> open daily for the execution of Cartes-de-Visite, Glass Pictures, &c. Views taken to order anywhere in the Province. Pictures of any description copied and enlarged to the life size by the Solar Camera. Photographs painted in Oil or Water Colour. Portraits taken at night, or in dark weather, by the Magnesium Light.

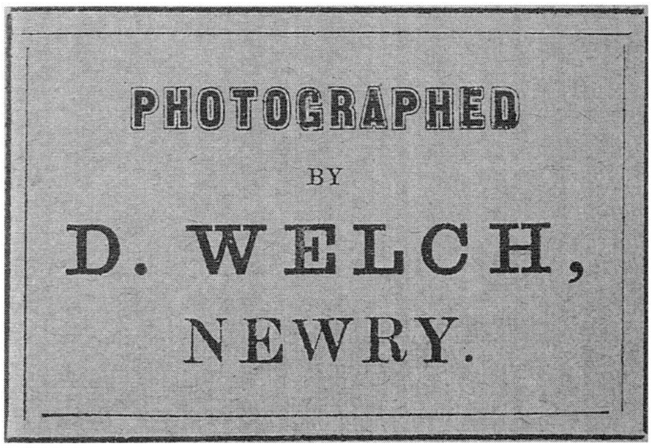

D. Welch, Newry, coloured album stamp, c. 1870.
MAGNI / UM

He did not appear in the 1868 directory but E. Huther is listed ten years later in 1878 at Carlisle Road, and Mrs Huther – presumably his widow – ran the studio there in 1880–2.

From this period and also from the north-west comes the unusually interesting figure of David Welch. A Scotsman from Kirkcudbright, Welch came to Ireland as a young man to work in the expanding linen industry, as 'agent' for a shirt manufacturer in Strabane, County Tyrone. There he met and in 1857 married a local girl of seventeen named Martha Graham who had artistic tastes (she was later to hand-colour some of his carte-de-visite portraits). He became increasingly interested in photography, to the extent that in 1863 he took it up professionally, establishing himself first in Enniskillen, where he and his growing family lived for the next five years. His sojourn in Strabane had brought him the patronage of the area's leading landowner, James Hamilton, 2nd Marquis of Abercorn. When Abercorn (a duke from 1868) was appointed lord lieutenant of

Ireland in 1865, Welch was able to call himself photographer by appointment to the viceroy.

In 1868 the Welch family moved to Newry in County Down, where they were to stay for the next three years or so, before migrating to England. There they settled for a short time at Leamington in Warwickshire. They soon returned to Ireland, however, at first to the south – in turn Kingstown (Dun Laoghaire), Carlow, Kildare and Kilkenny – before coming to rest again in the north, at Bangor. Welch died suddenly in 1875, leaving his widow to raise their six children as best she could.

David Welch's restless wanderings suggest that his photographic career was one of frustration. If so, it was not untypical: a shifting population of photographers, all more or less competent at the bread-and-butter (or bread-and-dripping) work of taking cheap portraits, roamed the country. It took exceptional talent, allied to good connections and a good head for business, to become well-established.

Surviving portraits, mostly in carte-de-visite form, show that Welch was as competent as most in that line. Apart from these, the evidence for his scope and competence as a photographer consists almost entirely of an album of original prints, some sixty in all, later compiled and annotated by his more famous son, Robert John Welch; this is now part of the Welch archive in the Ulster Museum.

These photographs, many of which are of great houses in Ireland, reflect the various locations of David Welch's career. From his Strabane days came views of

Belleek Pottery,
County Fermanagh, 1866,
by David Welch.

MAGNI / UM

This early view of the famous pottery at Belleek (the building had been completed only recently) was taken by Welch when he lived in Enniskillen.

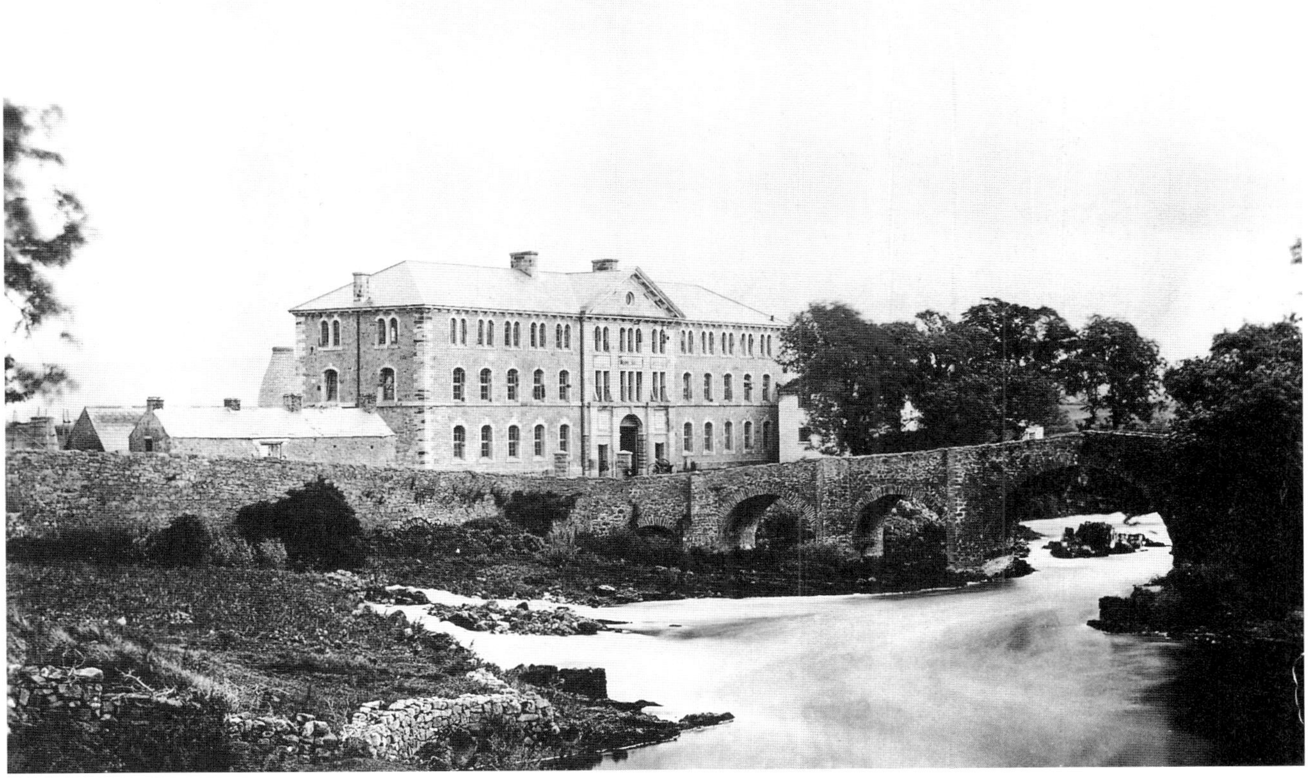

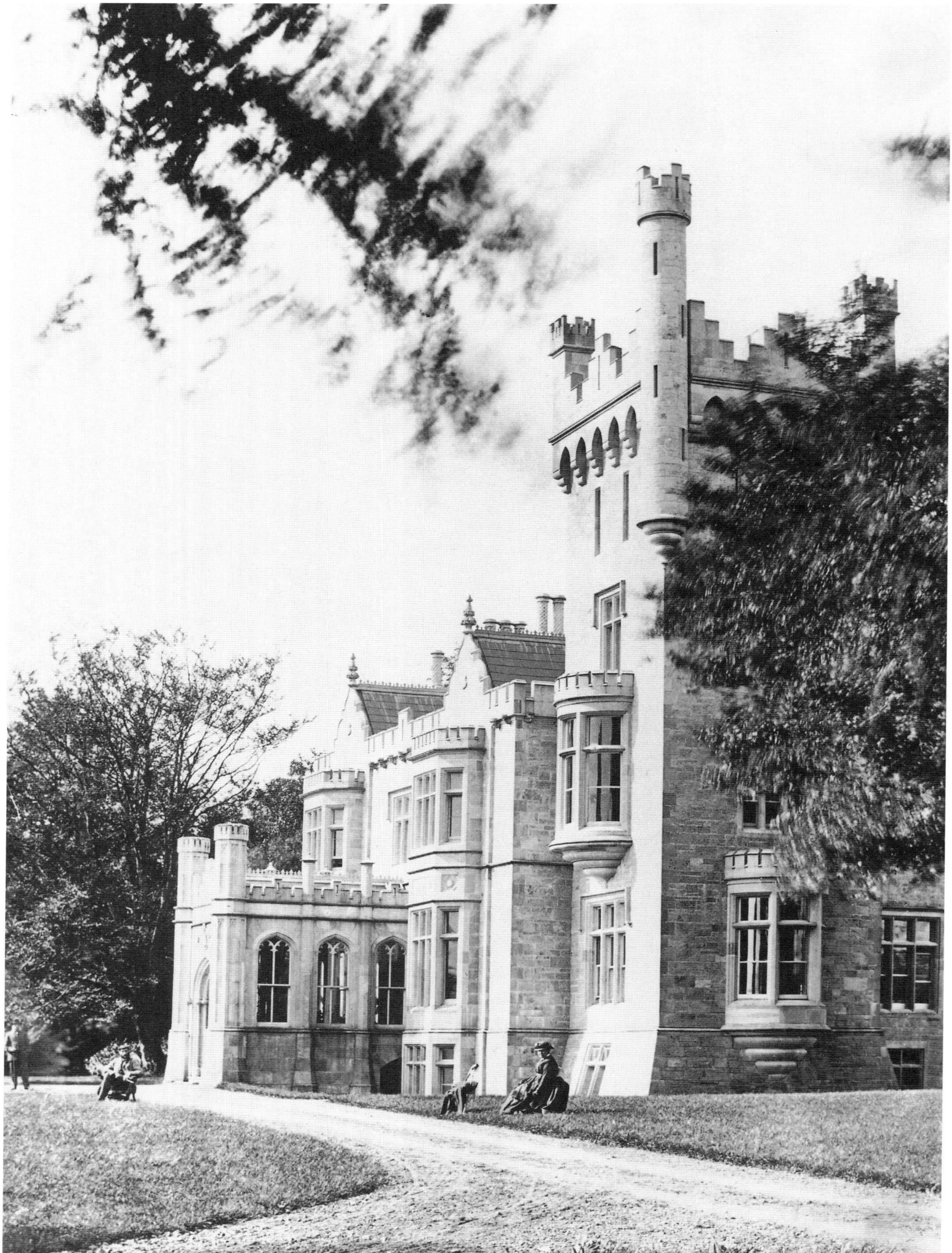

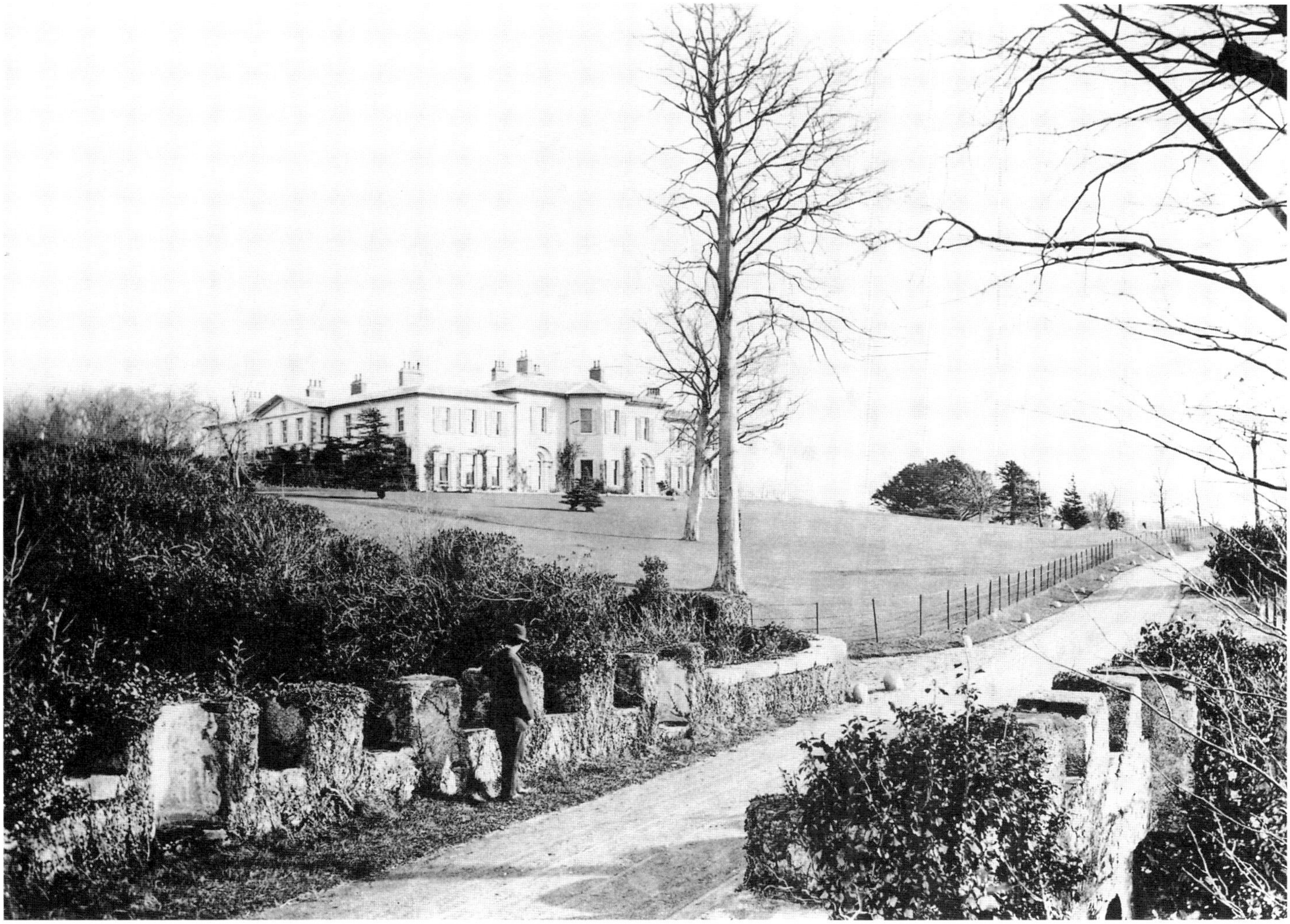

Baronscourt, his patron's Irish residence. From the Enniskillen studio come views of Florence Court, Magheramena Castle and the china works at Belleek; Lough Eske Castle in Donegal; Hilton Park, near Clones in County Monaghan; Farnham House, Ballyhaise House and other Cavan scenes. From the sojourn in Newry come views of Dromantine, Drumbanagher, Tollymore, Castlewellan, Mount Panther and other houses in County Down, as well as scenes from Rostrevor and Newcastle (where Welch ran a branch studio in the summer). The period in southern Ireland yields prints of Killarney, Powerscourt House and the great castle at Kilkenny; from his final days in Bangor, there are views of Bangor Castle and Clandeboye House. Lastly, souvenirs of the short spell in England include views of Stoneleigh Abbey, in Warwickshire, Bolton Abbey in Yorkshire and Eton College (with schoolboys). In fact, on the evidence of this album the elder Welch was a highly competent outdoor photographer.[19]

Other successful early photographers in the north-west were George Laidlaw, the first known photographer in Lifford and Strabane, who appears in the directories between 1868 and 1892, James Nimmocks in Coleraine and Castlerock (1868–80),

Tollymore Park, County Down, *c.* 1870, by David Welch.

MAGNI / UM

This view of Lord Roden's country seat was taken by Welch when he had his studio in Newry. The house was demolished in 1952 but the demesne is maintained as a forest park, open to the public.

Opposite
Lough Eske Castle, County Donegal, *c.* 1866, by David Welch.

MAGNI / UM

Built for a branch of the Brooke family, the castle was brand-new when this photograph was taken.

John Mack in Coleraine (from 1870), Thomas Predy in Limavady (from 1877) and William Watson in the town of Donegal (also from 1877). Even such a small place as Maghera had a photographer in 1877, one James Marks. In the south-west, David Welch's presence in Enniskillen from 1863 to 1868 has been mentioned earlier. For a short period in the 1860s there was also a studio in Ballyshannon, County Donegal (a garrison town): a Patrick Smyth, 'photographer, architect and grocer', was listed in 1868. Some years later, Miss E. Miller had her Mall Studio there. John McKendry, 'sewing agent and photographic artist', was to be found in Belturbet, County Cavan, in 1868. In Monaghan town, Joseph M. Graham was listed from 1868 to 1870. In mid-Ulster, Hugh Waide the schoolmaster was not the only early photographer in Cookstown; two others, Graham and Huey, were there in 1865 though gone by 1868. James Patterson established himself in the county and garrison town of Omagh in the mid-1860s; his widow was the proprietor in 1876.

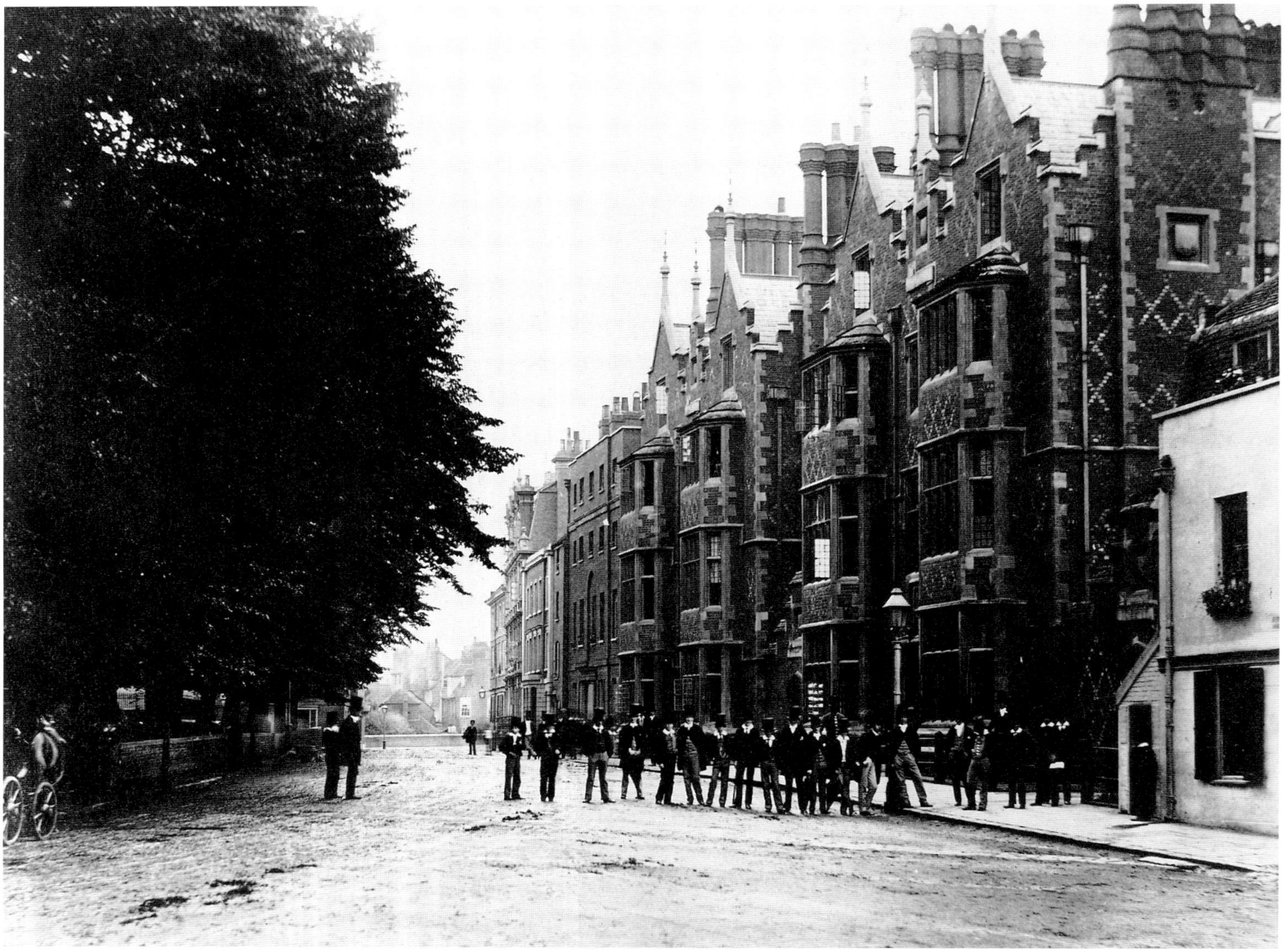

Eton College boys in the street, *c.* 1872, by David Welch.

MAGNI / UM

After leaving Newry, Welch and his family lived for a short time in England before returning to Ireland to settle eventually at Bangor, where he died suddenly in 1875.

Another early Omagh studio, which did not survive long, was that of Robert Nelson (1865–70); an Alexander Nelson is listed in Dungannon during the same period. John Thompson also operated in Omagh, but slightly later, between 1872 and 1877. Was he still there, as J.J. Thompson, twenty years later (1894–7)?

Holywood in County Down had a summer population of Belfast visitors sufficient to tempt William Ord (or Orde) to try his hand in 1870. Another early photographer in Holywood was James Kerr, whose premises in High Street included a fancy goods store as well as a studio. The Ulster Museum has an album of Holywood views, good professional work, which are almost certainly his. They are tipped-in original prints, datable from *c.* 1871 to *c.* 1885. Kerr was still going in 1897, when he photographed the town maypole decorated for Queen Victoria's jubilee, but disappeared from the directories shortly after that. The earliest recorded studio in County Down, however, was that of W. Wilson in Banbridge in 1861, though it is difficult to see how he could have obtained much business; in fact there was no sign of him in the town two years later. Newry, a port and garrison town not far from Banbridge, was a much more promising place and had a succession of studios from the mid-1860s when J.T. Cuming and George Wilson operated from Marcus Square and Mill Street. They were followed by David Welch in 1868. Welch's successor in the 1870s was an Englishman, W.B. Micklethwaite, who appears to have come from Biggleswade in Bedfordshire, since an address there is listed along with Newry and Newcastle on the back of one of his cartes.

Outside of Belfast and Londonderry, however, the best place in the North for early photographers was the ecclesiastical city of Armagh. Armagh had a population which included numbers of clergy, local officials and others who might wish to be photographed – not to mention the presence of a garrison, a county gaol and other institutions. By the mid-1860s it had three studios – McClelland's in Scotch Street, McKay's in Abbey Street and Bell's in Russell Street. All of these seem to have been out of business by the end of the decade, but another (Duncan's) opened up in the Mall in 1870 and was still listed in 1877, along with a new name in Abbey Street, Arthur Massey, 'portrait and landscape photographer, lithographer, engraver, copperplate printer, picture-framemaker, and insurance agent'. An elaborate two-page advertisement in the same directory expatiates at length on Massey's skill, his aristocratic patrons and 'the suitability of his Lenses for taking all kinds of Masonic, Orange, Oddfellow & other Lodge Groups'. He sold cameras and lenses and gave instruction in their use. He also operated a 'Lime Light Dissolving View Lantern', with which he was willing to visit any town or village in Ireland, and if a few local portraits were sent to him a few days previous to an engagement he could include them, life-size, in the evening's show. Furthermore, he was agent for the Mutual Life and Fire Insurance Companies, and promised that any

'Clergyman or Gentleman in the North giving a proposal for £500 on his own or friend's life' would be presented with 'Seven Copies of A.G. Massey's well-known 12 x 10 inch Views of his Church or Residence'. In addition to the studio in Armagh he had a branch studio in Monaghan for a time.

Massey was still in Abbey Street in 1880 (no mention of Monaghan), but by the end of that decade appears to have become a grocer in Scotch Street. In between, he appears briefly in the Belfast directory as proprietor of the Royal Ulster Fine Art Studio at 35 High Street. (An earlier Massey, Joseph, had had a studio in the same street, though not the same building, in the 1860s and early 1870s.) The custom of Armagh in the 1880s was largely in the hands of W.J. Hunter, whose Armagh Portrait Company was at 19 Scotch Street; Massey evidently turned to tea with the demise of the wet-plate process. Many of the early photographers came and went more quickly than that. The record may be held by Thomas Henry Hargrave, an Englishman from Cheshire who had been a photographer for nearly twenty years when he came to Keady, County Armagh, in March 1876. He had been there only a week when he fell down dead in front of an astonished customer named Mary Jane Armstrong. The *Armagh Guardian*, which carried an account of the inquest, reported revealingly: 'At first, it was thought that the vapour of the material used was the cause of death . . .', a reminder that in more ways than one photography did not necessarily provide a living.[20]

Some wet-plate amateurs

The wet collodion process was a challenge to technically minded amateurs, including a number of young army officers whose military careers entailed a good deal of

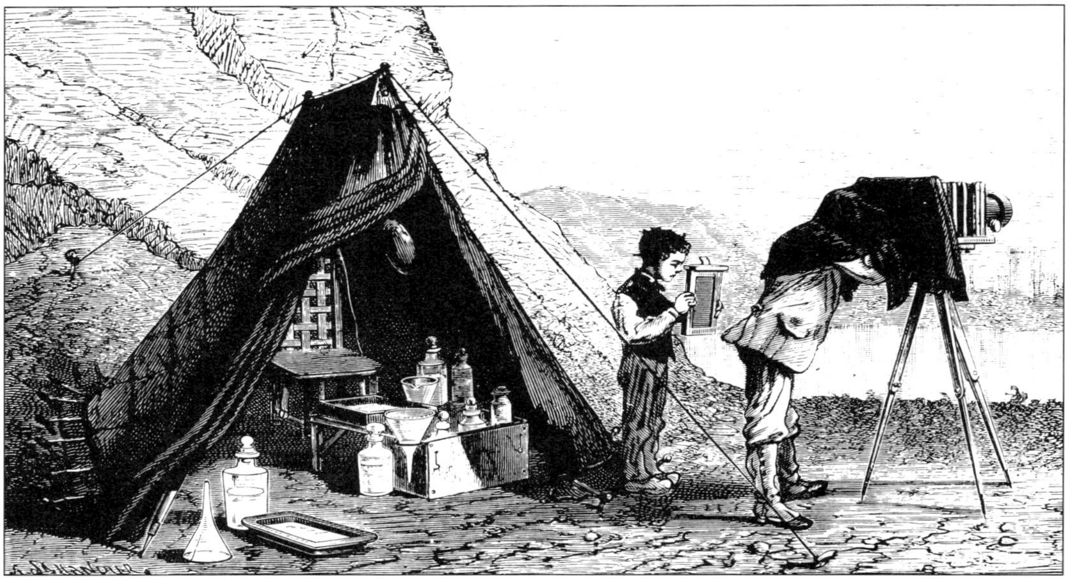

A wet-plate photographer at work out of doors, an engraving by Gaston Tissandier from his *History of Photography* (1876).

MAGNI / UM

Standard dry plates were soon to make this scene a thing of the past travel. One of the earliest and most successful of these gentlemen amateurs in the North of Ireland was Hugh Annesley of Castlewellan, County Down, a younger brother of the 4th Earl Annesley (whom he succeeded as 5th Earl in 1874). The earliest photographs in the Annesley albums, most of which are now in the Public Record Office of Northern Ireland, date from the early 1850s, when Hugh Annesley served as a junior officer in the Kaffir War in South Africa, 1851–3, in which he was badly wounded. Whether such curiosities as the photographs of a Kaffir skull and an ivory necklace and assegai were his own work or not is impossible to say with certainty, but they may well have been his first essays in an activity that was to interest him for the rest of his life. At any rate they were included in his first album, which is dated March 1855.

The first nine albums in the PRONI collection (others are in the hands of a descendant in Scotland but have been copied) consist mostly of Annesley's own photographs of army life and fellow officers and of the Castlewellan area and of Irish friends and relations, taken between the mid-1850s and the end of the 1870s. Those not his own are in most cases identified as the work of friends or of known professionals such as Cundall (who took a series of Crimean War soldiers for the Queen) or Howlett (of the great engineer Brunel and his ship *Leviathan*, later renamed *Great Eastern*). There are some interesting Crimean War photographs, though Annesley was not in the Crimea for long, being wounded at the battle of the Alma in October 1854, shortly after the British army landed; there is a picture, possibly a self-portrait, showing him with the black patch which

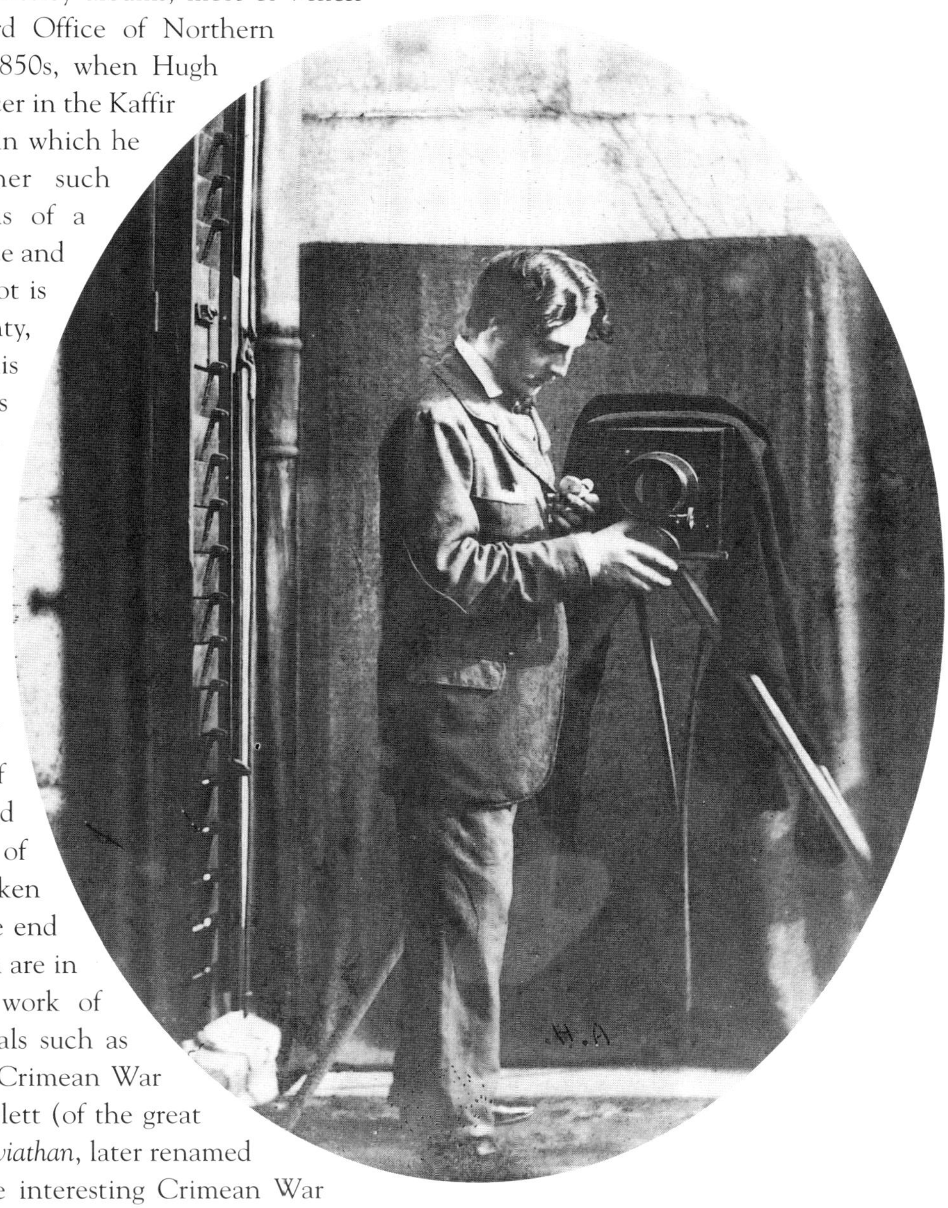

The Hon. Hugh Annesley with his camera, c. 1853.
PRONI (ANNESLEY COLLECTION, ALBUM 2/163)

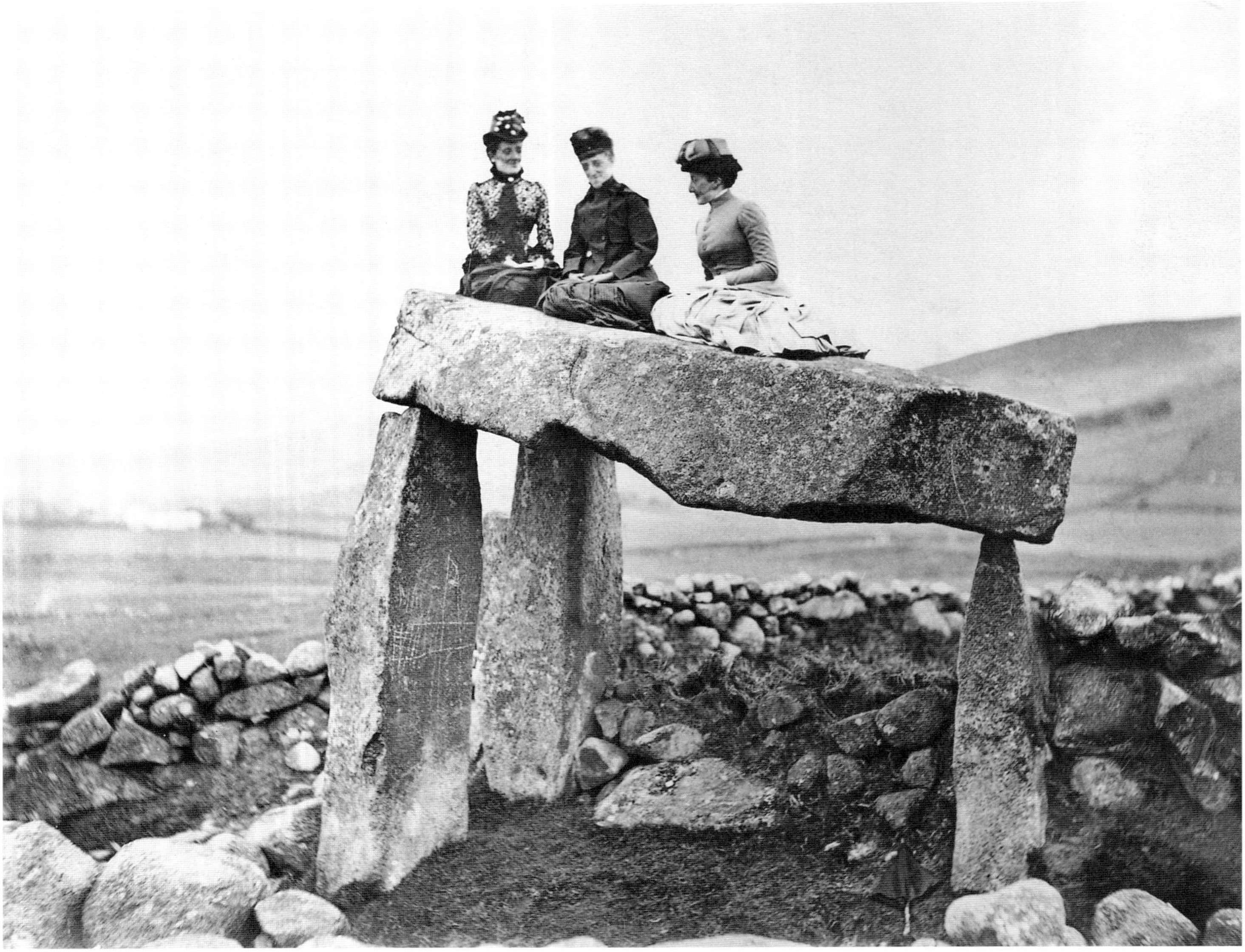

An outing to the Legananny dolmen, County Down, in the 1880s, by Hugh Annesley.
PRONI (ANNESLEY COLLECTION, ALBUM 5/84)

Being literally on the roadside, this notable ancient monument a few miles from Castlewellan was easily accessible to social climbers of all classes. Note the curious piebald effect, created by the wearing of veils, on the faces of the ladies from the castle.

covered the wound to his face.

From a local point of view his most interesting photographs are those of Castlewellan and Newcastle. These include pictures of various stages in the building of Castlewellan Castle, begun in 1856 and finished two years later, as well as views of and from Donard Lodge, on the slopes of Slieve Donard, where his widowed mother lived; also some portraits of employees of the estate.

His own 'photographic tent', used for preparing and developing his outdoor photographs, and his friend Lord Kilmorey's more elaborate 'photographic cab', are both illustrated in the albums. Though he later took advantage of the much more convenient dry-plate process to record journeys abroad, including an Indian tour in 1886–7, and the progress of his gardening improvements at Castlewellan, where he created a notable arboretum and published an account of it in 1903, illustrated with his own photographs, Annesley's best work as a photographer was done when

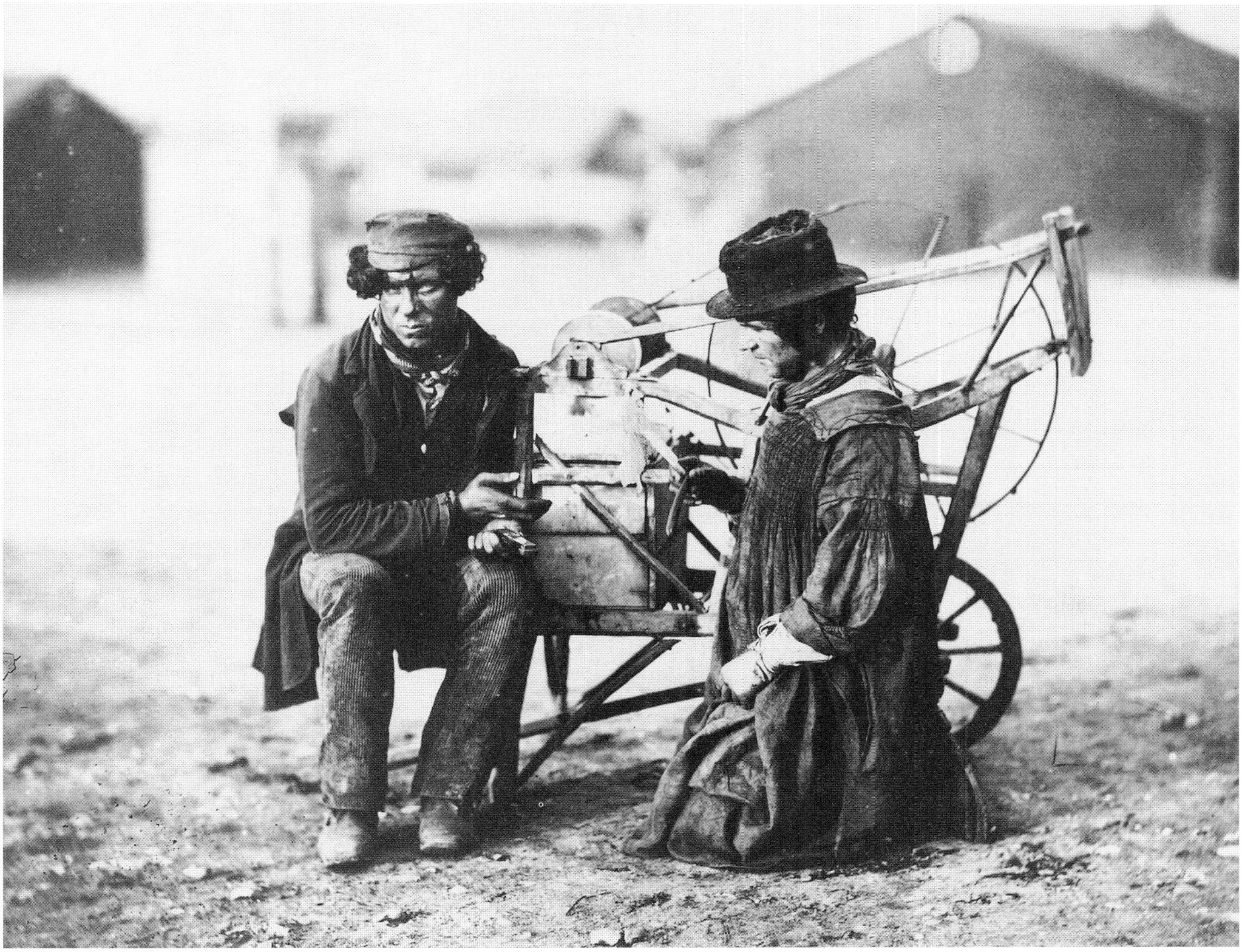

he was younger, as a skilled manipulator of the wet collodion process.

Similar albums can be found in a number of Irish country houses of the period, if usually on a smaller scale than those of the Annesley family and by a wider variety of hands. The 3rd Earl of Kilmorey, whose cab, mentioned above, shows him to have been another keen amateur, was a neighbouring landowner who lived at Mourne Park, Kilkeel, County Down. Born in 1842 and therefore some ten years younger than Annesley, he outlived him, surviving till 1915. Another and even closer neighbour was Robert, Viscount Jocelyn, son of the Earl of Roden, whose home was at Tollymore Park near Newcastle. It is not clear from the family albums to what extent Jocelyn himself was responsible for the photographs in the Roden albums; as usual, a good deal of swapping went on among these early photographers. His friend and fellow-soldier Charles Madden, a captain in the 8th King's Regiment, was undoubtedly an active and successful photographer in the 1860s.

'The seedy knife-grinder' at Aldershot Camp, Hampshire, 1860s, by Hugh Annesley.
PRONI (ANNESLEY COLLECTION, ALBUM 5/8)

The itinerant knife-grinder and his smocked assistant could have come straight from the pages of Charles Dickens.

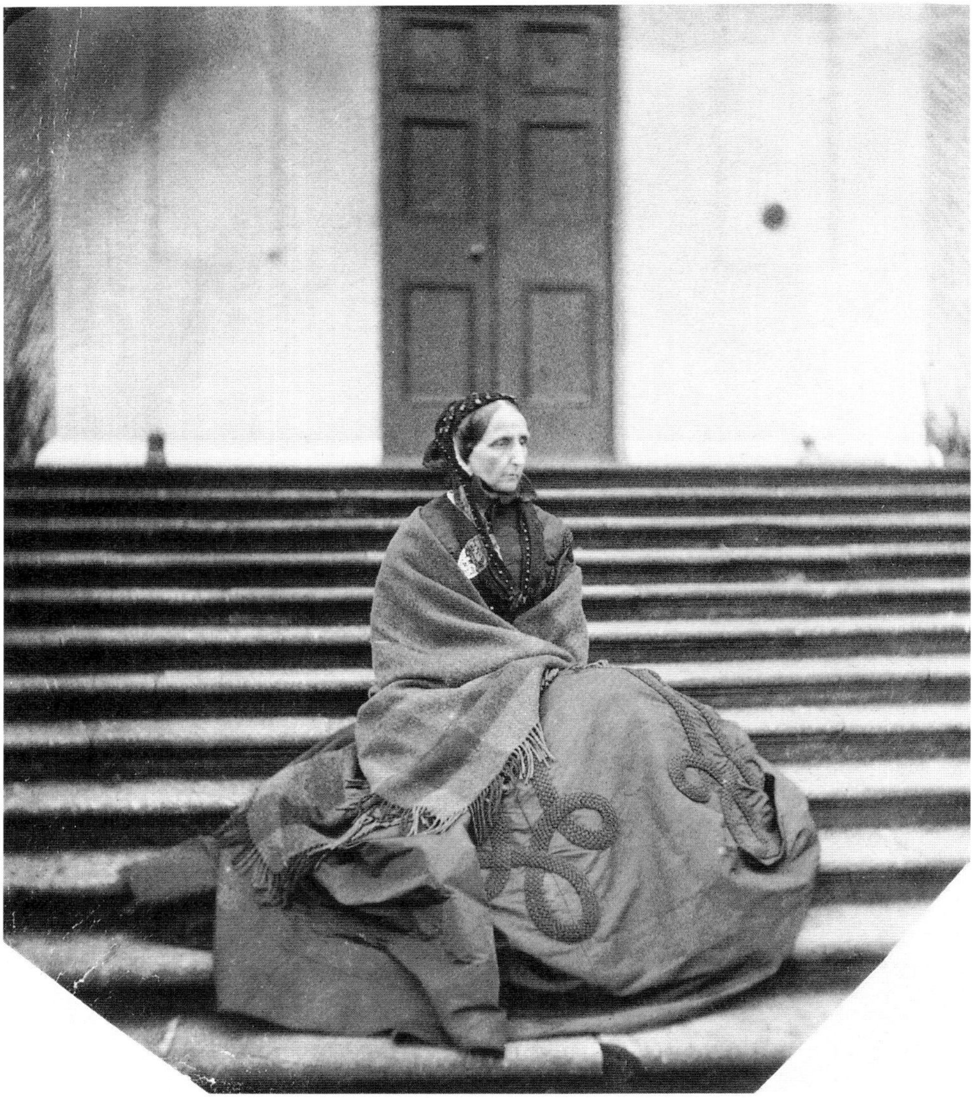

Mrs Mary Innes (née Wolseley) of Dromantine, Newry, *c.* 1860, by Captain C.D.R. Madden.
BY KIND PERMISSION OF J.S.D. MADDEN

Mrs Innes was related to the Madden family, and this striking portrait was taken at their home, Hilton Park, County Monaghan.

Born in 1839, he was one of the Maddens of Hilton Park, Clones, County Monaghan, where two interesting albums of his photographs are still preserved. These are of military groups and individuals in various garrison locations, including Malta, as well as of family members and friends. They date from 1856 to 1866 and include a charming self-portrait ('very young') with camera. He died young, of the plague, in Cork in 1874 at the age of thirty-five. He appears to have been responsible for some striking pictures of the elderly Earl of Roden, taken in 1868 at Tollymore Park, which appear in both the Roden and Madden albums.

One other County Down amateur of the period merits particular mention. Dudley Charles Fitzgerald de Ros, 24th Baron de Ros (1827–1907) was for many years an equerry in the Royal Household.[21] He was a keen photographer all his life, beginning as an exponent of the wet collodion process in the 1850s. Some forty of his portraits of Queen Victoria's family and Court circle are preserved in the royal albums. A much later album, commemorating the visit of Edward VII and Queen

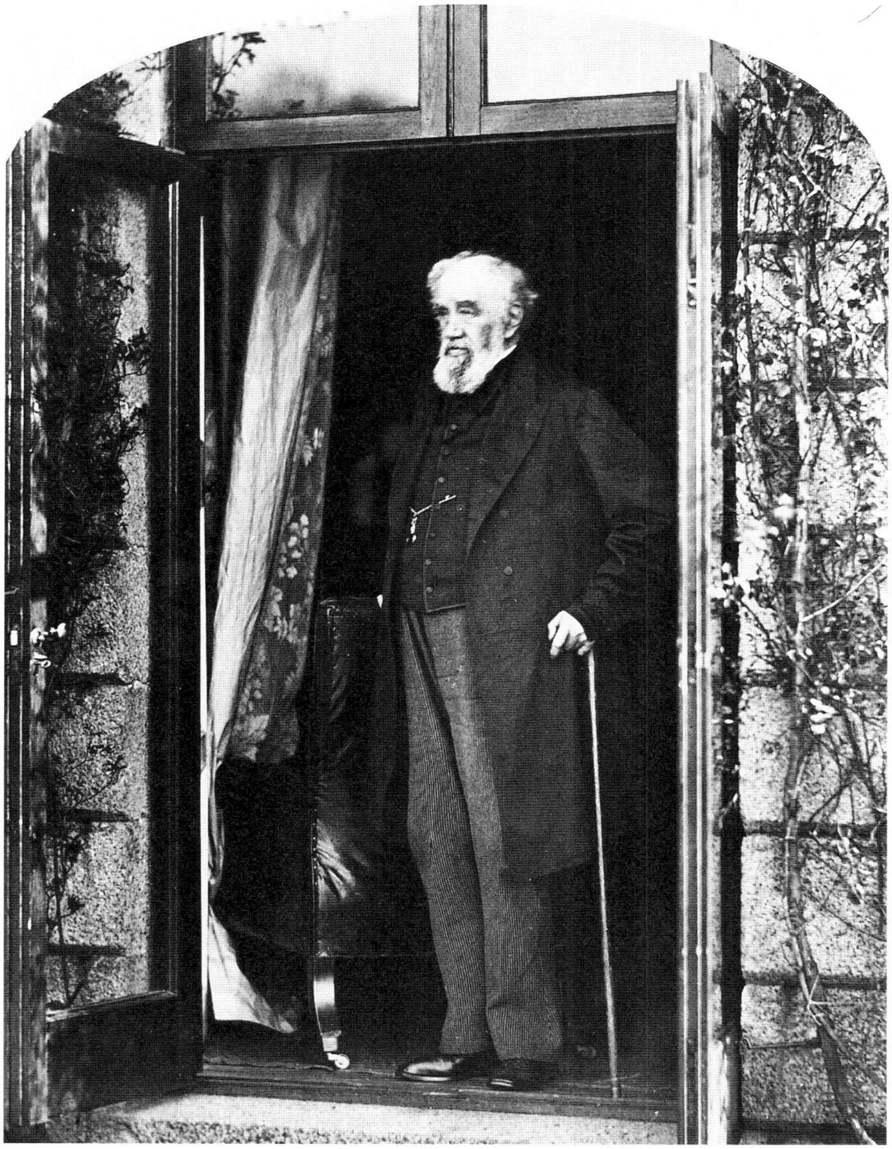

Robert Jocelyn, 3rd Earl of Roden (1788–1870), at home in Tollymore Park, County Down, in 1868, by Captain C.D.R. Madden.

BY KIND PERMISSION OF J.S.D. MADDEN

Alexandra to Ireland in 1903, contains three photographs by de Ros and his second wife showing their house at Strangford, County Down. No doubt the albums of other families contain evidence of more obscure amateurs, though not so many are as early in date as Annesley, Jocelyn, Madden and de Ros or have left such substantial evidence of their work. John Turnley of Drumnasole, a landowner in the Glens of Antrim, for example, was evidently a competent practitioner (PRONI has a fine photograph of Glenarm Castle taken by him about 1860) but little of his work survives. In the same area, though slightly later, between 1867 and 1870, the Glenarm doctor John Sinclair Holden was photographing local antiquities, geology, houses, harbours and shipping. Holden later went to live in England but some of his photographs survive and a few of them showing schooners and other craft have been published, notably in B.M. Walker's *Shadows on Glass*.

Roden was for many years Grand Master of the Orange Order in Ireland. Following a celebrated sectarian affray at Dolly's Brae in 1849, he was removed from the bench of magistrates. Madden, a friend of Roden's son and heir Lord Jocelyn, was a frequent visitor to Tollymore. If the evidence of one early portrait is to be believed, he started his photographic career as a schoolboy at Eton in 1852, aged thirteen or so.

The hitherto unknown work of another medical man of the same period, T. Agmondisham Vesey of Rostrevor, County Down, has survived in the shape of an album of thirty-two photographs, mostly of Rostrevor and district. Vesey was the dispensary doctor there for thirty years or more from the late 1860s. These photographs, all of which are signed and dated, were taken between 1872 and 1875 (when the album was presented to someone unknown, with a likeness of Vesey himself as frontispiece). The album is now in the Ulster Museum.

Studio equipment

So far as the props used by professional photographers for their studio portraits are concerned, we can tell from the portraits themselves how fashions changed. Those from the 1860s have comparatively simple, classical props – painted backcloths with columns, statuary and furniture. The following decade saw an outbreak of foliage and rustic landscapes. Marion and Company, the French firm of photographic publishers which supplied most of the stationery for our early photographers from its London branch (most early cartes and cabinets bear the legend 'Marion imp.'), also supplied rustic furniture and bridges. Later sets were more elaborate still – the deck of a steamship with wheel, funnel and bulwarks, for a mere £7, or even castellated ramparts with cannon, but no one in the north of Ireland went in for such elaboration. Robert Welch has left a photograph of the foyer of Church's studio in Belfast, where he worked *c.* 1880; it is full of statues, urns, pictures, flowers, ferns, and the inevitable piano.

We know from a detailed sale notice what Marcus Ward and Company's studio had contained in the way of props ten years earlier.[22] These included 'several valuable backgrounds, both landscape and interiors', several 'carved oak and other tables, rustic chairs, table and flower stand, walnut cabinet, polished walnut davenport, lady's easy carved walnut chair, walnut music stand, mahogany dressing table and mirror, pedestal basin stand, a number of elegant chairs in carved oak and walnut; gothic inlaid round table, two large gothic stands for exhibiting specimens, carved oak bookcase, stained wood counter, splendid Brussels carpet, 24´ x 21´. . . '

The same source tells us that the 'large and valuable stock of photographic apparatus' consisted of a carte-de-visite lens and a no. 4 portrait lens by Dallmeyer; a no. 4 triple lens, two carte-de-visite lenses and a portrait lens for a 10-by-10-inch camera, a no. 1 triple lens by Dallmeyer; a single sterescopic lens for children and focussing glass; a carte-de-visite camera and slide for a no. 23 lens by Ottewill, Collins and Company, diamond, cameo, back and slide for ditto, by Marion; a

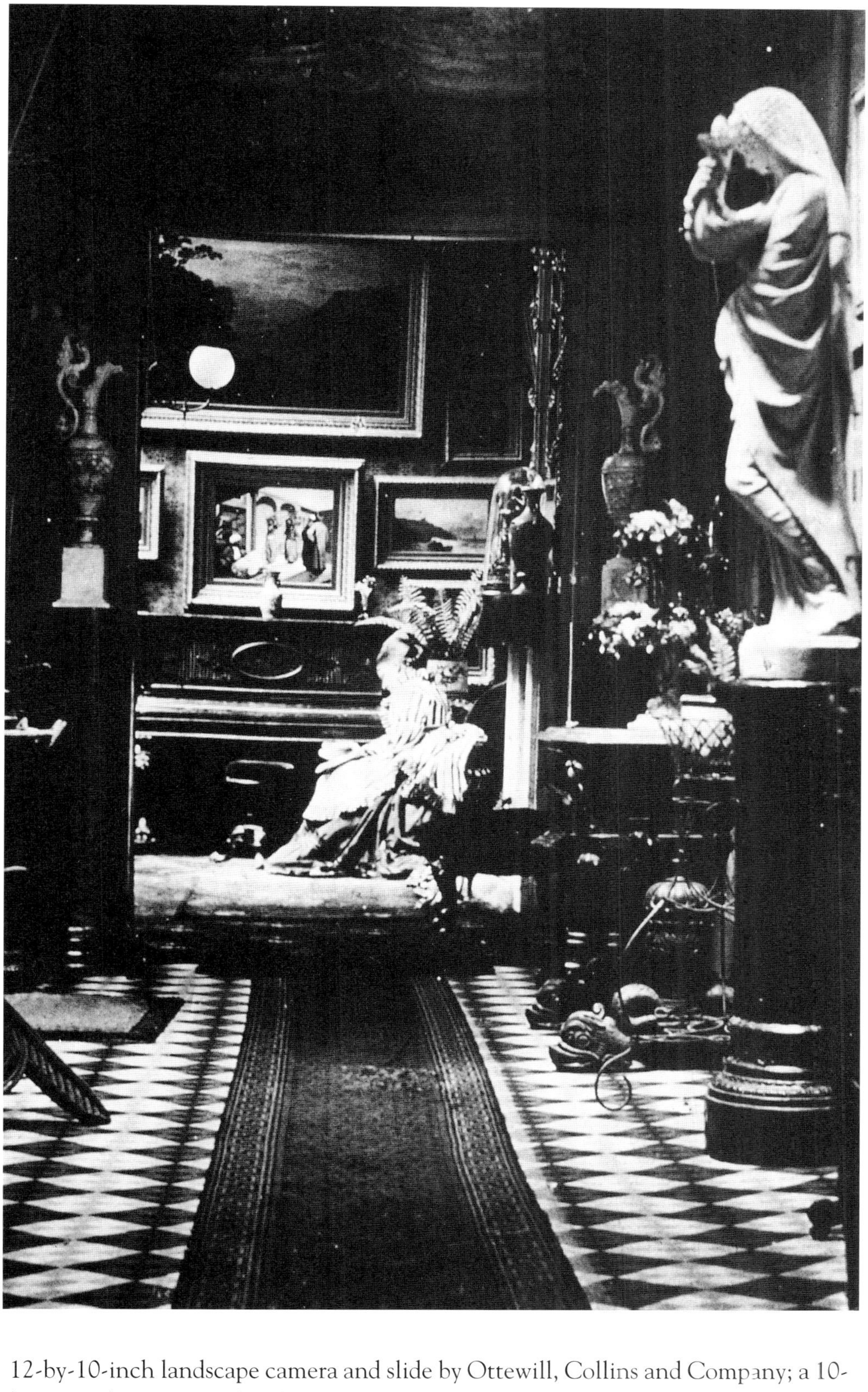

Foyer of E.T. Church's studio, Donegall Place, Belfast, c. 1880; from a carte de visite.
MAGNI / UM

12-by-10-inch landscape camera and slide by Ottewill, Collins and Company; a 10-by-10-inch camera and slide, carte-de-visite camera and slide, large portrait camera and two dark slides by Cranz; a double carte-de-visite camera; an enlarging camera

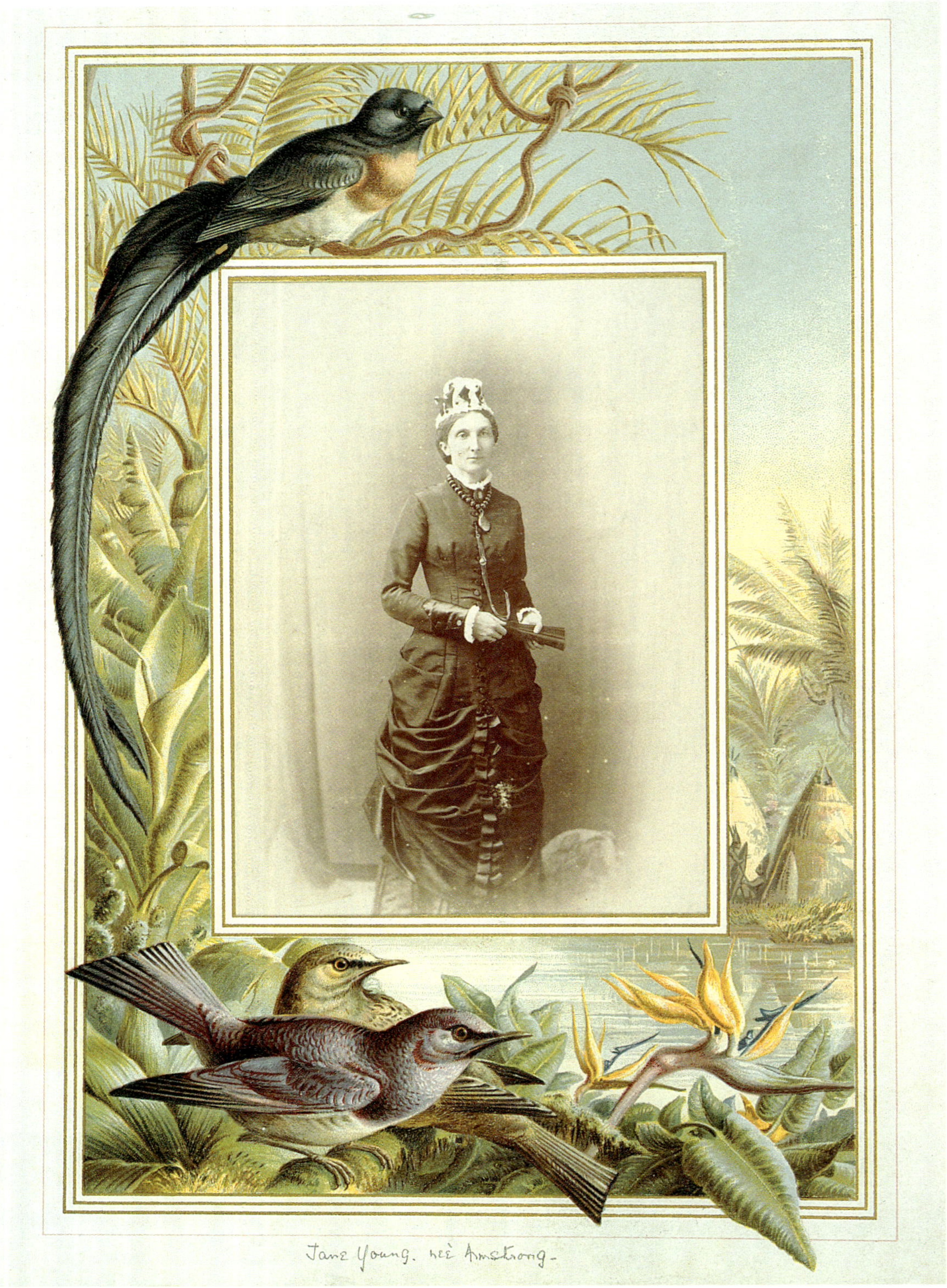

Mrs Jane Young, née Armstrong, c. 1880, from the 'Flower and Feather' Album belonging to the Young family, of Fenaghy, County Antrim.

BY KIND PERMISSION OF MRS ANNA STEWART

Most of the local portraits in the Young album, including this one, were taken by Thomas Erwin of Ballymena.

by Parsons, Richardson and Company, a portable camera stand; two large camera stands by Ottewill, Collins and Company; copying stand, baths, head rests, still, rolling machine by H. Bury and Company as well as washing troughs, plate boxes and printing frames. The operating gallery itself, with glass sides and roof, 26-by-10 feet, fitted complete with blinds on spring rollers, was also for sale, along with a stock of nearly ten thousand negatives, 'many of which were taken by Messrs Parkes and Gedge, but the greater portion were executed by Messrs Ward'. These were said to comprise 'most of the nobility and gentry of the North of Ireland, and a large number of clerical, musical, theatrical, literary, and other celebrities'.

The studio was being sold up because ill-health had forced the proprietor to retire. Since the Ward brothers were not themselves photographers, one is left wondering who the photographer was. Parkes and Gedge had earlier worked in the Marcus Ward studio, but by 1870 William Scott Parkes had his own studio in Donegall Place, two doors along from No. 13; he had taught at the Government School of Art, in Worcester. Horatius Gedge, another Englishman, had worked for Southwell Brothers, the great London firm with premises in Baker Street, before coming to Belfast, originally to Magill's. The two were in partnership in Belfast in 1870, 'having succeeded to Messrs M. Ward & Co's Artistic and Photographic Business', according to an advertisement in the directory for that year. So presumably they were the chief purchasers at the auction. One of their specialities was the Encaustic portrait or Mayerotype: 'Messrs P & G having painted nearly all the Portraits finished by this process at Messrs Ward and Magill's Establishment, beg to say they are now producing them superior to any in the United Kingdom.' They also advertised a Glass Room (whatever that was) on the first floor for the convenience of invalids. At some stage in these changes there seems to have been a connection between Parkes and Gedge and Galbraith, the proprietor of the studio in High Street, for a Galbraith carte of *c.* 1870 bears the information: 'Copies of our own, Marcus Ward & Co's or Parkes & Gedges Negatives may be had at any time at reduced prices.'

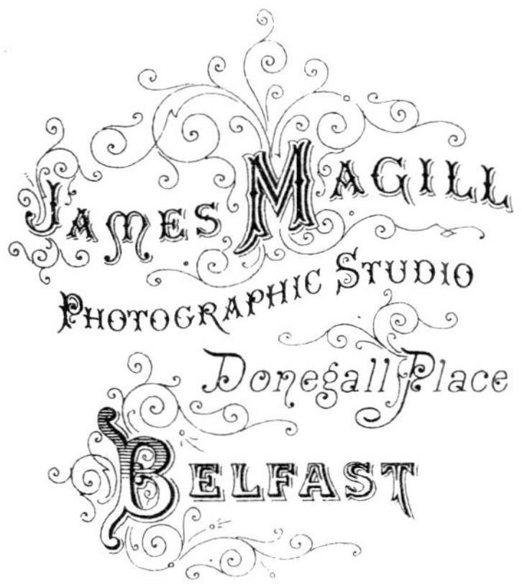

Unfortunately, there is a significant gap in the run of Belfast directories in the 1870s: after 1870, none was published till 1877. This reflected the slump in the linen industry, following the great boom of the previous decade. In 'Linenopolis' the whole local economy suffered when the mills and factories closed or went on short time. Undoubtedly business for photographers must also have suffered during the early 1870s, but in the absence of directories it is hard to guess how much. In 1870 there were seventeen studios, in 1877 the same number (including Marcus Ward and Company again, this time at their new premises off the Dublin Road, and eight new names) but neither Parkes nor Gedge is to be found and their premises in Donegall Place were being used for other than photographic purposes. By that time a new era in photography was beginning.

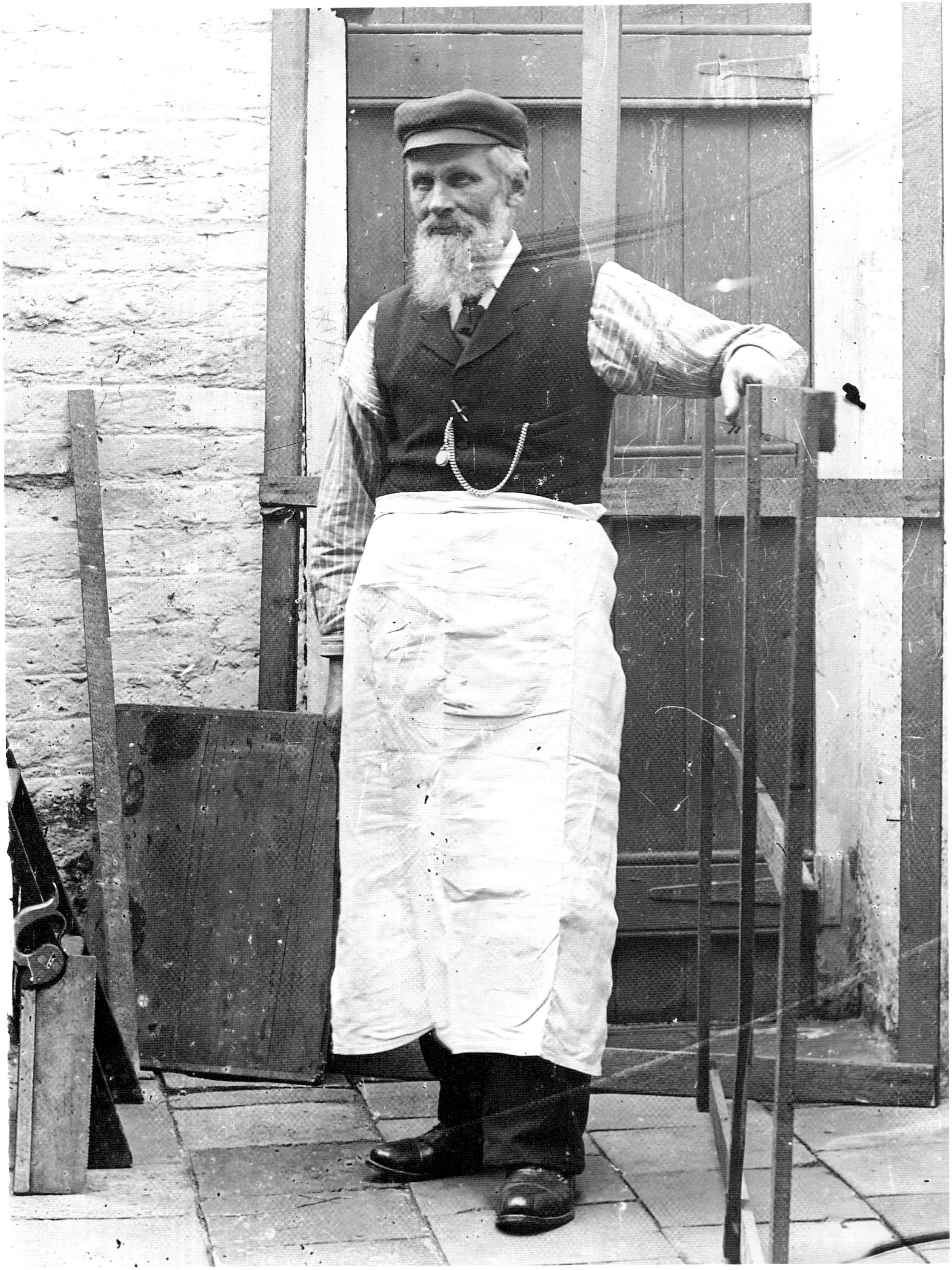

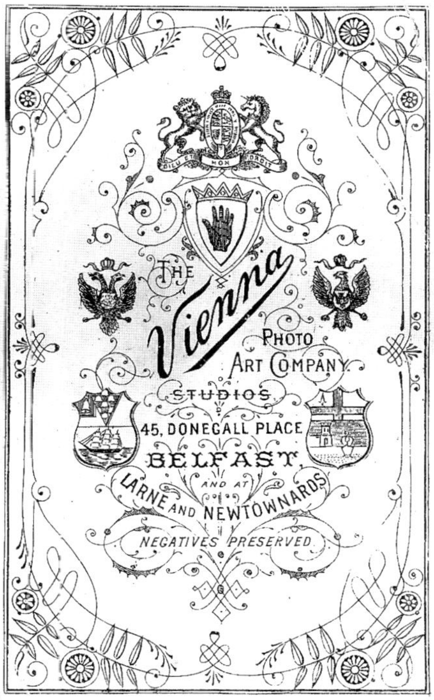

Developing in all directions

1880–1914

A whole new era in photography opened when the wet collodion process was replaced by the use of dry-plate negatives. Successful use of the wet plate had required a high degree of skill on the part of the photographer in preparing and applying the emulsion, in choosing the appropriate exposure and in developing the negatives. Various, more or less unsatisfactory, attempts to produce dry plates matching the wet ones in sensitivity were made during the 1860s. The first really promising recipe, however, was published by Dr Richard Leach Maddox in 1871. With the ability to retain their properties long enough, dry plate negatives were produced commercially.

The new glass plates, coated with an emulsion of silver bromide in a gelatin solution, were a major breakthrough and immediately made the more expensive and cumbersome wet collodion process obsolete. They were easy to make, very

Opposite
Samuel Weir, Belfast master carpenter and building contractor, *c.* 1900, by James McCaughan.
BY KIND PERMISSION OF MICHAEL McCAUGHAN

James McCaughan, by trade a painter and decorator, was an amateur photographer during the 1890s and early 1900s. Buying the components, he constructed his own camera and experimented with flash photography.

'The Band of Pipers' at the Glens of Antrim Feis, *c*. 1904, by J. Bland.

MAGNI / UM

F. J. Bigger's enthusiasm for all things Irish was largely responsible for the establishment of the Feis as an expression of cultural nationalism in the Glens. Bigger himself designed the costumes and persuaded people to wear them. At his weekend retreat in Ardglass, County Down, earnest revellers similarly tunicked and cross-gartered, or kilted in saffron, danced and played without the traditional stimulus of strong drink (their host was a noted temperance reformer).

sensitive, and could be kept for long periods. The greatest change they brought about was a significant reduction in exposure times. Even at its best, the wet collodion plate could not usually cope with moving objects of any kind. Now, 'instantaneous' photography became possible – though by modern standards exposures were still comparatively long. The new plates also had the advantage of being of standard quality, whereas wet plates had differed according to the method of preparation used by each individual photographer; so too had the appropriate exposure times. Standard sensitivity made it possible to calculate exposure times by measuring the light available in different conditions.

Professional photographers were quick to adopt the new process, which was not only a godsend for outdoor work but also simplified the taking of studio portraits and reduced their cost. The enthusiastic amateur was also greatly assisted. One result was the revival of amateur photographic societies.[1] In Belfast, where an earlier society had foundered in 1860, the Ulster Amateur Photographic Society was established in 1885 and met in the Belfast Natural History and Philosophical Society premises at the museum in College Square North from 1885 until 1910. Many members belonged to both bodies. One such was William Swanston, whose name often appears on photographs of scientific outings and excursions. Another noted amateur and BNHPS member was Mary Andrews, the youngest daughter of

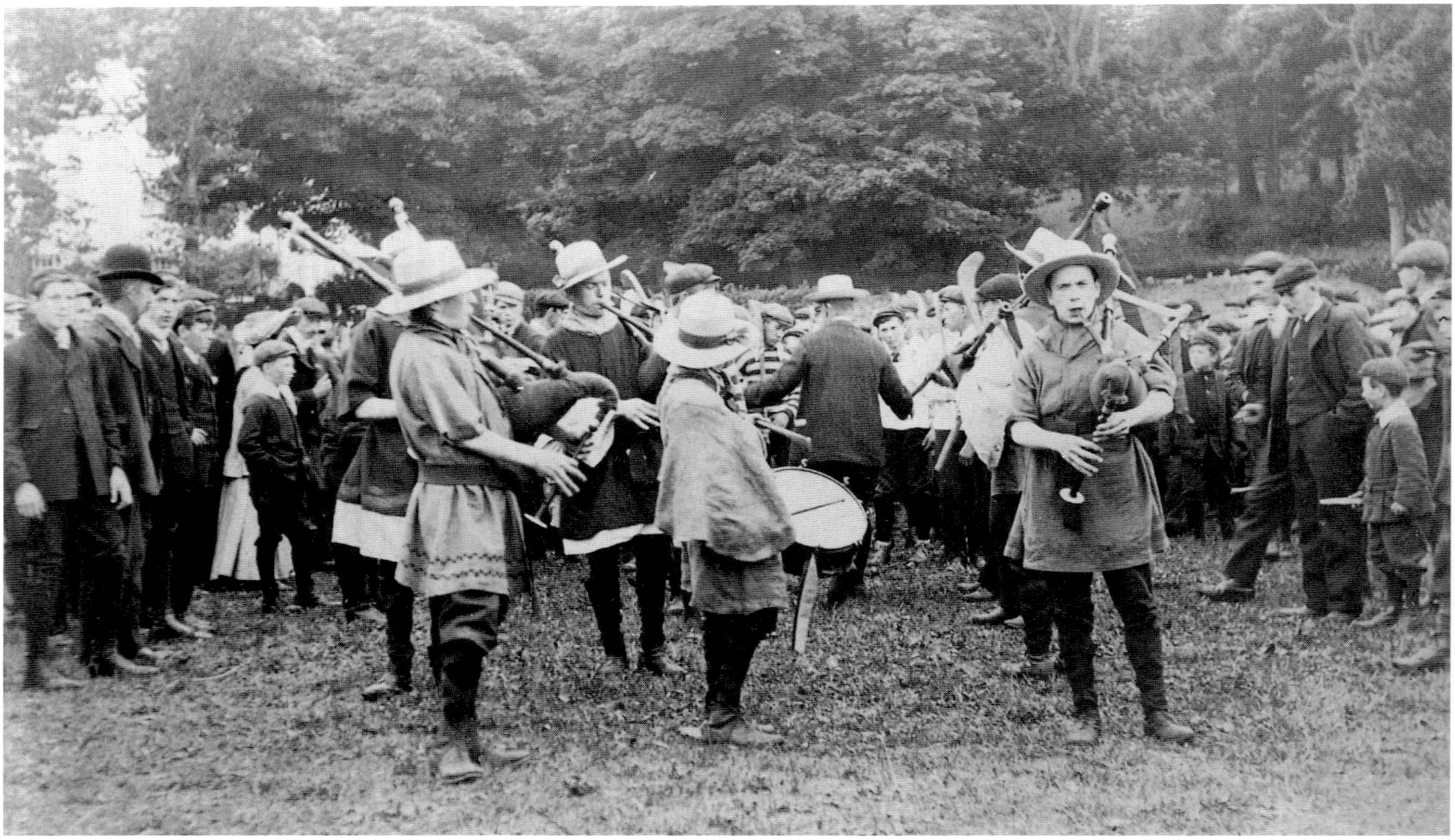

Dr Thomas Andrews, vice-president of the Queen's College, 1846–9, and subsequently professor of chemistry there. His daughter was a scholar in her own right, with a particular interest in geology. Many of her photographs of geological sites in Britain and Ireland, taken during the 1890s, were accepted for the British Association collection; the originals of these are now in the Ulster Museum. Another woman amateur, Anne Tate, had similar interests. So too had James Stelfox. Two other active amateur societies at the turn of the century were the City of Belfast Camera Club and the YMCA Camera Club. Both bodies organised annual exhibitions of members' work and awarded prizes.

One of the most extensive and interesting amateur collections to have survived from this period is that of Francis Joseph Bigger. Bigger was a solicitor by

Lambeg drums at Scarva, County Down, 13 July 1903.
MAGNI / UM

The Sham Fight at Scarva, re-enacting the victory of King William over King James at the Battle of the Boyne in 1690, is one of the traditional annual outings of the Orange Order. Bigger recorded this scene in another part of the battlefield.

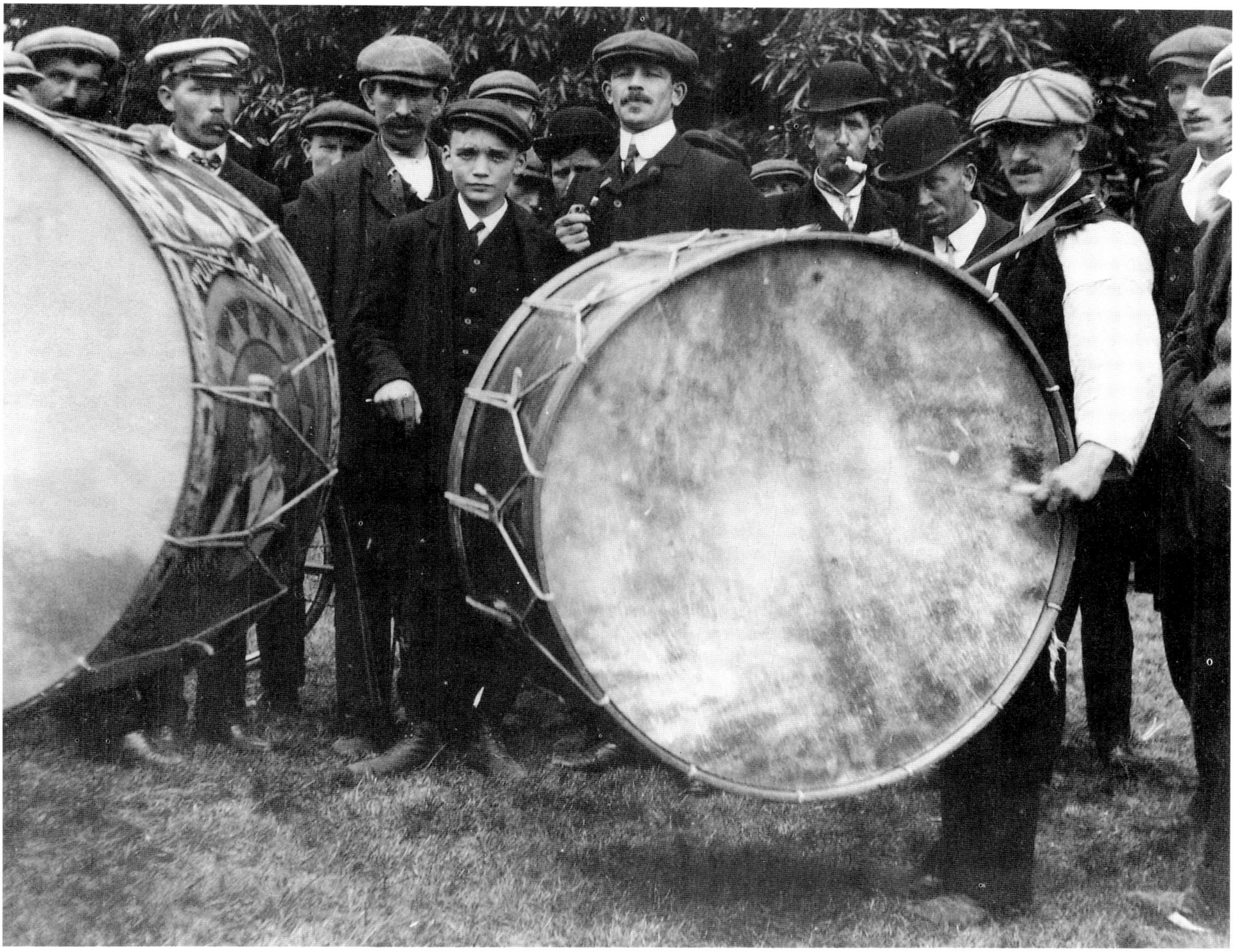

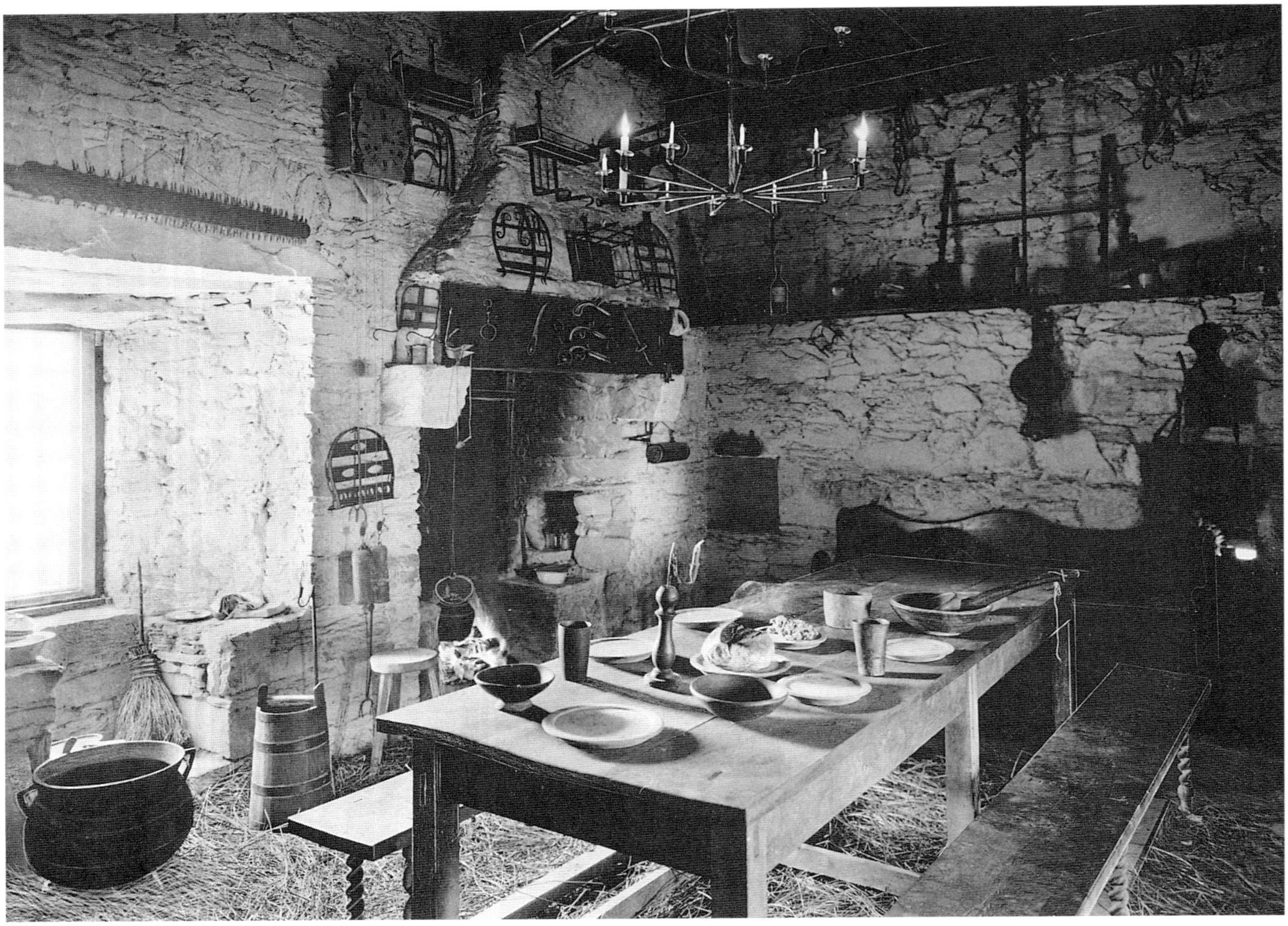

The kitchen in Jordan's Castle (Shane's Castle), F.J. Bigger's retreat at Ardglass, County Down, by R.J. Welch.
MAGNI / UM

profession, with a busy and successful practice in Belfast. The consuming passion of his life, however, was not the law but Irish history, ethnography and culture, all viewed from a strongly nationalist political viewpoint despite his Presbyterian background. Bigger played a leading part in the Gaelic revival in the North, but was known throughout Ireland. Individual to the point of eccentricity, and highly prejudiced in his historical judgements, he nevertheless – by example as well as advocacy – did a great deal to encourge public interest and activity in Irish culture.

Like his friends Welch, Robert Lloyd Praeger and A.W. Stelfox, Bigger was active in the Belfast Naturalists' Field Club, becoming secretary (a post he held for ten years) and president. Under Bigger's influence the club's excursions, all over the North of Ireland and beyond, increasingly catered for a wider range of interests than the purely scientific. Archaeology in particular attracted Bigger's attention in the 1890s. In 1894, along with the Belfast antiquarian R.M. Young, he relaunched the defunct *Ulster Journal of Archaeology*, soon becoming sole editor and remaining in charge until it expired again in 1911. He not only edited the journal, he contributed to every single issue. A member of the Royal Society of Antiquaries in Ireland since 1888, he was elected a Fellow in 1896; two years earlier he had been elected to membership of the Royal Irish Academy. An enthusiast for the Irish

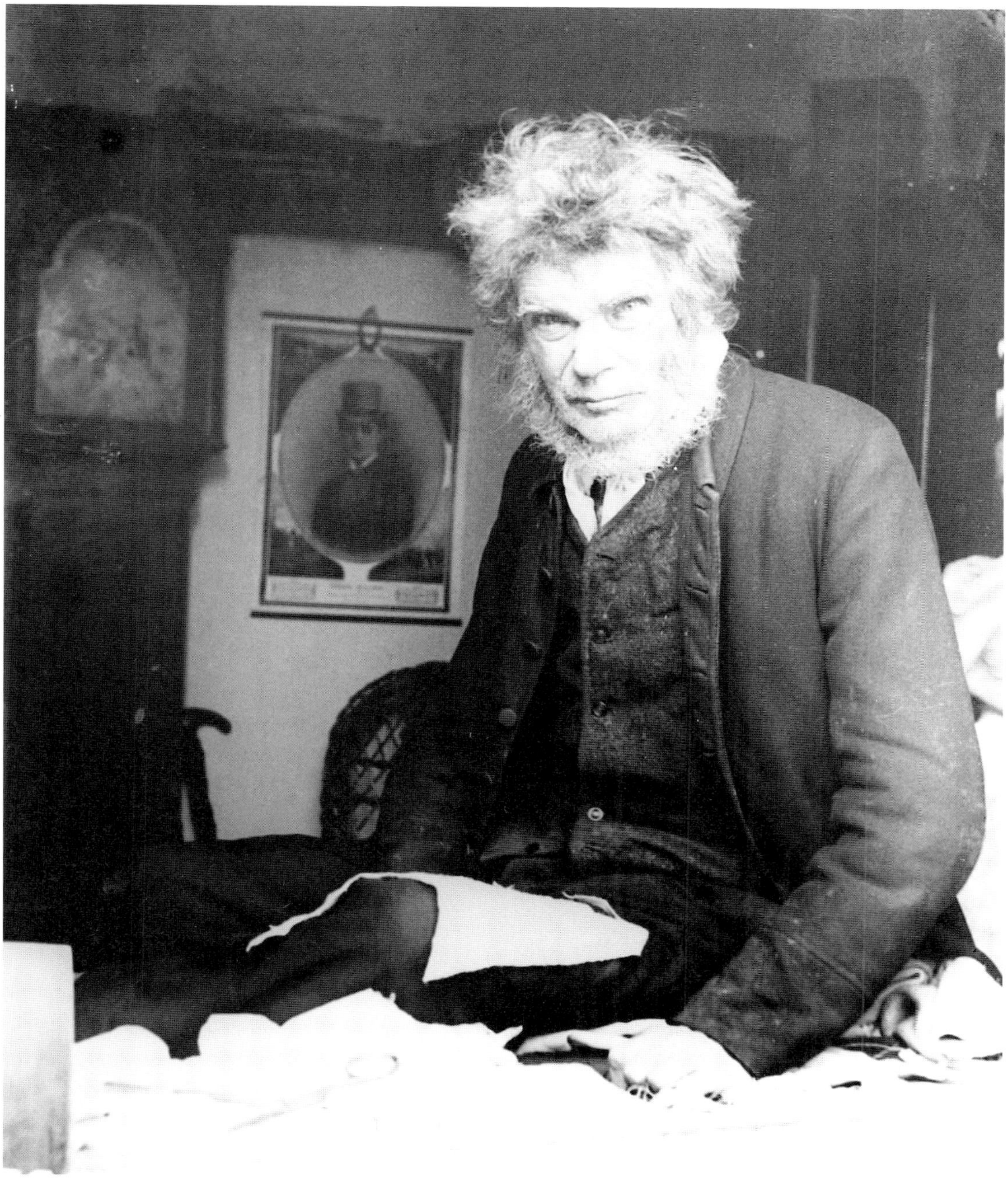

language, he belonged to the Coisde Gniotha of the Gaelic League, was president of the Coisde Ceanntair in Belfast and lectured on archaeology to the Irish School in Bank Street. Interest in traditional Irish music, costume and customs led to his patronage of the famous Belfast piper Francis McPeake. Bigger actually paid for McPeake to learn the pipes, after acquiring two rare sets of them for his own collection, importing a blind piper from Galway as teacher. He also revived (or invented) the Glens of Antrim Feis in 1904. The tower house in Ardglass, County Down, which he bought, restored and furnished in what he conceived to be the style of a traditional Irish chieftain and used as a holiday retreat, became a centre

Joshua Wells, itinerant tailor, at Sentry Hill farm, c. 1895, by W.F. McKinney.
MAGNI / UFTM (DUNDEE COLLECTION)

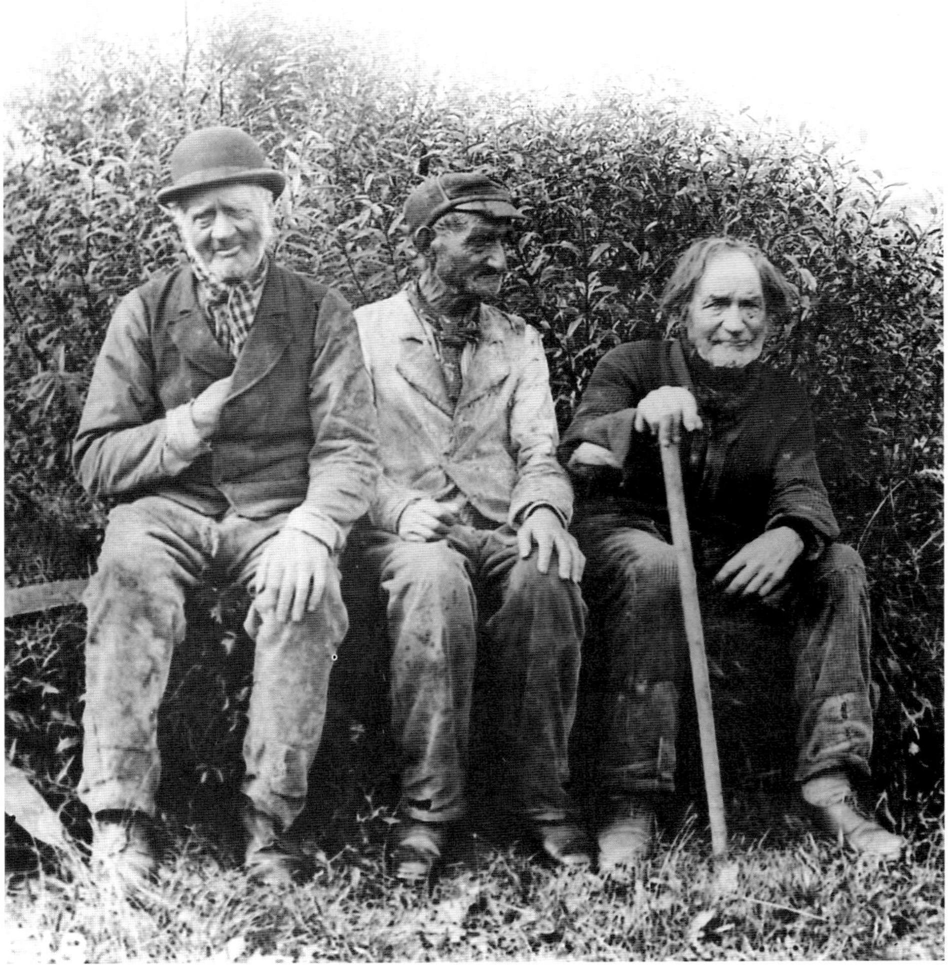

The three Guthrie brothers, King's Moss, County Antrim, c. 1895, by W.F. McKinney.
MAGNI / UFTM (DUNDEE COLLECTION)

The Guthries were small farmers who lived near Sentry Hill and were distantly related to the photographer. Like many in the area, they were descended from Scots who had settled there in the seventeenth century.

for such activities in fancy dress – an early heritage centre in fact. Both Welch and Green, among others, photographed Jordan's Castle (or Shane's Castle as Bigger preferred to call it, in honour of the sixteenth-century chieftain Shane O'Neill) and its curious contents.

Bigger's photographs went to the Belfast Museum and Art Gallery in 1927. The collection has been supplemented significantly in recent times by the purchase of his family albums. A few of the five thousand photographs are marked as the work of his friend, A.W. Stelfox, but most were presumably taken by Bigger himself or his brother. A catalogue is in the course of preparation.[2]

Bigger's family came from Carnmoney in County Antrim. In the same area in the late nineteenth century lived his kinsman and friend William Fee McKinney (1832–1917), who recorded his own life as a substantial farmer and that of the neighbourhood in photographs of exceptional interest. Many of them have been published in Brian Walker's book *Sentry Hill.*[3] Like Bigger, Welch and Hogg, McKinney belonged to the Belfast Naturalists' Field Club. He also acquired some

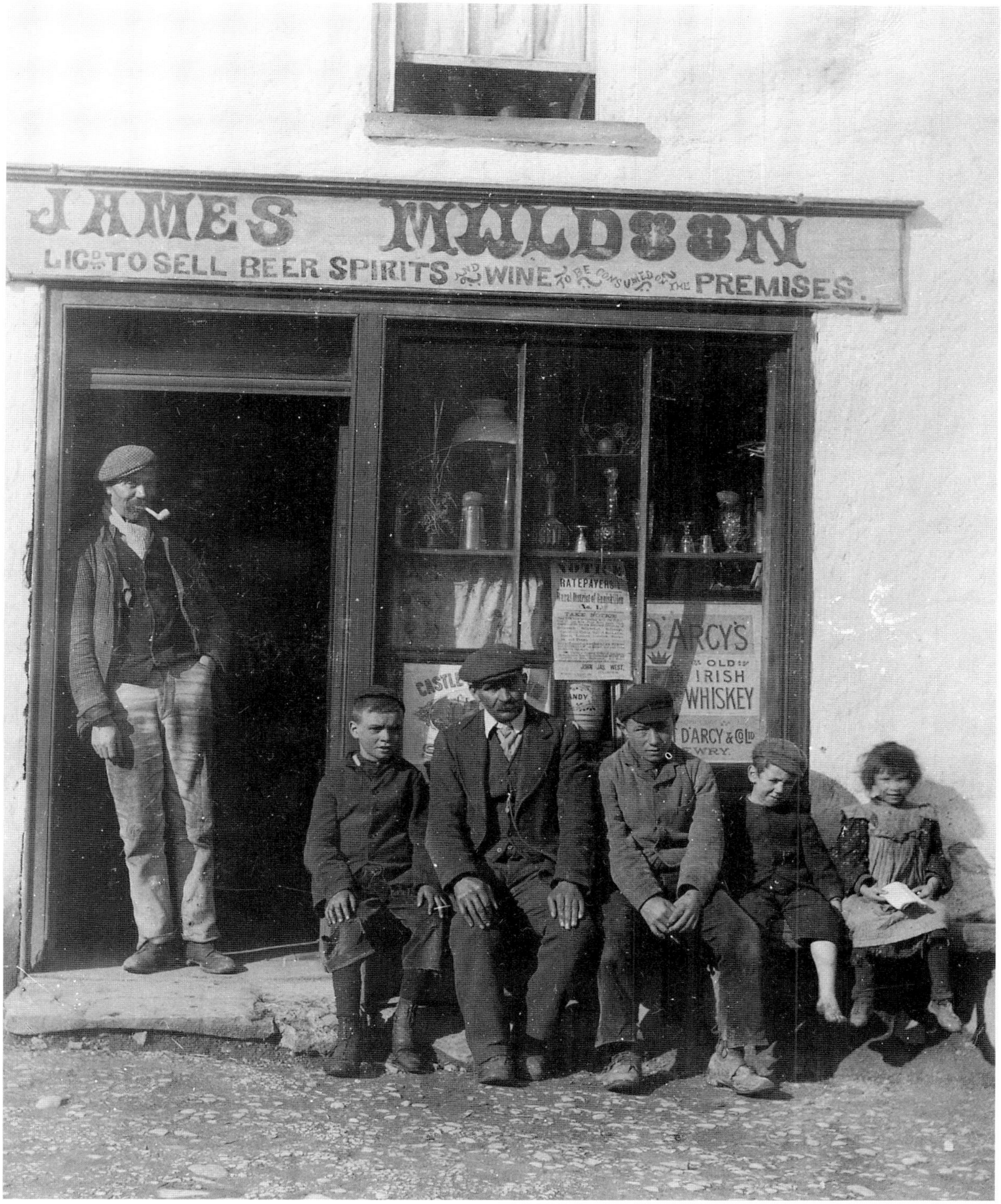

professional photographs by a short-lived Belfast photographer named Hale, who appeared in the directory for 1870 and went bankrupt in 1871, whereupon McKinney purchased the negatives for photographs of his own locality. Hale's work is otherwise unknown. The McKinney collection, which numbers about a thousand glass-plate negatives, is now in the Ulster Folk and Transport Museum.

'Muldoon's Whiskey Shop (one of 15) with Natives', by Charles Langham, 1899.
BY KIND PERMISSION OF SIR JAMES LANGHAM, BT.

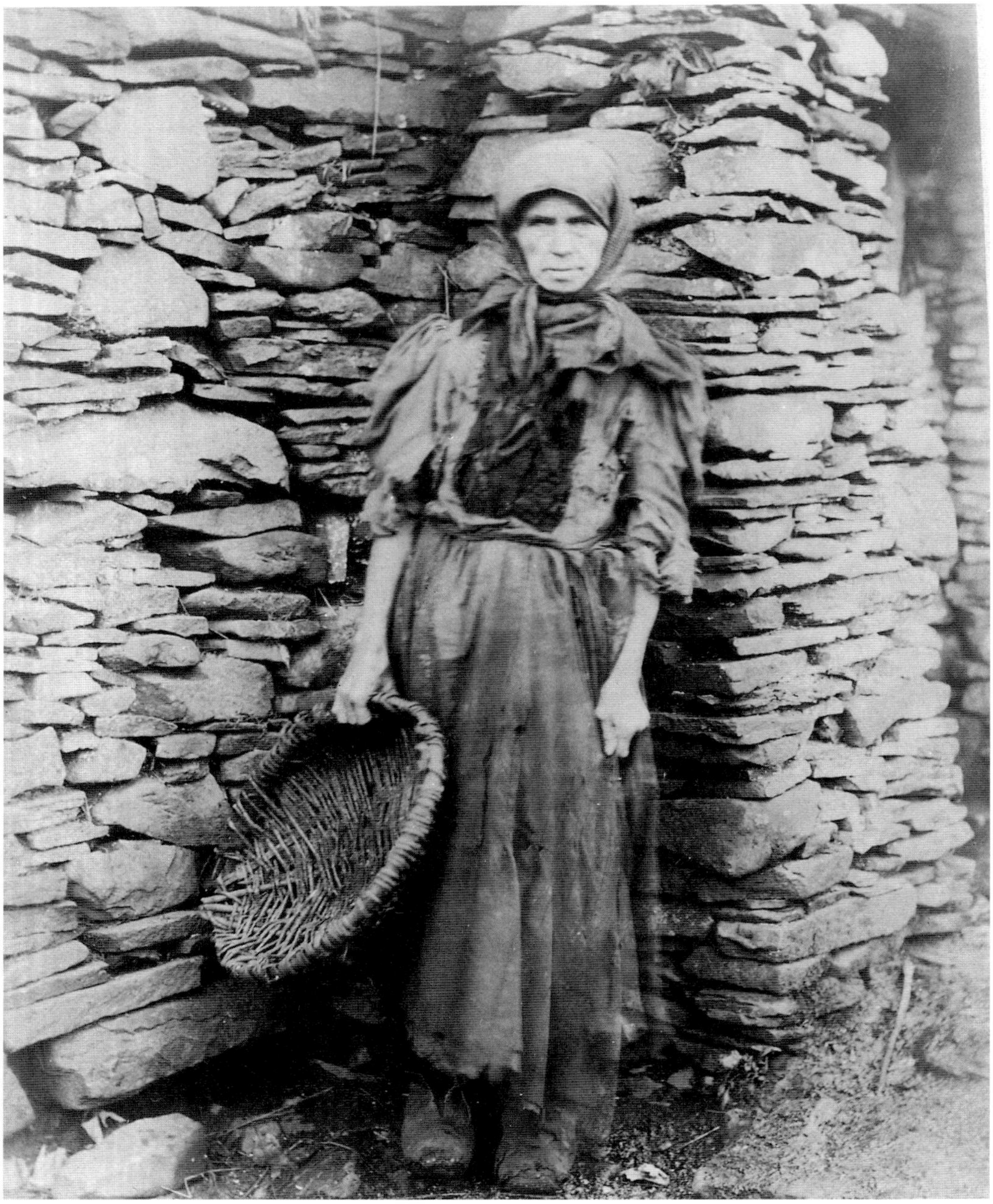

Potato-picker named McCaffrey, near Tempo, County Fermanagh, 1 November 1899, by Charles Langham.
BY KIND PERMISSION OF SIR JAMES LANGHAM, BT.

Had photographs been taken during the famine of the 1840s, this could have been one of them.

Incidentally, Welch took a group portrait of the McKinney family at Sentry Hill in 1893.

With the adoption of the dry plate, amateurs such as McKinney were able to produce photographs of good quality. In fact, some of them were encouraged by their success to become professionals. Country house photographers of the later nineteenth century and the early years of the twentieth usually adopted the Kodak camera, once available, in preference to the plate camera, but the more serious continued to use the latter. One such was Charles (later Sir Charles) Langham, of Tempo in County Fermanagh, an Englishman who had married the heiress to the Tempo Manor estate and had settled there. At the turn of the century he produced

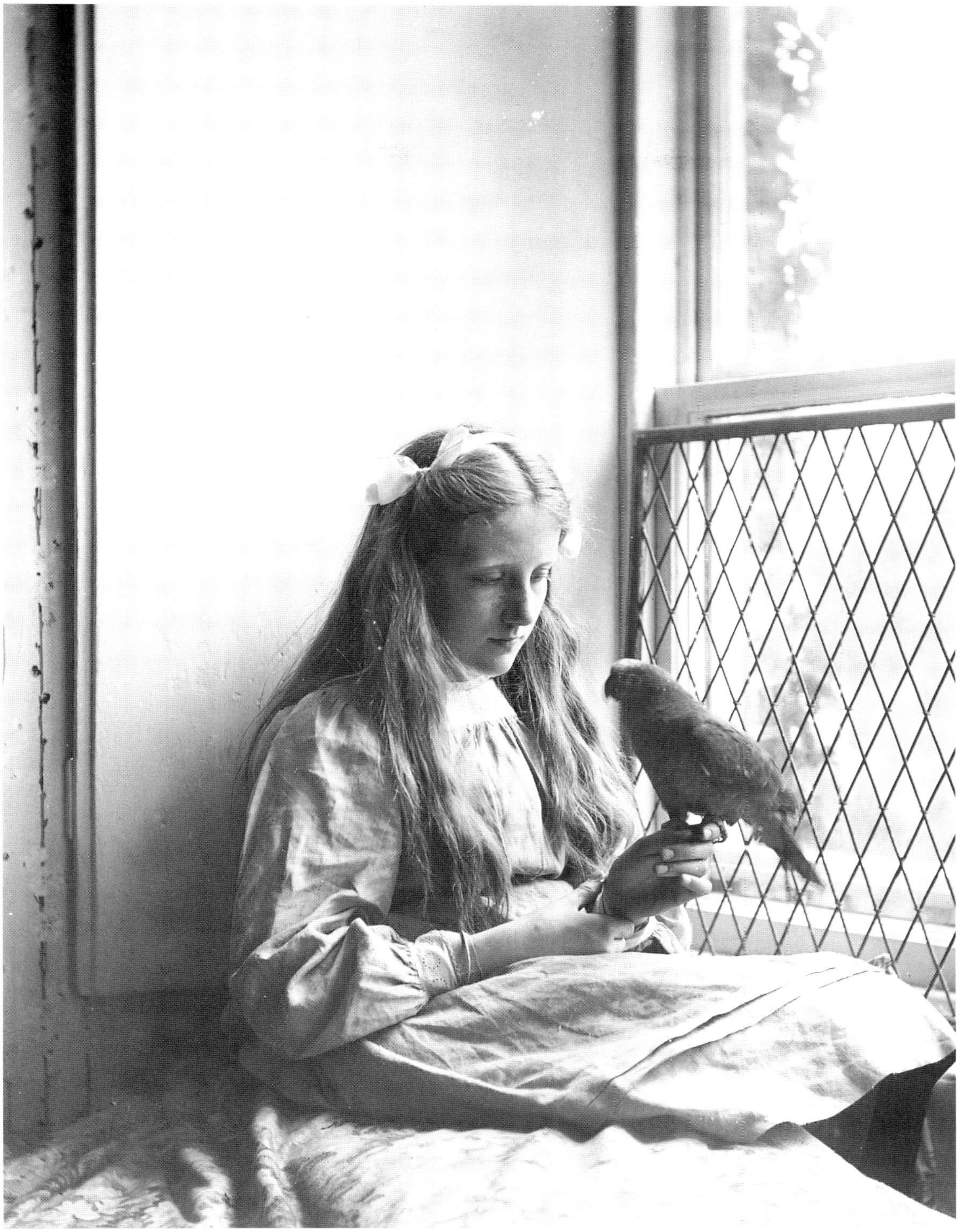

some very striking studies of people in and around the village. These 'natives', as he called them, included employees, local farmers and labourers and their families. One particularly powerful image is that of a 'woman named McCaffrey', a gaunt potato-gatherer dressed in rags – an image more reminiscent of the famine years of

Hilda Young (the photographer's daughter) with parrot, by Mary Alice Young.
PRONI AND THE HON. CHRISTOPHER BROOKE (YOUNG COLLECTION)

the 1840s than of the eve of the twentieth century. Langham's wife and his sister (who also settled in Ireland) were keen photographers too. They recorded local life and foreign travel more informally as well, in scores of excellent Kodak shots. Unusually, these negatives and prints were not only preserved carefully in the Kodak albums produced for the purpose but – rarer still – they were almost all identified and dated, a discipline learned by Langham and his wife in the course of amassing a notable collection of butterflies. The butterflies are now in the Ulster Museum. The photographs are still in the hands of the Langham family, but a selection of them was published a few years ago. Apart from the portraits mentioned above, they include interesting informal scenes from the Fair Day in the village in May 1900 and Twelfth of July scenes in the same year.[4] Other Fermanagh amateurs who produced good work during the same period were Annie King of Enniskillen (*c.* 1864–1920) and W.G. Eadie of Lisbellaw, who owned a woollen factory.[5]

A notable genteel amateur of the same period, but at the other end of the province, was Mary Alice Young of Galgorm Castle, Ballymena (1867–1946). Born at Bushmills, where her family, the Macnaghtens, were major landowners, she married John Young in 1893 and went to live at Galgorm a few years later. As a photographer she was active between 1890 and 1915. The Young Collection in PRONI contains over a thousand of the glass-plate negatives on which she recorded the life of her family and the neighbourhood of Galgorm, always competently, sometimes strikingly. A small selection of her work appears in Brian Walker's *Shadows on Glass*.[6]

Another interesting amateur photographer of country life – not the life of the gentry and the Big House this time but that of the common people – was Rose Shaw. Remarkably little is known for certain about the woman herself, apart from the fact that she came from Bath about 1888 to be governess to the children of a landowner named Moutray Gledstanes at Fardross, near Clogher in County Tyrone, and when no longer needed as governess returned to the area every summer to stay with the family as a guest. How she acquired her skill with the camera is unknown, but she was clearly an accomplished photographer. She seems to have become fascinated with the lives of the small tenant farmers of the Clogher Valley in the vicinity of Fardross, who scraped a living in circumstances that, to superficial view at least, had changed little since the days of William Carleton, whose native place this was. Her often charming, if always carefully composed, pictures of barefoot women at work on the mountainy farms dignify, while not concealing, the hard labour and simple lives of her 'peasants'. One can detect a touch of theatricality about some of her images – an arcadian artfulness – that tallies with the belief that at one stage of her life she had worked in the theatre, as a wardrobe mistress and producer of pageants. She certainly became fascinated by Carleton's stories of

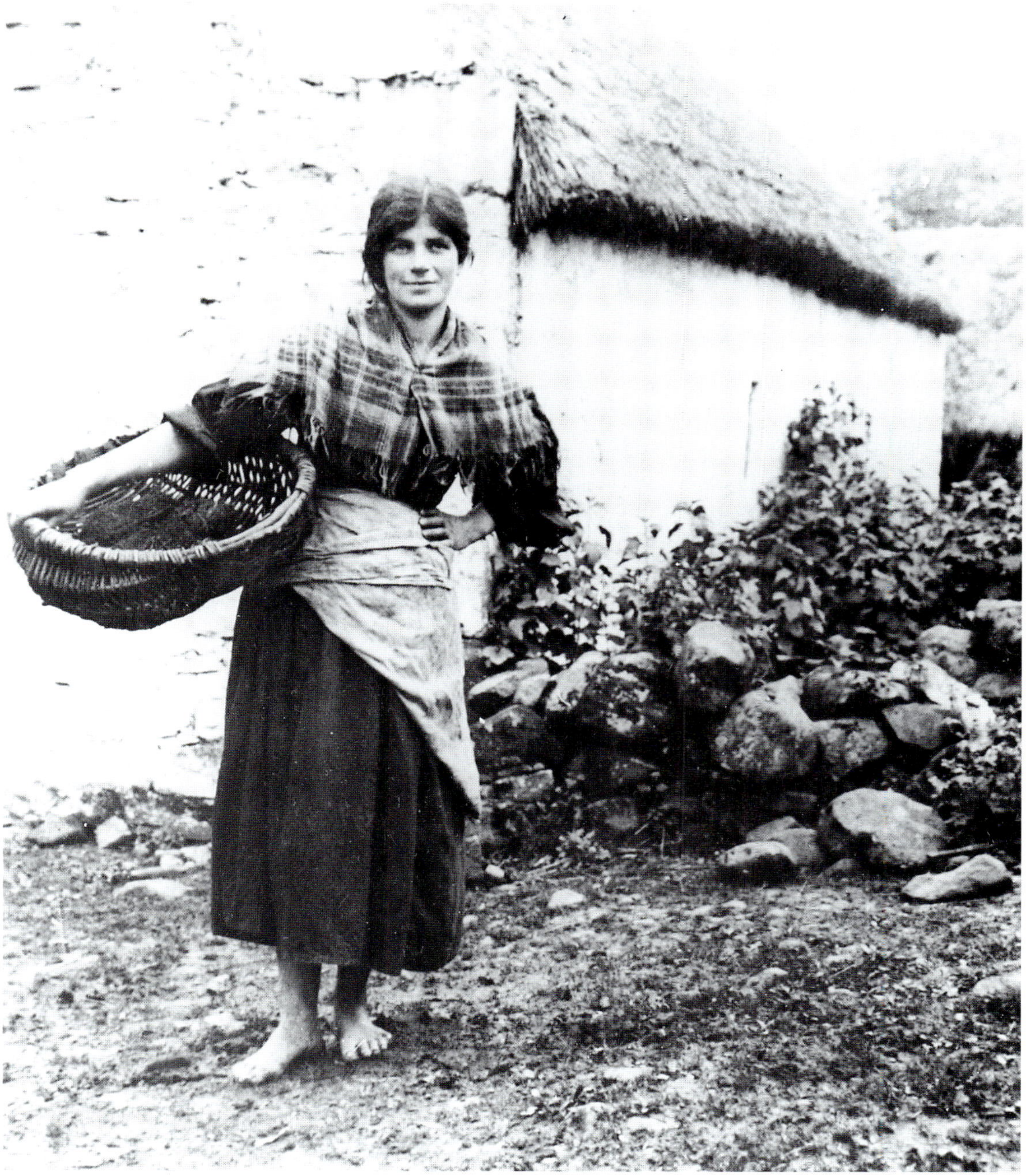

his Clogher upbringing, and seems to have made little distinction between that pre-Famine period and the early twentieth century in her book *Carleton's Country* (Dublin, 1930, with an introduction by Shane Leslie, a near neighbour of the Gledstanes family in County Monaghan). This volume was illustrated by sepia reproductions of some of her photographs. Thirty or so of her pictures – the only surviving evidence of her work – have been copied by the Ulster Folk and Transport Museum. Some of the most striking of them were published more recently in *Shadows on Glass*. None of the photographs is dated, but it is thought that most of them were taken in the early 1900s; one can be dated to about 1910. Rose

Clogher Valley 'peasant girl' with turf basket, c. 1920, by Rose Shaw.

MAGNI / UFTM

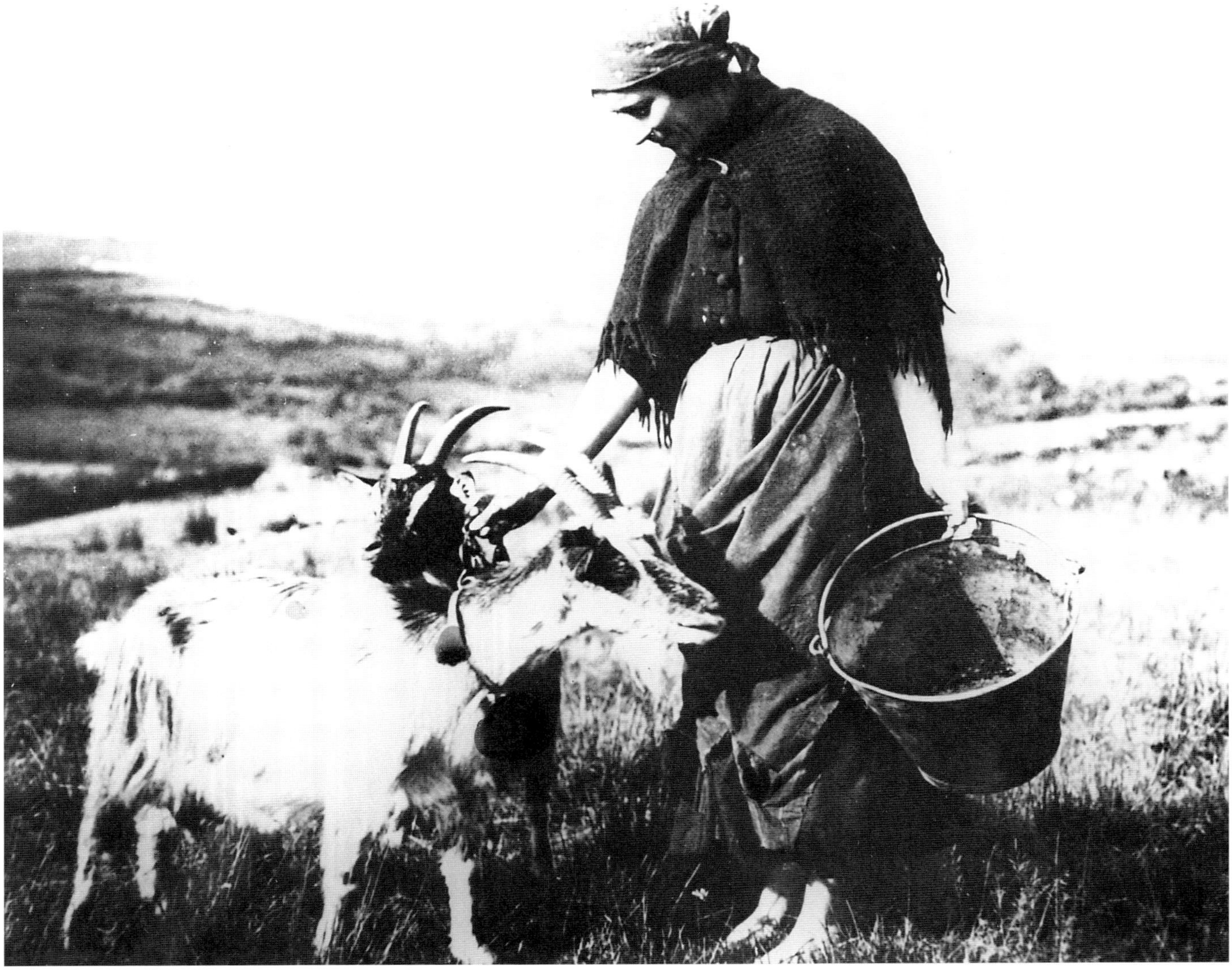

Clogher Valley woman with goats, by Rose Shaw.
MAGNI / UFTM

Shaw lived to a great age and died at Bath in the late 1940s.[7]

Dry plates made it much easier for travellers to record their travels. Far away from the County Down home she so seldom saw, Lady Dufferin, wife of the viceroy of India in the 1880s, took up photography to create her own unofficial souvenir of life at the top under the Raj. 'My first efforts in photography' by Hariot Dufferin, an album dated 1886, is now in the Public Record Office of Northern Ireland. PRONI's extensive holdings of family papers contain a number of such collections, large and small – the visual records of some of the many less prominent people from the North of Ireland who made their careers somehwere in the far-flung Empire or in commerce with foreign lands. Similar material can be found in the Ulster Museum; a good example is the collection of photographs from the Davidson family, Ceylon tea planters and founders of the Sirocco Works in east Belfast.

David James Hogg, a Belfast schoolmaster and brother of the successful professional Alex Hogg, was a competent amateur whose work is known mainly from an album of 1909 which illustrates the work of a Belfast police court missionary named Collins. The subject matter is exceptionally interesting because rarely recorded, but, apart from that, the photographs are clearly by a practised hand; like his brother (before he turned professional), David Hogg was active in several camera clubs and entered his work for exhibitions.[8]

The general effect of enabling amateurs to produce good photographs more easily was a marked decline in the number of existing professional studios. At least, this was the effect in Dublin. Belfast was different, for the simple reason that its population expanded enormously after 1880, particularly during the 1890s when boom conditions in shipbuilding, engineering and the building trade attracted very large numbers of immigrants from the countryside. The number of studios did actually fall slightly during the 1880s, from 16 to 14, but by 1892 it had risen to 19 and by 1899 it was 27. With considerable fluctuations, which reflect the industrial and commercial fortunes of the city, the number of studios went on rising in the years before the outbreak of the First World War – 23 in 1900–1 (coinciding with the Boer War), 28 in 1902–3, 30 in 1904–5, a peak of 48 in 1907, down to 38 in 1913. During this period, the prospect of good business attracted three leading firms from other parts of the United Kingdom to establish studios in Belfast. In 1880 Thomas Williams and Company of Plymouth opened a branch at 25 Castle Place. Though one comes across examples of their cartes fairly often, the move was evidently not a success and they had gone from Belfast by 1884. The Glasgow firm of Turnbull and Sons started in the mid-1880s at 23 Garfield Street, advertising their 'Patent Luxograph Apparatus', which enabled them to 'take photographs at all times and in all weathers, after dark as well as during the day', and their use of other patented processes. Turnbull's remained in Belfast for many years, till the end of the 1920s. Lafayette, the great Dublin firm with branches in several British cities, opened a studio in Donegall Place at the turn of the century; it too lasted until the end of the twenties. For a time Lafayette's had a studio in Larne as well, competing for the ferry and tourist trade with James Boyd, E.W. Mack and others.

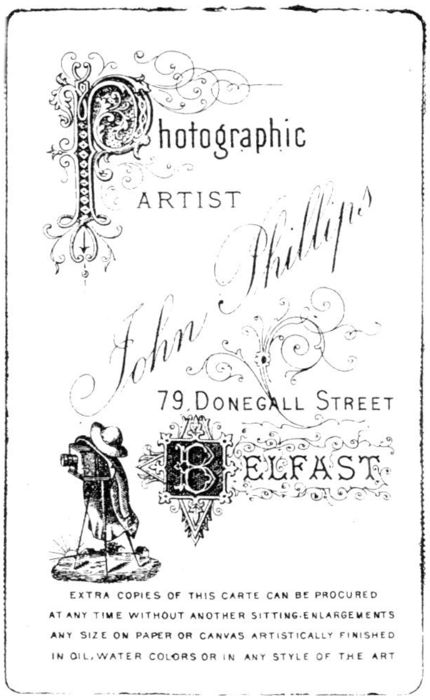

As always, the photographic profession during this period consisted, on the one hand, of a core of well-established and relatively prosperous firms, and on the other hand of a changing cast of photographers who came and went fairly rapidly. In fact photography was never a profession in any proper meaning of the term, since entry to it was entirely uncontrolled and there were no agreed standards. On the contrary, anyone could set up as a photographer, and cut-throat competition was the rule. This is not to say that individual photographers did not have professional standards, priding themselves on doing work of consistently good quality and even exercising some professional courtesy in their dealings with each other once established in an area. It is difficult to imagine anyone going to greater trouble to achieve perfect results, with the equipment available to him, than Robert Welch.

There was no attempt at this stage, however, to form any kind of professional organisation. Individuality was highly prized: it is noticeable that partnerships seldom lasted any length of time, artistic temperaments (or business plans) all too easily clashing.

By far the most successful of the portrait photographers in the North of Ireland during the late nineteenth and early twentieth centuries was William Abernethy. Nothing much is known about his origins, but he is thought to have come from a farm near Comber in County Down, and apparently learned his trade with a Belfast photographer named Phillips, the proprietor of a successful studio first in Donegall Street then in Royal Avenue. Abernethy set up on his own in 1886, at 29 High Street, which was to remain his chief studio when he later expanded into numerous branches. Phillips, to whom Abernethy must have been a rival for the next thirty years, claimed in 1899 to have the largest and best-lighted studio in the city, and the longest established; also that the Prince of Wales and the lord lieutenant were his patrons and that he was 'unsurpassed' in outdoor photography and the taking of groups. At the turn of the century he was still making a good living, to judge from the fact that his private residence was a substantial house in Duncairn Gardens, off the Antrim Road.

Abernethy was the coming man, however, and his studio was to enjoy the same

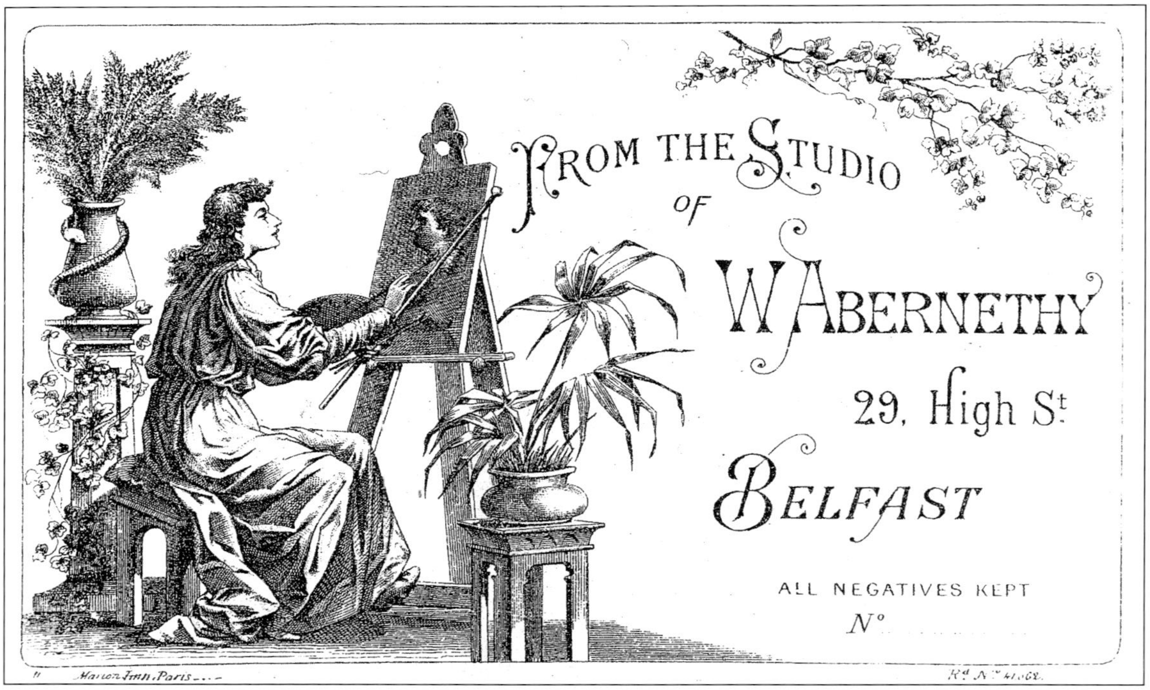

Back of a cabinet portrait, William Abernethy's studio, c. 1900.

MAGNI / UM

This particular design, linking art and photography, one of a range supplied by the French firm, Marion and Company, was a popular choice among studio owners. Abenethy was the most fashionable and most successful portrait photographer in the North of Ireland from the 1880s to the 1920s. Queen Victoria gave him the royal warrant, one of only four in Ireland awarded during her reign.

esteem and success in his own generation as Magill's had enjoyed in the previous one. One comes across his photographs everywhere – portraits of all sizes, from cartes to life-size, and groups of all kinds. His work was good, and well presented, with a look of bourgeois solidity about it that must have reassured his extensive clientele. The substantial entry under his name in *Industries of Ireland* tells us that he 'commenced business at the above address [29 High Street] some five years ago, where he occupies several floors of a large and handsome building'. The entrance hall, where specimens of the photographer's work were displayed, led to a reception room – 'an elegantly-furnished apartment' – with a ladies' dressing room beyond. One flight up, there was another waiting room, with dressing rooms for both sexes. The studio itself was 45 feet long, 'replete with every modern requisite, [such] as patent blinds to regulate the light on any part of the group or figure, a large variety of backgrounds of different tints to suit various complexions, dresses, &c., of the sitters, scenery on patent rollers, &c.'.

Technical equipment was also of the latest kind, such as the Meagher patent camera with Dallmeyer lens and instantaneous shutter ('specially adapted for photographing children or pet animals'). Abernethy also claimed to employ 'one of the largest cameras in the kingdom for the production of the new popular panel photos', as well as 'one of the largest and most approved appliances for photographing family groups, pic-nic parties, landscapes, buildings, machinery, &c.'. By that time he had a considerable business, employing 'upwards of twenty experienced assistants' in various departments; he claimed that, taking Saturday and Monday as average days, 'upwards of three hundred clients are photographed'. A few years later, in an advertisement of 1895, Abernethy said he had photographed over eighteen thousand people at his studios within the previous year. At his large printing and finishing works at Bloomfield, it was said, only the most skilled men were employed.

Later still, he opened branch studios in Belfast (two of them in High Street), as well as others in Bangor, Newry and Dundalk. Abernethy could afford to live well. His two sons were sent to boarding schools, after which one went to university to read medicine, the other to the Slade School of Art; one of the daughters, an early graduate of Trinity College, Dublin, became headmistress of a Dublin girls' school. He and his wife travelled to Paris, he himself (accompanied by the incumbent of the church he attended, and whose fare he paid) to the Holy Land, and he was reputedly equally generous to numerous relations. When he died in 1930 he still left £6,350, in modern terms a substantial amount of money. His sons – who carried on running the business during the 1930s, till one retired from it and the other one died – were less successful, partly, it was said, because of the advent of the polyfoto. In any case, Belfast was a depressed area during the 1930s, in industrial and commercial terms. Abernethy's widow continued to run the studio, through a manager, until the 1950s.[9]

Abernethy's affluence at the close of his long career was in sharp contrast to the unaccountably small estate left by James Glass, the noted Londonderry photographer, who died in 1931 apparently worth only £189. Yet the two beneficiaries of his will, his spinster daughters, appear to have lived comfortably, and themselves left estates valued at over £2,800 and £8,500. Glass, born in 1847, had started at 65 Carlisle Road about 1875, at first in partnership; the 1878 directory lists the studio of Young and Glass at that address. Young soon disappeared, however. In an advertisement of 1890 in the *Londonderry Almanac* Glass tendered his 'sincere Thanks to his numerous Patrons for the very liberal support accorded him during the last Fourteen Years'. His entries in *Industries of the North* a year later says he 'entered into business some sixteen years ago by opening a first-class studio at No. 65, Carlisle Road, and pursued his artistic avocation with such ardour that ten had not elapsed before he was called upon to vastly increase his accommodation by the institution of a second studio at No. 31 in the same busy thoroughfare as a branch establishment'. As well as portraits of all kinds, Glass produced outdoor photographs, enlargements 'finished superbly' in crayon, oil and watercolour, and 'exquisitely executed examples of work on porcelain, of which he makes a speciality, and in which he particularly excels'.

Apart possibly from descendants of the sitters themselves – most of whom were what might be called local obscurities – Glass's portraits are of limited interest to posterity. All the negatives from his career of more than half a century have in any case disappeared, but an album of twenty-four original prints he took in the Gweedore district of Donegal survives and illustrates a famous episode in local and

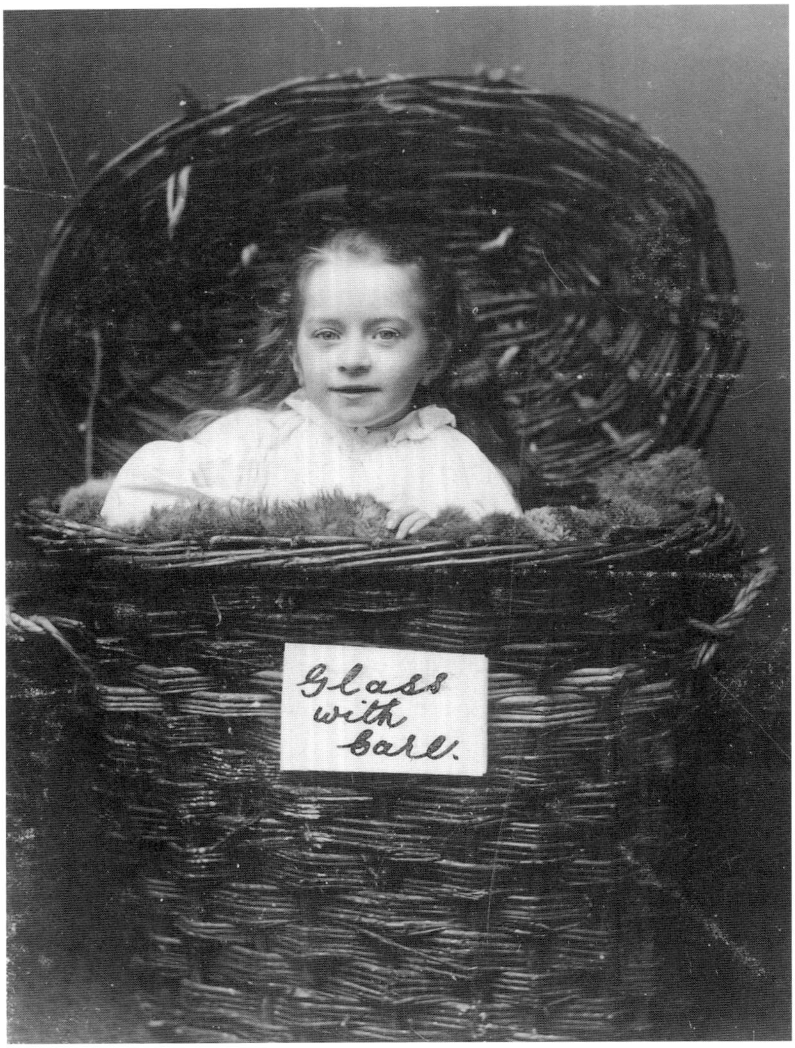

'Glass with Care', by James Glass, *c.* 1880.
MAGNI / UM

Glass's amusing portrait of his daughter Ellie, posed in one of the wicker containers used for transporting photographic chemicals.

national history. Gweedore, an area of extreme harshness, with scarcely any fertile land and an excessive population of impoverished people barely able to subsist at the best of times, let alone pay rent to a landlord, became a test case in the land war of the 1870s and 1880s. Following evictions on the Nixon and Olpherts estates, the parish priest of Gweedore, Father McFadden, who famously declared on one occasion, 'I am the law in Gweedore', led a campaign of resistance. When early in 1889 the police inspector sent to arrest him at his presbytery was killed by an angry crowd, the priest and a number of his parishioners were indicted for murder. The Gweedore case was taken up by both unionists and nationalists in Ireland and by their partisans in Great Britain, where the Liberal press strongly championed the anti-landlord and anti-coercion cause.

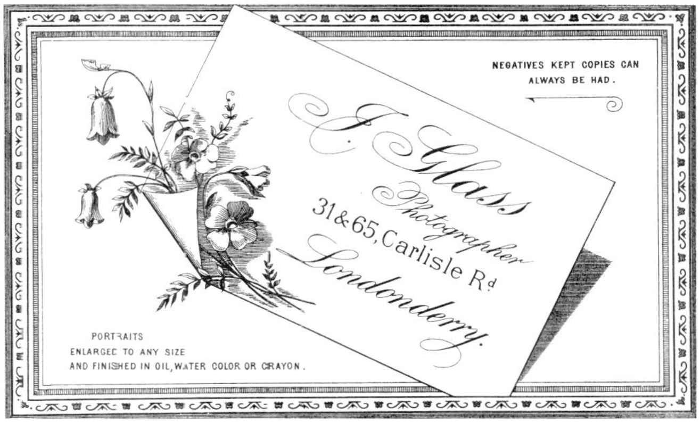

The trial of the Gweedore prisoners was transferred from Donegal to Maryborough (modern Portlaoise) in Queen's County (Laois), where it was heard

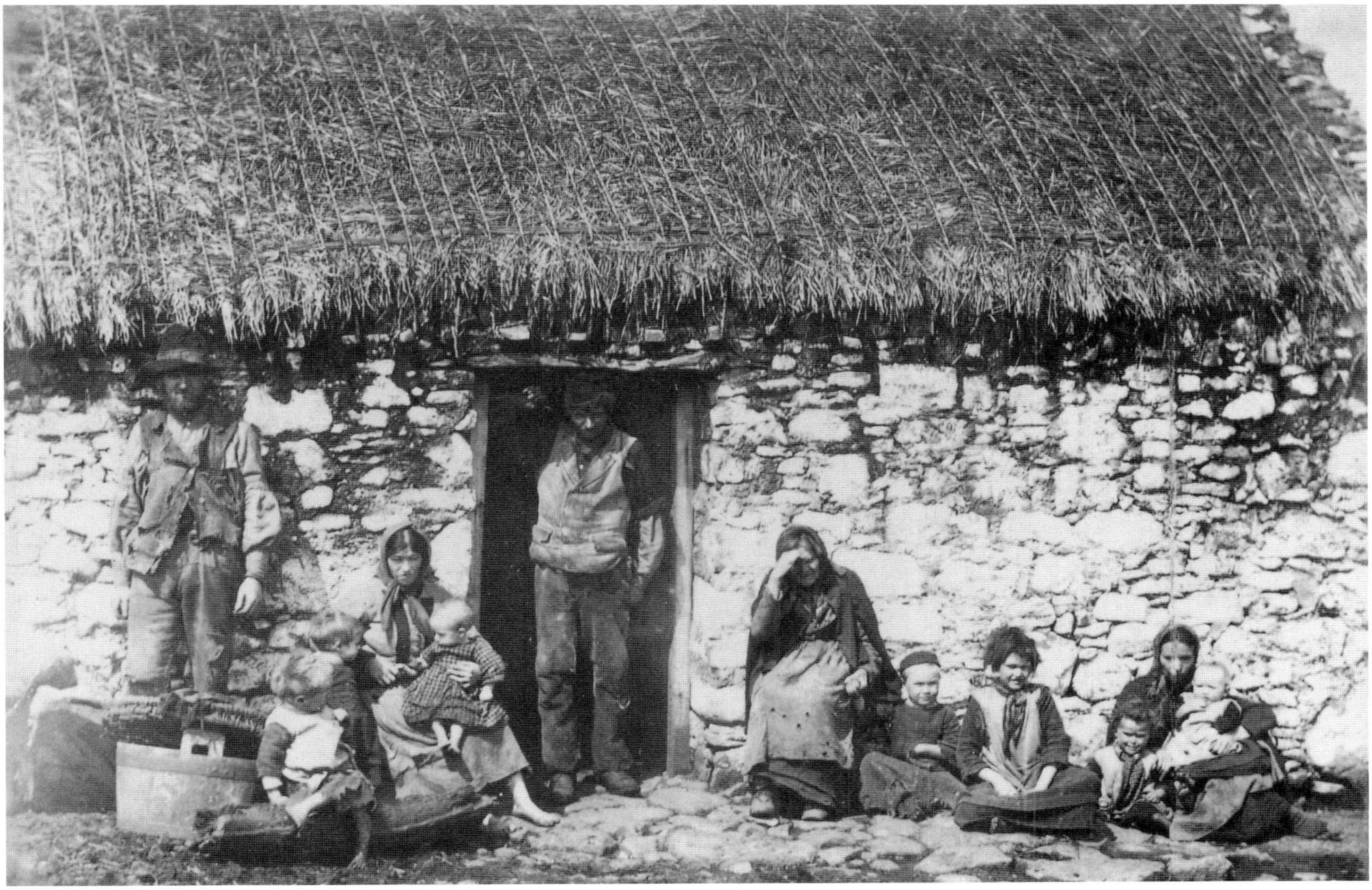

People of Gweedore, County Donegal, a scene from the album compiled by James Glass, *c.* 1889, for the Gweedore murder case.

MAGNI / UM

by a special jury of landowners and property owners, only one of whom was a Catholic. The attorney general led for the prosecution, assisted by Edward Carson among others. An application to the judge to allow members of the jury to visit Gweedore, to see for themselves the scene of the crime, was opposed by the crown and rejected. Instead, James Glass provided a collection of photographs consisting of a visual record of the extreme poverty and backwardness in the area, along with views of Father McFadden's presbytery, the village of Falcarragh and other locations mentioned in the pleadings. The views of Gweedore and its inhabitants appear to be wet collodion prints, considerably earlier in date than the rest, late 1870s or early 1880s. An influential pamphlet about the trial by H.W. Massingham, a leading Liberal journalist, was illustrated by a couple of Glass's photographs in the form of simple engravings. As to the outcome, a compromise was eventually agreed by the defence whereby the accused admitted guilt (though not murder) and were given sentences ranging from two months to ten years. Those still in prison in 1892 were released by the new Liberal administration in Ireland.[10]

William Allison, who left an estate valued at £1,100 when he died in 1923, was

Advertisement for James Boyd, Larne, 1899, from *Larne Grand Fete and Fancy Fair.*

MAGNI / UM

Like other shopkeepers pursuing the tourist trade, Boyd invested in the publication (ostensibly by himself) of selections of local views. *Boyd's Popular Album of Larne and the Grand Antrim Coast Scenery*, printed in Germany *c.* 1895, consists of thirty-one engravings of anonymous photographs.

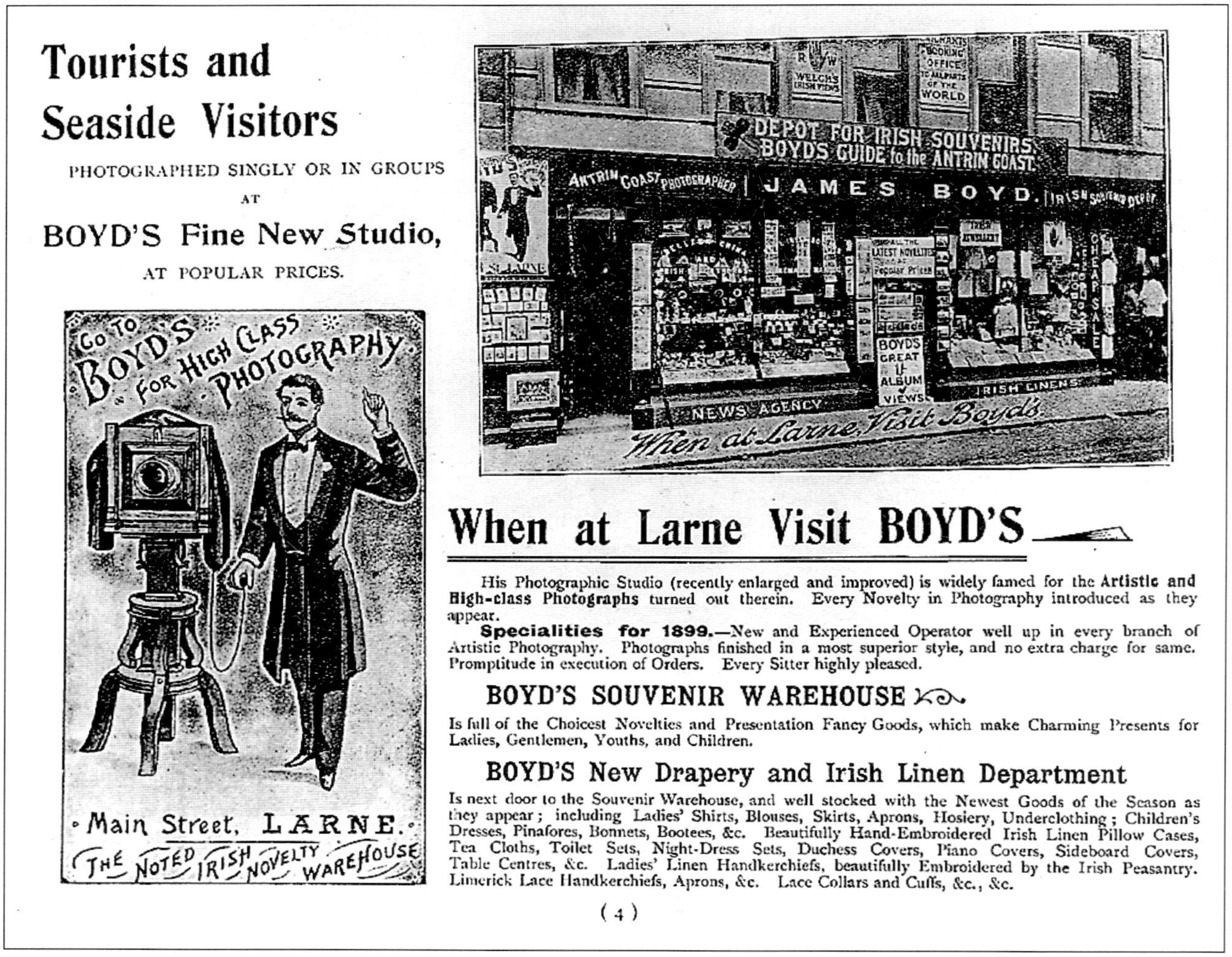

a Yorkshireman who had come to Belfast with his cousin Herbert in 1881 and had been a photographer's assistant in Oxford before the two of them established their studio at 13 Donegall Square North. In the 1890s the business had prospered and Allison and Allison had secured a good share of the Belfast portrait trade, expanding to take over the Vienna Photo Art Company's studio in Queen's Arcade about 1892, opening a branch in Clanbrassil Street, Dundalk, in 1896, acquiring the well-established firm of W.J. Hunter in Armagh in 1900 from the photographer's widow and opening in Newry in 1903.

By 1904 William Allison was 'instructing' students in the Municipal Technical Institute (his appointment as Instructor was noted on the firm's letterhead) and in that year applied for the post of teacher of the subject. His letter of application gives his qualifications for the post as 'over twenty years practical experience as a professional photographer – 12 years of that time as one of the principals of my firm' – during which he had practised every branch of photography except the photo-mechanical department, of which he possessed only a theoretical

Dr Gilbert Marshall of Markethill, County Armagh, at the wheel of his new Humberette, 1908, by Herbert Allison.

PRONI (ALLISON COLLECTION)

Dr Marshall was evidently well pleased with his car. He later remarked that when he had had a horse he used to arrive home at ten o'clock at night dead tired but could now travel fifty miles and be home by five o'clock without being exhausted.

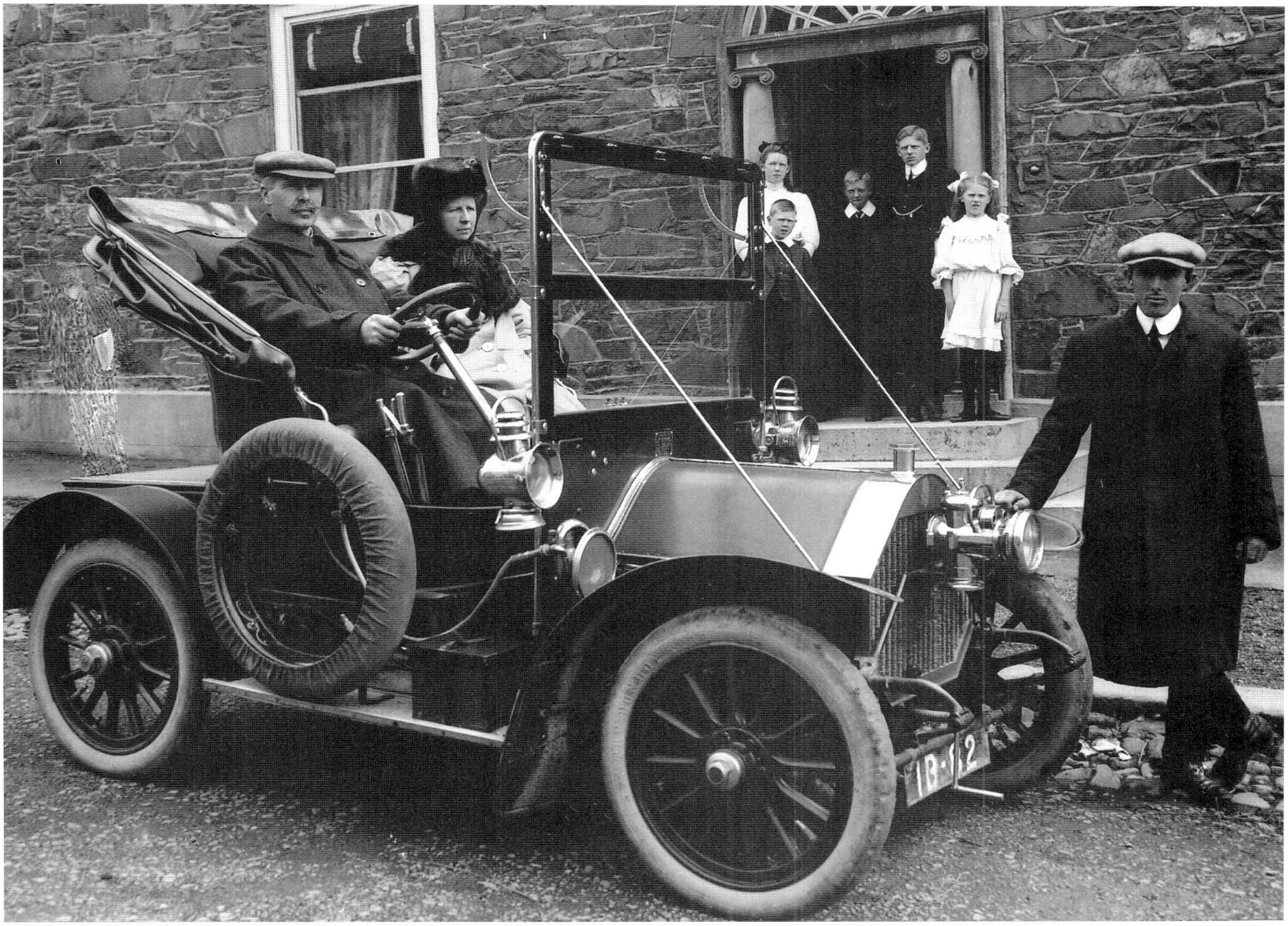

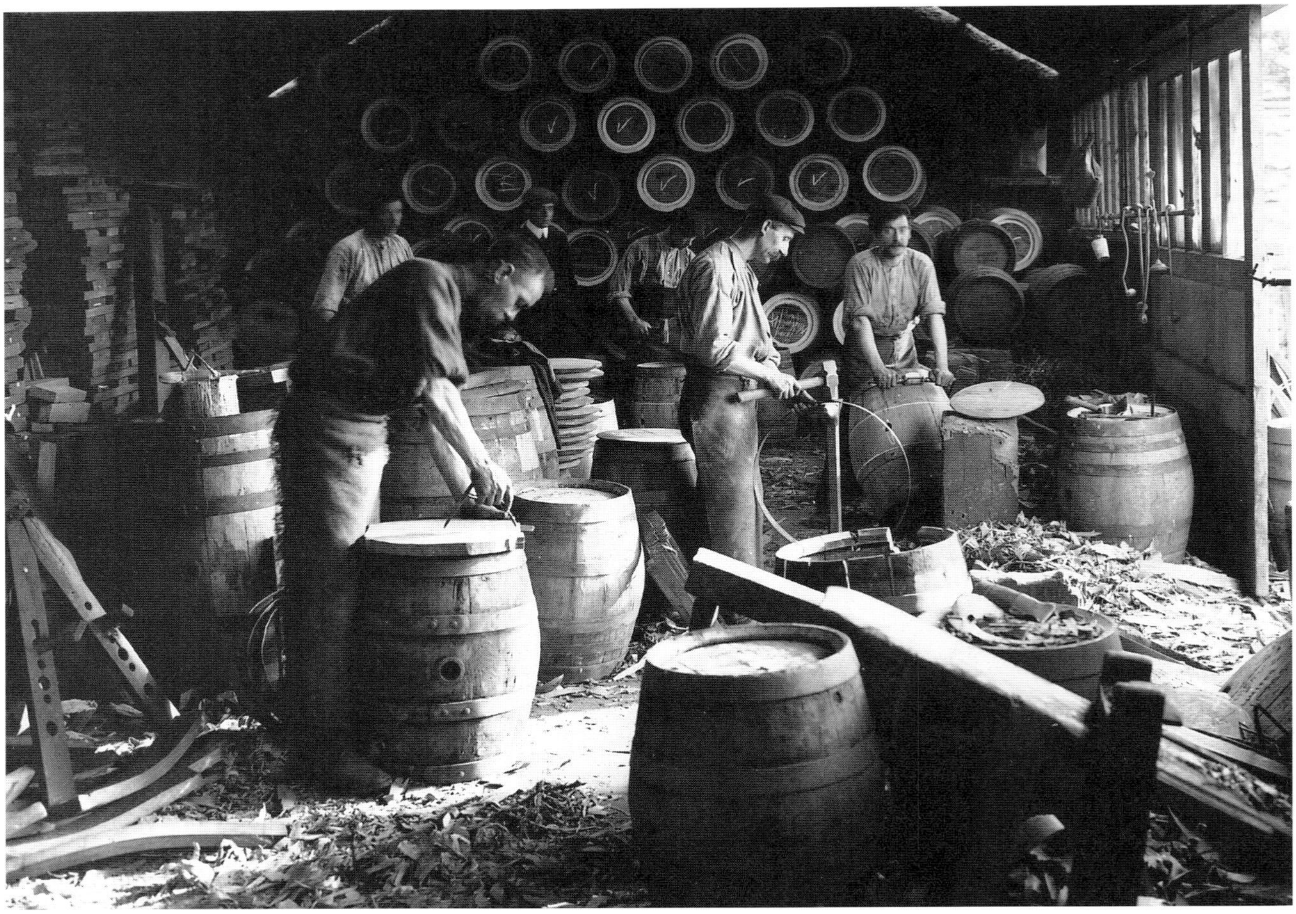

Coopers at work in the Great Northern Brewery, Dundalk, County Louth, c. 1910, by Herbert Allison.
PRONI (ALLISON COLLECTION)

knowledge. He had exhibited at several London and provincial exhibitions, including that of the Royal Photographic Society, and held one of only four certificates awarded for excellence in 1903, in a competition where over six hundred professionals from all over the UK had entered their work. The Technical College post on this occasion went to A.R. Hogg, who was comparatively new to the professional ranks, but Allison was appointed later and evidently made a success of it.[11]

At the time he appears to have been promised a share of the institute's commissions, for he was writing in 1905 to the principal to remind him: 'You promised some time ago that I should be given a fair share of what was going, and I feel that so long as I hold the position of teacher & am professionally engaged in Photography I should be given a fair amount of the work.' In 1905 the Allison partnership broke up. William remained in Belfast, while Herbert Allison moved to live at Warrenpoint, where he set up another studio and from where he ran the two in Newry and Dundalk and kept an eye on the main business in Armagh, which was managed by his son, Herbert junior, from 1903. In the 1920s and 1930s Herbert senior travelled to Armagh by train from the two County Down studios (the one in Dundalk closed when Ireland was partitioned in 1921), where all the processing work was done, collected the prints from the previous week and returned home.

Apart from Herbert junior, who did well out of the monopoly business in

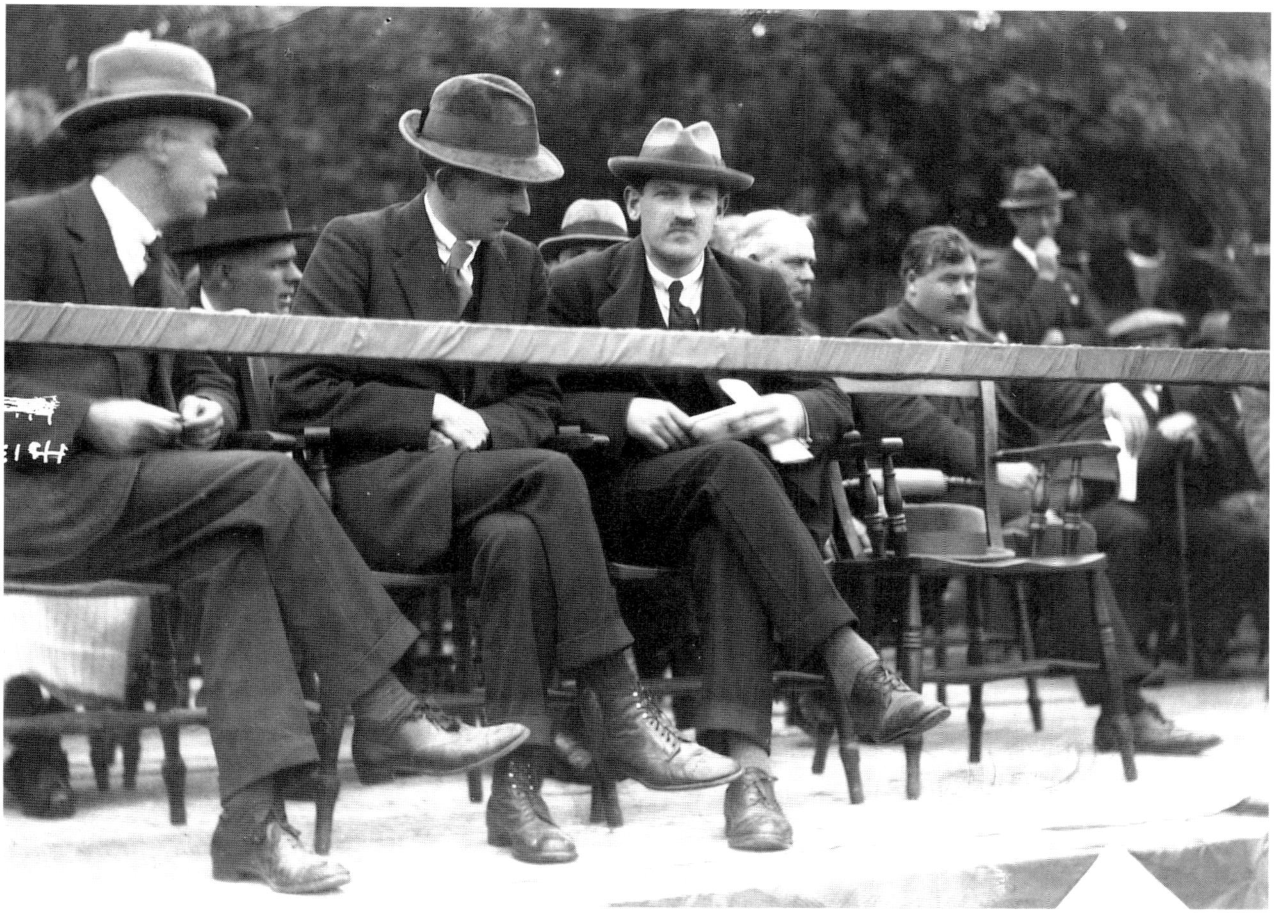

Armagh and became a pillar of the community there, Herbert Allison had another son, who became a dentist in England, and two daughters, one of whom married a prominent Belfast solicitor. He himself played a very active part in local affairs, as a Justice of the Peace and town councillor, before dying at Warrenpoint in 1947 at the age of ninety-four, just ten years before his elder son. An excellent selection of the surviving photographs from the Armagh studio, which are now in the Public Record Office of Northern Ireland, has been published by Fitzgerald and Weatherup with a useful introduction on Herbert Allison's life and career. That it was a successful career may be judged from the fact that when he died he left £8,500.[12]

Allison and Allison, along with Abernethy and others, exhibited in 1895 at the Belfast Art and Industrial Exhibition. The Allisons were awarded a silver medal and diploma. The Ulster Museum has a number of interesting photographs of their studio in Donegall Square which date from about this time. We also know a good deal about the Vienna Photo Art Company which they had recently acquired. The name of this firm, and the imperial eagle which it used as a trademark, derived from the fact that the photographer who established it about 1881, F. Charles, was an Austrian. Charles's business partner, whom he had met in Liverpool, was one Robert Little, who came from County Cavan. Little, who had had a successful

Michael Collins in Armagh, 4 September 1921, by Herbert Allison.
PRONI (ALLISON COLLECTION)

This is one of those interesting occasions when local and national history coincide. Collins, third from left, had been elected MP for Armagh in the new parliament of Northern Ireland. He is shown here on the platform of a Sinn Féin meeting attended by more than twenty thousand people, his first appearance in public since the truce that ended the Irish War of Independence.

business in Liverpool selling pictures and picture frames, provided the finance for the business but was not himself a photographer. The partnership broke up in the mid-1880s. Charles became sole proprietor of the Vienna Photo Art Company, while Little set up a rival concern, the Queen's Photo Art Company in Royal Avenue, employing a photographer named Welsh (not to be confused with Robert Welch) as manager. Little soon gave up his interest in the photographic business, Welsh becoming proprietor. Little remained in Belfast but reverted to his former trade as picture-frame maker, carver and gilder, with premises first in Royal Avenue, and later in York Street.[13] By 1892 Allison and Allison were proprietors of the Vienna Art Company. Whether or not Charles remained in Belfast to become the partner in the firm of Charles and Russell (51 Ann Street until 1900, 10 Royal Avenue thereafter until the early 1920s) has not been established.

Another Austrian, who worked in Belfast slightly later than Charles, was Carl Rubens, whose Austrian Studio was at 39 Dublin Road in the 1890s. He does not appear in the directories until 1899, but judging from the fact that he was awarded a medal in the Belfast exhibition of 1894 he must have been in the city for some time before that. In an advertisement of 1899 he claimed to have been awarded a special diploma of honour in Vienna in 1891, and also claimed the patronage of HRH Maria Theresa of Austria. Other patrons were the Princess of Wales, the Duchess of Albany, Lord Salisbury and W.E. Gladstone ('Special Sittings, Testimonials for same'). The same source tells us that the studio was managed by a Mr Dawson; two years later, Dawson and Company were the proprietors.[14] J.B. De Voto, perhaps of Italian origin, appears in the directories briefly in the mid-1890s at 13 Fleetwood Street, a small street off the Crumlin Road; a Miss De Voto, at the same address, was a music teacher. There was no entry under the name in the Belfast directory in 1894; subsequently, it appears in connection with coal and flour merchants (the name still survives in Devoto and Hassan, coal merchants) but there is no further sign of the photographer after 1895.

Mavius and Vivash, an exotic-sounding pair but both, evidently, English, ran a studio in Ann Street for the ten years up to 1893, when the partnership broke up. Mavius, then described as 'late of Mavius & Vivash', became 'Photographic Artist' at the studio of Hugh Adair in Donegall Place. Adair was a printer and stationer with an established business in Arthur Street and a branch in Donegall Place which sold fancy goods, including photograph frames. Along with Mavius's services he purchased the entire Mavius and Vivash stock of negatives, lenses and cameras. Thus equipped, Adair urged 'Ladies or Gentlemen who may have been unable to obtain a satisfactory likeness' to give Mr Mavius a sitting, 'as difficult subjects are his speciality'.[15]

A striking number of photographers in the north of Ireland in the nineteenth

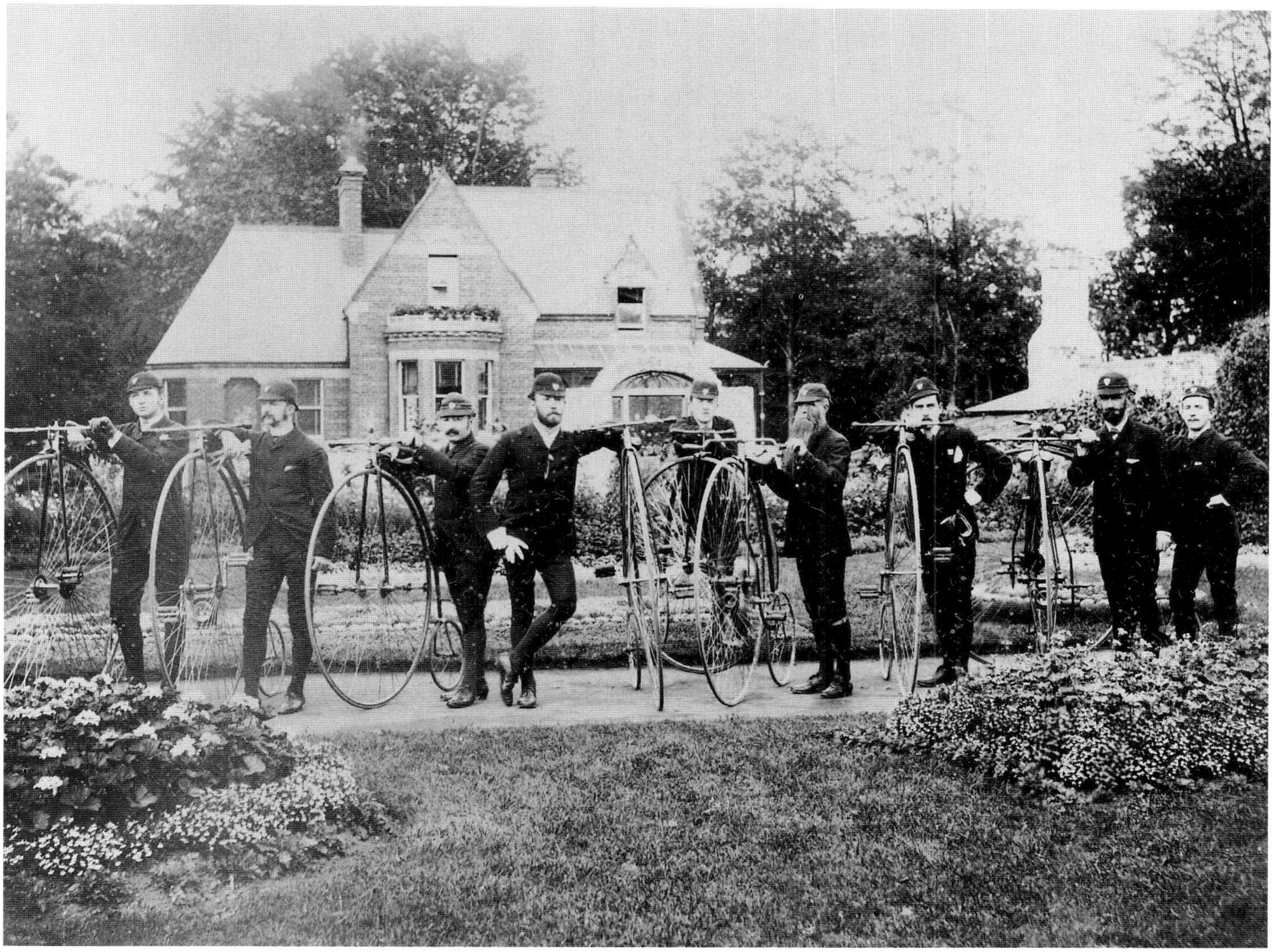

century were immigrants. One obvious explanation for this was the population explosion in Belfast; the fact was that most Belfast people came from somewhere else, either the Irish countryside or Great Britain. One newcomer during the 1880s was Harry Douglas (1862–1934), who after coming to Belfast from Edinburgh in 1884 worked as a photographer, first with August Neilson, then for Magill's. When Magill's studio closed down (in 1893 after a fire), Douglas set up on his own at 35 Royal Avenue, then worked as a portrait painter at the same address for the rest of his life (he died in 1934 leaving £654). It was as a portrait painter that he made a successful career recording successive lord mayors and other civic dignitaries whose artistic tastes would not have welcomed anything other than the strictly conventional.[16] So much of the work of the better portrait photographers was artistic in nature – the colouring and retouching in particular – that the term 'Photographic Artist', under which photographers were for so long listed in the directories, was a pretty accurate description as well as a claim to artistic respectability.

Members of the Northern Cycling Club in Ormeau Park, Belfast, *c.* 1880, by Robert Seggons.

MAGNI / UM

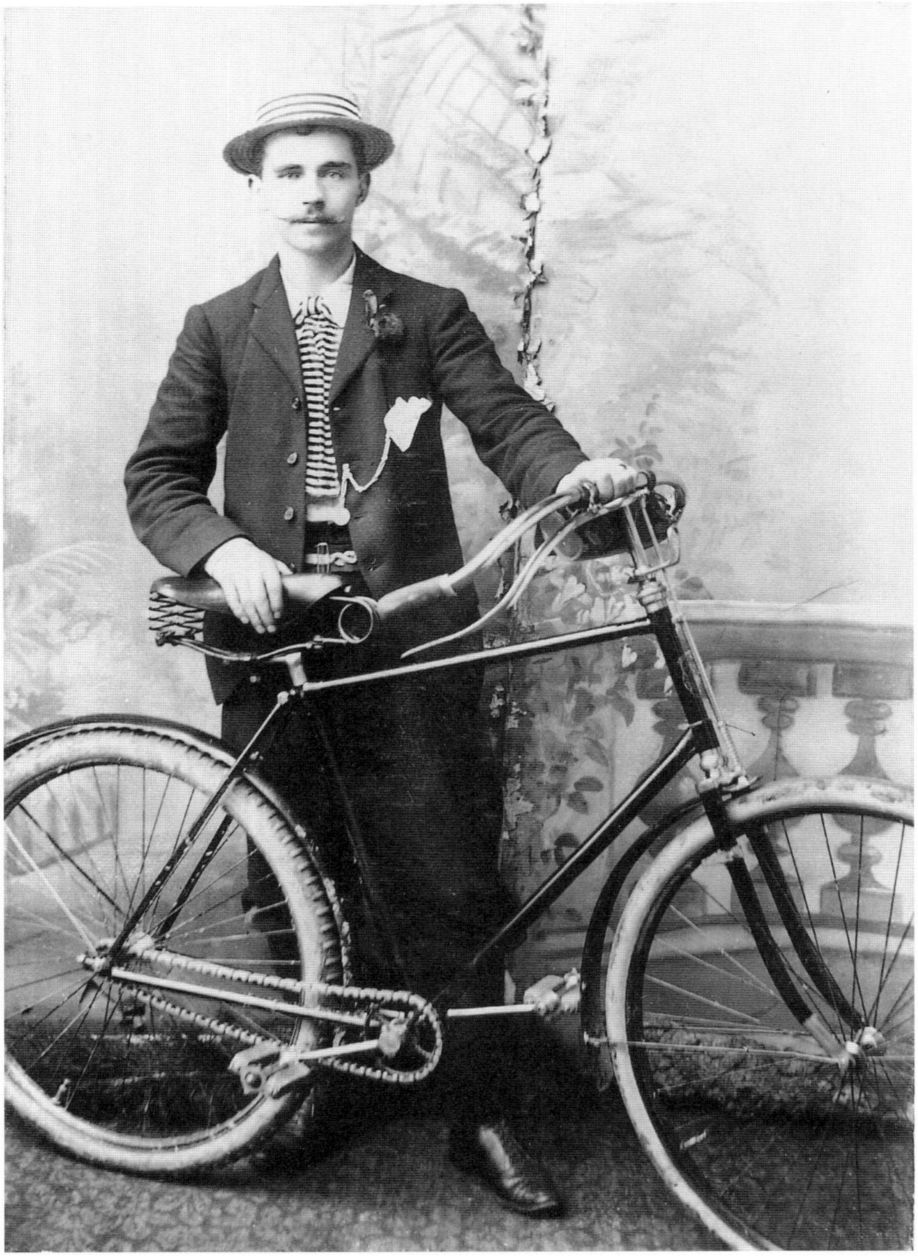

James Mitchell (1867–1941) with his bicycle, *c.* 1896, by G.V. Simmons, Portadown.
BY KIND PERMISSION OF MRS BRENDA COLLINS

A gents' outfitter by trade, born in Coleraine, married to a Coleraine girl and settled in Dublin, the subject's presence in Portadown is a family mystery.

Robert Seggons, briefly mentioned earlier as having started as an assistant in Sarony's gallery in the early 1860s, acquired his own studio in Castle Place sometime in the early 1870s and for the next twenty-five or thirty years was successful both as a taker of portraits and as a general photographer. He exhibited at the Belfast International Exhibition and Bazaar in 1876. His surviving photographs (in addition to numerous cartes and cabinets) include two group portraits of cycling club members in Ormeau Park in the early 1880s, photographs of gasworks

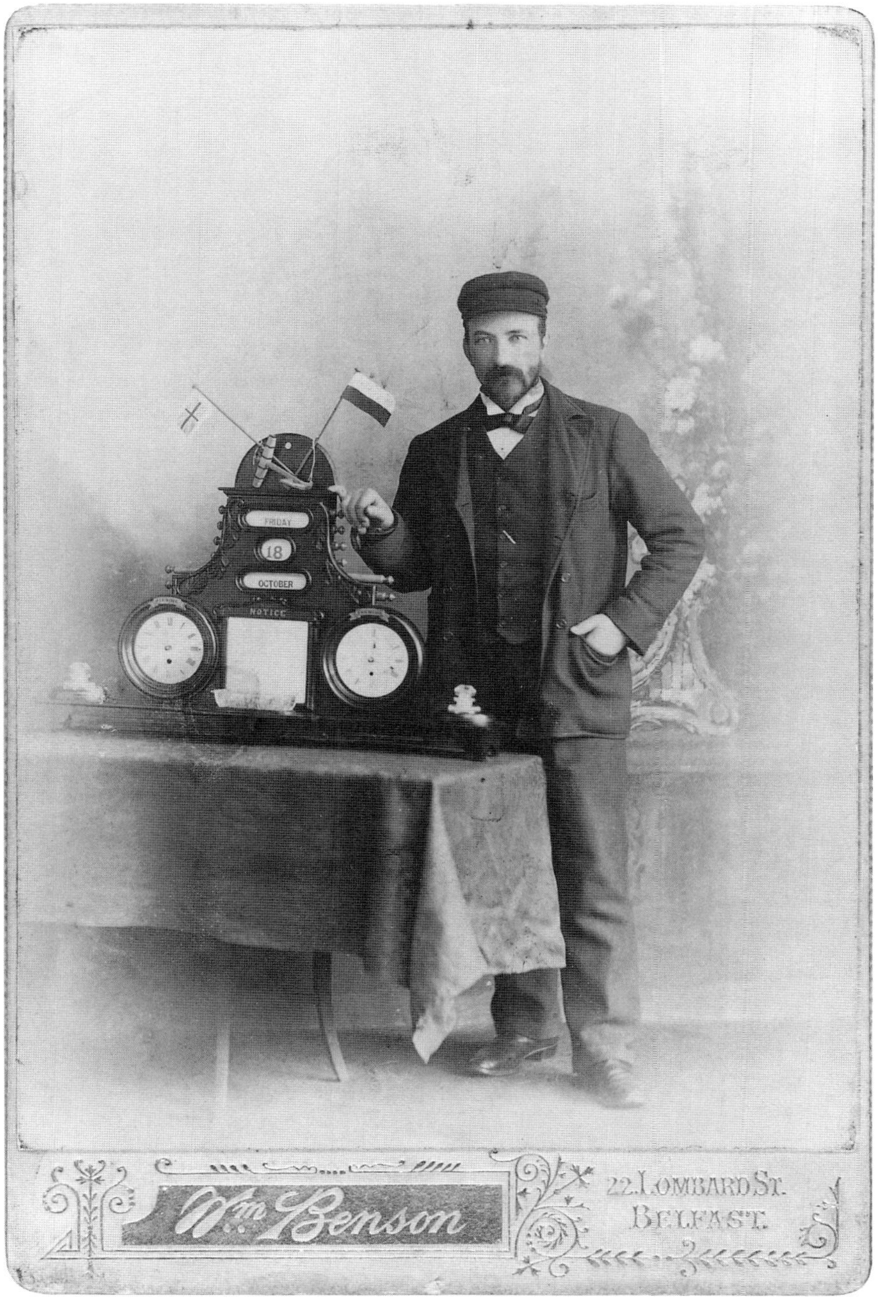

Robert James Benson (d. 1931), Belfast harbour pilot, with his 'invention', photographed by his brother William, c. 1900.

BY KIND PERMISSION OF MRS P. McLEAN

employees and extensions to the gasworks of the same period, a set of the ceremonial decorated arches erected in Belfast in 1885 for the visit of the Prince of Wales, and one of the 5th Dragoon Guards, the Black Watch and the Royal Irish Constabulary on picket duty at the Sirocco Works in east Belfast during the anti-Home Rule riots of 1886. By 1890 Seggons was doing sufficiently well to move house from Wellesley Avenue (a respectable but modest street of brick terrace houses) to a more imposing address in Wellington Park nearby. He called his new home Camera House. When he died there early in 1905 he left the sum of £1,695.

The Benson family provided pilots in successive generations, as far back as this man's great-grandfather. The precise purpose of his invention is now obscure but the two dials, labelled MORNING and EVENING, presumably refer to the daily tides.

Among anonymous survivals of some interest, the Ulster Museum has a small collection of full-plate glass negatives, professional in quality but bearing no photographer's name or any other mark. All are dated, on their original paper envelopes, 1895. One group depicts views of textile machine shops in Combe Barbour's engineering works; another consists of views of Elmwood Presbyterian Church, mostly interiors. The remainder include exceptionally rare and interesting views of the White Linen Hall in its last days, transformed, by a mock castellated entrance and a huge temporary structure covering its inner courtyard, into the venue for the Belfast Exhibition of 1895. Immediately after the close of the exhibition, work began on the demolition of the building, to clear the site for the erection of the new City Hall. One of the photographs shows the demolition men at work. The rooms inside which had for many years housed the Linen Hall Library (hence its name) were photographed by R.J. Welch shortly before the removal of this well-known Belfast landmark, which dated from 1785.

The spread of organised sport, from the 1880s on, provided a growing amount of work for photographers. The Irish Football Association was formed in Belfast in 1880. Seggons, and later Abernethy, photographed football teams and other sporting groups in the years before and after the turn of the century. From about 1910, however, the official photographer to the IFA was Robert Lyttle, whose studio at that time was at 44 Dublin Road. He moved in the early 1920s to 12 High Street and later still opened a branch in Donegall Place, as well as one in Londonderry. Lyttle had trained in Belfast with a photographer named Thompson, then worked for Abernethy for ten years, according to the information on his photograph of Broadway Football Club in 1911. In a move up-market in the 1920s he changed his business name to R. Clements Lyttle, 'photographer in commerce and industry', and it was under this new name that he ran a studio in Dublin for a time, at 30 Westmoreland Street (I have seen a postcard with the Dublin address, overstamped 'R. Lyttle, 44 Dublin Road, Belfast'). Lyttle later acquired a warrant from the government of Northern Ireland and was also appointed a Justice of the Peace. Sports teams continued to provide much of his bread-and-butter work, however. Fading family mementoes of an earlier generation's prowess at many a Belfast school or club bear his name. He died in 1950 comfortably off, leaving an estate valued at £4,515.

Trademark of Robert Lyttle, official photographer to the Irish Football Association, c. 1912, redrawn by Deirdre Crone.
MAGNI / UM

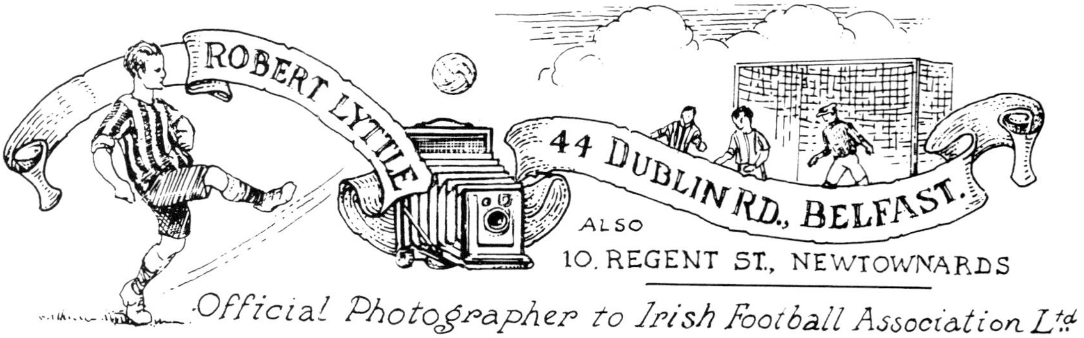

Outside Belfast, the largest surviving collection of glass-plate negatives had its origin in Strabane in the years before the First World War. In 1901 J.W. Burrows set up his studio there and during the next twelve years took portraits, photographed events and occasions of all kinds in the town and round about, as well as running a cinema and a dance hall. In 1913 he sold the business to a Londoner, Herbert Cooper, who was the town's photographer until he died in 1960 at the age of eighty-six. By his will Cooper left nearly £7,000. All the surviving negatives of Burrows and Cooper were subsequently purchased by the Public Record Office of Northern Ireland, where the Cooper Collection (as it is called) is now to be found. At more than approximately 30,000 glass plates, it is one of the largest commercial collections in Ireland. The portraits which form a large part of that number are of limited interest but the rest are a fascinating record of small-town life in the north-west over six decades. Some examples of Burrows's work from the early years – pictures of a visiting circus, a local dance and flower show, processions of Orangemen

Catch-My-Pal demonstation, at Baronscourt, County Tyrone, in 1910, by J.W. Burrows.

PRONI (COOPER COLLECTION)

The Protestant Total Abstinence Union, or Catch-My-Pal Movement as it was usually called, was started by a Presbyterian minister in Armagh in 1909 and spread rapidly in the North of Ireland. The Duke of Abercorn, the owner of Baronscourt, lent his support by allowing his grounds to be used by local organisers.

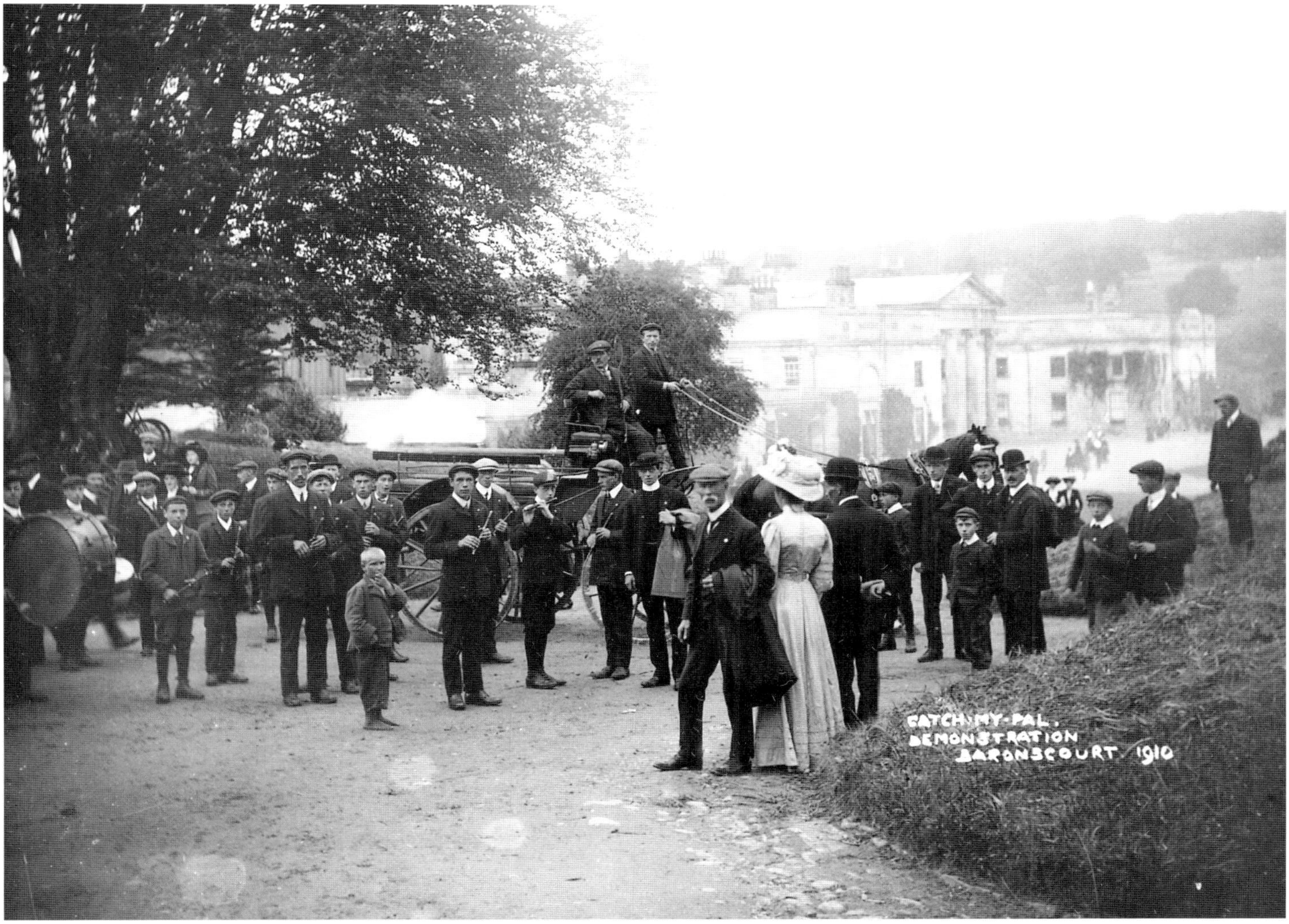

and Hibernians – are illustrated in B.M. Walker's books *Shadows on Glass* and *Faces of the Past*, but most are as yet unknown to the general public, though increasingly used by local historians.[17]

In County Cavan during this period, with one notable exception, there was an almost complete absence of such development. In particular, the directories show no sign of any well-established professional studio in the county town of Cavan itself. There is no obvious explanation for this, apart from population decline and the absence of the kind of changing clientele that a military garrison or tourist attractions would have provided. The exception was to be found in the small town of Bailieborough, where the enterprise of a local man established what was to become a local institution. James Coleman was the son of the assistant county surveyor. After some training in Belfast, he set up his Bailieboro' Studio in 1904,

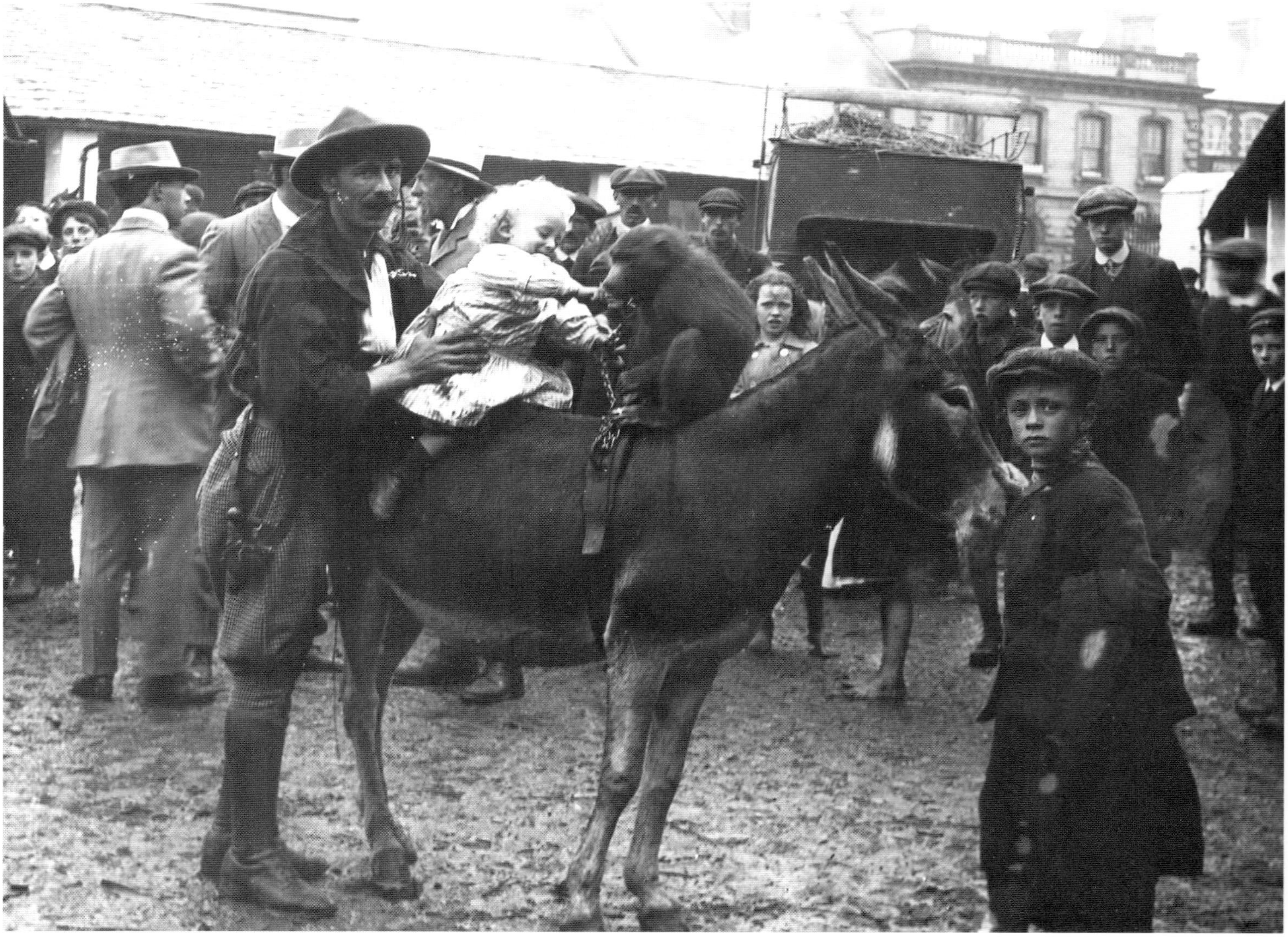

Circus folk with child and monkey in Strabane, c. 1910, by J.W. Burrows.
PRONI (COOPER COLLECTION)

The circus in question was Buff Bill's, run by William Kayes, which visited Strabane several times in the years before 1914.

running it till he died at his work forty-two years later, when his son William succeeded him. An advertisement of 1914 for reconstructed premises mentions a studio of 40 feet by 16 with modern facilities. The illustration features a large studio camera, and portraits were clearly the staple work, supplemented by the publication of numerous 'J.A.C.' picture postcards. In 1914 Coleman was already a member of the London-based Professional Photographers' Association – an unusual affiliation for any photographer in Ulster at this early date, perhaps to be accounted for by a determination to maintain standards.

The north coast of County Antrim generated more photographs than any other part of Ulster with the exception of Donegal. Picturesque scenery, archaeological remains, geological oddities (notably the Giant's Causeway), archaic survivals in agriculture, transport and customs (as in the Glens), popular tourist resorts such as Portrush – all attracted visitors, who wished to record both the things they had come to see and their own presence there. Visiting professional photographers –

Homespun woollen market in the town of Ardara, County Donegal, c. 1920, by H.F. Cooper.

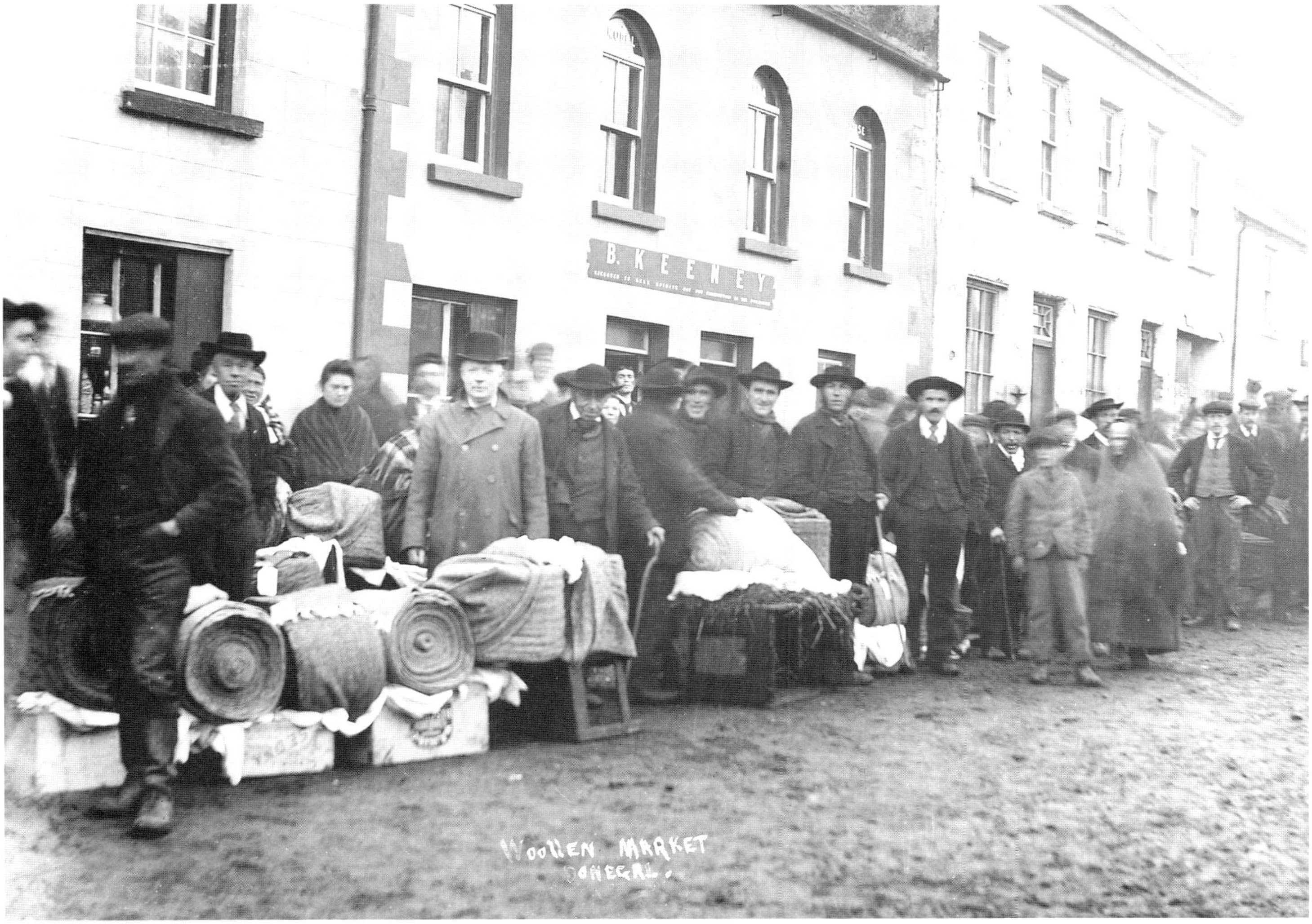

Lawrence, Valentine, Welch – produced numerous series of photographs for general sale, as prints or postcards or for publication in books or folders. Amateurs of all sorts produced their own. Then there were a small number of resident professionals whose main living was provided by summer visitors but who got some custom throughout the year. Such studios were often run in conjunction with some other kind of business.

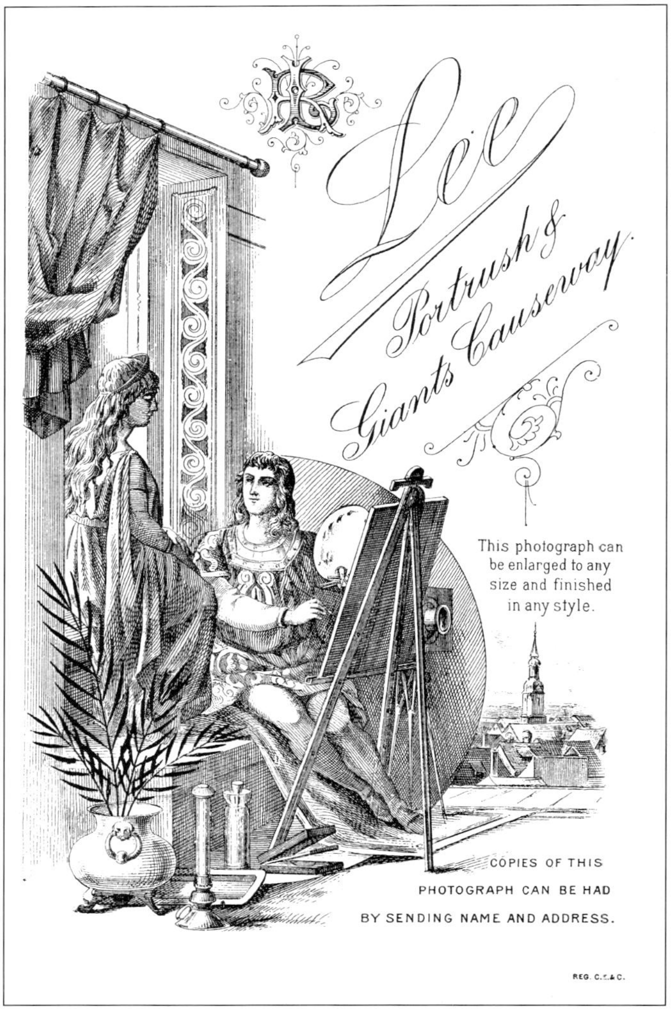

Opposite
Double portrait, taken at the Giant's Causeway by Lee, Portrush, c. 1910.
MAGNI / UM

The leading photographers in Portrush in the late nineteenth century and early twentieth century were the Lee family. Robert Lee, 'artist and photographer', is listed in Bassett's *Guide to County Antrim* (1888) at Causeway View, Portrush. Two years later, Robert Lee and Son were at work there. By the turn of the century the studio had moved to Lansdowne Crescent. The Lees apparently came from Ballycastle but had moved to England, where Robert Lee learned photography, before returning to settle in Portrush. The two sons, Robert junior and Alex, both became photographers; so too did their sister Henrietta. During or after the Boer War the brothers went to South Africa for a time, where they had a studio in Cape Town with mounts bearing the exotic legend, 'Lee's Studios at Cape Town, Portrush and the Giant's Causeway'. When they returned to Portrush they set up separate studios, Robert in Main Street, Alex at Bath Cottage (where his sister Henrietta also worked). Alex had another studio in Coleraine, which he visited twice weekly, as well as the one at the Causeway. This last, used only during the summer, was a wooden chalet. Having travelled from Portrush on the electric tram, itself a much-photographed phenomenon, Lee would set up his camera in front of the rock formation known as the 'Wishing Chair' and photograph visitors. Processing was done back at Bath Cottage, so presumably his clients paid in advance. Later, in order to supplement his income, he bought a Kodak dealership (this involved purchasing at least £100 worth of Kodak equipment) and went in for developing and processing.

Professionals had always developed and processed their own work but in the early days most of the amateurs in a growing market put their work in the hands of pharmaceutical chemists. By providing a 24-hour service and then a twice-daily

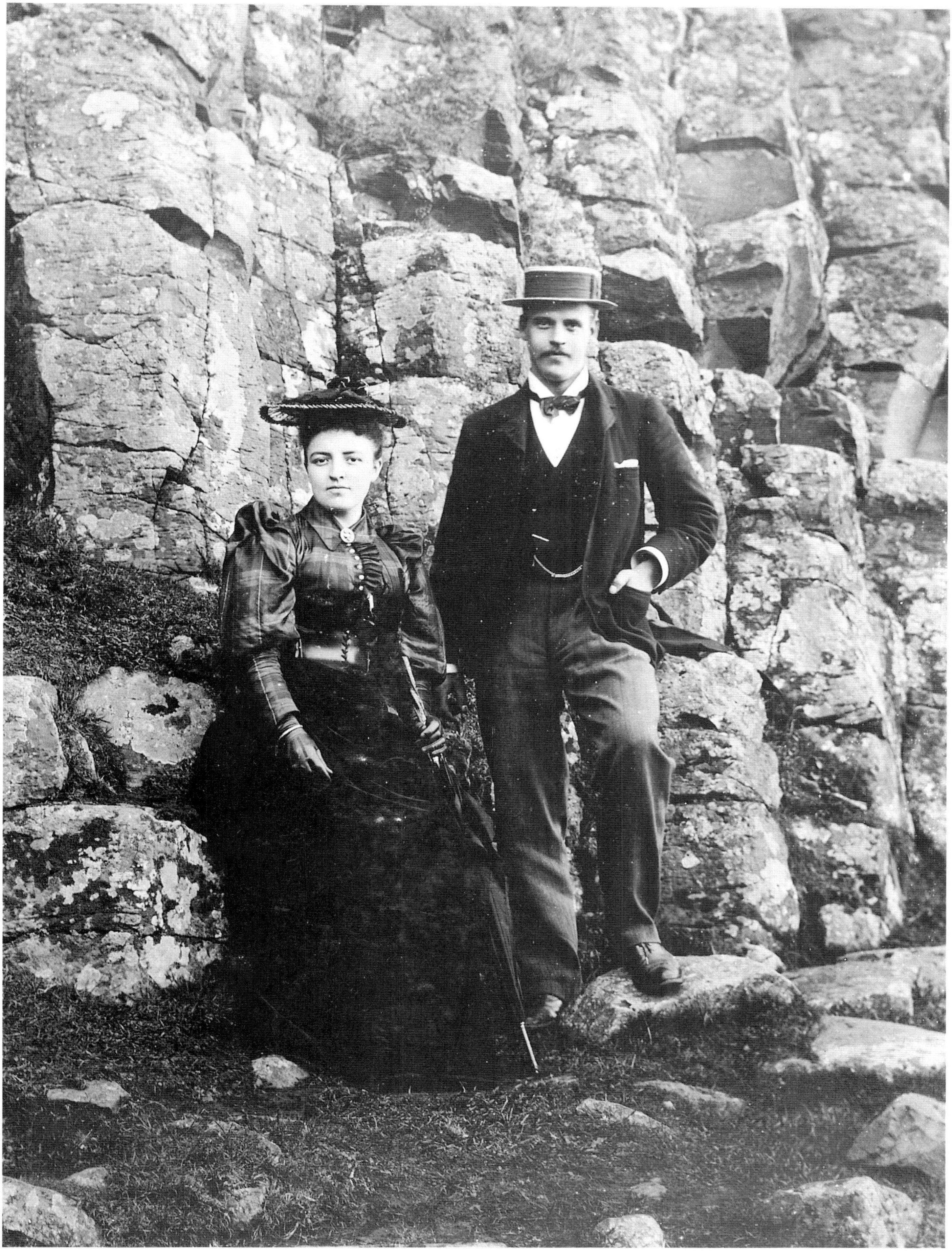

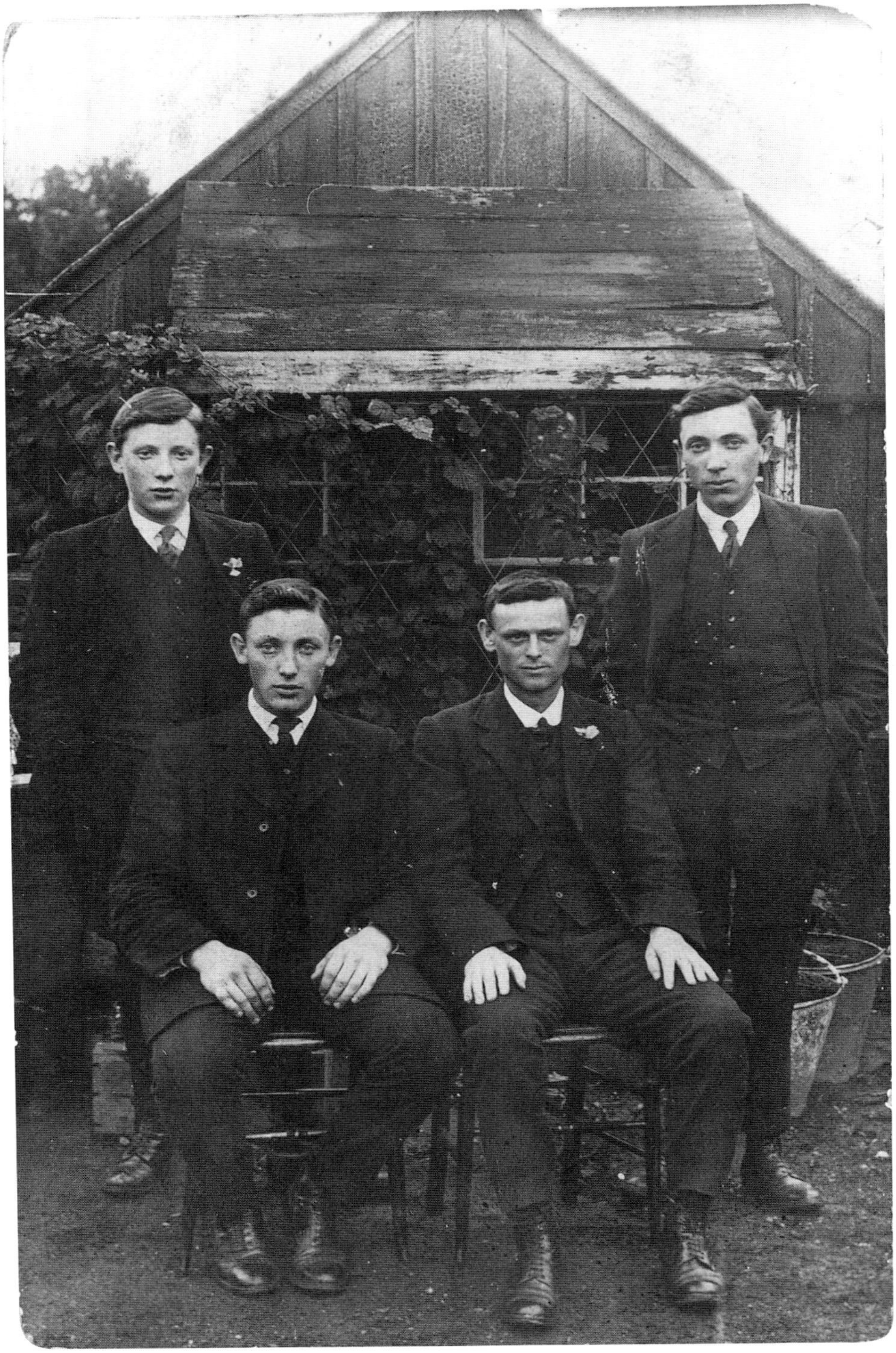

The three Dugan brothers (first, second and fourth from left) with their cousin, Robert Stewart, taken in the back yard of the latter's spirit grocery at Drumbeg, County Down, *c.* 1915. The photographer was probably an itinerant Italian named Bertie Bruno, who used a wooden hut nearby for his occasional visits.
BY KIND PERMISSION OF DR EILEEN BLACK

service Alex Lee soon took most of the trade from the chemists and finally ended up by processing their films for them. Views of Portrush taken in the summer for use as postcards were processed during the quiet winter months, selling either under Lee's own name or that of Valentine, who purchased some of his work. As well as providing material for postcards, Lee's views of the north coast were used to illustrate tourist guides such as *The North of Ireland: An Ideal Holiday Resort,* published by the Bournemouth firm of W. Mate and Sons, in which thirty-nine of the sixty illustrations were Lee's photographs.[18]

Farther down the scale of success from Lee (who did well enough to send one of his sons to boarding school and university, where he qualified as a doctor) were two photographers named Merten and Francis who like him sought custom at the Causeway in the years before the First World War. They are listed in the Bushmills section of the directories between 1908 and 1911 but were evidently operating some years earlier than 1908, for a postcard view of Ballycastle, published by 'Merten & Co., Bushmills', was posted by them in Ballycastle in August 1904. The message on the card read: 'We are busy there [at the Causeway] just now and cannot leave for 6 weeks.' Another of their surviving postcards shows the main street of the village of Cullybackey, County Antrim. Lower still in the ranking of photographers was Bertie Bruno – possibly an itinerant Italian – who is known only by a single photograph dating from about 1915.[19]

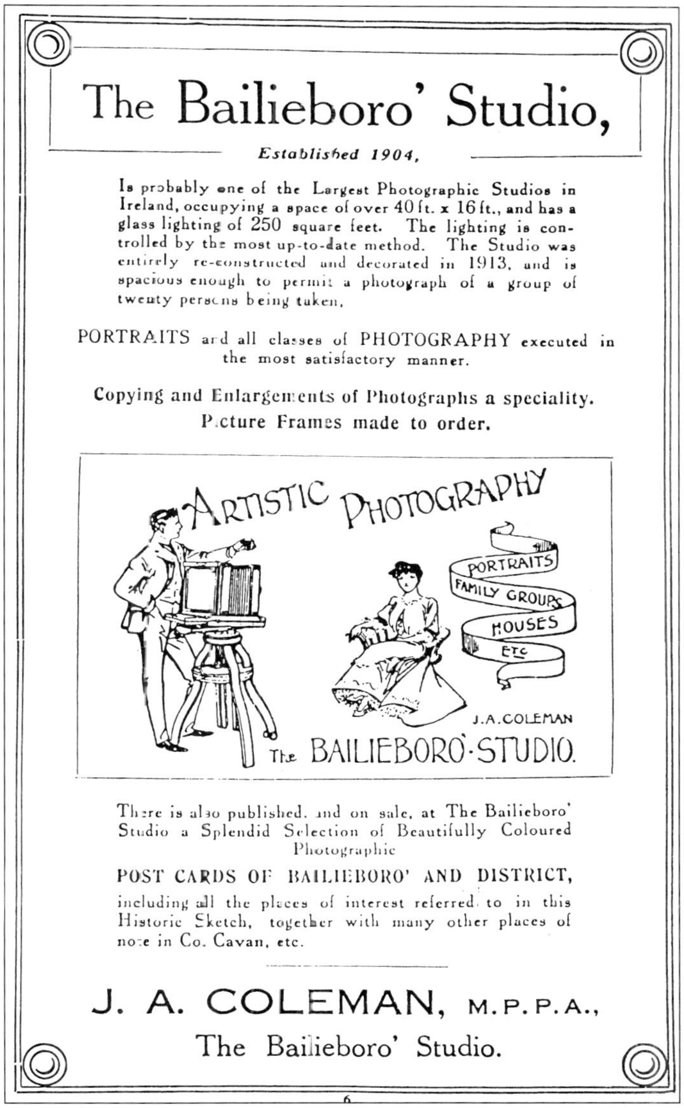

Advertisement for J.A. Coleman's studio in Balieborough, County Cavan, 1914, from the photographer's own history of the town and its neighbourhood.

BY KIND PERMISSION OF W.G. COLEMAN

Another obscure photographer who published postcards was W.J. Napier, of Scarva, County Down. Born about 1870 on a farm near Scarva, Napier was a bright pupil at elementary school who gained a scholarship to Portadown College, where among other subjects he studied chemistry. His hopes of becoming a chemist, however, were dashed when at the age of nineteen he developed 'hip disease' (tuberculosis of the bones) and had to have a leg amputated. The nature of the operation precluded the fitting of an artificial limb. He took up photography for a living, travelling by pony and trap and developing his photographs at home. The advent of the picture postcard encouraged him to publish a series of local views. The cards that survive show work of good quality. In his forties Napier developed kidney trouble and, when operated upon at the private hospital run by his two sisters in Lancashire, died there in 1919. Local historical research has recently rescued this very local photographer from total obscurity.[20]

Scarcely any professional women photographers appear as owners of studios

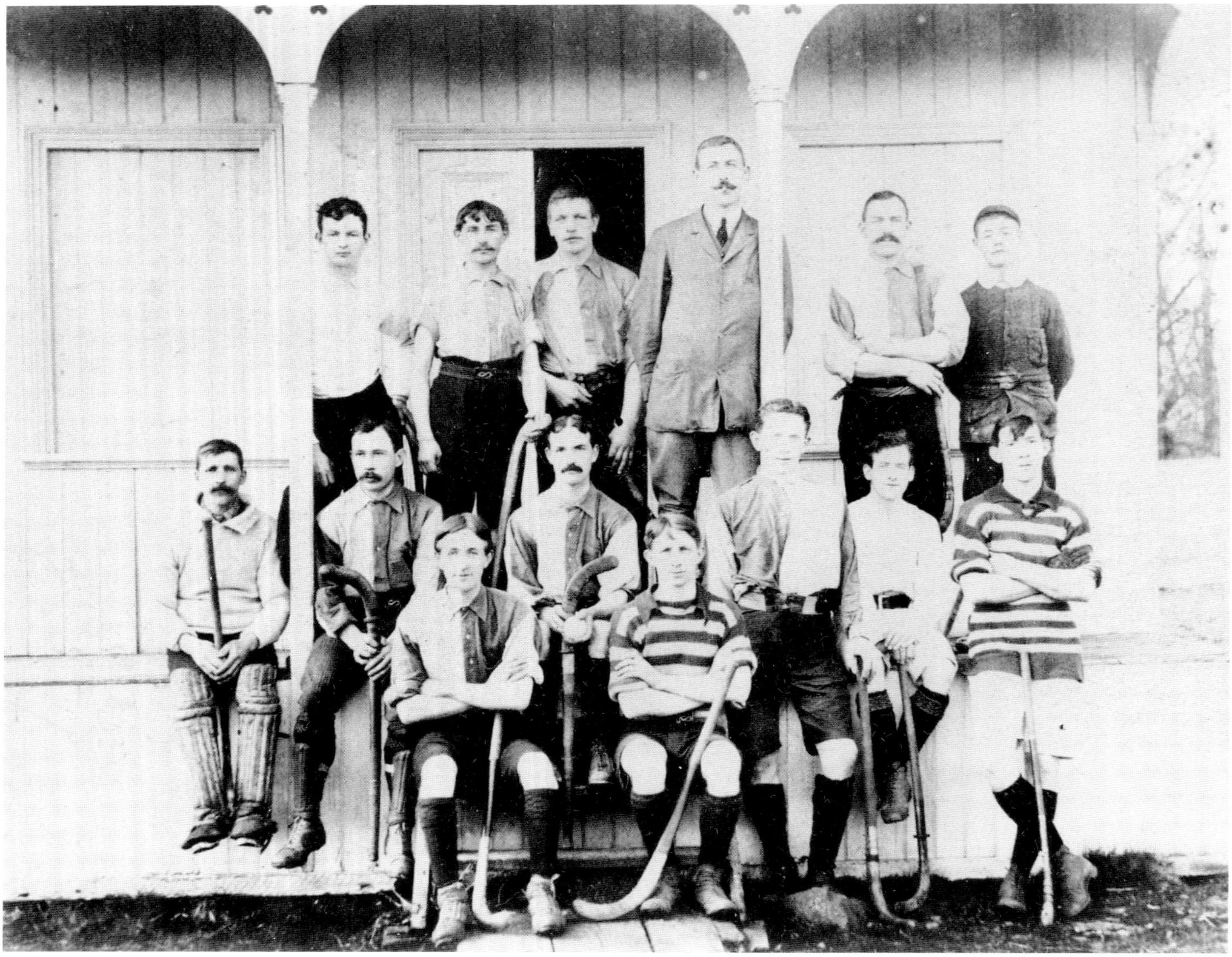

Randalstown Hockey Club, County Antrim, c. 1905, by Annie Booth.
BY KIND PERMISSION OF JAMES KILPATRICK

Miss Booth became a professional photographer in Randalstown just after the turn of the century, recording the topography, social life and economic activities of this mill and market town and its farming hinterland. An earlier photographer named Stuart had operated there in the 1880s.

before the 1920s. Those that do, such as Miss Galway in Clones, County Monaghan, Miss Woods in Portrush and Coleraine or Mrs Hunter in Armagh, are either daughters or widows who had inherited a family business. Miss Woods's studio in Portrush, which claimed to specialise in portraits of children, was part of a bookseller's and stationery business and included a fancy warehouse for Irish novelties (Belleek china, Connemara marble, bog oak souvenirs), a not uncommon combination in tourist areas. Another local female photographer during this period, Annie Booth, of Randalstown in County Antrim, was unusual in several respects. With no family connection to encourage her (her father was a 'car owner' in the village), she appears to have taken up photography out of sheer interest after attending a science class in her late teens and winning a prize. In the intervals between keeping house for her father and brother, she became a competent photographer. Her name first appears in directories in 1906, but she was at work at

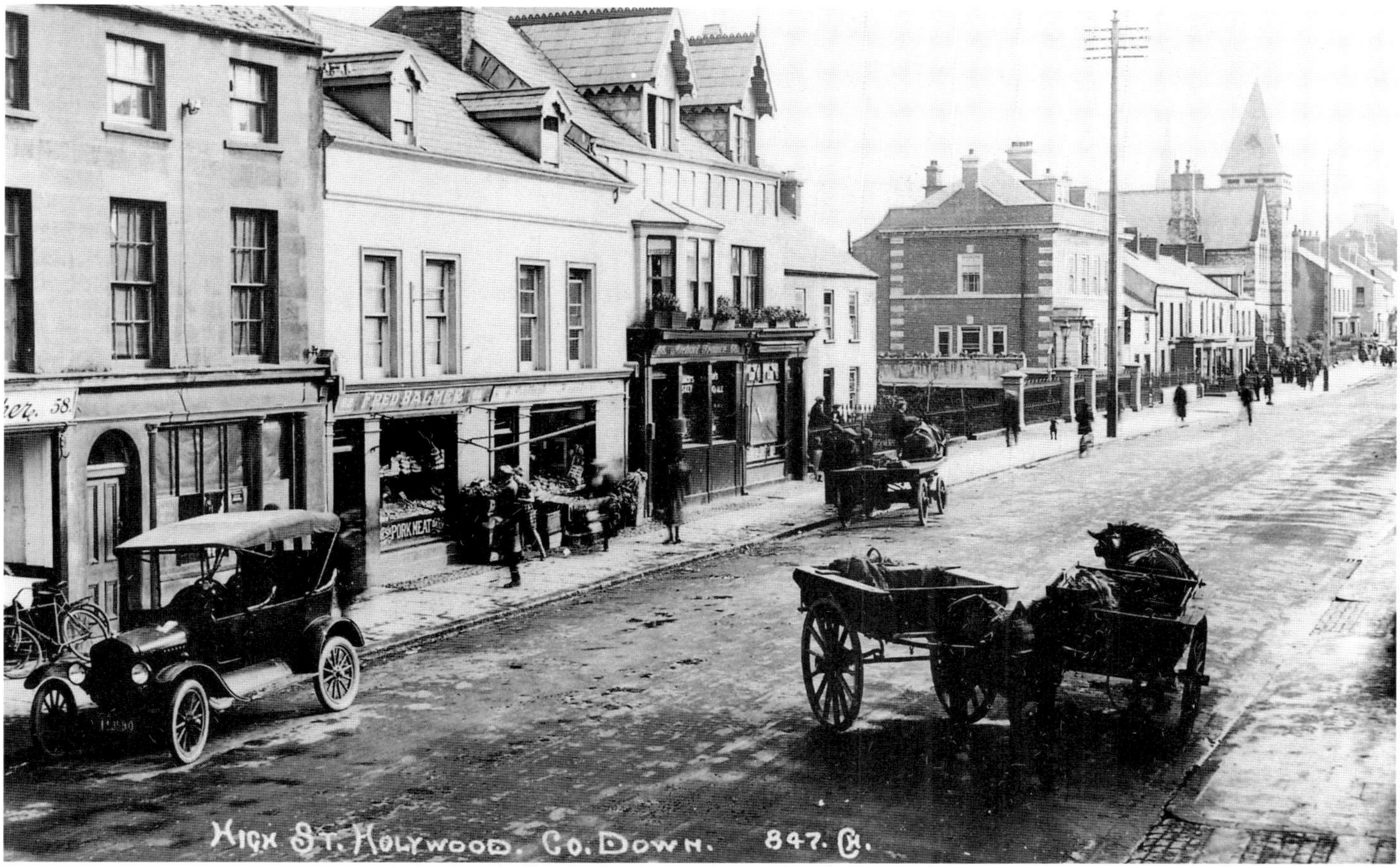

Postcard view of High Street, Holywood, County Down, in the 1920s, by C[laude] H[enfrey].
BY KIND PERMISSION OF DESMOND QUAIL

least three years earlier, from the evidence of one of her postcard views of the locality. This suggests that she was a very late starter, in her mid-forties at least. She continued until the 1920s, for a time in partnership with a companion named Miss Milner (Booth and Milner postcards appear from about 1910). Annie Booth is yet another example of the importance of the picture postcard in providing a living of some sort for small local photographers.[21]

Lastly, for a few years between the wars some remarkably good photographs of Holywood, Carrickfergus and other parts of north Down and south Antrim were published in postcard form by Claude Henfrey. Henfrey was an Englishman, who came to the area around the end of the First World War. There is no sign of him in directories, but some of his work survives and is now eagerly sought by postcard collectors. He appears to have given up his photographic activities quite abruptly, reappearing in Belfast later as proprietor of a confectionery business. When he died in the 1950s, he left over £22,000, far more than he could ever have made from his camera.[22]

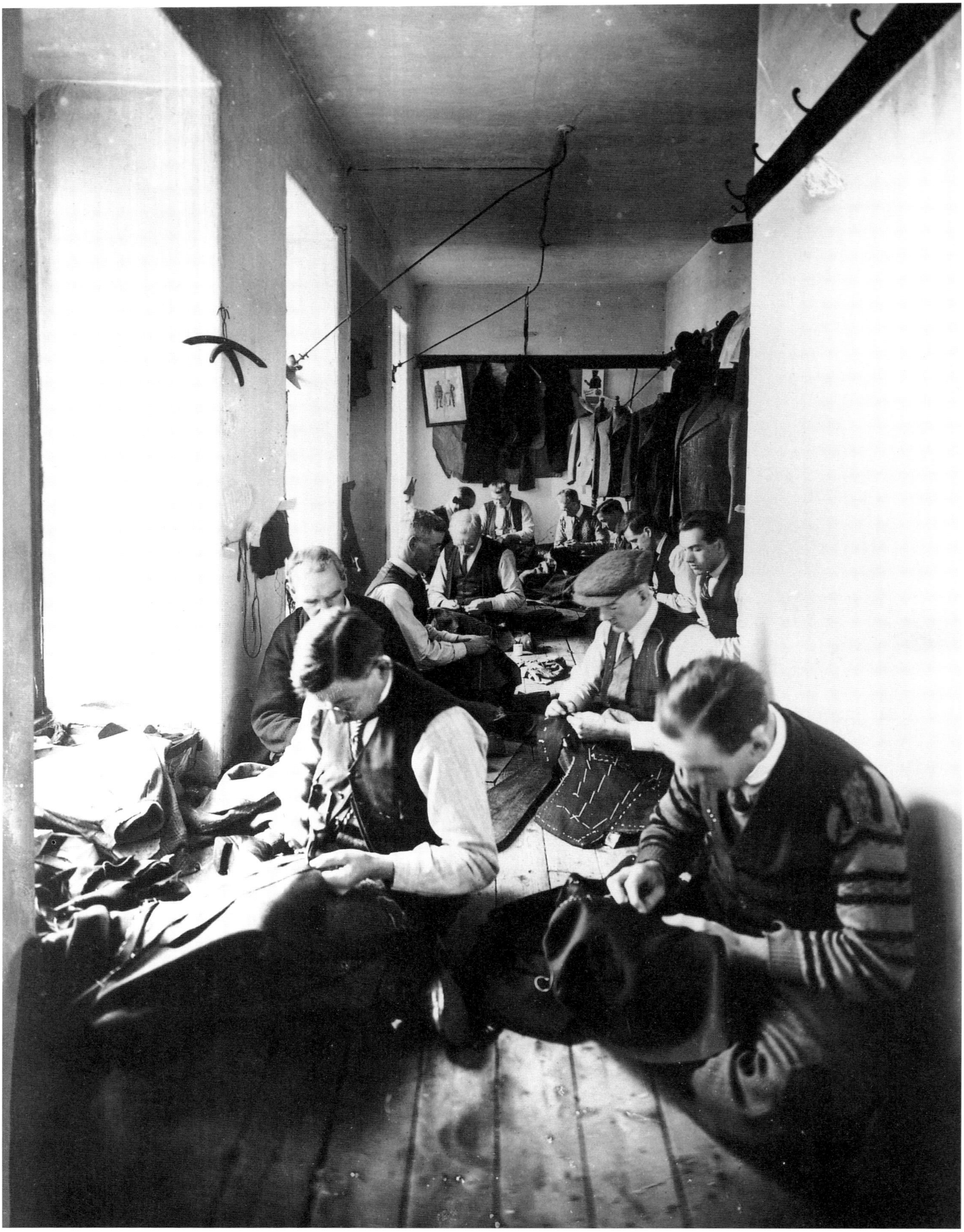

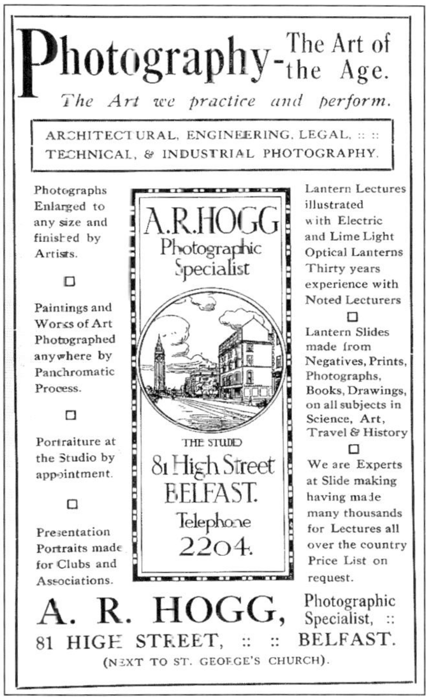

Professional amateurs: Welch, Hogg and Green

Most professional photographers made (and still make) their livings, if not their fortunes, by taking portraits, while supplementing their incomes by commissions of other kinds or by speculative work. Three outstanding Ulster photographers of the late nineteenth and early twentieth centuries, however, did little or no portrait work. Instead they specialised, so to speak, in everything else.

Opposite
Tailors at work in the sewing room of Messrs W.J. Marshall, 37 High Street, Belfast, 7 February 1931, by A.R. Hogg.
MAGNI / ULSTER MUSEUM (HOGG COLLECTION)

Robert Welch

The eldest and most important of the three photographers, who also exerted a

Robert Welch at the Grey Man's Path, Fair Head, County Antrim, c. 1892.
MAGNI / ULSTER MUSEUM (WELCH COLLECTION)

Instructed by Welch, a local lad took this shot of the photographer, perched above a sheer drop of 400 feet. Welch noted that the rocks at the top were sharp enough to cut twine.

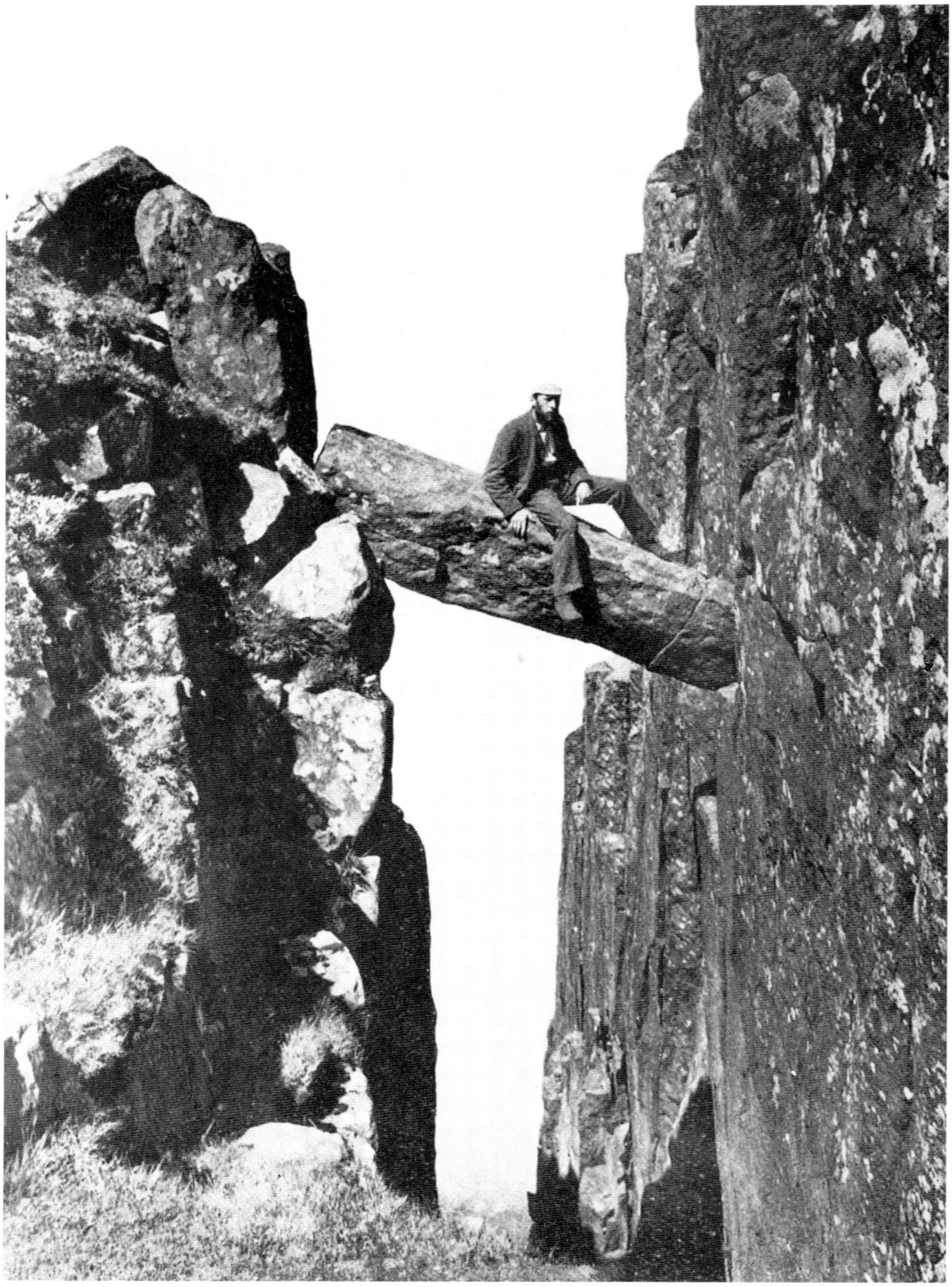

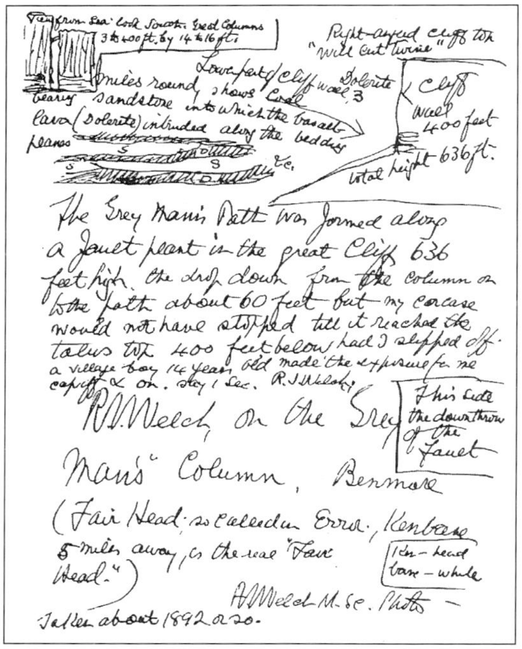

from Sea: look South: Great Columns 3 to 400 ft. by 14 to 16 ft.

Right-angled cliff top "will cut twine"

Lower part of Cliff wall 3 miles round shows Coal bearing sandstone into which the basalt lava (Dolerite) intruded along the bedding planes &c.

Dolerite

Cliff wall 400 feet

total height 636 ft.

The Grey Man's Path was formed along a fault plane in the great Cliff 636 feet high. The drop down from the column on to the path about 60 feet but my carcase would not have stopped till it reached the talus top 400 feet below had I slipped off. a village boy 14 years old made the exposure for me cap off & on. say 1 sec. R.J.Welch.

R.J. Welch on the Grey Man's Column, Benmore (Fair Head, so called in Error, Kenbane 5 miles away, is the real "Fair Head.")

This side the downthrow of the Fault

Ken – head
bane – white

R.J.Welch M.Sc. Photo –
Taken about 1892 or 90.

A page from Welch's notebook, written in 1930, containing his vivid recollection of how he had his photograph taken at the Grey Man's Path nearly forty years earlier.
MAGNI / ULSTER MUSEUM (WELCH COLLECTION)

considerable influence on the other two, was Robert John Welch (1859–1936). Since his father David was a professional photographer, Welch's apprenticeship began early. Even as a boy excursions with his father gave him an unusually wide knowledge of the topography and antiquities of Ireland, particularly Ulster. His father's death in 1875 made it necessary for him to become a professional photographer himself, instead of entering Queen's College as an undergraduate, as he had hoped. For several years he was an assistant in the studio of E.T. Church, then set up in 1883 on his own, working from the house at 49 Lonsdale Street where he lived with his mother and where he was to spend the rest of his life.

To begin with Welch specialised in landscape and legal work, and made his reputation first by his 'Irish Views'. These included much antiquarian, geological and ethnographic subject-matter. In a lecture he gave in 1926 to a meeting of the recently established Northern Ireland branch of the Professional Photographers' Association he claimed to have travelled eighty thousand miles in Ireland to photograph antiquities alone.[1]

Welch's 'Irish Views' became very widely known through displays of his prints in railway carriages (the LMS Railway Company was a valued client), hotels and transatlantic liners, and by their use as illustrations in tourist guides and travel books. Welch had a genuine interest in encouraging tourists, long before any organisation existed for that purpose. He used to make up sheets of maps, annotated by notes in his own hand describing and commenting upon the outstanding local sights and illustrated by his own photographs.[2] He presented these to hotel owners in Donegal, Antrim, Fermanagh and Sligo for the edification of their guests; some of them still exist.

Welch's views of the west of Ireland led directly to the award of a royal warrant in 1900. During Queen Victoria's visit to Ireland in that year, the Congested Districts Board (a government development department which was set up in 1891)

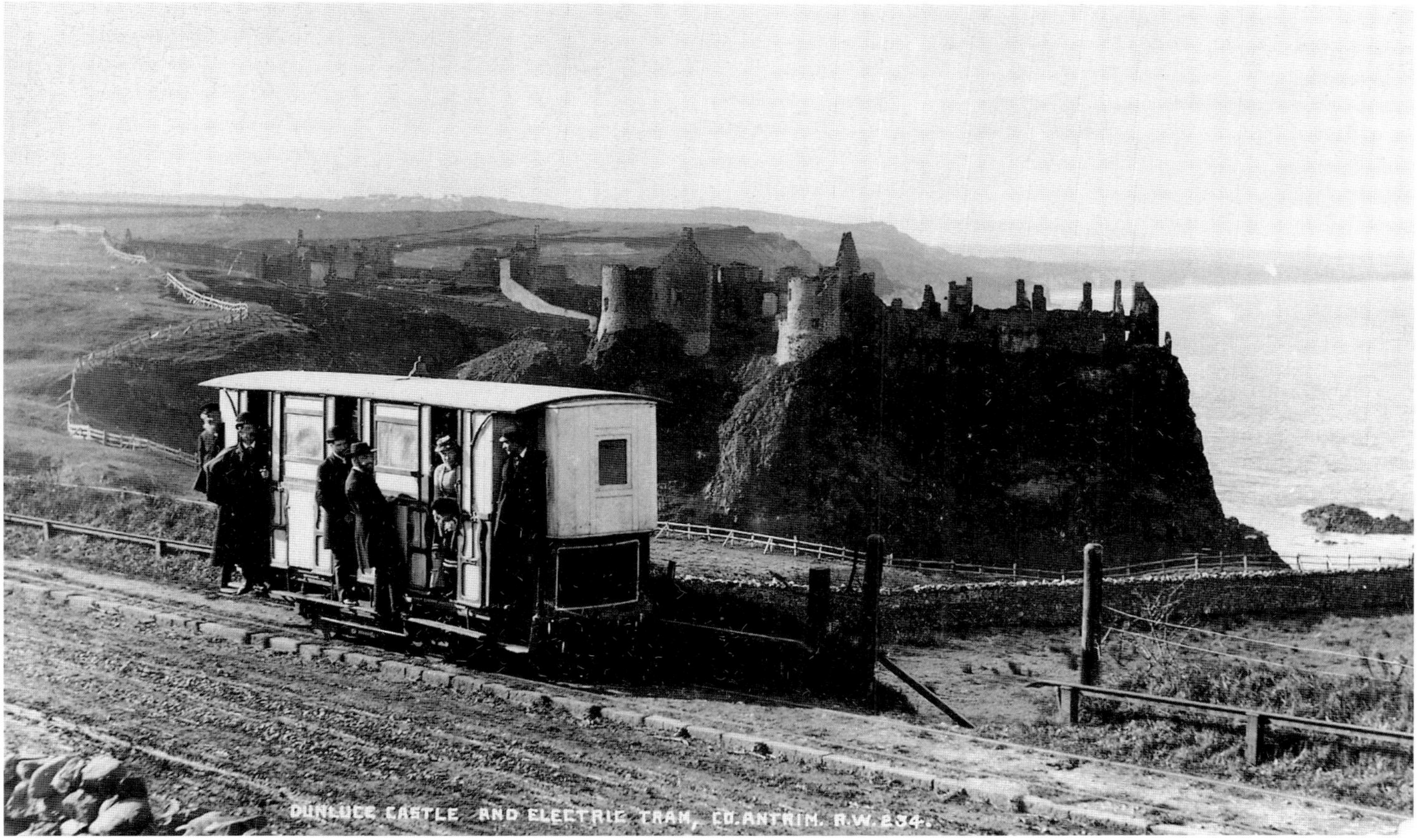

'Dunluce Castle and Electric Tram, County Antrim', c. 1895, by R.J. Welch.

MAGNI / ULSTER MUSEUM (WELCH COLLECTION)

The tramway (the world's first hydro-electric railway, opened in 1883, closed in 1949) ran between Portrush and the Causeway, passing the picturesque ruins of the old castle of the MacDonnells. This early picture shows the raised conduction rail alongside the track, before it was replaced in 1899 by an overhead trolley system. Lee of Portrush and other photographers travelled by the tram to photograph summer visitors at the Causeway.

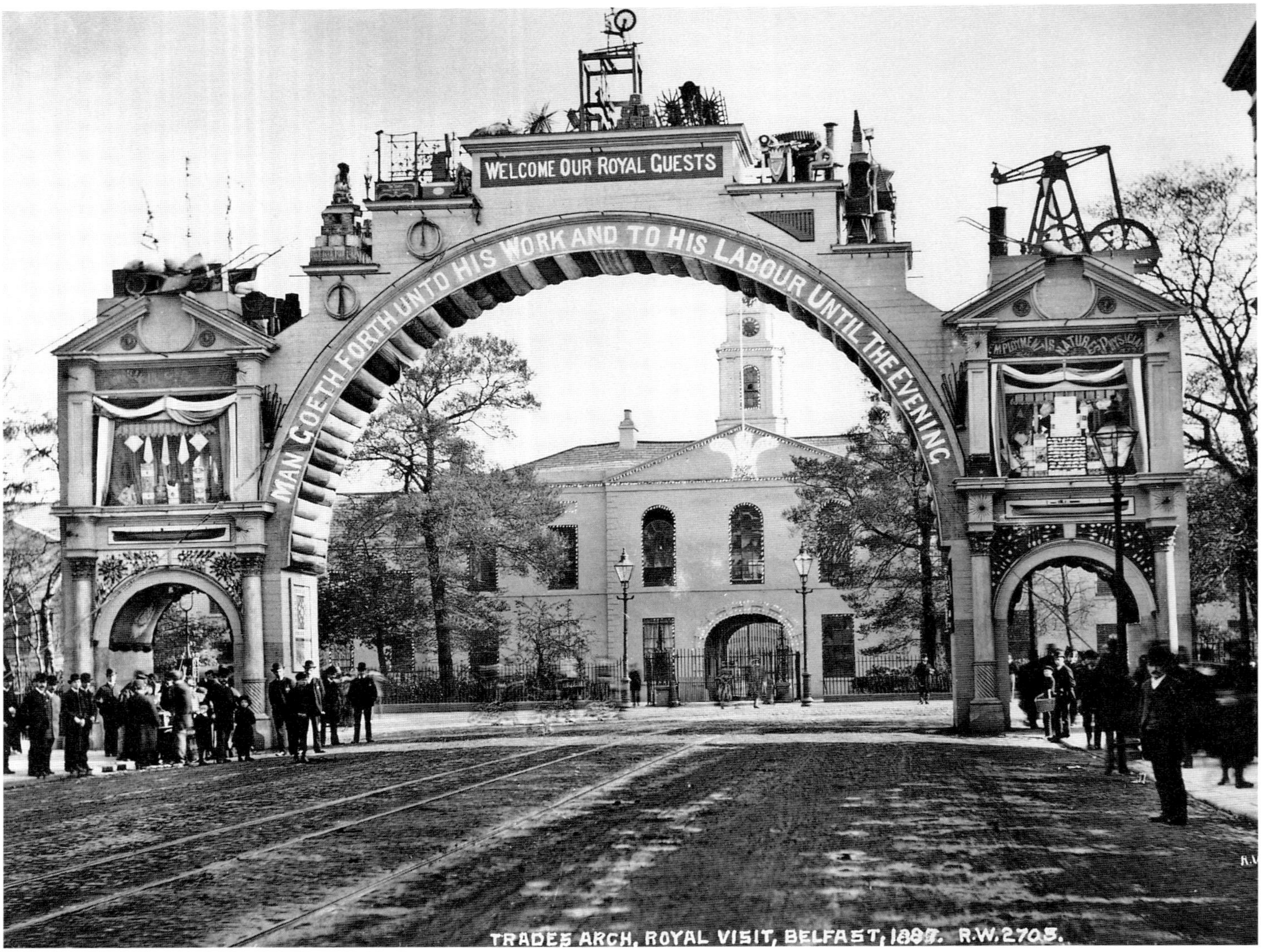

'Trades Arch, Royal Visit, Belfast, 1885', by R.J. Welch.

MAGNI / ULSTER MUSEUM (WELCH COLLECTION)

One of several street arches erected in Belfast for the visit of the Prince of Wales (later Edward VII) and his wife Alexandra. Welch, recently established as a photographer, had his 'first real success' with a set of photographs of these decorations. The old White Linen Hall, on the site of the present City Hall, forms the background here.

selected Welch's photographs to show the Queen what life was like for some of her subjects in the most impoverished areas of the western seaboard.[3] The only other holders of the royal warrant in Ireland in Victoria's reign were Lafayette and Chancellor, of Dublin (1887 and 1899), and Abernethy of Belfast (1900), so the grant was signal recognition of Welch's standing and achievement. During the entire reign, warrants were granted to only fifty-one photographers, ten of them from outside the British Isles.[4]

Royal visits were always good for business. Welch later recorded in his 'Excursions Diary' that in April 1885, when the Princess of Wales came to Belfast, he had achieved his first real commercial success with a series of views of the street arches and other decorations that were put up for the occasion: 'These did well, being a much longer series & handier in size than the 12″ x 10″ of the other Photogrs. Many of the latter were returned on the stationers etc. hands when my set appeared.' He went on to say that if the bromide processes had been known he could have trebled his profit: 'Platino was known, but too dear & not too good.'[5] The platinotype, in which pure platinum instead of the usual silver salts was used in making up the final photographic print, was introduced as early as 1873 by William Willis. When fully developed it was an extremely high-quality print, generally grey in colour but very fine-toned and resistant to fading. Welch's best work was produced by this method. The platinotype for most photographers came to an end during the First World War, when platinum became scarce and very expensive, but Welch seems to have had a stock of the paper, for he went on producing platinotypes well into the 1920s. (One of his competitors on the occasion of the royal visit of 1885 was Robert Seggons, who also produced a series of photographs of the street arches; at least one set has survived.)

In 1886 Welch took a series of views for the Royal Commission of Enquiry of the damage caused in Belfast by the anti-Home Rule riots of that year – an early instance of the employment of photography in this way, though it had been used

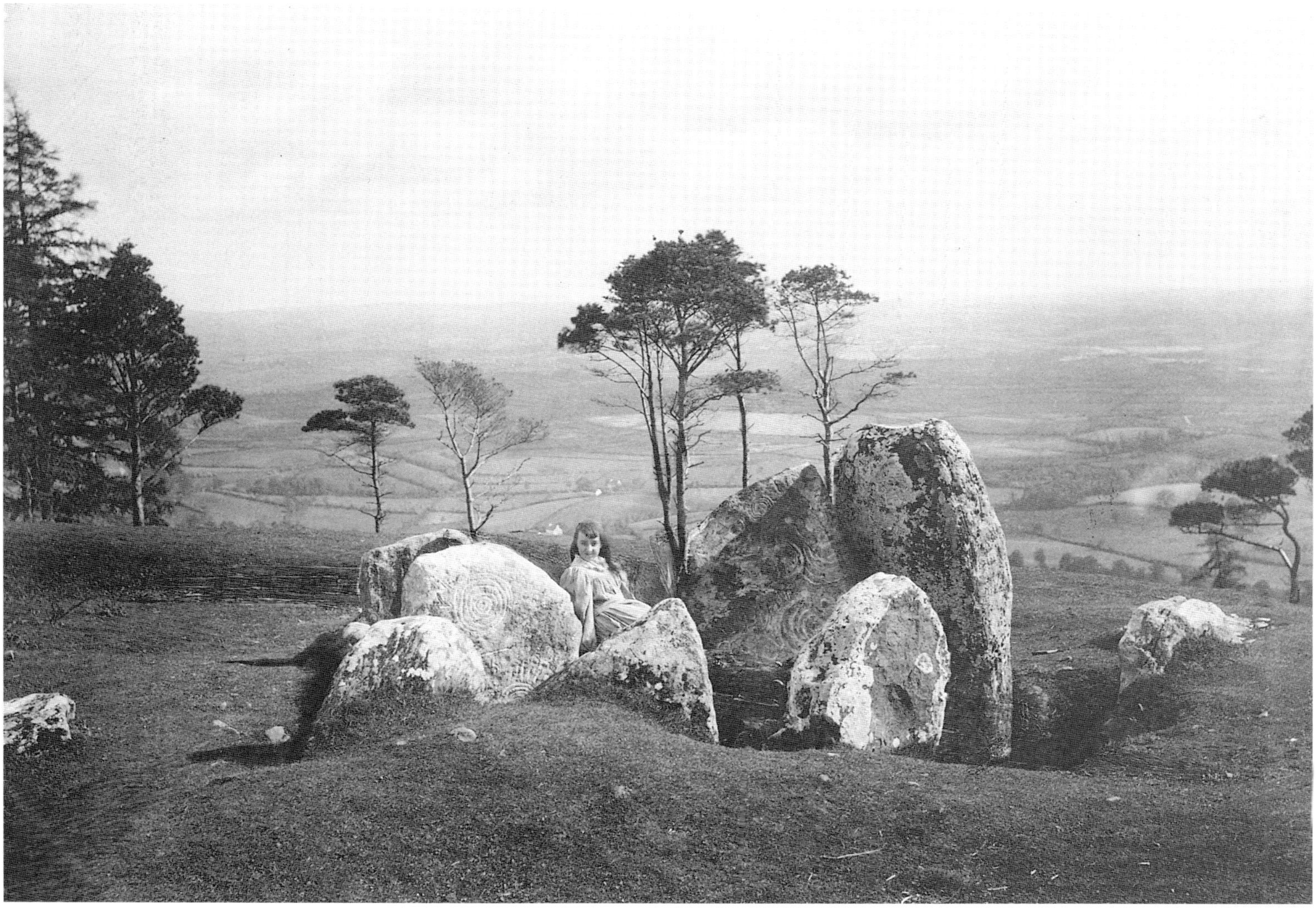

Knockmany cairn, County Tyrone, by R.J. Welch, from an original platinotype print.
MAGNI / ULSTER MUSEUM (WELCH COLLECTION)

Welch photographed hundreds of such ancient monuments all over Ireland for his 'Irish Views' or for the records of the Office of Public Works.

for some time in recording the likenesses of convicted criminals and lunatics. Inmates of Holywell Asylum at Antrim were photographed in a systematic way from an early period.

From the early 1880s Welch produced a series of Linen Trade views that also proved popular, the first of a number of photographs by northern photographers recording the industry in its heyday before the First World War. Some of these early photographs appear rather static and lifeless – spinning rooms and weaving sheds full of machinery without a worker in sight – either because the mill owners wanted views of machinery alone or, as in many similar cases, because Welch's equipment at the time could not cope with human figures or any other moving objects and he had removed them from the negative. By contrast, the photographs he took of the various departments of the Belfast Ropeworks and their operations in 1899 do show workers, including the office staff. These were used in the firm's illustrated brochure, produced in the same year. Commissions of this kind constantly added to Welch's stock of potentially useful negatives, which could be called upon for various purposes, such as a new series of prints or a set of lantern slides.

In 1888 Welch noted taking a series of old castles in the Ards peninsula and

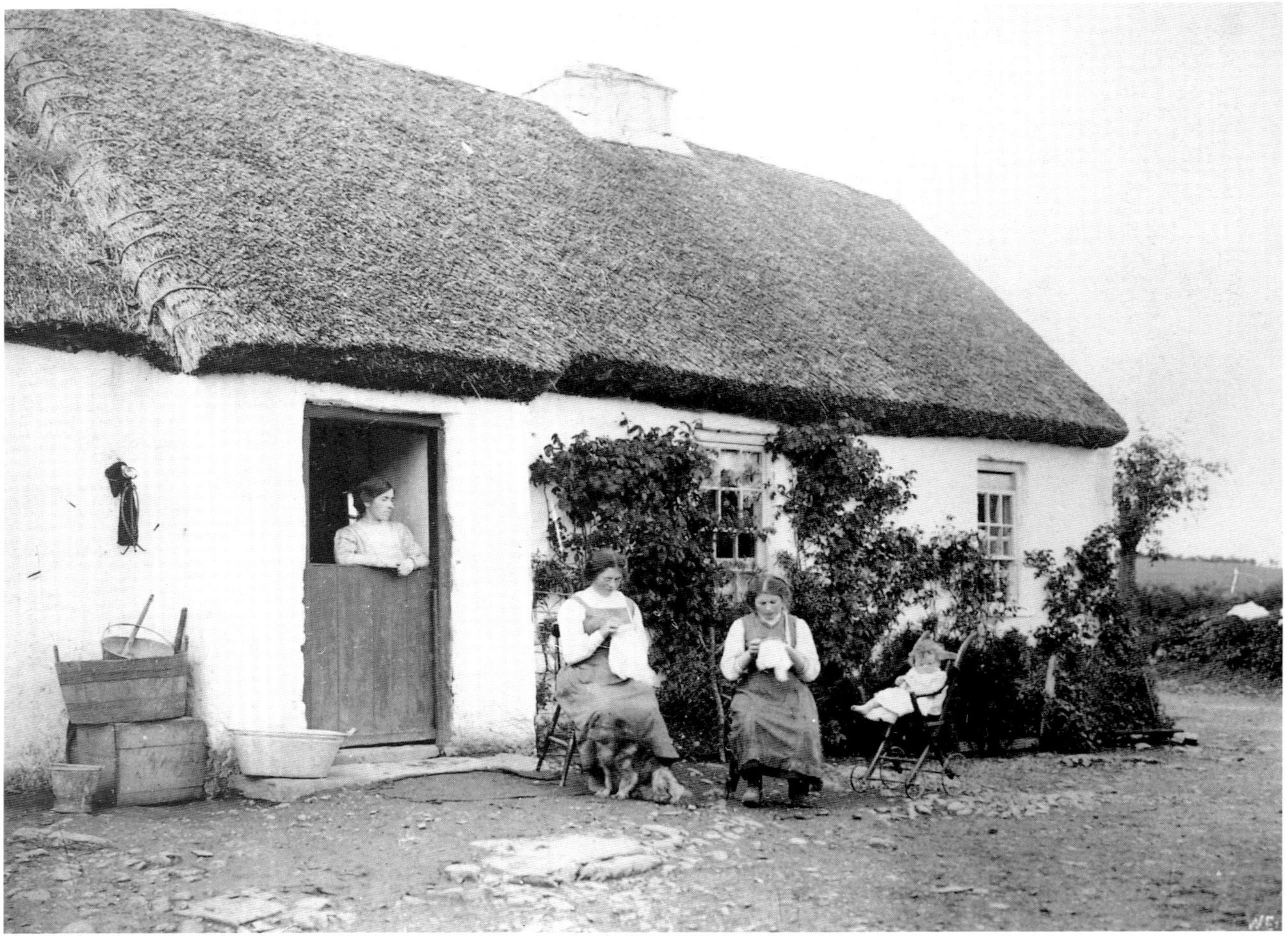

'Flowering' linen in County Down, c. 1912, by R.J. Welch.

MAGNI / ULSTER MUSEUM (WELCH COLLECTION)

This is one of a series of photographs on the linen industry, commissioned from Welch in 1912 by Marshall Field and Company of Chicago. Embroidering linen goods was an important source of income for many farm women in the north of Ireland.

around Strangford Lough for the publishers Marcus Ward and Company, commissioned to illustrate Professor Savage Armstrong's book *The Savages of the Ards*. He noted that he 'had already done Mahee Castle on a BNFC excursion and Sketrick also' – the latter luckily, since it had subsequently fallen down. Along with other photographers, he recorded ancient monuments such as those for the Office of Public Works, or at any rate sold some of his prints to the OPW. A recently published selection from that source includes a photograph of Inch Abbey, County Down, by the Belfast photographer John Phillips, as well as several by Welch.[6] On the excursions of the Belfast Naturalists' Field Club, Welch constantly added to his stock of such views, for these outings frequently included visits to antiquarian or archaeological sites as well as those of more scientific interest.

From the mid-1890s Welch was the official photographer to the shipbuilding firm of Harland and Wolff, then in its period of greatest expansion and prestige. From 1894 he photographed an increasingly large and impressive series of transatlantic liners from the laying of the keels to the sea trials, culminating in the *Olympic* and her sister ship *Titanic*. He guessed that his photographs of the launch in 1910 of the *Olympic*, which appeared in newspapers and other publications all

Turning shop in the engineering department of Harland and Wolff, Belfast, 1897, by R.J. Welch.
MAGNI / UFTM (HARLAND AND WOLFF COLLECTION)

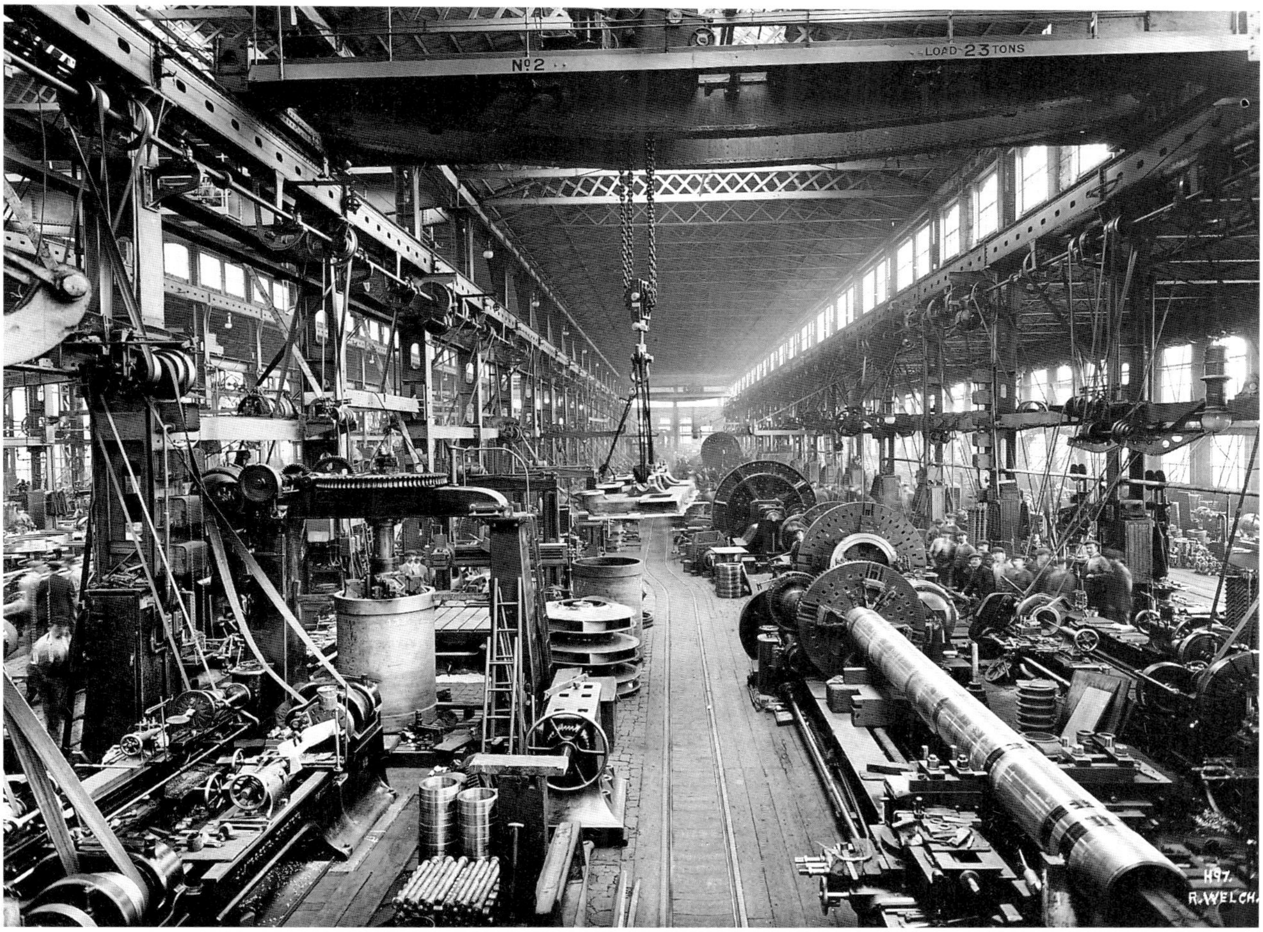

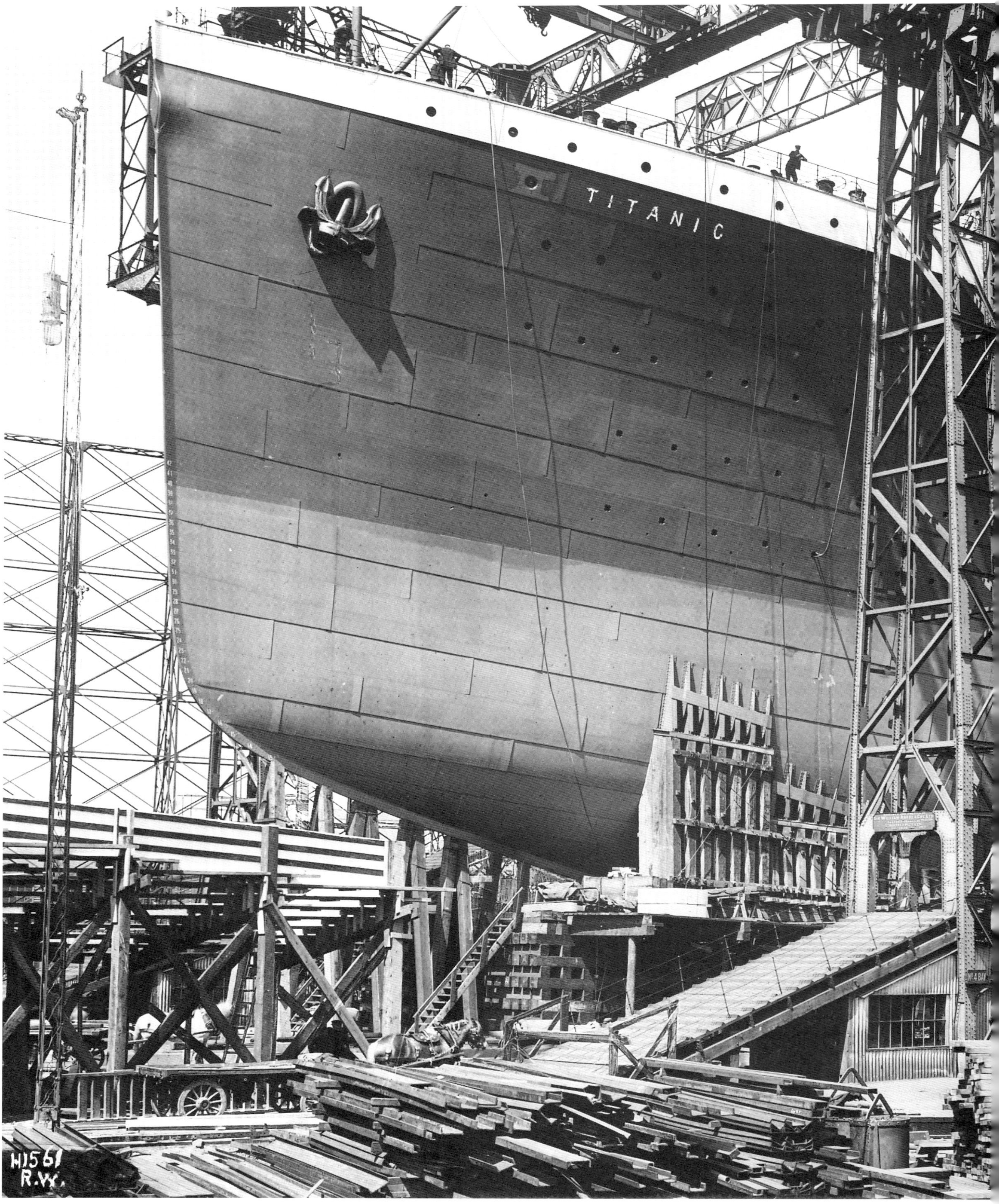
TITANIC
H1561
R.W.

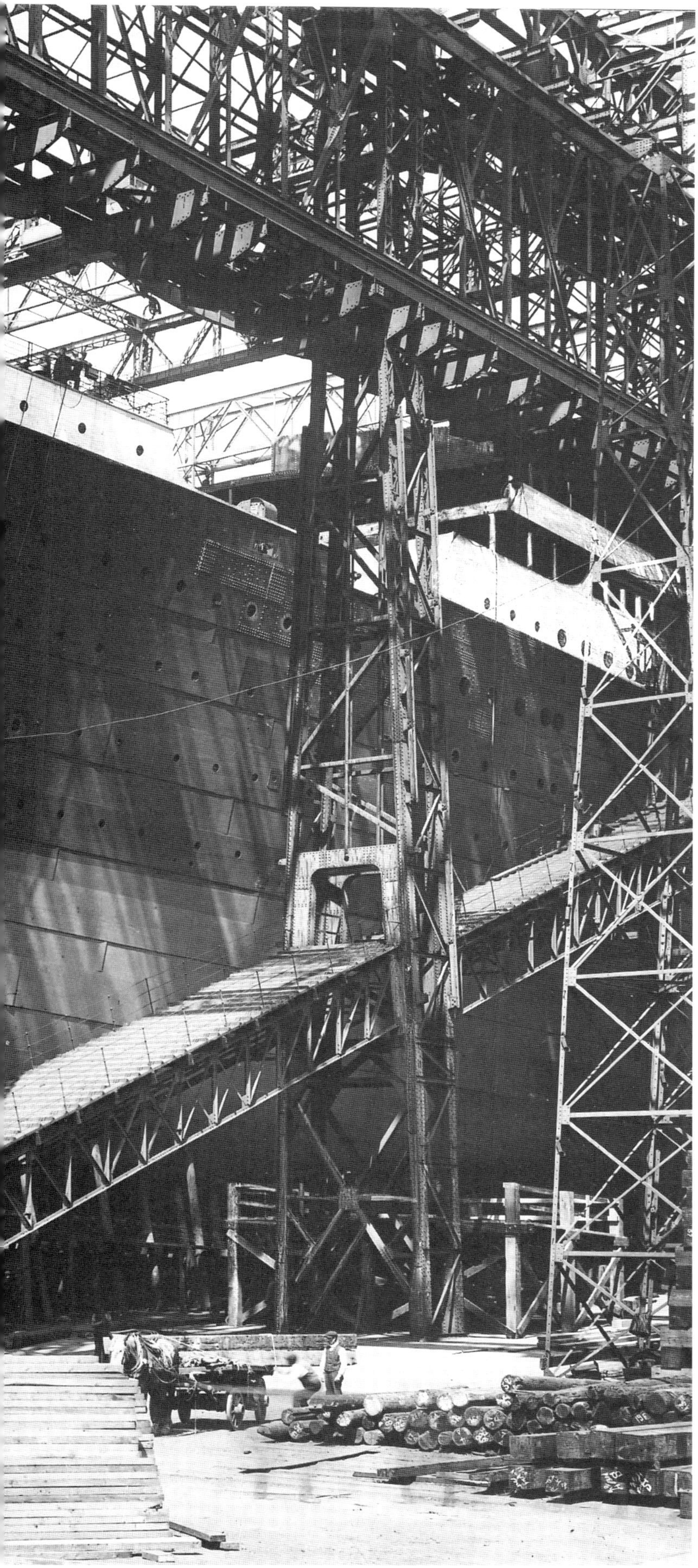

Titanic in the final stages of construction, May 1911, by R.J. Welch.
MAGNI / UFTM
(HARLAND AND WOLFF COLLECTION)

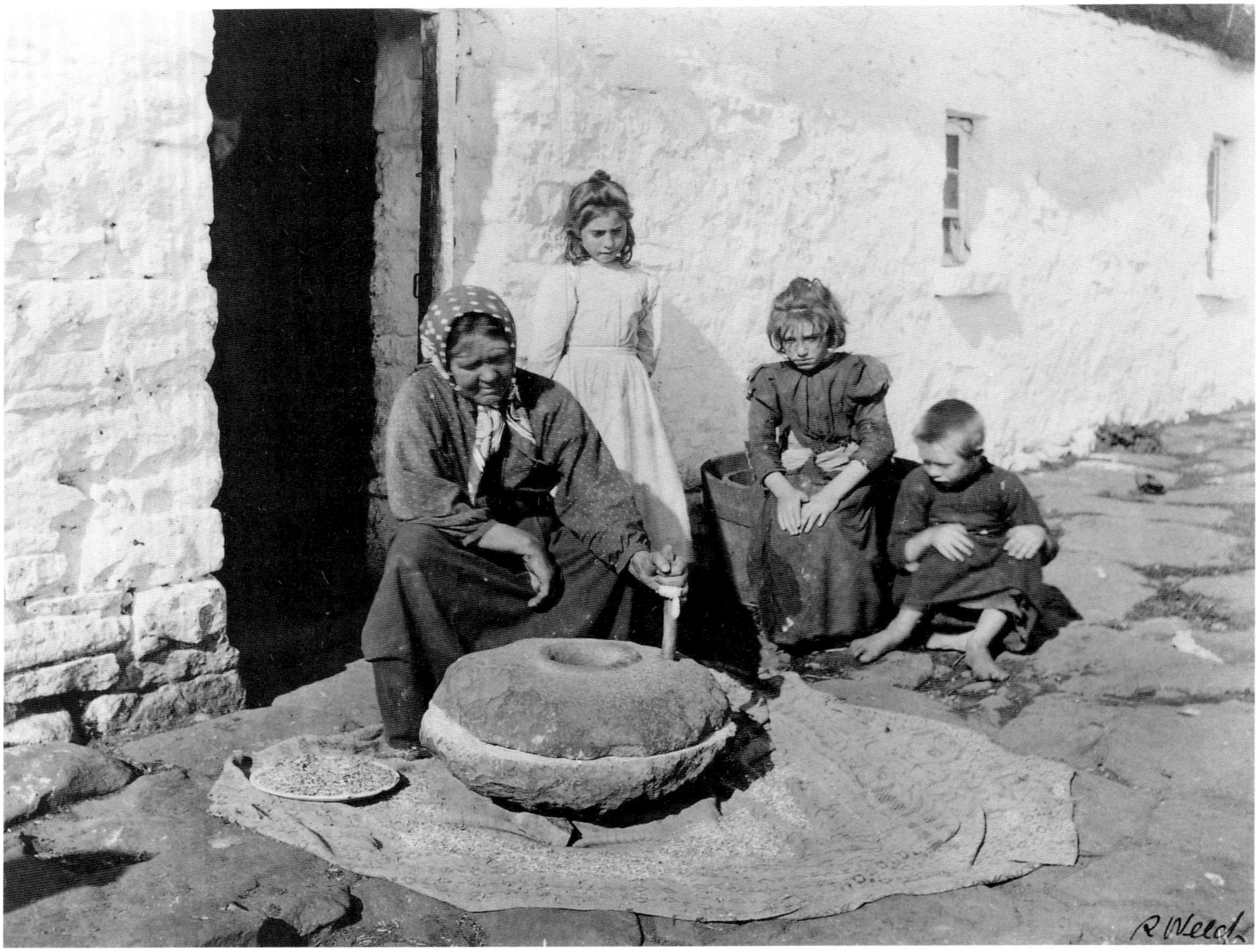

Mary Heraghty demonstrating the use of a rotary quern, Inishmurray, County Sligo, 12 September 1900, by R.J. Welch.

MAGNI / ULSTER MUSEUM (WELCH COLLECTION)

On the island of Inishmurray, this ancient method of grinding corn lasted into the early twentieth century. By that date it was used mainly to grind the barley for making poteen.

over the world, must have been reproduced about 700 million times.[7] The official negatives, which were acquired by the firm as part of the commission, are now in the Harland and Wolff collection in the Ulster Folk and Transport Museum. Welch took additional shots on his own account, however, and many of these are in the main Welch Collection in the Ulster Museum.

Welch was enormously proud of his connection with Belfast's greatest industry. Such work had its dangers, however. Apart from the risk of falling from scaffolding, Welch narrowly escaped death from a flying red-hot rivet on one occasion and on another lost his camera and was nearly drowned in the wash of a launching. He was intrepid in such matters, and prepared to take almost any risk in order to get a really satisfactory picture. In 1921, then aged sixty-two, he had himself hauled at the end of a rope, without any safety cradle, to the top of a 150-foot chimney at the Ropeworks, where he was able to observe the fact (later recorded in his diary) that 'the Chimney was swaying 6 ins from plum[b] each way with the high wind' – this despite his poor head for heights.[8]

Welch's technical skill, and the enormous pains he took to achieve the best possible results, were equally displayed in his scientific photographs. These were labours of love as well as commissions: his friend Hogg recalled how he would spend half an hour on successive exposures of a flower on a windy day in order to get the result he wanted. His photographs of rare Irish plants, such as those of the Burren in County Clare, were famous among botanists. Both these and his geological photographs were extensively used, and greatly admired, as illustrations in textbooks and learned articles. Someone remarked that Welch's illustrations were often the highlight of other people's work.[9]

Welch's diaries frequently mention the equipment he used. So far as plate size was concerned he started with the 10-by-12-inch ones he had inherited from his

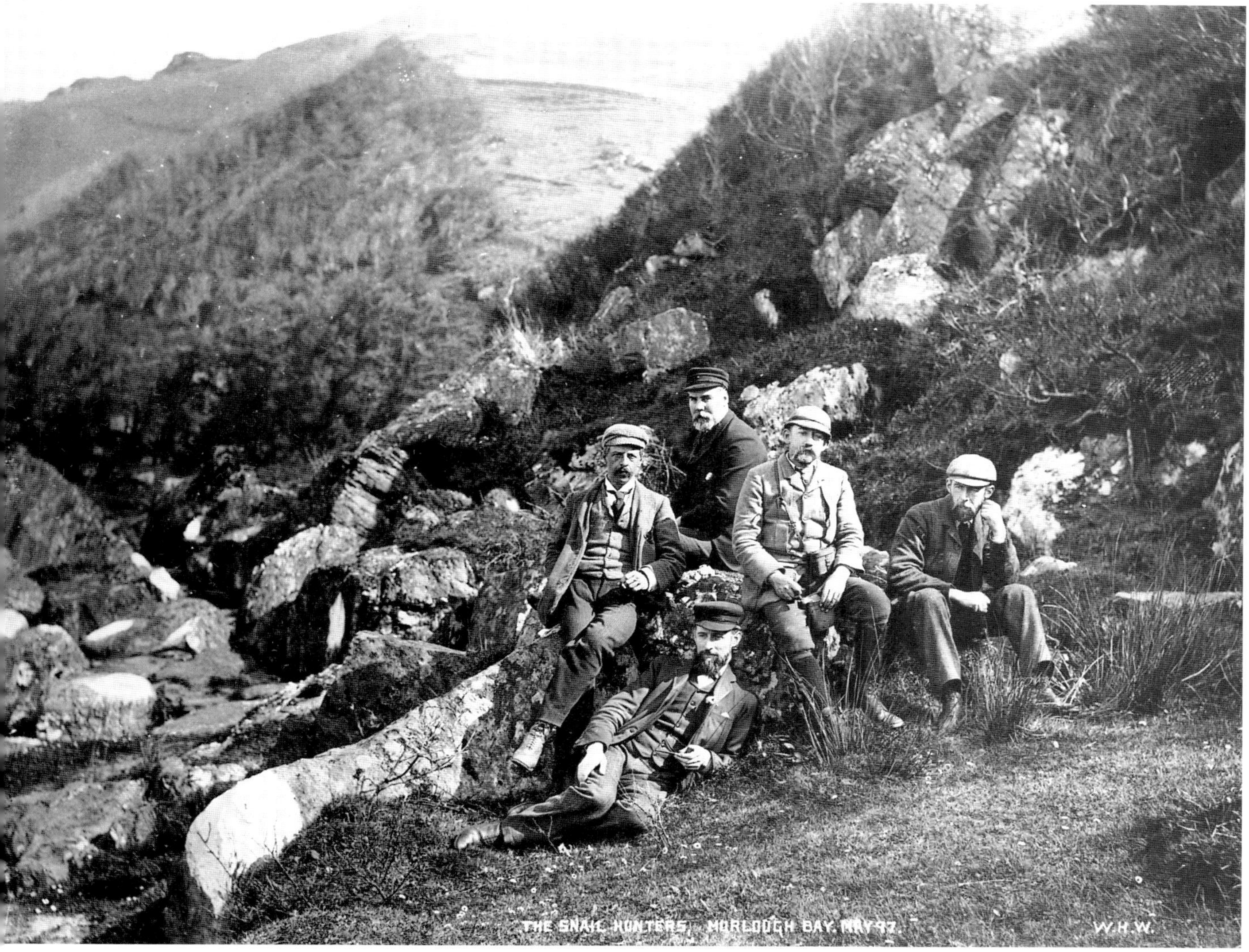

'The Snail Hunters, at Murlough Bay', May 1897, by W.H.W.

MAGNI / ULSTER MUSEUM (WELCH COLLECTION)

Welch, seen here on the right, was a keen member of the British Conchological Society, becoming its president in 1922. Someone else took this souvenir of a day's snail-hunting on the north coast of County Antrim.

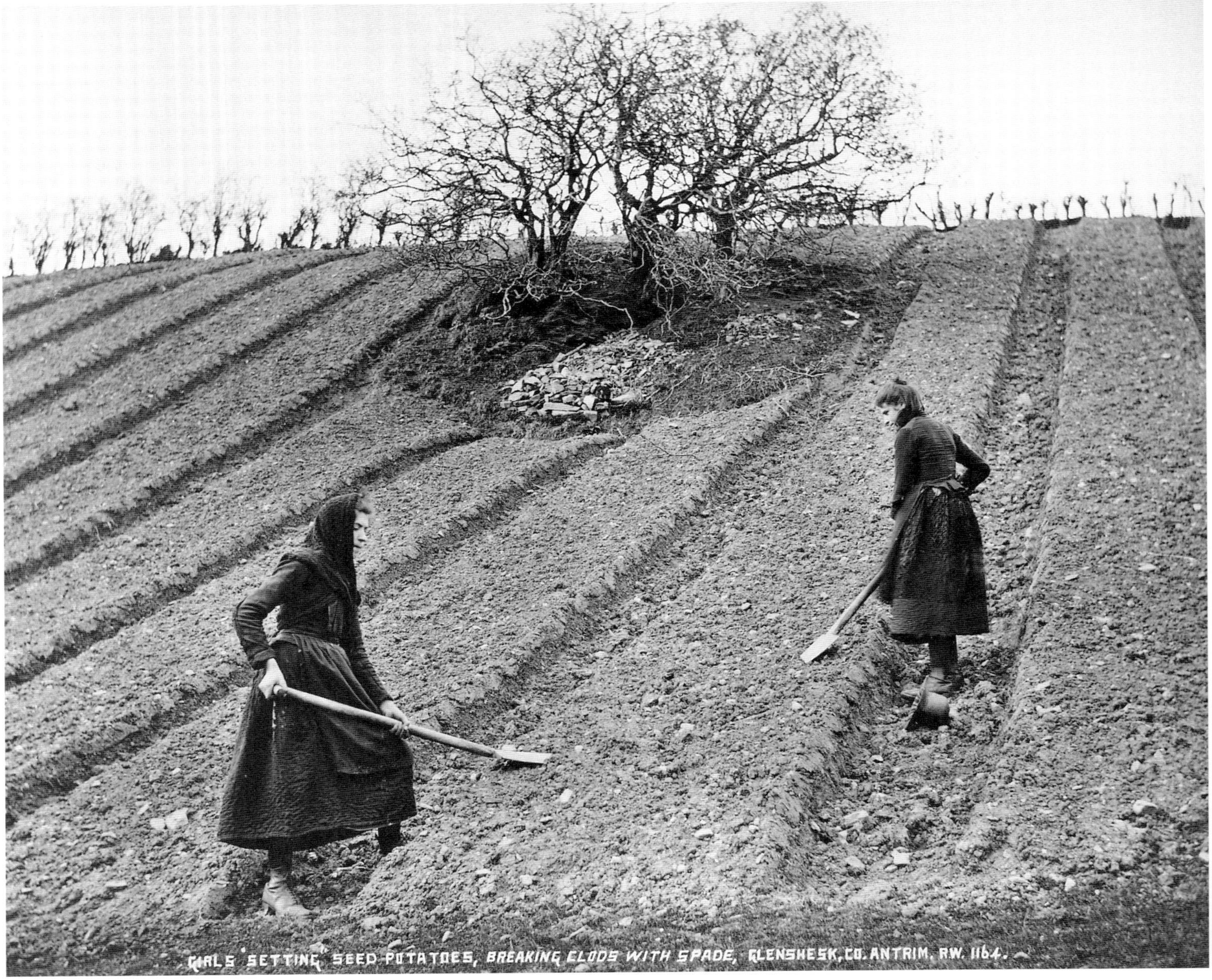

'Girls "setting" seed potatoes . . . Glenshesk, County Antrim', by R.J. Welch.
MAGNI / ULSTER MUSEUM (WELCH COLLECTION)

father, but by 1885 he had acquired the more convenient 8½-by-6½-inch size. As to lenses, before 1894 he used Ross's 7- and 10-inch portable symmetrical lenses, often with a back combination of a 7-inch lens. He noted: 'This though slow I found to be the most excellent single landscape and indeed architectural lense. In later years I replaced it with Ross-Goerz of about the same focal length (6 inches), which was much more rapid.' Down to about 1900 Welch used Castle plates, later Imperial. In 1912 he first used the new Hydra plates of the Paget Plate Company and was greatly impressed, describing them as 'a godsend to anyone undertaking such a varied class of work as mine, exterior and interior, scientific, industrial, engineering and commercial etc.'. This was because of the latitude they gave with exposure times. Welch claimed to have allowed four or five times the correct exposure when in doubt, with successful results.[10]

Welch's academic activities were largely channelled through membership of the

Belfast Naturalists' Field Club and its various subject groups. His father had taken him to lectures of the British Association when it met in Belfast in 1874, and Edmund Church also encouraged him. Welch joined the Field Club in 1880, became one of its most active and enthusiastic members and remained so for the rest of his life, serving as secretary in 1908–9 and president in 1910–12. He acquired through field-work and observation an impressive knowledge of practical science, recording what he saw in photographs of superb quality. His photographs of birds' nests on Rathlin Island in 1889 were apparently the first of their kind. Archaeology was another keen interest. Welch became a major contributor to the portfolio of photographs of archaeological remains in the north of Ireland compiled by the Field Club. His 1890 view of a 'horned cairn' or court grave in Donegal was another first. During the 1890s he was also the most prolific photographer of geological sites in Ireland. The publication in 1894 of his catalogue of geological views, accompanied by scholarly comment from Professor Grenville Cole, was a landmark in the study of the subject.

At the same time, as a member of the Field Club's ethnography committee he was taking views of what he called 'Irish country life'. This interest was displayed at the British Association meeting in Belfast in 1902, when he was very active in preparations behind the scenes. This involvement can be seen in the many photographs included in the Guide produced for the occasion. Lastly, his enthusiasm for conchology (the study and collection of mollusc shells) brought him wider recognition, as a collector (he discovered and described two important Irish species) and as an authority. He served on the council of the Conchological Society of Great Britain and Ireland and was its president in 1922–3.[11]

Though lacking any formal educational qualification of a higher sort, beyond diplomas in drawing, geology and physiography (geomorphology or physical geography) acquired in his teens, Welch was elected a Member of the Royal Irish Academy in 1904. Nearly twenty years later, in 1923, Queen's University awarded him an honorary M.Sc. He was rightly proud of both distinctions.

As mentioned earlier, for a photographer of such distinction Welch died comparatively poor, leaving an estate valued at less than £500. His mother, left a widow in 1875 with half a dozen children to raise, had struggled to keep the photographic business going from the little house in Lonsdale Street, Belfast, to which she had moved from Bangor. Robert became the family's main support. His mother looked after him and kept the books of his business until her death in 1908; thereafter his sister Sara, who lived with them, took over, until she too died in 1915. Welch later revealed in a very frank letter to one of his scientific friends in England that after Sara's death he had a complete nervous breakdown. His anxiety was caused in part by financial worries. His elder brother and family, he said, had plundered his resources 'almost to the limit' before he paid to ship them all off to Canada sometime before the First World War broke out. He went on: 'I had not recovered but was doing well when the war came on and caught me out badly . . . almost every little investment I had shut down, all building and almost all shipbuilding work (except for a little Admiralty work in 1915 only) shut down . . . '[12] The lean war years were followed by civil strife and the partition of Ireland, which also affected Welch's photographic business. Writing in April 1922 he asserted that the war 'had stopped all my class [of] work except about 5 to 10% first 2 years & nothing at all afterwards. I have done more business last 10 days . . . than in all the four years ending 1921.' He also mentioned

> dire family trouble with my second brother, which kept me in a *very bad nervous* state for nearly 2 years till his death. He was a traveller for a big Whiskey Company, was seldom sober after 1 p.m., was travelling with a big 6 shooter (a heavy one) and very large amounts of money, he often collected up to £130 per day, now fancy that & his condition, his very bad short temper when he had liquor in. He would have shot a man, with as little compunction, if irritated in any argument on any subject & he was travelling in very hot corners, Armagh, Cavan, Leitrim, South Tyrone . . . *I was the guarantor to the Co.* for him & any day I might have been called on to pay up anything up to £160 or so, stolen from him when very badly in liquor.[13]

Photographic business eventually picked up again, but Welch had lost most of the money he had made in his heyday before the war. He was no longer at the peak of his profession, and he missed the business skills and companionship of his mother and sister. In 1927 his friends eventually persuaded the government of Northern Ireland to award him a civil list pension of £100 a year.

Welch retained his remarkable vitality almost to the end of his life. According to his diary, on 18 August 1935, then aged seventy-six, he 'played 54 games of tennis between 4.15 and 8.45, with a 45 minute break for tea', adding, 'I was not tired when bad light stopped play.'[14] The last diary entry, noting the death of George V, was written on 20 January 1936. Play finally stopped for the indefatigable photographer himself eight months later, on 28 September.

Alexander Hogg

Alexander Robert Hogg (1870–1939), Welch's younger contemporary, began as an amateur. From an early age he was a keen and competent photographer; his

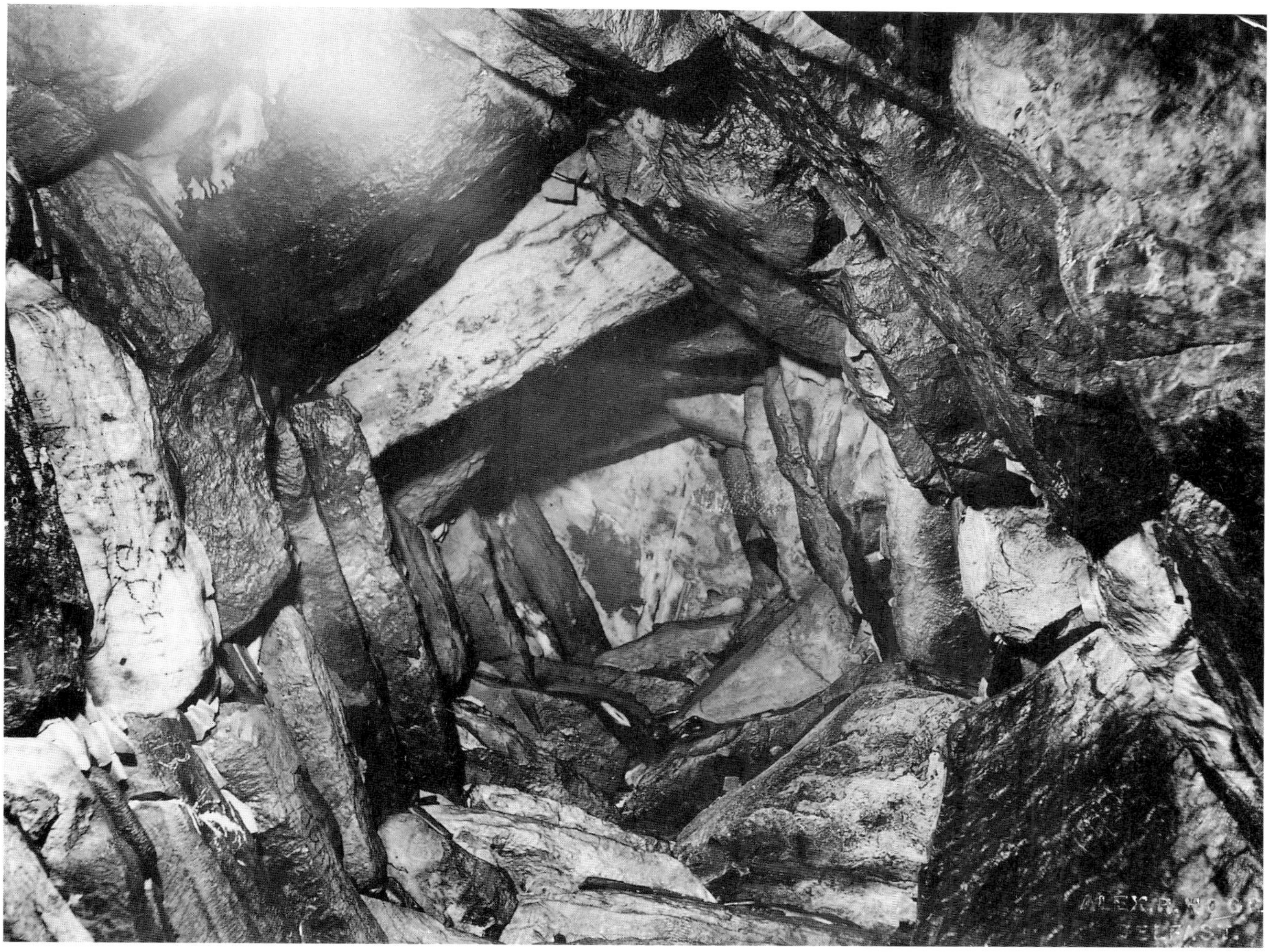

The burial chamber, Newgrange, County Meath, looking up at the capstone, taken by flashlight, c. 1900, from an original print by A.R. Hogg.
MAGNI / ULSTER MUSEUM (HOGG COLLECTION)

Hogg described this as a 'rare photograph'.

earliest extant photograph, a view of the façade of Townsend Street Presbyterian Church in Belfast, is dated 1884, when he was just fourteen. Though born and brought up in the country, in County Down, he moved to Belfast as soon as he left school and was to live there for the rest of his life. After serving his time as a druggist's apprentice with an uncle, James Hogg, who had a business in York Street, Hogg was employed for some years by the firm of Dobbin and Company, 'grocers, druggists and general merchants' in North Street. Sometime in the late 1890s, no doubt in consequence of his considerable experience in such matters – he was awarded a prize medal for his lantern slides in 1895, and became expert in manipulating the apparatus – he was taken on as lanternist by the firm of J. Lizars, 'manufacturing opticians and dealers in photographic apparatus' as the directory entries describe them. Their premises were at that time in Victoria Street (the firm is still in business in Belfast, now in Wellington Place).[15]

If Hogg had not turned professional he might well be remembered as an outstanding amateur photographer, for he was very active in local groups, such as the Ulster Amateur Photographic Society, and won many prizes in their exhibitions. On the technical side he was particularly interested in flashlight photography. A surviving lantern slide shows a meeting of the UAPS taken by flashlight in 1895. Two years later, on a visit to County Fermanagh, he and some friends, equipped with a Todd-Forret lamp and a wide-angle lens, penetrated the limestone caves at Boho and took the first pictures of the interior. The 'lecturette' describing the expedition, which he delivered to the YMCA Camera Club, was subsequently published in the *Amateur Photographer*. In 1899, during an expedition to the Boyne Valley which resulted in many interesting pictures, Hogg photographed the roof of the burial chamber at Newgrange by means of flashlight, describing the result as a 'rare photograph'.[16]

By the time he was thirty Hogg was sufficiently confident in his skills to give up the security of a regular salary for the uncertain career of a professional photographer. He made the change in 1901, setting up his studio in Trinity Street, where he was to work for the next two decades. He appeared in the Belfast directory the following year, as 'photographic and lantern specialist'. This description soon became, on his attractive Celtic Revival letterhead with its shamrock device and round tower, 'photographic specialist, lanternist and cinematographer'. Up to the end of the First World War Hogg gave regular weekly cinematograph shows in the Belfast

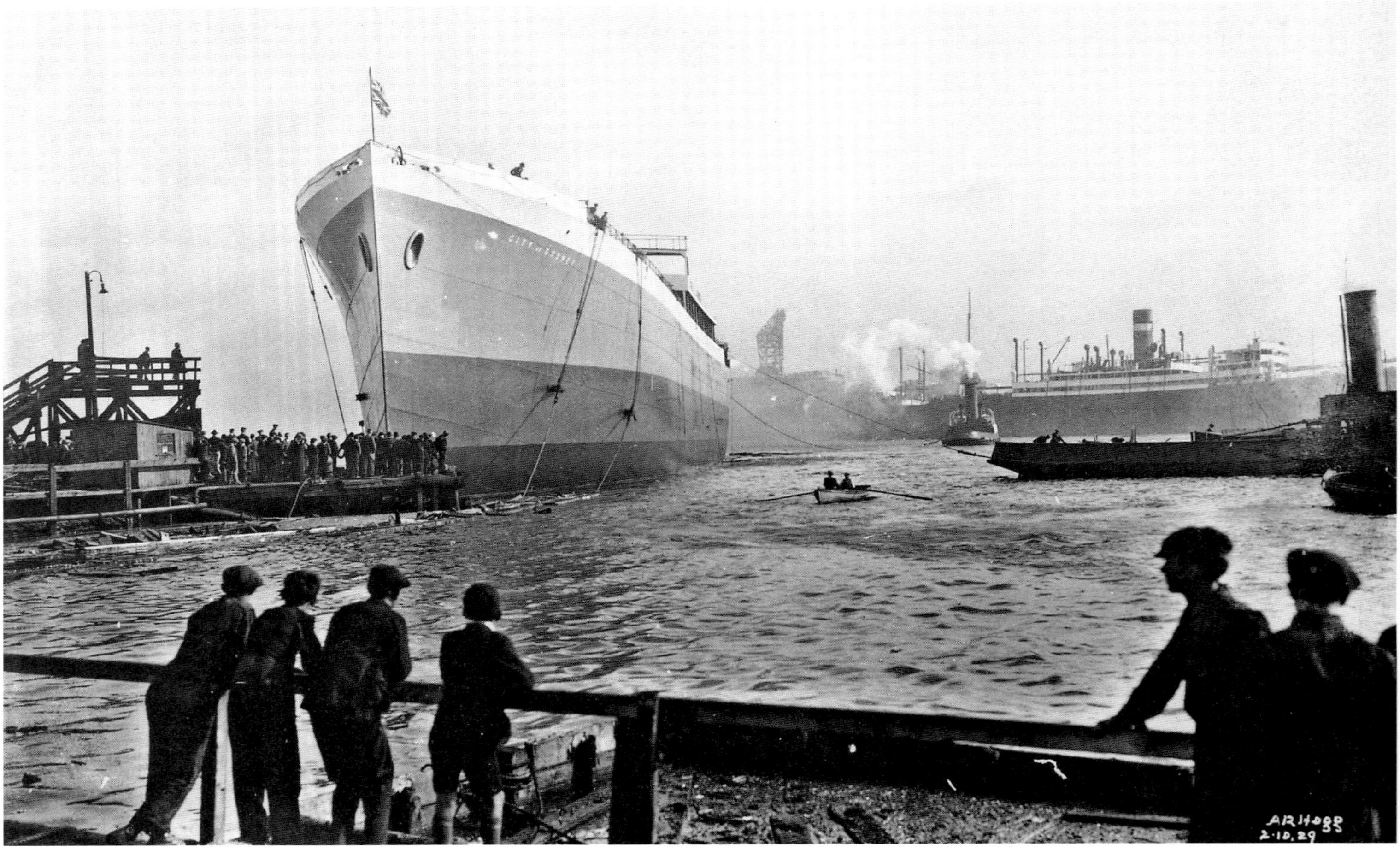

Launch of the *City of Sydney* at Workman Clark's yard in Belfast, 2 October 1929, by A.R. Hogg.
MAGNI / ULSTER MUSEUM (HOGG COLLECTION)

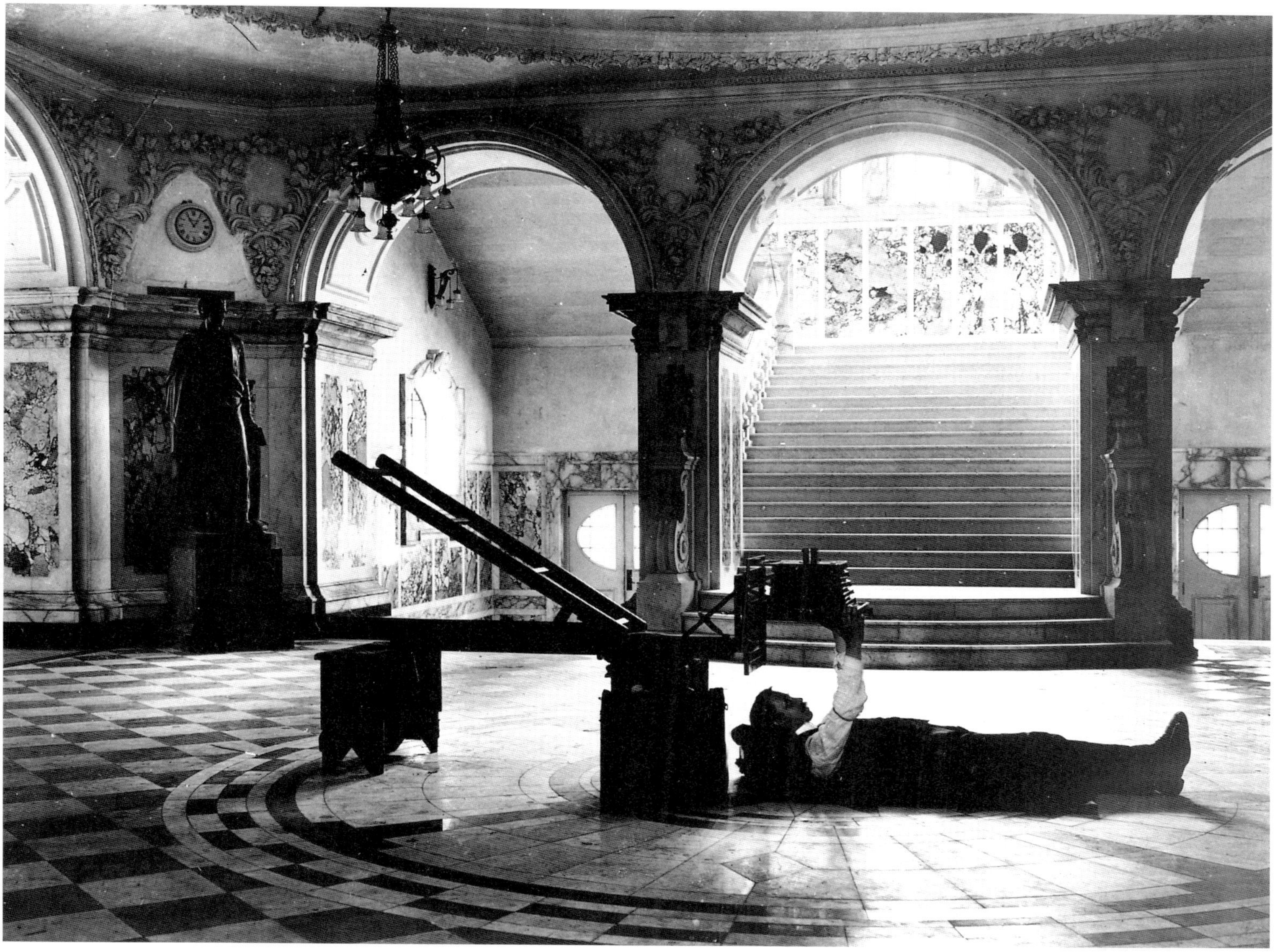

Central Mission's Grosvenor Hall and the Presbyterian headquarters, the Assembly Hall. When he married in 1907 and set up house he called his new home 'Kineto', indicating his interest in moving pictures at this stage. An advertisement in a guide to Dungannon, published in 1909, concentrates on his cinematograph exhibitions – 'No other form of Entertainment is so attractive, interesting, or amusing as the Moving Pictures' – no doubt because there was little custom for his photography outside of Belfast, whereas the visiting cinematographer was still a comparatively rare bird in country areas. The spread of commercial cinemas largely put an end to such work, but lantern slide shows and lectures remained popular and contributed to Hogg's income (as lecturer, lantern operator, maker of slides and proprietor of a lending library of slides) for many years. Today the particular interest of his slide collection is that many of his most interesting early photographs are preserved only in this form, the original negatives having apparently been lost or destroyed.

Alex Hogg photographing the interior of the dome of the new City Hall in Belfast, 1906.
MAGNI / ULSTER MUSEUM (HOGG COLLECTION)

The statue on the left is that of Frederick Richard Chichester, Earl of Belfast. Its unveiling in 1855, on the site now occupied by a statue of the Reverend Dr Henry Cooke, was the subject of one of the earliest surviving photographs taken in Belfast.

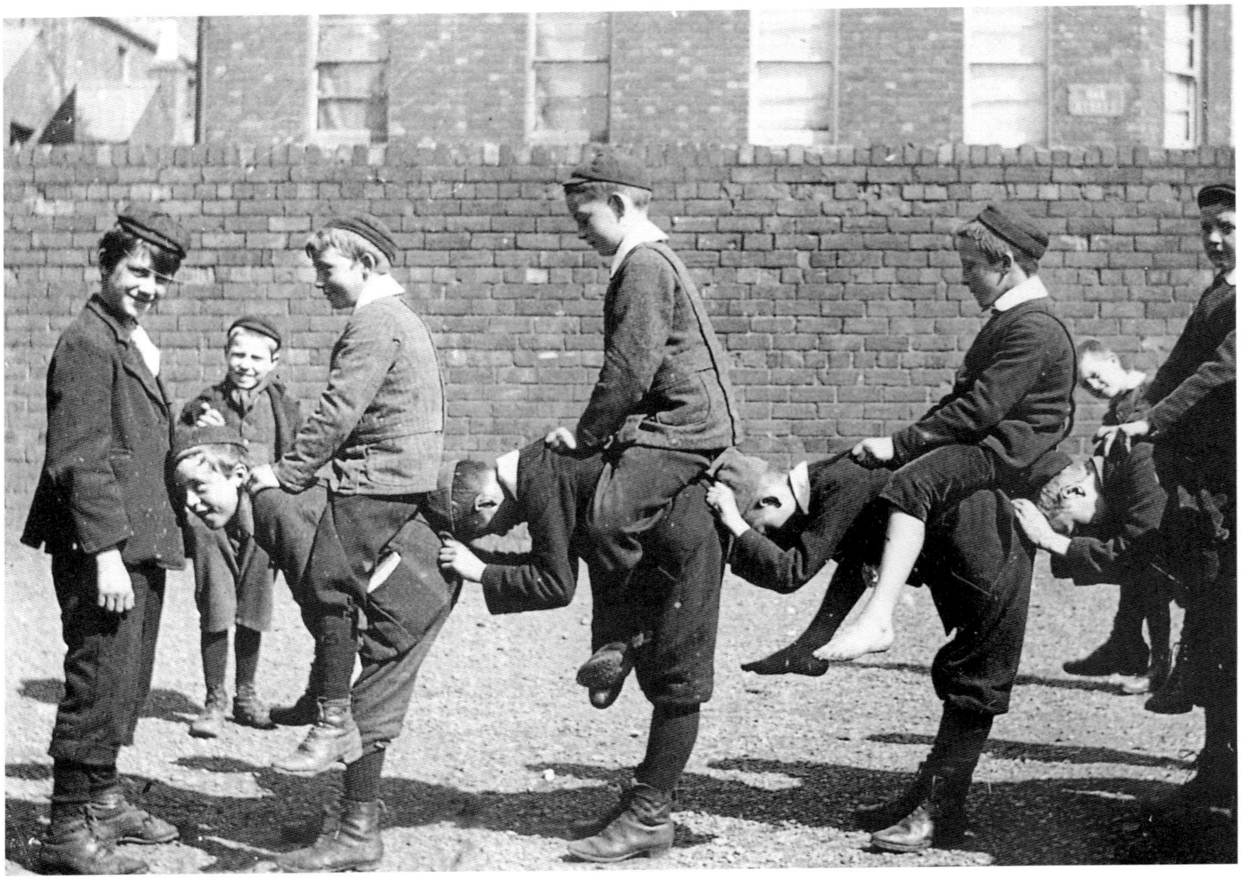

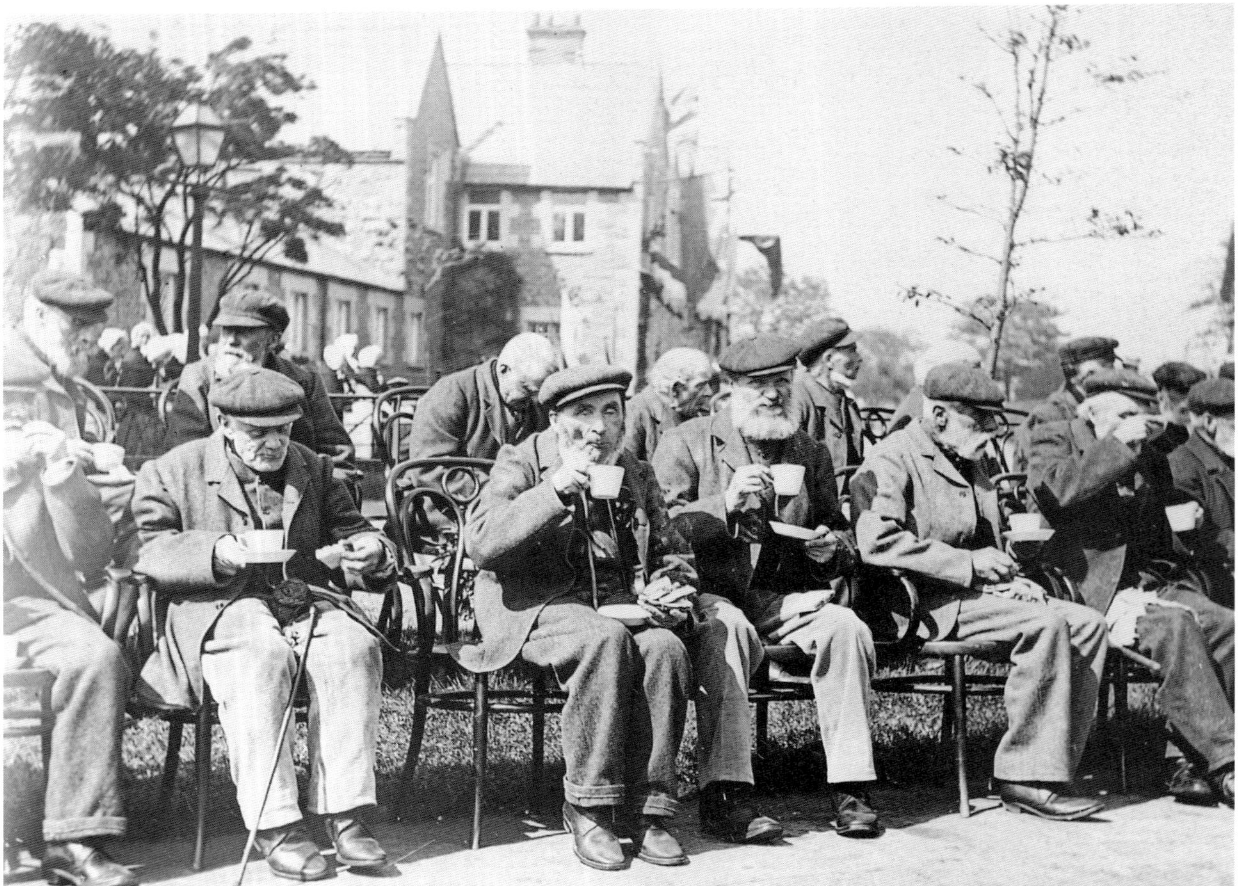

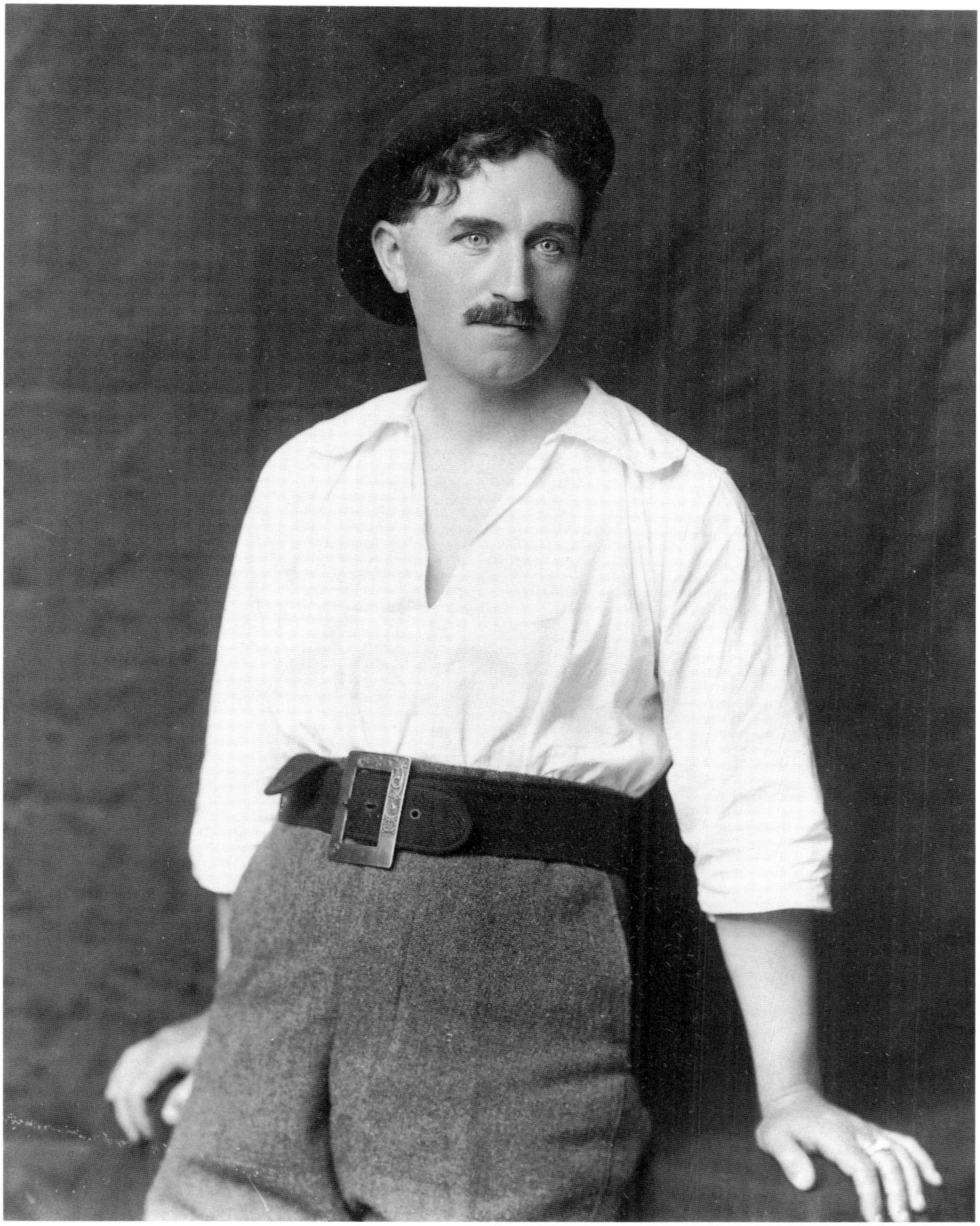

Opposite top
Boys playing a posed version of 'Churchie' (a very robust version of leapfrog) in the playground of McQuiston National School, Belfast, in 1902, from a lantern slide by A.R. Hogg.
MAGNI / ULSTER MUSEUM (HOGG COLLECTION)

Opposite bottom
Paupers having tea outside the Belfast Union Workhouse, while awaiting a royal procession, 1903; from a lantern slide by A.R. Hogg.
MAGNI / ULSTER MUSEUM (HOGG COLLECTION)

Left
Cathal O'Byrne, author, by A.R. Hogg, 1917.
MAGNI / ULSTER MUSEUM (HOGG COLLECTION)

Best remembered now for a collection of short historical pieces entitled *As I Roved Out* (Dublin, 1946), O'Byrne was a devoted admirer of F.J. Bigger, to whose memory he dedicated that book. In this portrait, dated August 1917, Hogg caught the spirit of romantic nationalism very well.

The bulk of Hogg's surviving work as a photographer of shipbuilding, linen manufacture and other industrial processes was done during the latter part of his career. He did a considerable amount, however, before 1914, when Welch was in his prime. Though Welch was the official Harland and Wolff photographer, the

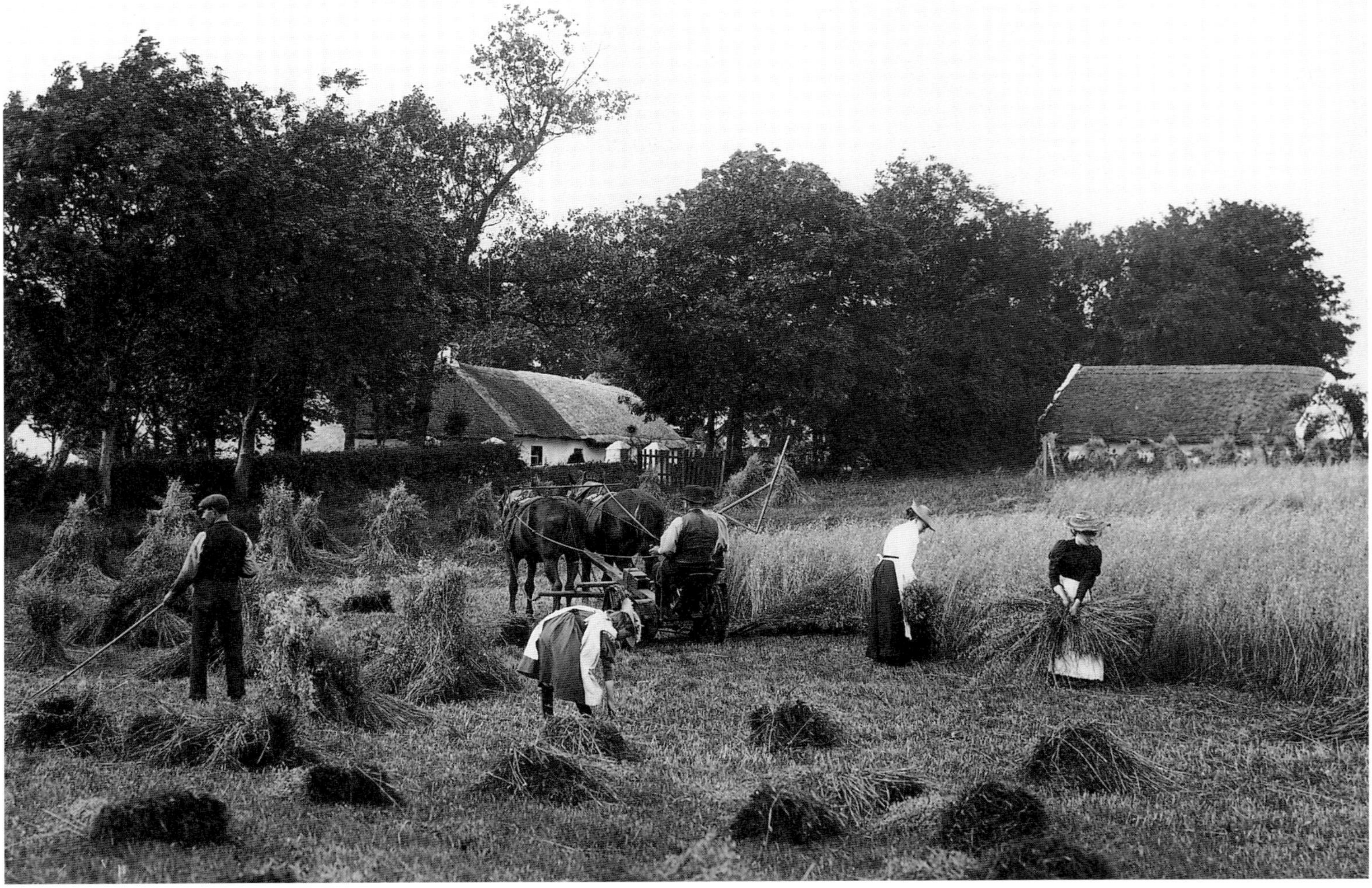

Cutting the corn on Isaac Montgomery's farm at Lisnalinchy, County Antrim, c. 1904, by A.R. Hogg.

MAGNI / ULSTER MUSEUM (HOGG COLLECTION)

launches of the company's great ocean liners such as *Olympic* and *Titanic* were public events and most leading photographers covered them. In the 1920s Hogg was to become the official photographer to the other Belfast shipyard, that of Workman Clark and Company. Another event in Belfast in the early 1900s which provided scope for the speculative photographer was the dockers' strike of 1907. Using a hand-held camera Hogg took many pictures of incidents during the strike, including some which may well be the earliest of a Belfast riot mob in action, hurling stones at a detachment of the Cameron Highlanders marching along the Grosvenor Road. To judge from the quality of the prints he may not have succeeded in selling any of these for publication. He did, however, sell to *Commercial Motor* photographs of 'picket-proof motor wagons' used during the strike.[17]

Most of the collection of glass-plate negatives now in the Ulster Museum date from the latter part of Hogg's career, the 1920s and 1930s. He appears to have rationalised his stock either about 1912 (when he started using a new negative register, which fortunately survives) or at the time he moved his studio from Trinity Street to High Street in 1921. The interesting exceptions include many of the very large (15-by-18-inch) glass-plate negatives of the new City Hall, opened in 1906. Hogg took the photographs used in the official brochure, and similar ones for the Municipal College of Technology, both before and after the opening of its splendid new building in 1907. These large plates also include views of the entire audience of the Grand Opera House during the performance of a play in 1917. Some of the couples in the front rows, who evidently wanted to remain anonymous, are carefully shielding their faces from the camera.[18]

Hogg was fortunate in getting numerous commissions from various departments of Belfast Corporation throughout his professional career. His earliest photographs of the Municipal Technical Institute and its surroundings in College Square are

Laying out linen for bleaching at the Old Bleach factory, Randalstown, County Antrim, 1930s, by A.R. Hogg.
MAGNI / ULSTER MUSEUM (HOGG COLLECTION)

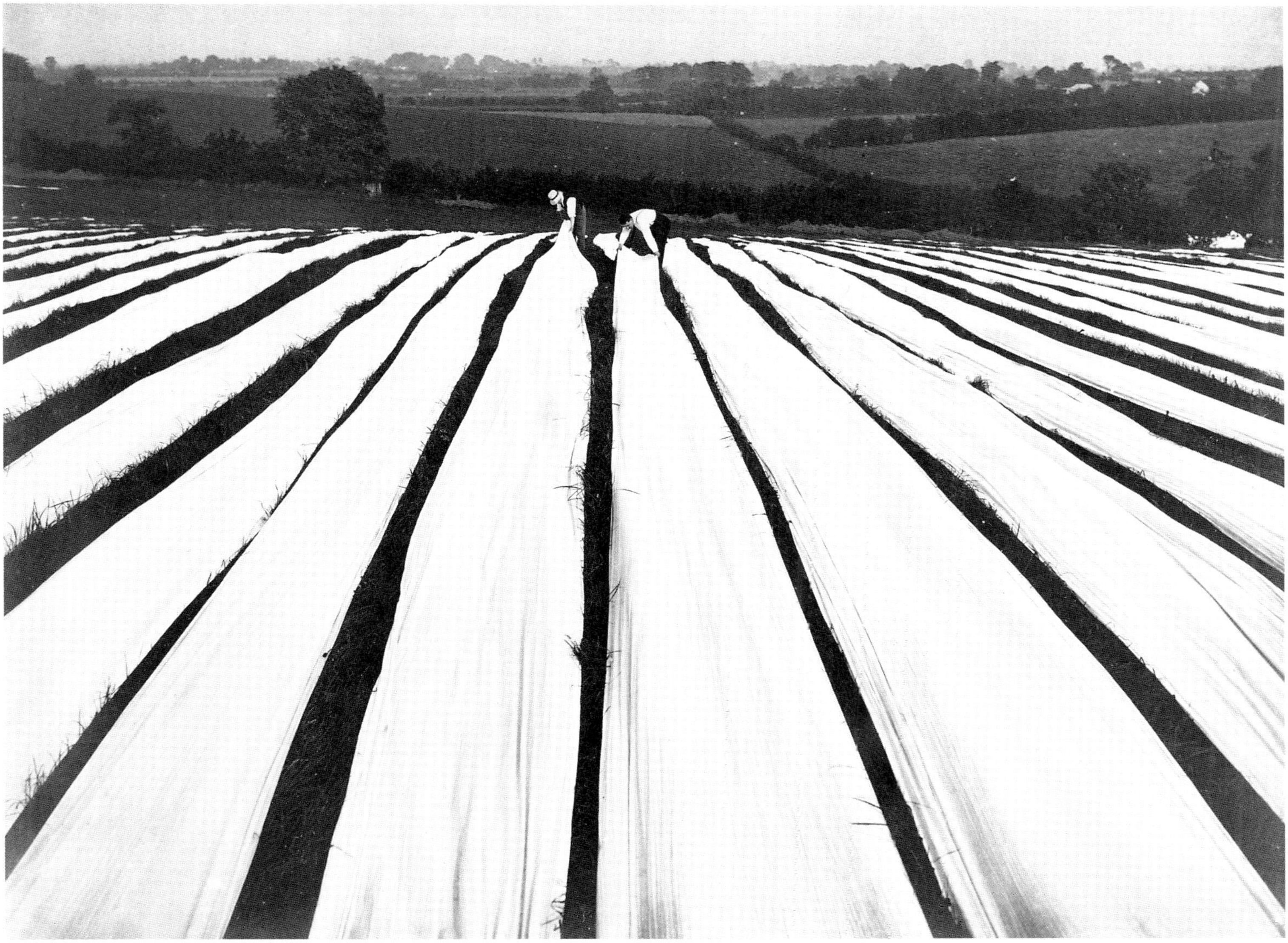

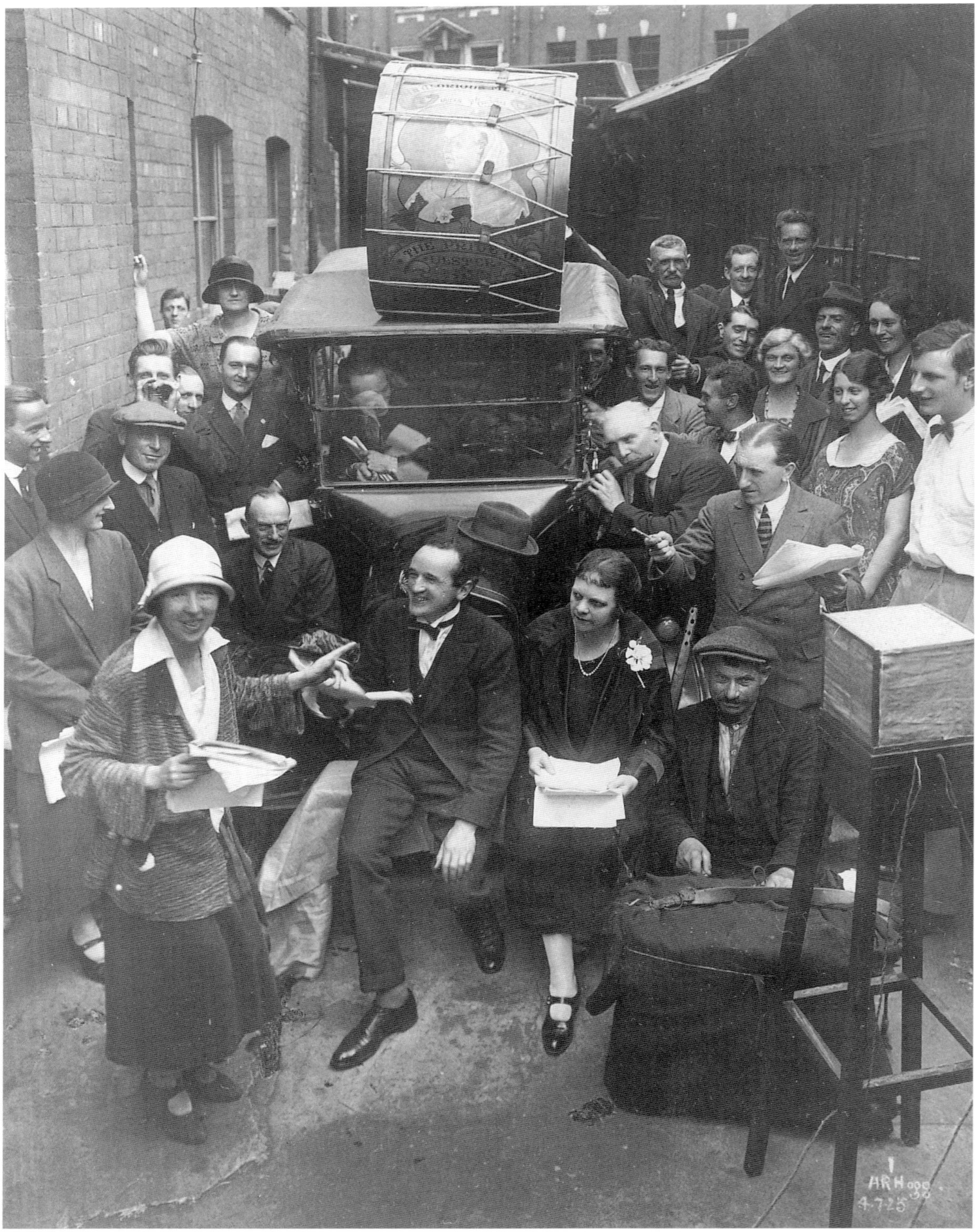

British Broadcasting Company concert party, Linenhall Street, Belfast, 1925, by A.R. Hogg.
MAGNI / ULSTER MUSEUM (HOGG COLLECTION)

The young man in shirt sleeves on the right is Tyrone Guthrie (1900–71), the notable theatrical director, whose first job after coming down from Oxford was that of junior assistant to the head of the new broadcasting station in Belfast. The man in the centre front is Richard Hayward (1898–1964), dramatist, local dialogue expert, Irish travel writer and traditional music enthusiast.

dated 1902, the year after he set up his studio; thereafter the Tech and its activities provided him with regular work. From the 1920s, when the corporation's Education Committee became responsible for the city's primary schools, Hogg photographed

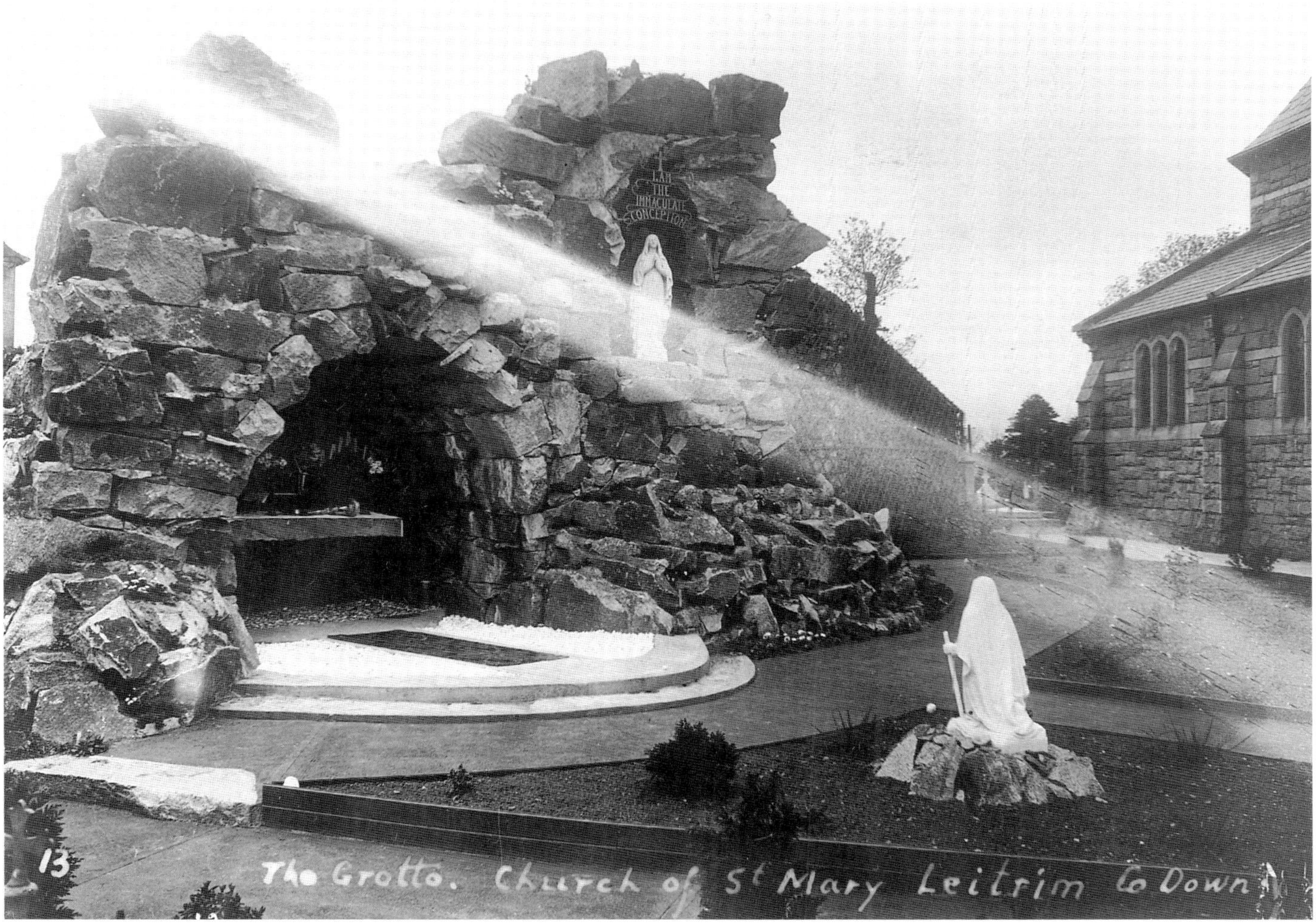

most of the new facilities, built at public expense, that were provided to replace the worst of the National Schools. The new schools were a belated answer to a desperate need which Hogg's own photographs had illustrated more than twenty years earlier in 1902, when he had been employed by the eye surgeon and educational reformer Dr W.A. McKeown to record conditions in the city's National Schools for an article in the *Belfast Weekly Telegraph*.[19] As McKeown himself said, every picture of Hogg's was worth a thousand words of his – even though, with limited printing techniques, the photographs could be used only in the form of engravings. Many of the series survive as lantern slides, in which form their full impact was no doubt felt by the audiences McKeown lectured to in person.

Another corporation department which provided Hogg with work over a long period was the transport department. Privately owned and operated till 1904, Belfast's tramways were electrified the following year and thereafter expanded rapidly. In 1910 the corporation purchased the Cavehill and Whitewell Tramway Company, along with forty acres of recreational land at Bellevue which were later developed as places of public recreation. Hogg seems to have taken most of the

The new Lourdes grotto at St Mary's Church, Leitrim, County Down, consecrated on 26 May 1929. By A.R. Hogg, from an album of prints produced for the church authorities.

MAGNI / ULSTER MUSEUM (HOGG COLLECTION)

The general opinion is that the mysterious shaft of light was the result of trick photography, presumably devised to enhance the effect of the solemn occasion, rather than divine intervention.

official photographs of the Tramway Company's stock and activities including, in the 1930s, such features as the Floral Hall at Hazelwood and the zoo at Bellevue. Most of the surviving pictures of the tramcars are now in the Public Record Office of Northern Ireland, the rest in the Ulster Museum.

The Electricity Department provided an increasing number of commissions as the demand for its product and its services increased. Again Hogg was employed almost from the beginning, his earliest photographs being those of the new power station which opened in 1903. Twenty years later the opening of a much larger power station greatly increased the department's activities. Electricity with its 'clean' image was seen as the fuel of the future both for industry and the home. The corporation's efforts to exploit its possibilities, which included the establishment of showrooms and the demonstration of domestic appliances, were recorded by Hogg in a series of interesting pictures, including one of the first 'all-electric' house, in Balmoral Avenue in 1928.

Improved public housing, however reluctant the corporation was about providing it, was an unavoidable necessity in Belfast in the early 1900s. An Improvement Order was eventually obtained in 1910 and two years later Hogg was employed to photograph a large number of slum properties in the decayed central areas of the city which were scheduled for removal. Many of these pictures, which are of interest to social historians, survive either as lantern slides or glass-plate negatives. Hogg subsequently photographed some of the new homes that were eventually built to replace the slums – I say eventually because councillors dragged their feet, unwilling to lose potential voters from their own wards. The housing record of the corporation between the wars was if anything more dismal than before, but a few subsidised estates were built and again Hogg was the photographer employed to record them in all their bare newness.

While the corporation supplied Hogg with a good deal of bread-and-butter work, he also had a very wide variety of business and other clients, ranging from owners of shops, hotels and restaurants to artists, architects, lawyers, insurance companies, churches and cinemas. Four decades of urban life and work are illustrated in his surviving photographs, quite apart from his views of the Ulster countryside. Only his friend Welch rivalled his achievement as a recorder of the life of his time, and in some respects – the portrayal of people at work in particular – Hogg was better than Welch. By the time he died in 1939 Hogg was regarded as the leading practitioner in the north. Years before, in the mid-1920s, he had taken the lead in establishing the Ulster branch of the Professional Photographers' Association, and in the 1930s he served on its national council. Reports of his death in local newspapers remarked that while his work covered every class of commercial and technical photography he was best known for his views of Ulster beauty spots, which were used

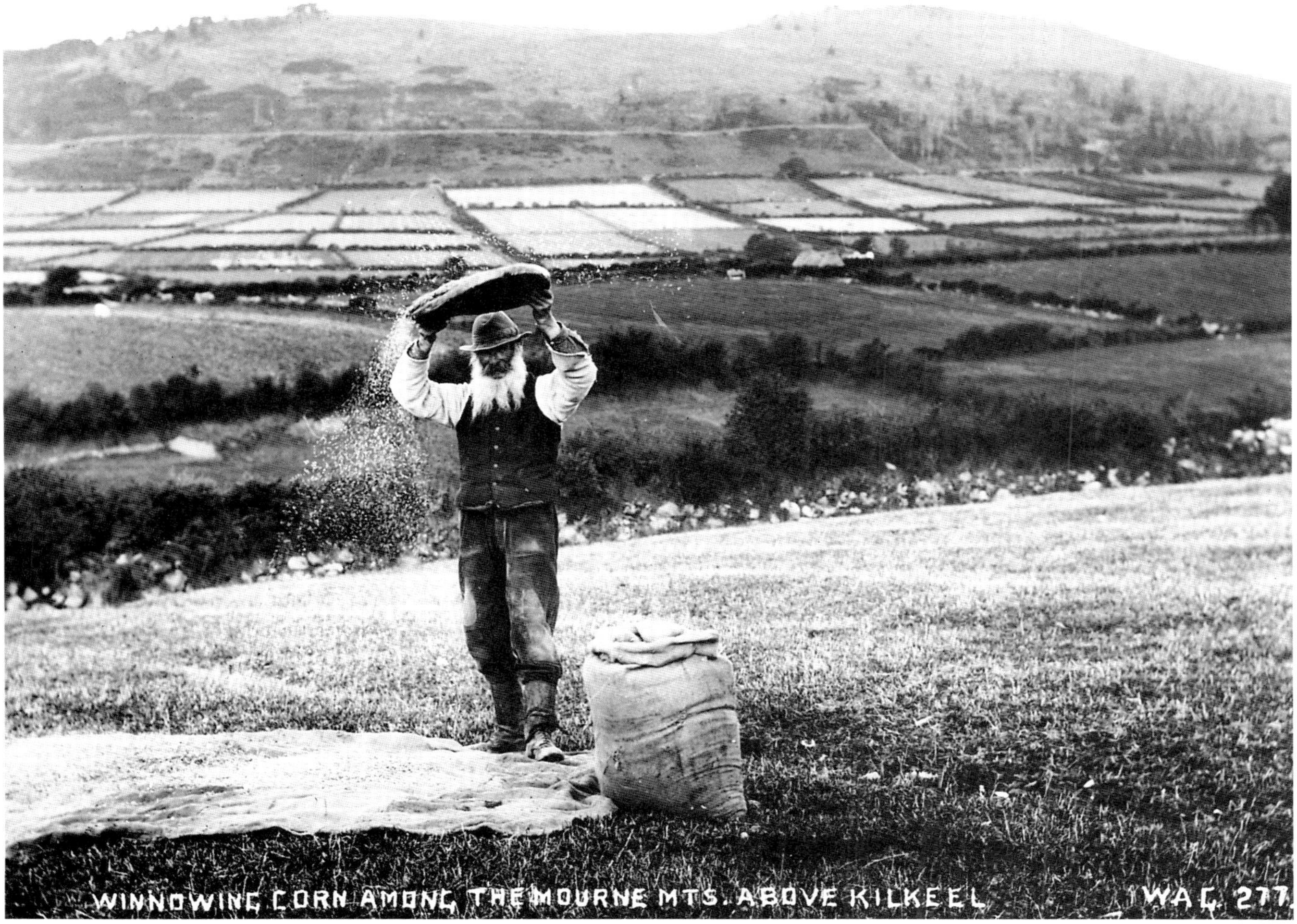

'Winnowing corn among the Mourne Mountains, above Kilkeel', by W.A. Green.

MAGNI / UFTM (GREEN COLLECTION)

The patriarchal appearance of the figure adds greatly to the effect in this photograph of an ancient agricultural practice, no doubt specially staged for the camera. We do not know exactly when the photograph was taken, but the negative number (277) is an early one in Green's professional career, c. 1910.

in numerous travel and tourist publications. Today, it is the range of his photographs and the way they reflect humdrum life that excites those who use them.

William Green

William Alfred Green (1870–1958), Hogg's exact contemporary, came from a different background and became a professional photographer even later in life. Green was born in Newry, County Down, where his father had a tea and grocery business. The whole Green connection were Quakers. Green's great-uncle, Forster Green, became the leading tea merchant in Belfast, where his premises in High Street were adorned with a great golden tea-canister. Forster Green was a noted philanthropist, generous particularly to victims of tuberculosis – a disease which carried off most of his own family – for whom he endowed a hospital on the outskirts of the city.[20]

Young Green was sent to board at the Friends' School in Lisburn. When both his parents died while he was quite young and the business in Newry was sold, he was taken on as an apprentice by his great-uncle, moving to Belfast and into the tea business. This may not have been good for his health, which was said to be delicate. Alternatively, he may not have been cut out for the life. In any case he did not remain in the firm, which eventually passed out of the family's direct control. When Forster Green died in 1903 he left £3,250 to his grand-nephew, William, and a further £250 to William's wife (who was a grand-niece). This, together with their own inheritances, left them comfortable if not well-off.

Green's spare time was employed in scholarly pursuits of an amateur kind. Like Welch he was an active member of the Belfast Naturalists' Field Club, and he later became a Fellow of the Royal Society of Antiquaries of Ireland. He took up

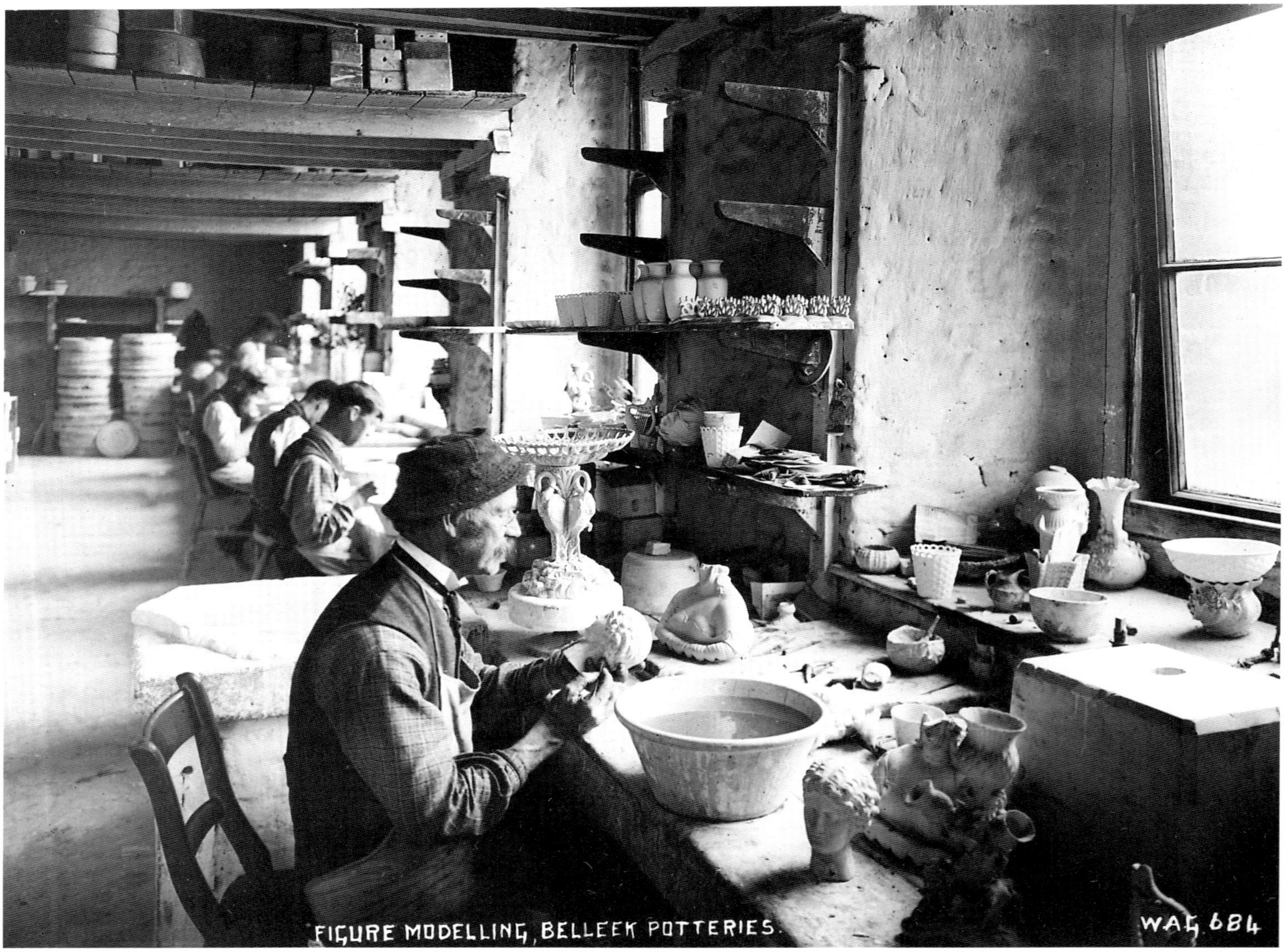

'Figure modelling, Belleek Potteries', County Fermanagh, by W.A. Green.
MAGNI / UFTM (GREEN COLLECTION)

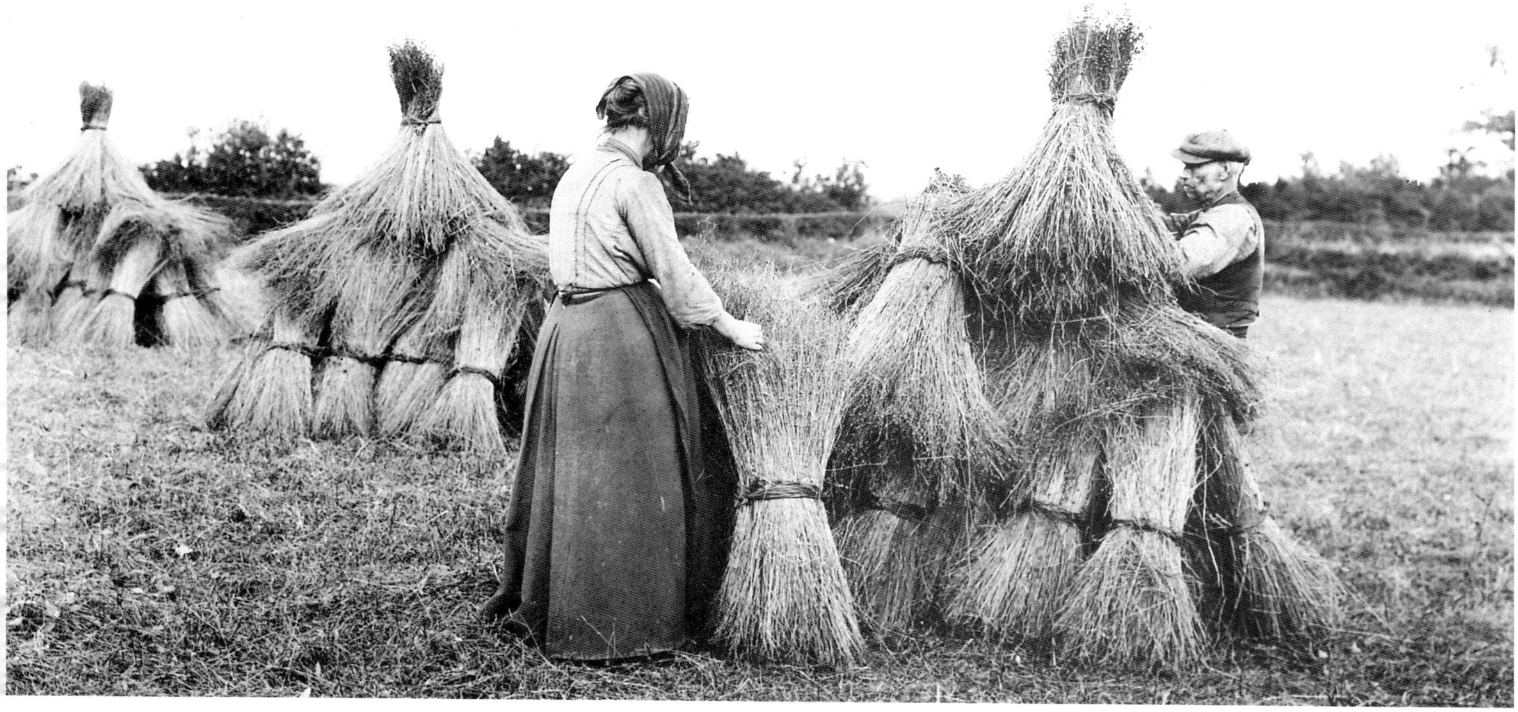

taxidermy (or birdstuffing, as it was commonly called) and collected specimens for his private museum. The development of these interests led him to apply for the post of Curator of the Municipal Art Gallery and Museum (then housed on the top floor of the Public Library in Royal Avenue) when it fell vacant in 1905. Though his application was supported by an impressive array of testimonials from his scientific acquaintances, it was not successful. As he himself admitted, he was not a trained specialist in anything, but he claimed that he had had 'for many years the keen desire to associate myself with Museum Work, and with that object I have devoted all the spare time at my disposal to the study of our local Ethnography, Geology, Conchology, etc., and I have also, through patient practice, acquired a fair workable knowledge of Taxidermy'.[21]

'Stooking the flax, Toome, County Antrim', by W.A. Green.

MAGNI / UFTM (GREEN COLLECTION)

The pagoda-like architecture of the stooks contributes to a striking composition.

Oddly enough, Green's application for the museum post makes no mention of his interest in photography, though the earliest photograph in the Green Collection in the Ulster Folk and Transport Museum is dated 1887. Green was certainly not so prominent an amateur photographer as Hogg, but he clearly became pretty competent. It is generally believed that before setting up as a professional he

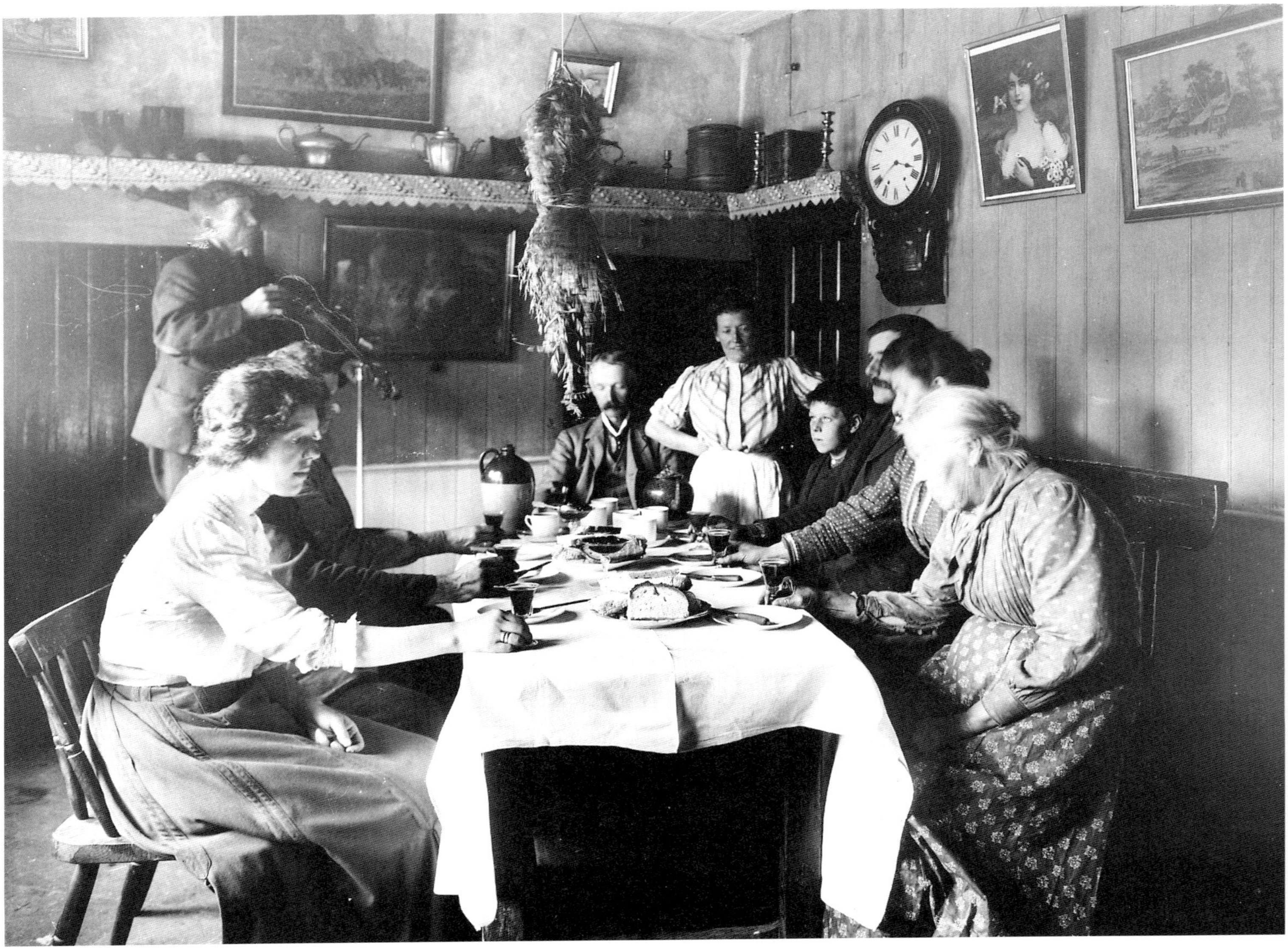

'The Churn or Harvest Home, Toome, County Antrim', by W.A. Green.
MAGNI / UFTM (GREEN COLLECTION)

The ceremonial 'calliagh' or last sheaf is suspended above the simple feast. The workers appear to be exhausted, but in any case – like the fiddler with his fiddle – needed to keep still for the camera since the dimly lit kitchen must have necessitated a fairly long exposure.

trained under Welch. Whether there was any formal training or not, he certainly accompanied Welch on photographic outings and must have learned a good deal from him before launching out on his own in 1910, aged forty.

Green billed himself as a landscape and scientific photographer but offered in addition hand-painted views, calendars, photographs and slides of Irish scenery, country life, industries, antiquities and natural history. He also published two series of 'Irish Views' postcards – the 'Wagtail' series (a pun on his initials WAG), which dates from about 1914, and a later, very fine, series printed by the expensive collotype method. The quality of his work was excellent, a fact reflected in the selections of local views published in recent years by Friar's Bush Press from the original negatives in the Green Collection.[22]

This staple work, however good, is not nowadays Green's chief claim to be regarded as an important Irish photographer. Instead, it is the work he did out of

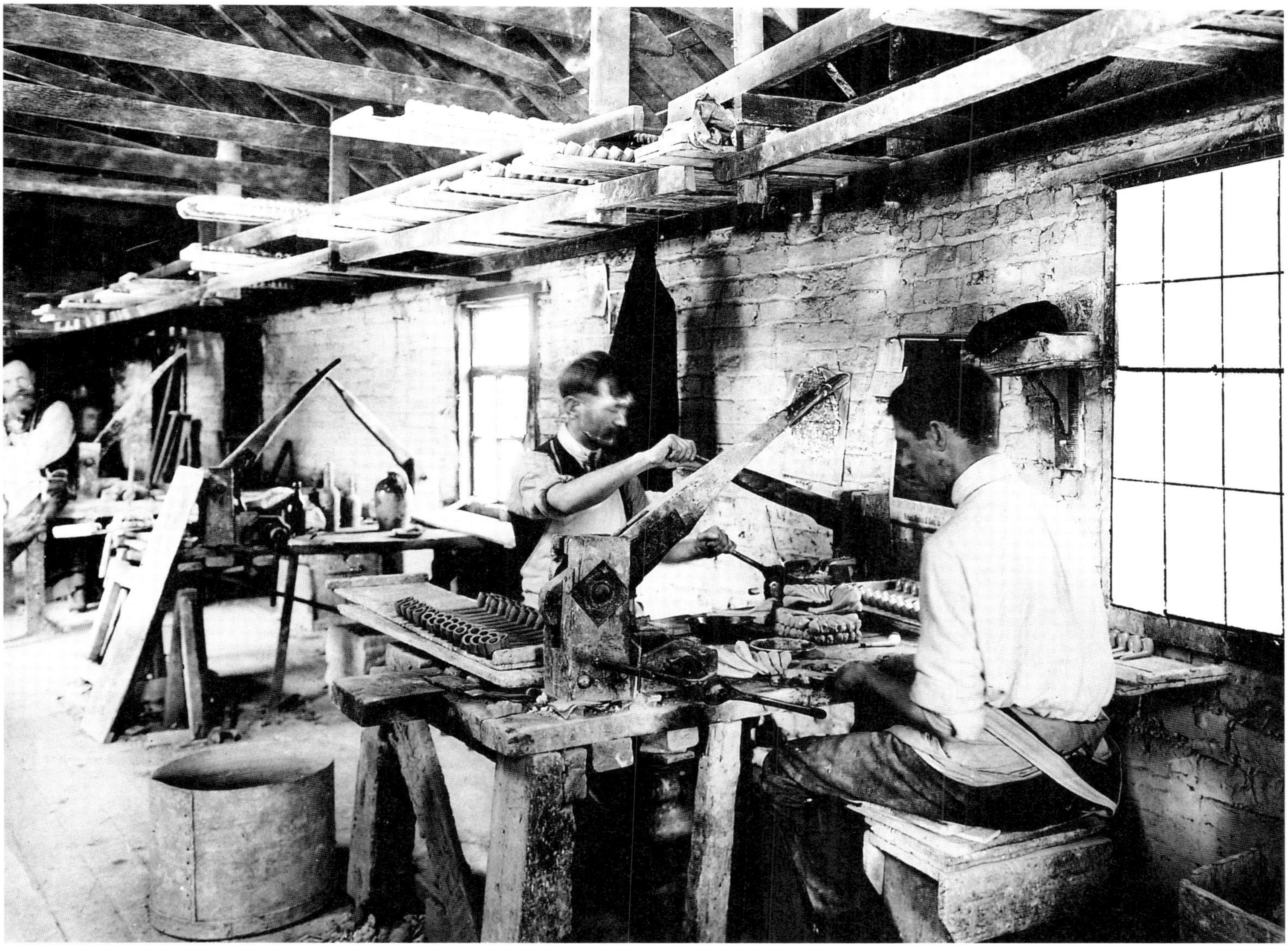

his own personal interest, in recording old rural craft methods and social customs, that seems most striking. In a talk to the Field Club in 1921 he explained how he had become interested in a world that was rapidly passing out of existence:

> Some years ago I happened to be in the Toome [County Antrim] district doing some general photography, and saw some people steeping flax. I was sufficiently interested to take a photograph and the friend who was with me told me that the scutching stock [a very primitive device] was still in use in the locality. To make a long story short, I stayed a fortnight with him and he drove me round the district. I got pictures of several of the old methods used in the country in the manipulation of flax – hand scutching, breaking, cloving, hand hackling etc. Curiously enough most of the people engaged in these primitive operations are since dead, and as they appear to be the last to use them, I think they are now obsolete.[23]

'Piercing and moulding clay pipes', by W.A. Green, 1914.

MAGNI / UFTM (GREEN COLLECTION)

This is one of a series of seven photographs recording the processes by which clay pipes were still being made in Belfast in the early twentieth century. The firm concerned, Hamilton's of Winetavern Street, finally closed during the 1930s.

He went on to say that in the same district he got photographs of an old Irish custom at the corn harvest – 'cutting the calliagh' or last sheaf. Other archaic customs he recorded were concerned with May Day, St Patrick's Day and Wedding Maskers.

Like both Welch and Hogg, Green photographed the various stages of producing linen in the spinning mills and weaving factories then so common in Ulster. He also photographed all the stages of the homespun woollen industry in County Donegal, from the shearing of the sheep to the production of finished garments; carpet making at Killybegs; china production at Belleek; and clay pipe making in Belfast. He was particularly interested in the area around Lough Neagh, where he recorded the ancient ways of the eel fishers at Toome and the pollan fishers. Here he was following directly in Welch's footsteps.

Green moved to Antrim in 1924, to a house he inherited from an uncle, and lived there till he died in 1958. In 1921 the Greens had lost their only child, a son

'Donegal carpet hand-loom weaving at Killybegs', by W.A. Green.
MAGNI / UFTM (GREEN COLLECTION)

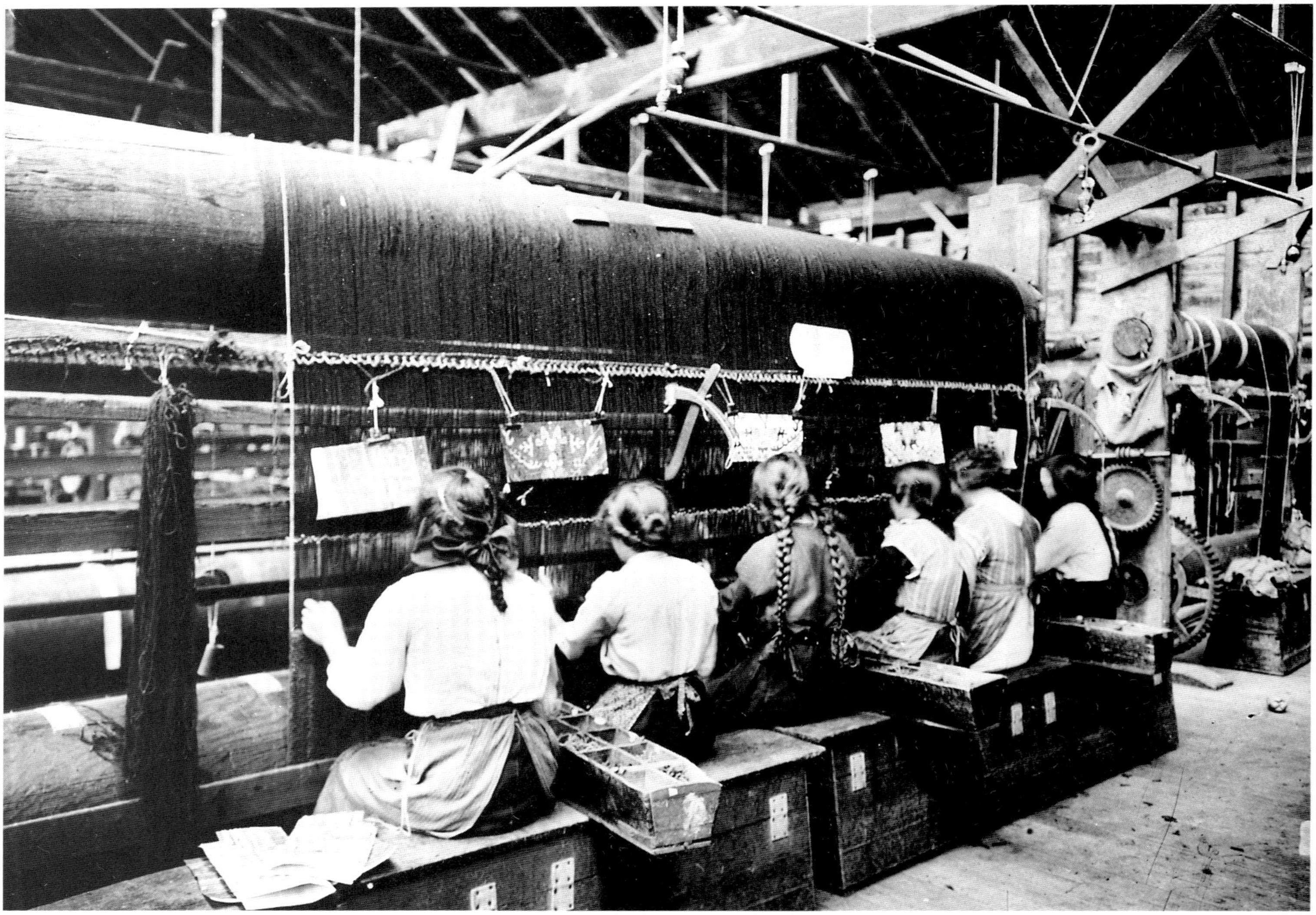

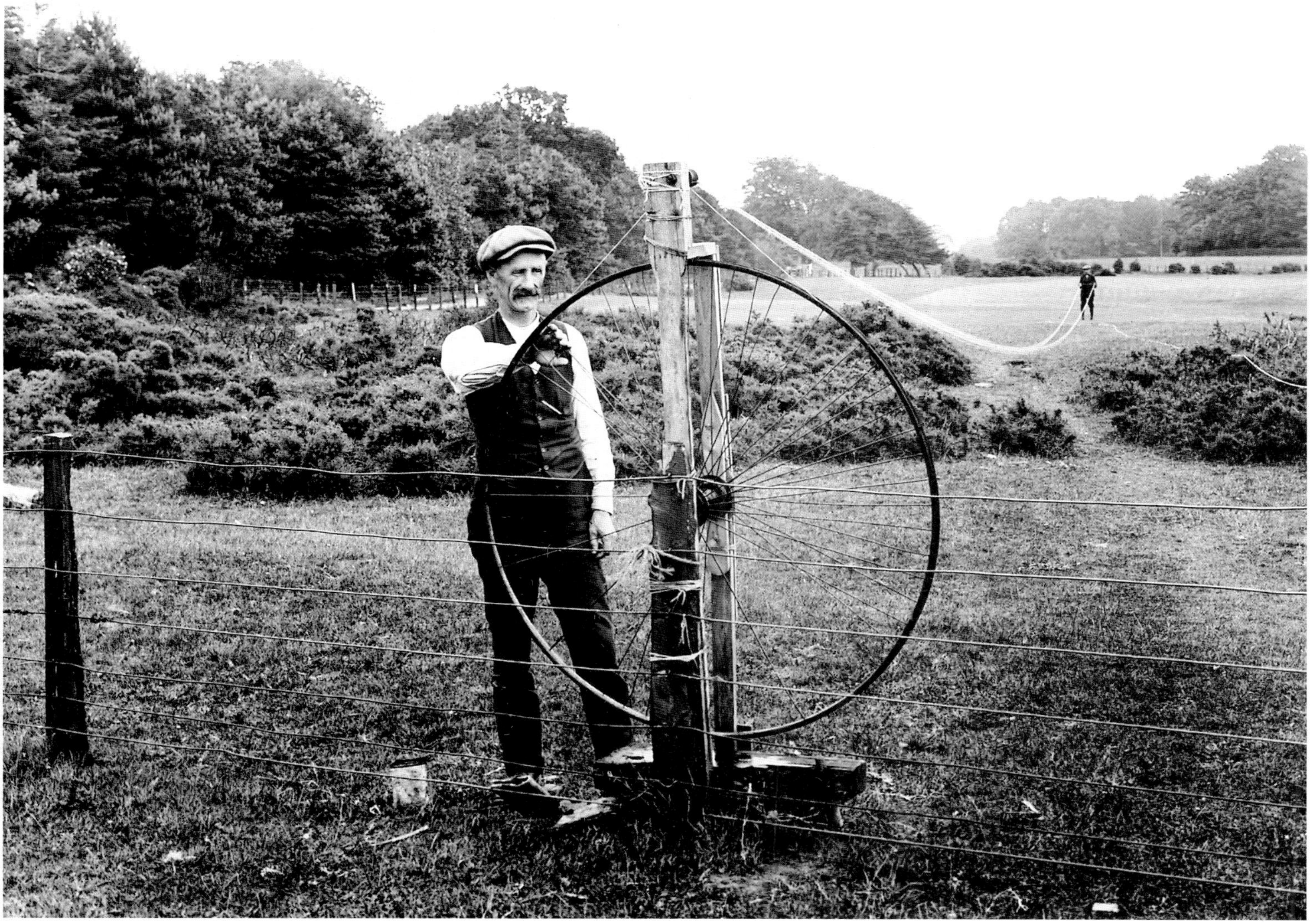

named Edmund, who died as the result of an incident at the Friends' School in Lisburn, where he was a trainee teacher – 'accidentally killed, experimenting with gas mask' according to the school records.[24] (He had been a pupil there for four years, before going to Bootham, the Quaker school at York, from which he had recently returned.) Father and son had been extremely close (the boy appears as a figure in many of the early photographs) and Green was devastated. It used to be thought that he gave up photography in consequence, but this was not the case. He did effectively retire in the mid-1930s, however, so for all practical purposes his career came to an end at the same time as that of his mentor Welch and his contemporary Hogg.

All three men were typical of a certain period in Irish photography and a certain

'Pollan fishers twisting lines for nets, Lough Neagh', by W.A. Green.
MAGNI / UFTM (GREEN COLLECTION)

Apart from eels, which were a valuable export crop, Lough Neagh produced large quantities of the species of white fish known as pollan, which were mainly for local consumption.

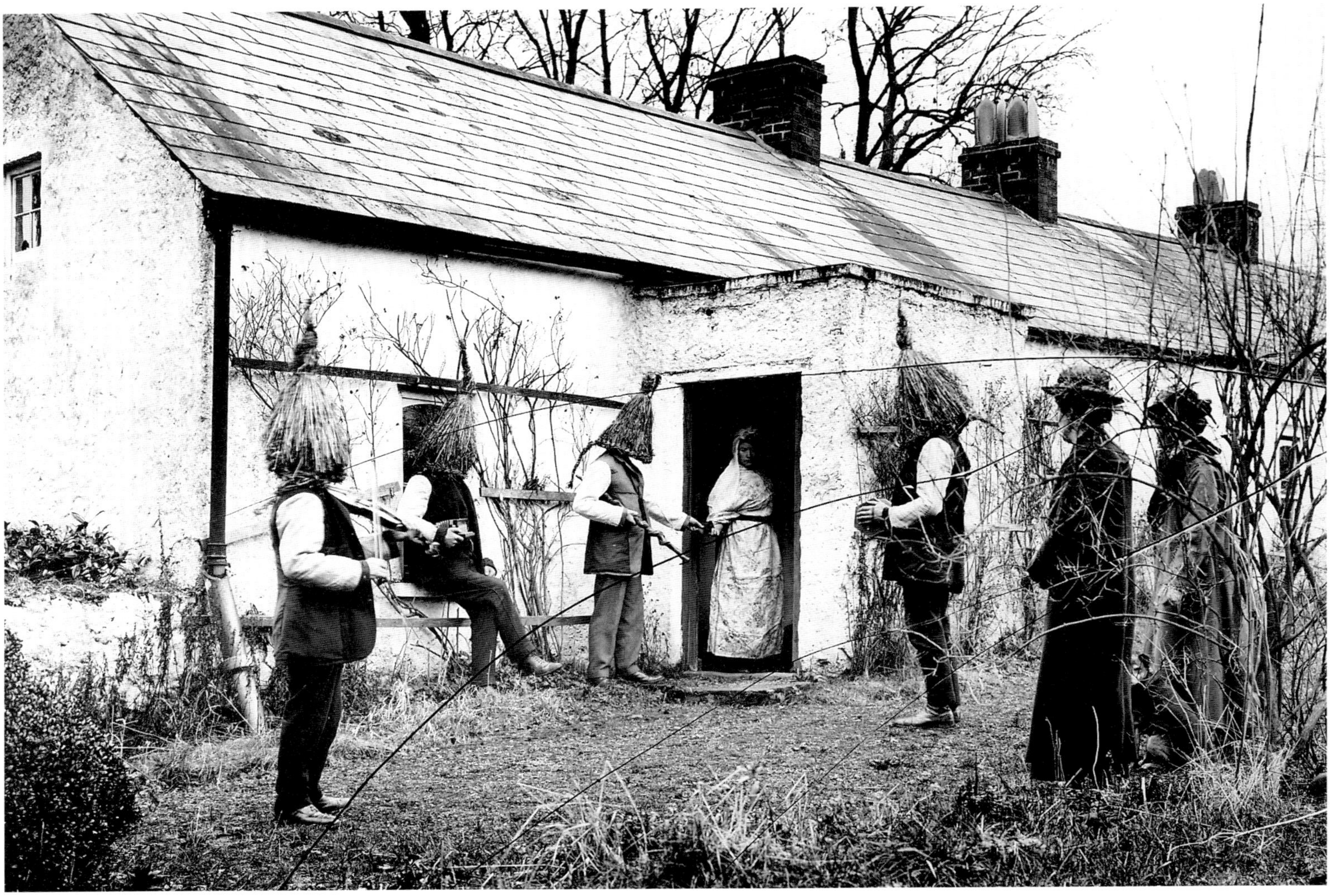

'Wedding Maskers, a Sligo marriage custom', by W.A. Green.
MAGNI / UFTM (GREEN COLLECTION)

Although large glass negatives gave excellent definition, one drawback was their fragility, as the cracks on this photograph show.

kind of Irish photographer – one with scholarly interests, the enthusiasm of the amateur, and strong links to the Field Club and similar societies. The next generation of general specialists would be more purely professional in approach. Nevertheless, it was still possible in the 1930s for someone entering the photographic profession to begin as an amateur. One example was Lionel Symes, a young stockbroker from Dublin who preferred photography to stocks and shares. He moved north to Belfast because the northern capital's industrial and business life gave scope for the kind of photography he wanted to do, and set up in 1935 under the name A and C Photography. The initials stood for Artistic and Commercial. A and C, still in business, took up where Welch, Hogg and Green left off.[25]

Movers and shakers

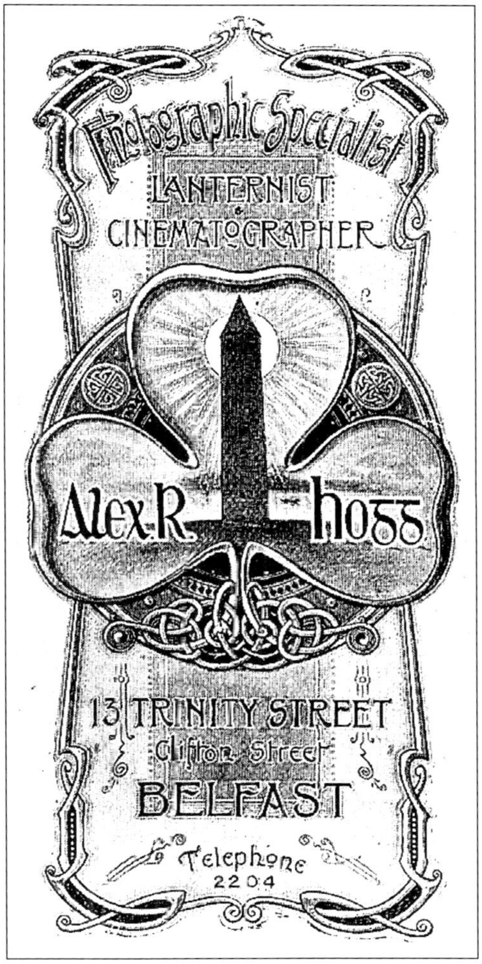

A.R. Hogg's Celtic Revival letterhead, c. 1902, describing himself as a cinematographer.
MAGNI / UM (HOGG COLLECTION)

At least one of the leading photographers of his day – Alex Hogg – also described himself as a cinematographer during the early years of his professional career. He was of course keenly interested in the exciting new world of moving pictures, as the choice of 'Kineto' for the name of his new house clearly showed. On further examination of the available evidence, however, it becomes plain that he was no pioneer, either as movie photographer or showman. He became a skilful operator of the cinematograph (and its successful operation required considerable skill) rather than a film maker or entrepreneur. It does appear, all the same, that movie-making of some sort was on the syllabus of his Technical College class, for a notice circulated by the principal to members of the class, about arrangements for a forthcoming outdoor meeting, includes the announcement, 'Mr Hogg intends taking a cinematograph film of "Life on the Lagan".'[1] So far as we know, Hogg did not own a movie camera himself, whereas cinematograph projectors were part of his stock in trade. One machine used by him in his long-running series of shows at the Grosvenor Hall survives in the Ulster Museum. At any rate, he never advertised his programme as containing films of his own making.

The first (projected) moving pictures shown in the north of Ireland were seen by the patrons of Belfast's Empire Theatre of Varieties on 16 November 1896.[2] This novelty item in the evening's programme created a sensation, despite its brevity (each film was only fifty feet long and lasted only about sixty seconds). Both the films and the projector used to show them on this occasion were the work of the French brothers Auguste and Louis Lumière, chemists and cinema pioneers; the projectionist was their agent in the United Kingdom, a Frenchman named Trewey. While in Belfast, Trewey and his colleagues photographed street scenes at Castle Junction and the Queen's Bridge which were included in the programme on their return visit to the Empire a few weeks later.

The sight that transfixed those first cinemagoers was *The Arrival of a Train*, which opened with a scene showing a stretch of railway receding into the distance. An express train comes into view, hurtles towards the audience, steams into a station, stops and disgorges its passengers, who alight and walk jerkily towards the camera. The projector, lit by a lamp-box fuelled by an acetylene burner emitting an intense naked flame, had to be cranked by hand. Its operator tried to project at the same speed as that used in the taking of the film. For a speed of sixteen frames a second, waltz tempo was apparently a good guide. Until the arrival of constant speed electric motors, projectionists were therefore much given to humming or whistling as they worked.[3]

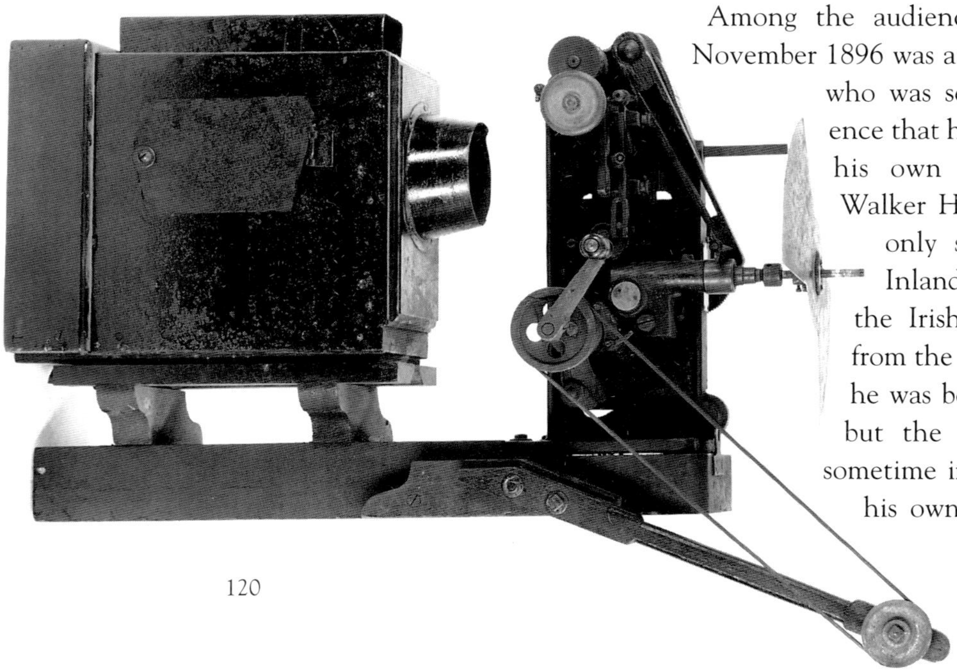

Hand-cranked cinematograph projector belonging to A.R. Hogg.
MAGNI / UM (HOGG COLLECTION)

This model, no. 105 by Ross of London, dates from the early 1900s.

Among the audience at the Empire on 16 November 1896 was a hotel owner named Hicks, who was so enthused by the experience that he at once set out to acquire his own movie equipment. John Walker Hicks (1863–1938) was the only son of an official in the Inland Revenue department of the Irish civil service.[4] We know from the census returns of 1901 that he was born in County Fermanagh, but the family moved to Belfast sometime in the 1870s. According to his own account, in an interview with a journalist in 1900, Hicks attended the Government School of Art and there became interested in photography. From a fellow-student he learned about the new dry-plate process, and claimed to be one of the first amateurs in Belfast to use it.[5] In 1890 he married, at Rathfarnham near Dublin, Marie Elizabeth Hanna. She came from Ballyshannon, County Donegal, and her father is described on the marriage certificate as 'gentleman'. In the same year, the Hickses opened the Shaftesbury Hotel at 5 College Square North, Belfast, expanding presently to take in No. 6 next door. An advertisement for the business, published a few months later, includes this special note in bold type: 'The only Hotel in Belfast fitted with PHOTOGRAPHIC DEVELOPING ROOM to which visitors have Free access.' The couple's first child, a boy they named Cyril William Hanna, was born in 1891. A second son, John Henry Victor, born three years later, testified to his father's enthusiasm for photography by bearing the additonal forename Daguerre.

No sooner had Hicks acquired a cinematograph than he was approached to exhibit it. In January 1897 the secretary of the Fête Committee of the St Vincent de Paul Society in Dublin was instructed 'to secure the services of the Hibernian Cinematograph Company for their cinematograph now exhibiting in Paris'. Hicks had recently established his Hibernian Vitagraph Company as a dealership, based at his hotel. It advertised itself as selling 'Cinematography, Gramophones, Phonographs, Optical Lanterns and Photographic Apparatus'. The 'Vitagraphe' was a French-made film camera which apparently, could also be adapted for use as a printer and projector.[6] Hicks was engaged to show films at the St Vincent de Paul Society's Granada Bazaar, as it was called, which was held at the Rotunda in Sackville (now O'Connell) Street in February 1897.

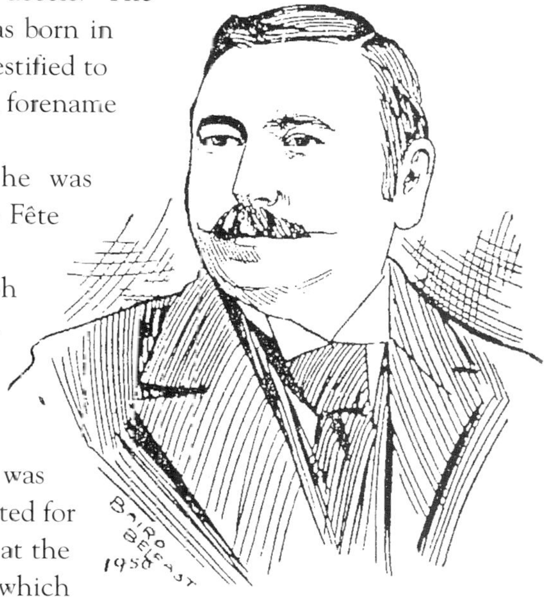

Professor Kineto (J.W. Hicks) in 1900, from *Irish Playgoer*, 19 April 1900.

WITH ACKNOWLEDGEMENTS TO JOHN MARTIN

Adopting the stage name 'Professor Kineto', he attracted large crowds and rave reviews. One of the visitors, the principal of Knock College, invited him to give a lecture and exhibition at the College. It was the success of these two entertainments, he later said, that persuaded him to pursue a professional career. During the next couple of years he lectured and performed in twenty-six of the leading schools in Ireland, including Blackrock, Clongowes Wood, Wesley College and Portora, and gave public 'seances' (as they were sometimes called) everywhere from Antrim in the north to Tipperary in the south. There was universal praise for the quality of the showings, in particular for the remarkable lack of flicker in the projected images – 'unquestionably superior to any heretofore seen in the city [of Dublin]'; 'almost entirely free from vibration'; 'remarkable for steadiness'; 'the best of its class we have had since the original Lumière's', and so on. This improvement, Hicks said, was due to his own refinement of the French apparatus.

Much was evidently due to the skilful manipulation of the operator, and also to his showmanship. Hicks himself recalled that as a boy he had given magic-lantern shows in the attic of the house in Belfast, charging his friends in cash or in kind. As a public performer he was evidently also a renowned storyteller, whose 'witty little yarns were received with roars of laughter'. The content of his early programmes consisted largely if not entirely of films bought in or hired from France and England; one that sounded of his own making, showing the ocean dashing wildly in a 'Donegal cave', was perhaps only locally labelled, like another stock piece, showing a fire brigade turning out, which was billed as local wherever it was shown. The repertoire was considerably enlarged in 1900 by the inclusion of films about the Boer War. In that year Professor Kineto and his Anglo-Parisienne Biorama ran for no less than six consecutive weeks at the Empire Theatre. One evening in March, when the Irish and Welsh rugby teams, along with Distillery and Blackburn Rovers football teams, were entertained by the theatre management, Kineto 'made a hit with a number of bioramic portraits of the captains'. When Kineto 'turned out the light and turned on his Biocinoramaniatograph', as one humorous reviewer called it, audiences were invariably well pleased by the varied programme he presented.

The high point of Kineto's achievement as showman and film-maker came in April 1900. As the *Irish Playgoer* of 19 April reported:

> The enterprising Belfast Cinematographer . . . made a big record on the occasion of the Queen's entry into Dublin. He started from Belfast by the early train, with his assistants and apparatus, got into position along the route of the Queen's procession in Dublin, took two separate films in perfect style, left Dublin by the quarter to three train, got to Belfast at six, carried out all the necessary developments in a remarkably quick time, and at ten o'clock the same night the Queen's entry into Dublin was exhibited in the Empire Theatre in Belfast. This is undoubtedly a record in the new and popular art, for though the Derby Race was exhibited at the Palace Cinematograph in London on the evening of the race last year, still it might be remembered that the operators were in the developing room a considerable time before six in the evening. Professor Kineto and the managers of the Empire Theatre in Belfast were, we understand, receiving numerous telegrams of congratulation during the night from the managers and proprietors of many of the largest music halls across the water.

Several Belfast newspapers reported that Kineto's films were actually developed on the train; and there was apparently a private viewing before the public one at the

Empire. Later showings to large crowds at the Ulster Hall in Belfast and the Guildhall in Londonderry were received with equal enthusiasm.

In April 1901 Kineto was appearing at the Alhambra Theatre in Belfast. By that time his varied repertoire included films of ship launches – *Celtic* and *Shamrock* – as well as more football teams (Cliftonville and the Freebooters, a Dublin amateur side). As a columnist in *Nomad's Weekly* (4 May) put it: 'The truth is Kineto is a wonderfully up-to-date little man who would, I verily believe, be first to biograph the aborigines of the moon – if he was only tall enough to reach it.' As at the Empire, he was re-engaged week after week. He was in Scotland in January 1902, but the following month was back in Belfast, when he showed a film – one of his own, apparently – of the Ireland v. Wales rugby match at Swansea the year before. This and his film of a match between Collegians FC and Mountain Ash went down well at a Collegians concert held in the YMCA.

In Kineto's book of press cuttings, the source of all this information, there are no more entries until December 1908.[7] By that time, Hicks had given up the Metropole Hotel (as it was then known), which in 1908 was acquired by the Presbyterian Mission to the Deaf and Dumb, and had left Belfast. Under the heading 'Franco-British Honour for Belfast Man', an English newspaper printed the following, which one could believe to have been written by Hicks himself, were it not for the misspelling of his name:

> In May last during a business visit to Belfast, Mr J.W. Hix, the well known cinematographer and art photographer, was telegraphed for by the promoters of the Ballymaclinton Village at the Franco-British Exhibition to proceed immediately to London for the purpose of taking cinematograph views of the King's visit to the world-famed village. Mr Hix carried out the commission to the complete satisfaction of all concerned, and the pictures have since been extensively exhibited with marked success. The experience was not a novel one, for Mr Hix, as will be recalled by many, executed a similar commission for the management of the Empire Theatre on the day of the arrival of the late Queen Victoria in Ireland, taking cinematograph views at Kingstown and Dublin, developing the films in the train, and showing them in Belfast the same evening to a crowded audience. At the Franco-British Exhibition Mr Hix had full control of the photographic work in connection with Ballymaclinton, and had the honour of being awarded a gold medal by the judges for a collection of large art portraits of celebrities, including the Lord Bishop of Down and Connor and Dromore, the Countess of Battersea, Father Bernard Vaughan, Lieutenant Shackleton (Antarctic explorer), the Bishop of Exeter. Mr Hix is to be warmly congratulated on the tribute thus paid to his skill and enterprise in the photographic world.

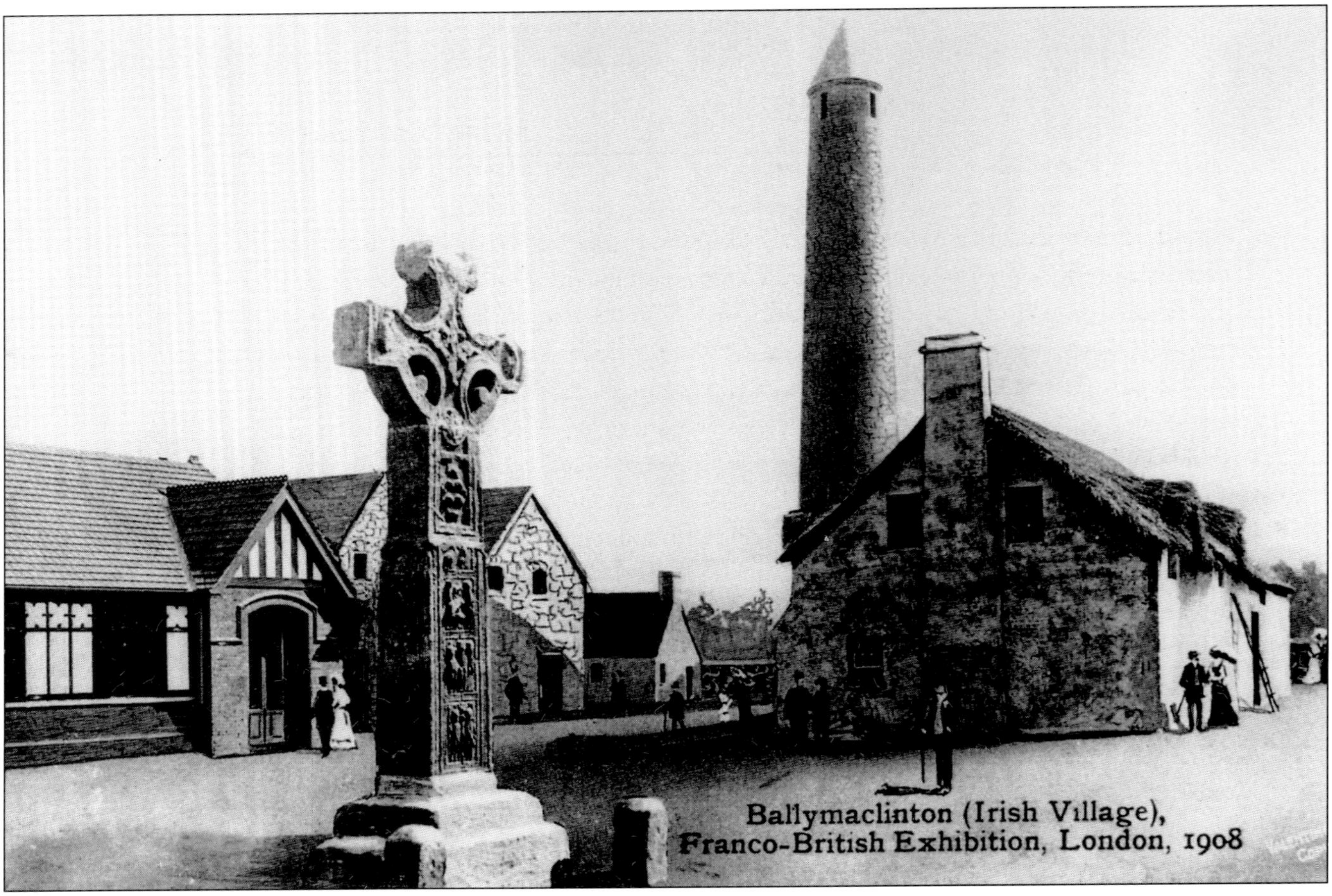

Ballymaclinton village, at the Franco-British Exhibition of 1908, from a postcard by Valentine.
MAGNI / UM

The Belfast firm of McClinton and Thompson was notable for its 'Barilla' soap. It was taken over by Brown's of Donaghmore, sponsors of the village. 'Ballybrown', however, would have sounded less Irish.

The Exhibition took place at the White City in London. Afterwards, for two weeks, in what so far as his cuttings book is concerned was the swansong of Professor Kineto, Hicks showed his films of the King with President Fallières and *Life in Ballymaclinton* to audiences in Tunbridge Wells. The views of Ballymaclinton claimed to show 'the ordinary life of the Irish Colleens, their dances and their native surroundings'. In fact Ballymaclinton, an advertising vehicle for McClinton's soap, was based upon the actual village of Donaghmore, County Tyrone. It featured replicas of an imaginary round tower and of the actual Celtic high cross in Donaghmore, the latter a favourite subject for photographers.

It is difficult to believe that Hicks and his Biorama retired completely from public view at this point. The advent of permanent cinemas, however, must have driven Kineto off the stage. Biographical details thereafter are scarce. His younger son, who died in England in 1946, left a son, who was born in Kensington in 1922. The eldest son, described as an 'advertising contractor', settled at Herne Bay in Kent. One descendant became a professional photographer and was working in London about twenty years ago. Hicks himself died in Chelsea in February 1938, leaving no will and an estate of less than a thousand pounds. His death certificate describes him as 'retired hotel proprietor', so he may have reverted to his former employment. His wife survived him by a few years, dying in 1943.

Hicks does appear to have been the leading native pioneer of moving pictures in Ireland, both as a cinematographer and as a maker of films. Such was the speed of technical change and commercial development in the new medium that his heyday did not last very long but, while it did, Professor Kineto's name achieved a more than local reputation. Though St John Ervine, the noted Irish playwright, was later to recall 'the days when the cinematograph was a despised turn in music-halls', showmanship was to be the essential element in the success of this great new development in the history of photography.[8]

Another enterprising photographer and cinematographer operating in the North of Ireland was Hicks's contemporary A.D. Coon. Allen Daniel Coon (1867–1938) was an American, born in Buffalo, New York. His father was a Baptist minister, his mother reputedly a native American, though he seldom spoke of his origins and early life. He knew, and was possibly related to, George Eastman, the founder of Kodak, who came from the same area. After studying law at university in New York state he set up in his home town as an attorney. But the law was evidently far too sedentary a profession for someone as restless and enterprising as Coon. After spells in California and Alaska prospecting for gold he came to England about 1900, apparently in the company of Eastman, and then to Ireland. In 1902 he set up Coon's Genuine American Living Picture and Variety Company and his picture postcard publishing business. His 'permanent address' at this stage was South Wall, Londonderry, but his letterhead included the words 'Also On Tour'. He was to be on tour for the rest of his life, more or less, till he died in Sligo, still travelling, in 1938.[9]

The combination of cinematographic travelling showman and photographic publisher that was Coon's peculiar contribution to the history of photography in the North of Ireland was extensively listed in his first letterhead. He provided 'outfits and films for hire; lantern slides from any picture, design, or drawing; blocks, enlargements, and photo postcards, in any process', and announced himself as publisher of the 'Coon' series of pictorial postcards. Theatres, music halls, organisations, schools, clergymen, private parties etcetera were offered 'First-class Living Picture Entertainment – Educational and Scientific – combined with Mirth, Music, Melody, and Mystery'. Encouraging testimonials from satisfied patrons in the west of the province were reproduced.

After his marriage to Clara Nelson, who was an active partner in his photographic enterprises in between producing seven children, Coon moved his base of operations to Letterkenny in County Donegal. There he became involved in a number of other commercial activities, as a dealer in motor cars, agent for Rex-Jap motorcycles and managing director of a haulage company that ran lorries and a charabanc between Letterkenny and Londonderry. From Letterkenny he toured the country with his travelling cinema. He also established permanent cinemas in Letterkenny, Buncrana and Killybegs. At Letterkenny, where the venue was the town's Literary Institute, the first three rows of seats were bookable in advance and those who occupied them were served free tea, biscuits and cigarettes during the inevitably frequent intervals. Another ingenious idea was the rooftop light which told the inhabitants of Killybegs that the film show was on. The cinema at Buncrana, which opened in 1916, was a commission from the government, to provide entertainment for the soldiers and sailors stationed in and around Lough Swilly during the First World War.[10]

Coon may also have had a hand in the establishment in 1910 of one of the first

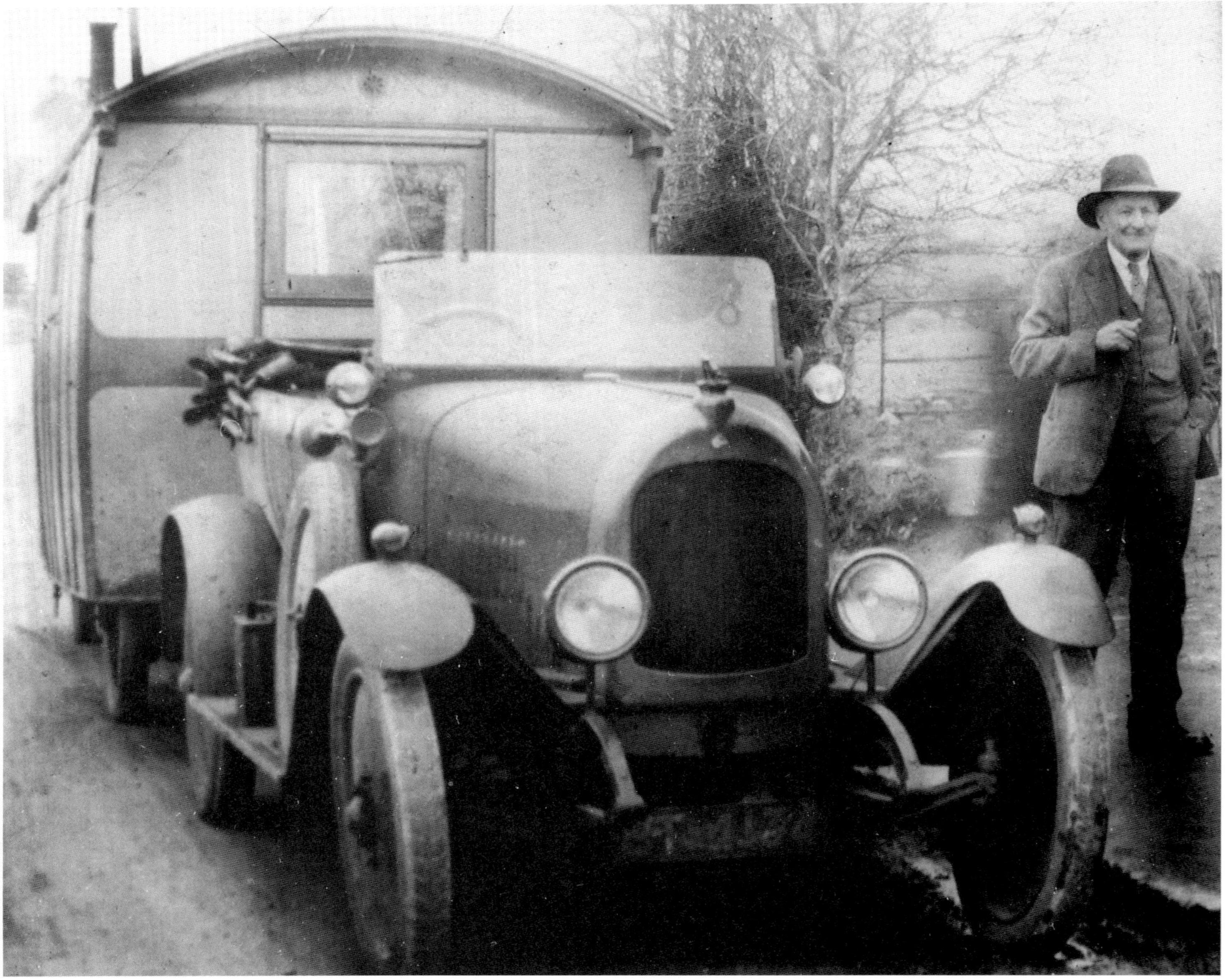

A.D. Coon on the road with his travelling show, c. 1930.
BY KIND PERMISSION OF ALLEN COON

cinemas in Belfast, the Princess Picture Palace on the Newtownards Road, though its main proprietor was a local greengrocer named Anderson. Despite its name, the Princess was anything but palatial: its 1,200 seats consisted of wooden benches, and the slightly better ones in the raised back stalls were separated from would-be social climbers in the pit by barbed wire.[11]

In essence, however, Coon was a travelling showman, taking to the road every summer with his motor-drawn caravans (one a studio-cum-darkroom, the other living quarters, supplemented on occasion by a tent). When he arrived at his destination for the night, he would proceed to take a 16 mm film of the place and some of its people. Enlivened by his commentary, this 'News Reel' fascinated the audience at the subsequent performance. At one stage Coon owned a complete set of early Chaplin films, the kind of material that would have formed the staple of a travelling show. During the day, he took portraits and views which he later added to his list of picture postcards. The latter, straightforward photographs of good quality in sepia tones, were printed in Germany and retailed through local shops. They cost the retailer, whose name appeared on them, less than £5 for 2,000.[12] As well as these topographical postcards, other 'Irish Views' contained topical comment, such as the picture of an aged couple near Downings in County Donegal with their well-laden donkey. This is entitled 'Bringing Home the Old-Age Pension (Bread, Tobacco, Tea, Paraffin, Potatoes, Sugar, Coals, etc.)' – a reference to the recent introduction of Lloyd George's great reform.

In 1921, when Ireland was partitioned, Coon and his family left Letterkenny, now in the Irish Free State, and based themselves at Moira, County Down, where when not on the move they lived in their caravans at a quarry (Quarry View was their address). A prospectus of the late 1920s shows us that the Letterkenny end was maintained, however, so Coon could continue to operate throughout the North of Ireland. An advertising photograph of the same date shows the impressive range of equipment – cameras, lenses, spotlights and so on – that Coon had at his disposal at that time. Some had been purchased recently from the studio of the late William Allison and from the Belfast branch of Turnbull and Sons, the Glasgow firm which closed in 1929. Pictures of Coon show an energetic-looking, heavily moustached figure with a glint in his eye and a wide-brimmed Stetson on his head, very different from the sober image of most photographers. He remained an extrovert showman to the end, still giving a weekly showing of films in the Orange Hall in Moira until shortly before his death. When he died, the body was brought from Sligo and buried in the Unitarian churchyard at Moira. His estate was valued at only £200. His more substantial legacy consisted of his postcard views, many of which survive now as collectors' items. The task of such collectors is made easier by Coon's own system of numbering and dating: each postcard bears a number

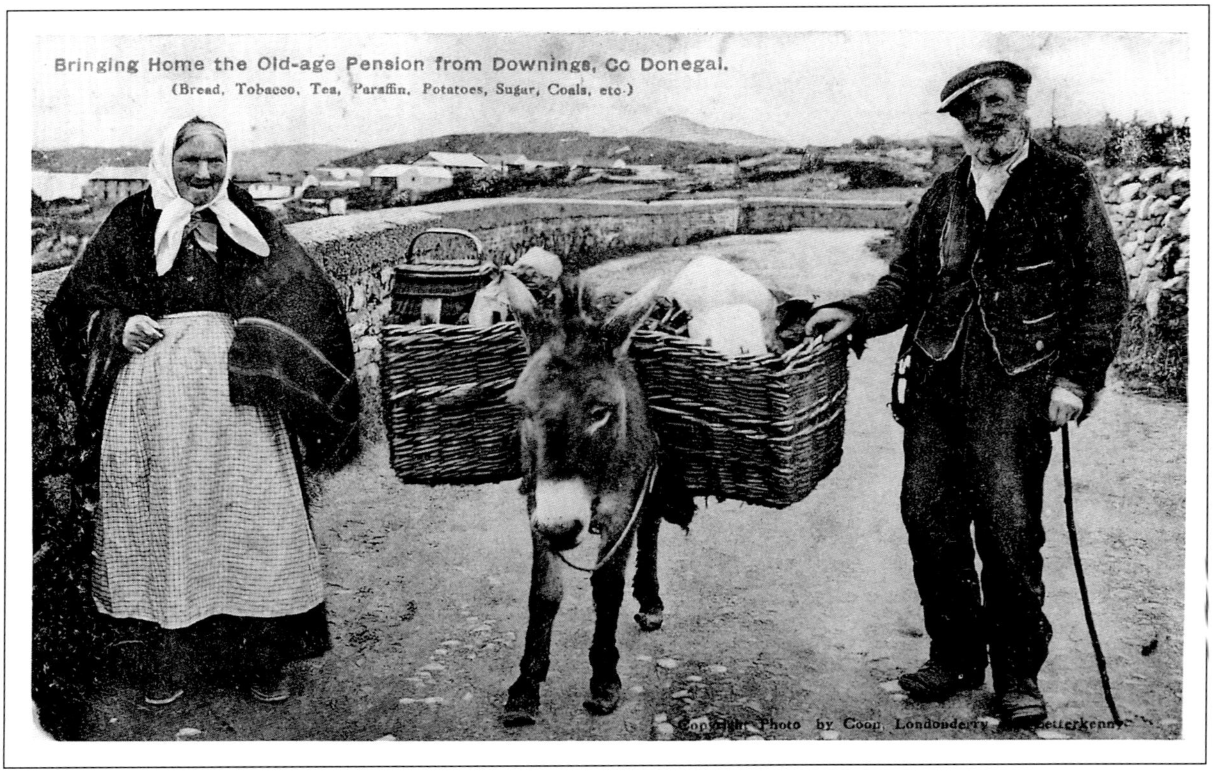

Postcard by A.D. Coon, c. 1910.
BY KIND PERMISSION OF ALLEN COON

made up of the last two figures of the year, followed by a running number.[13]

Two of his children, a daughter Gladys and a son Gaynor, had become interested in photography and assisted him in his latter years. After his death they kept the strictly photographic side of the business going for a while, but the outbreak of the war in 1939 soon made it impossible to continue. The caravans and their contents decayed at Quarry View till abandoned and eventually destroyed. A more dramatic tale, that in a last act of showmanship Coon gathered everything together and deliberately tipped it all into the flooded quarry, appears to be without foundation, but no doubt indicates a well-founded reputation for flamboyant behaviour.

Other developments
1890–1939

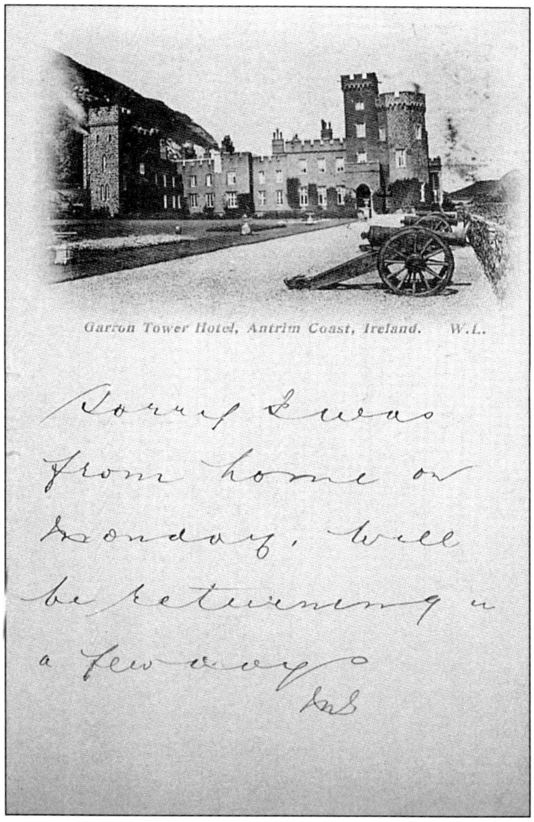

Postcard by W. Lawerence, Dublin, featuring Garron Tower Hotel, County Antrim, 1902.

BY KIND PERMISSION OF DESMOND QUAIL

Next to the discovery and development of moving pictures, the most important advances during the half-century before the outbreak of the Second World War were in colour photography and photographic publication. Attempts to produce coloured photographs went right back to the daguerreotype itself. The realistic appearance of daguerreotype portraits could be enhanced by tinting or painting, but it proved difficult to find an entirely satisfactory or practical method of doing so.[1] Highlighting details of feature or costume, rather than attempting to imitate an entire painted portrait, sometimes gave the best results. Later photographs on paper or canvas were easier to colour convincingly. The best of these retouched images were very good indeed, almost indistinguishable from traditional portraiture when mounted and framed, especially if done to a small scale. Most 'artist

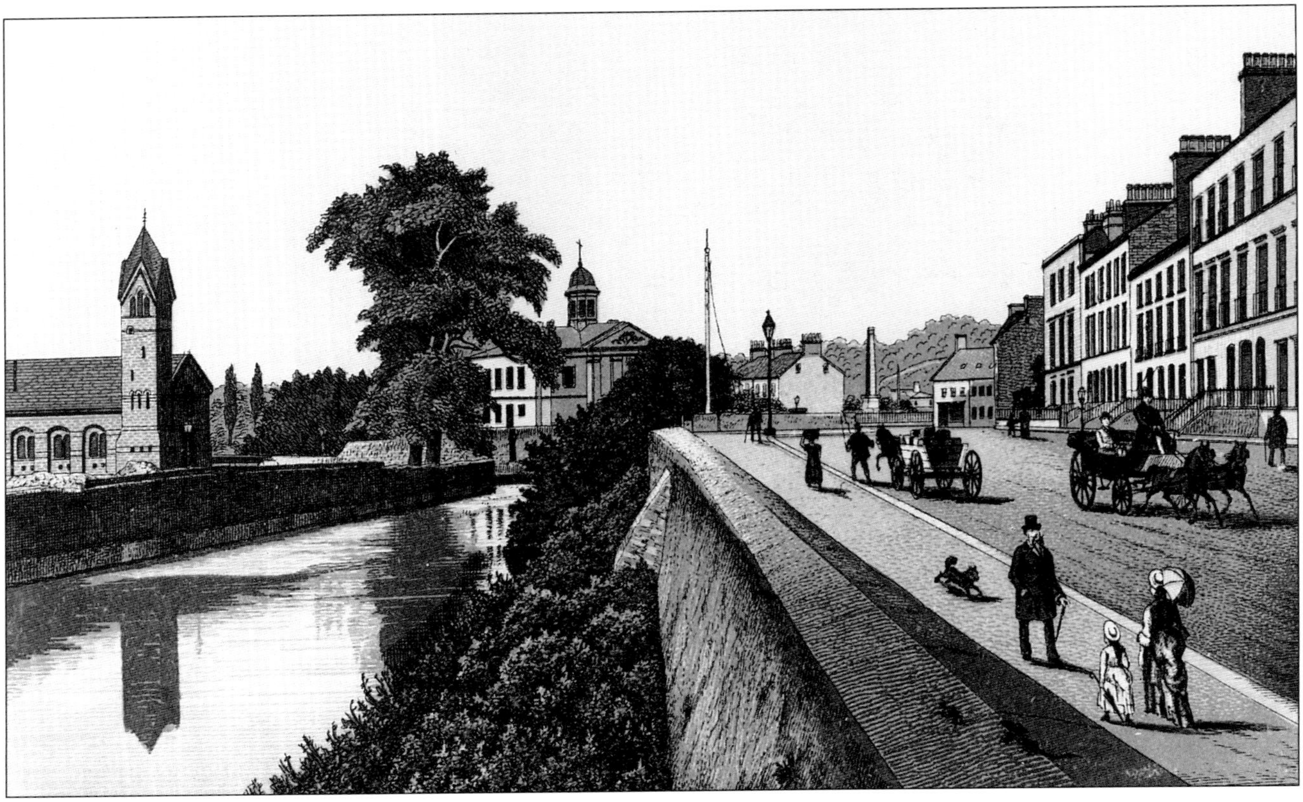

Court House and Trevor Hill, Newry, *c.* 1885, from *Album of Newry and Bessbrook* by W. Lawrence, Dublin.
MAGNI / UM

These early Lawrence albums, and others like them, consisted of photographs redrawn as engravings, giving an unnaturally well-defined look. Publishers could also insert human and animal figures beyond the reach of the cameras of the time.

photographers' prided themselves on their ability to do such work, or employed competent people to do it for them.

Not until the 1890s was a practicable colour photography process invented. In 1892, John Joly, professor of biology at Trinity College, Dublin, announced a method which involved the creation of a rather crude colour transparency by sandwiching monochrome plates together with special screens inscribed with red, green and blue lines (about 30 to the inch).[2] Though important historically, Joly's process was soon superseded in practice by a much superior one – the autochrome, patented by the Lumière brothers in France in 1904 and marketed by them in an improved form three years later.[3] Easy to use, though expensive and requiring long exposures, it produced subtle if not always reliable colouring. The chief drawback of the autochrome, however, was that being a positive glass plate it was only capable of being used with a viewer; there was no simple and efficient method, at the time, for turning these transparencies into colour prints. Consequently, the process was of interest mostly to amateurs and experimental art photographers.

Examples of Irish autochromes are hard to come by. The only published record of early Irish subjects, dating from 1913, has appeared recently in France. Funded by the wealthy banker Albert Kahn, two young Frenchwomen named Mespoulet and Mignon were despatched to Ireland in that year to record in colour some of the architectural and ethnographic scenes already widely familiar in black and white. This excursion was part of an enormous project, covering traditional life in many areas of the world, which produced thousands of autochromes, now housed in a

Paris museum. Mespoulet and Mignon took seventy-five colour photographs, all but two of which were successful. They visited Galway, Clonmacnoise, Glendalough and the Boyne Valley (the farthest north they went) photographing ancient monuments, women of the Claddagh in their distinctive costume, and survivals such as the coracle fishermen on the Boyne. The best of these pictures, with their soft tints, are very pleasing indeed.[4]

For all the interest in autochromes and other processes – such as those of Louis Dufay, another Frenchman, and of the Agfa Company in Germany – by which it became more and more achievable, by 1939 colour photography still had some way to go before it could claim anything like perfection in the rendering and fixing of true chromatic values. Much remained to be achieved in that direction after the Second World War. By contrast, the half-century after 1890 was notable for another major development that was largely complete by 1939, namely the revolution in photographic reproduction in black and white by means of the half-tone process.

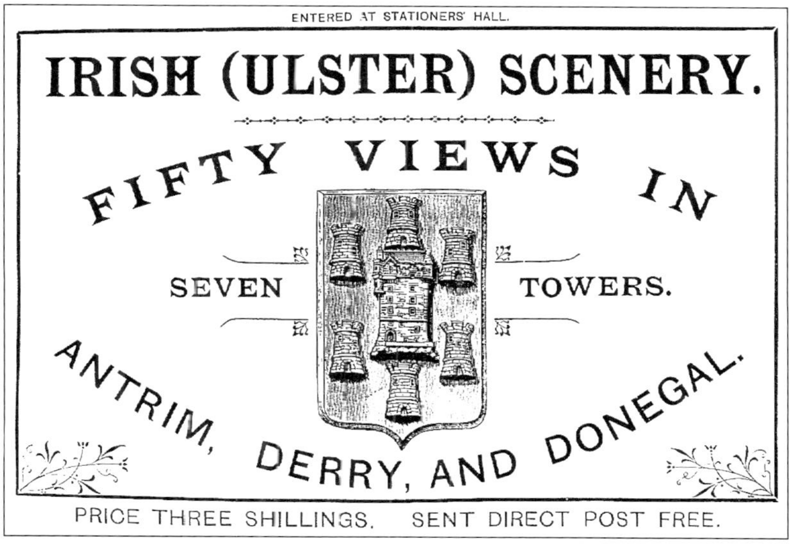
ENTERED AT STATIONERS' HALL.

IRISH (ULSTER) SCENERY.

FIFTY VIEWS IN

SEVEN TOWERS.

ANTRIM, DERRY, AND DONEGAL.

PRICE THREE SHILLINGS. SENT DIRECT POST FREE.

Title page of *Irish (Ulster) Scenery: Fifty Views in Antrim, Derry and Donegal.* (Ballymena, c. 1910).
MAGNI / UM

This well-produced volume consists of half-tone reproductions (from blocks made by Meisenbach and Company, the London branch of a German firm) of photographs by Welch (35), Lawrence (8), Valentine (3), Lee, Mayer and Fullerton. The publisher was Thomas Rigby, a Lancashire man who for thirty years was stationmaster of the Belfast and Northern Counties Railway in Ballymena, retiring in 1903. His first venture in tourist publishing – 'Rigby's Guide', a booklet costing one shilling – had great success in the north of England and was reprinted.

Before the 1890s, reproduction of photographs on a large scale had been restricted by the lack of a technically satisfactory and economically viable method of printing. The first photographs used for book illustration were actual prints tipped-in, such as those by the Dublin photographer F.H. Mares, whose 'Irish Views' were used in a series issued by a Glasgow publisher in 1867, one of which was entitled *The Giant's Causeway and the North*. Alternatively, they had to be transformed by artists into engravings or woodcuts before they could be printed. The best early processes were the Woodburytype, invented by Walter Woodbury as far back as 1866, and the carbon print. Though these gave good results, in the sense that they provided convincing copies of the originals from which they were taken, neither could be printed directly onto the page by a printing machine. They were therefore unsuitable for mass publication.

The principle of half-tone reproduction, or photo-engraving, was known as early as 1852. It was not practically feasible, however, until 1881, when F.E. Ives first patented his work in the United States. Ives refined his method by later modifications. By the turn of the century the whole business of presenting photographic images to the public had been revolutionised by making it possible to print both type and illustration in the one operation. From the early 1890s, half-tone illustrations began to appear in books, magazines and pamphlets, even to a limited extent in newspapers. (The poor quality of newsprint, however, long deterred most daily papers from adopting photography as early or as extensively as the weekly journals did; 'a crisp handmade drawing seemed preferable to an indistinct camera image'.[5]) In Dublin, a new weekly called the *Illustrograph* appeared, profusely illustrated with photographs by both professionals and amateurs.

The advent of the half-tone process block soon had an effect on the way 'views' photographers published and marketed their work. The trade in original prints declined, to be increasingly replaced by the sale of souvenir booklets of reproduced photographs.[6] Lawrence's series of *Emerald Isle* albums, introduced in the 1890s, included several relating to the North of Ireland. Welch, whose famous 'Irish Views' rivalled those of Lawrence in scope and quality if not in quantity and sophistication of marketing, went on producing albums of original prints for special occasions and purposes. For example, the photographs he took of the construction and launching of a whole succession of Harland and Wolff liners were made up into albums. A later one, now in the Ulster Museum collection, appears to have been compiled for the Slieve Donard Hotel at Newcastle, County Down; apart from views of the hotel itself and the Newcastle area, it includes a photograph of a group of wounded soldiers entertained for tea in 1915. The success of Welch's scientific photographs as academic illustrations is mentioned elsewhere.

Publication for the tourist market provided a substantial and growing outlet for the work of many photographers. The *Giant's Causeway* volume in the 'Camera Series', published *c.* 1890 by the Liverpool firm of Brown and Rawcliffe, contained over forty views by Welch; all appear to be engravings. A later railway guide, *The North of Ireland Illustrated*, published by the Bournemouth firm of W. Mate and Sons, consisted of over sixty excellent half-tones by Ayton, Lee, Hogg and others. By 1907 it had run to a fifth edition. Ayton's view of Shipquay Place in Londonderry gives a good view of his own impressive studio. *Picturesque Donegal*, published in London the following year and illustrated by the photographs of its author, Edgar Shrubsole, was another railway guide, this time for the Great Northern Railway (Ireland) Company. From the same period, but lacking either the photographer's name or the date, come productions published in the names of local tradesmen, such as *Warrenpoint, Rostrevor and District*, an album of eighteen views published by Jones, Sons and Company of Warrenpoint, chemists and druggists, or a similar *Views of Newry and District*, published by James Irwin and Company, booksellers and stationers of Newry. In both cases, the quality of the reproductions is good. A particularly interesting venture was the 'Irish View Scenery' series of cigarette cards, issued by Gallaher's between 1897 and 1910 – six hundred views in all, genuine miniature bromides produced by a photographic rather than a printing process to begin with, later reproduced from letterpress blocks; many were Lawrence views, others by Welch.[7] Increasingly, reproduced photographs were used directly in advertising and marketing material, such as the brochure produced by Belfast Ropeworks in 1899, which was entirely (and extensively) illustrated by Welch's work. Hogg's photographs filled the brochures produced for the official opening of the new City Hall in Belfast in 1906 and the new College of Technology the following year. In the 1930s Hogg was a major, if unacknowledged, contributor to the lavishly illustrated annual publication of the new Ulster Tourist Development Association. Once started, the process became endless and, more and more, the work of the photographers concerned was credited to them.

It is less easy to trace the early photographers who worked directly for newspapers as employees. They tended to be backroom boys, sometimes with other tasks to perform: the first photographer employed by the *Londonderry Standard* in the mid-1920s, a man of European origin named Lackner, was also the process engraver, the person who made the block or zinc plate used in the printing.[8] The

Camera room at McCaw, Stevenson and Orr Ltd, Belfast printers, December 1925, by A.R. Hogg.

MAGNI / UM (HOGG COLLECTION)

MSO's new 'Marcotype' colour printing process, perfected in the early 1920s, involved the making of four-colour separations by camera work – one example of the increasing use of photography in commercial printing of all kinds. Note the curious effect to the right of this picture, where unrelated bits of two different operatives appear.

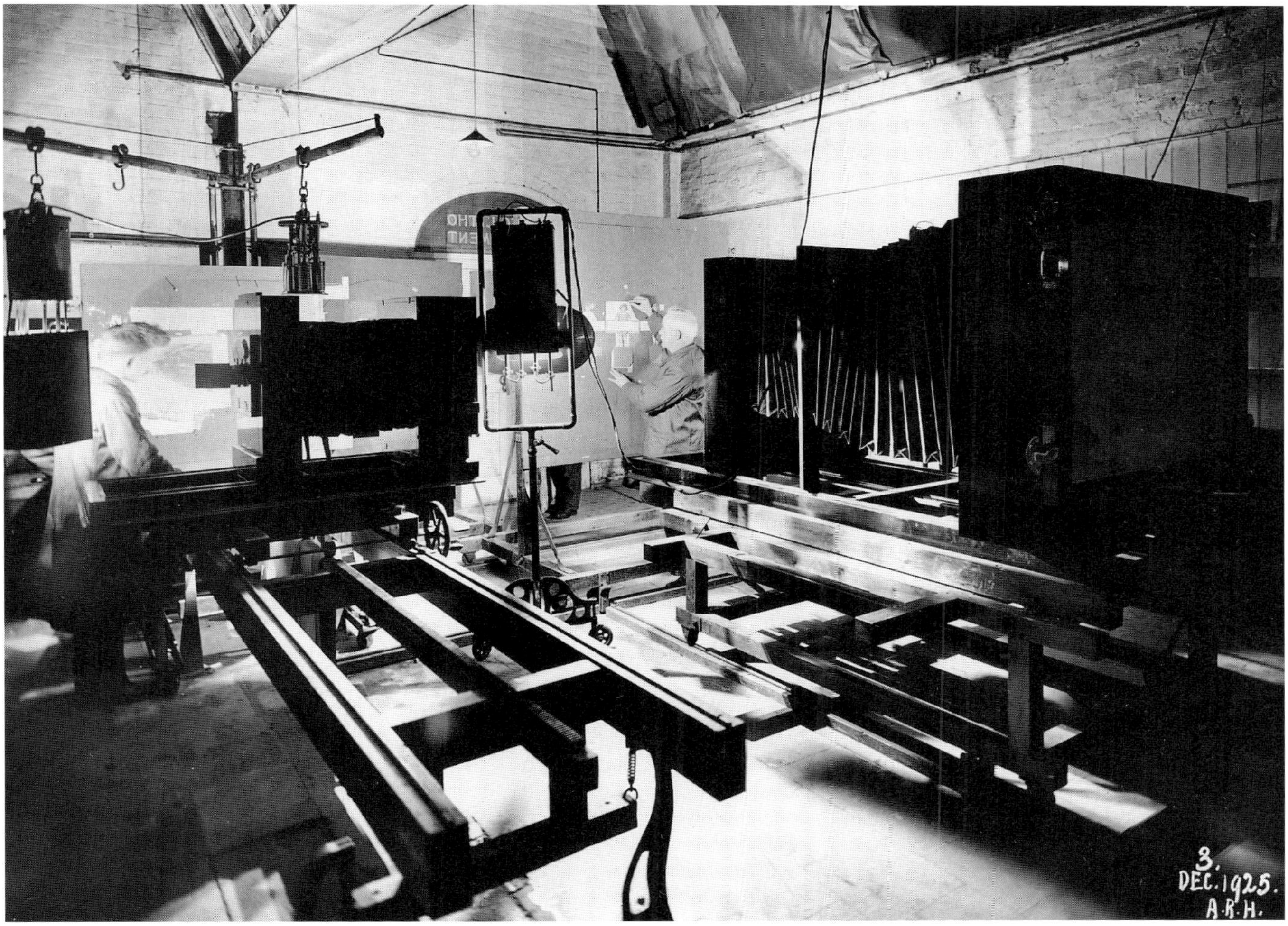

official history of the *Belfast Telegraph* asserts that from 1907 onward the paper 'backed the major advances being made in photography to such an extent that technologically the *Telegraph* was years ahead of its contemporaries'.[9] This was undoubtedly true, for its owners, W. and G. Baird, had a large general printing business and were major suppliers of process blocks for all kinds of purposes, but no names of its staff photographers survive earlier than the 1920s; even then they were obscure figures. They were by no means the *Telegraph's* only source of images of course. Among others, the artist Arthur Campbell, who was employed as a print designer on the staff, sold some of his interesting amateur photographs to the paper in the 1930s.[10] The story of photographers in the city's morning dailies – the *Belfast News-Letter*, the *Northern Whig* and the *Irish News* – is equally obscure in this period. By 1939, however, photographs were an indispensable feature of most newspapers.

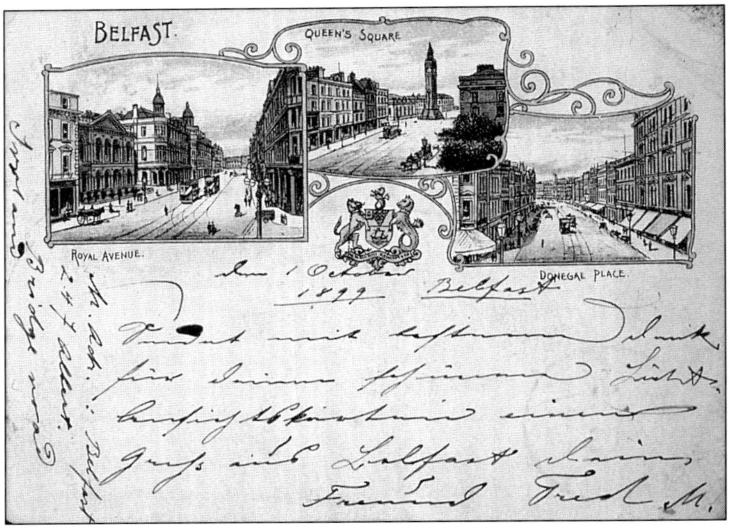

An early greetings card from Belfast, with engraved views based on photographs. This particular card was sent on 1 October 1899 to a correspondent in St Petersburg, Russia.

BY KIND PERMISSION OF DESMOND QUAIL

Lastly, in this brief survey of the use of photographic reproduction and its effect on photographers in the north of Ireland, we come to the interesting question of the picture postcard. The idea of an 'open post-sheet' (*offenes Postblatt*) at a reduced postal rate was proposed in 1865 by an official of the Post Office of the North German Confederation, the forerunner of the German Empire. The suggestion was rejected at the time, but four years later something very similar was adopted throughout the Austrian Empire (Austria-Hungary) and the postcard was launched. Germany and the United Kingdom followed suit in 1870, France and other European countries and the United States soon after. Success was immediate – in Austria-Hungary, there were sales of nearly 3 million in the first three months. Sixty million were sold in the first six months in the USA. In the United Kingdom, where postage was set at a halfpenny, some objections were at first raised by people who thought the cheap rate demeaning to correspondents (or deplorable on the grounds that anyone who liked, such as one's servants,

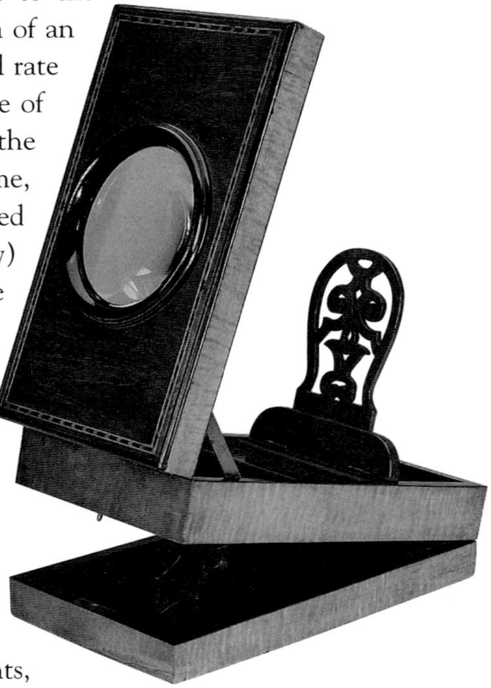

Right
Postcard viewer, *c.* 1905.

MAGNI / UM

The postcard-collecting craze of the 1890s and early 1900s gave rise to the manufacture and sale of various accessories – chiefly albums, but also postcard viewers with built-in magnifiers. At the upper end of the market these were handsome things, like the one illustrated here.

PRIVATE COLLECTION

could read the message). Gladstone, however, was an enthusiastic user and no fewer than 575,000 cards were sold by the GPO on the first day and 75 million in the first year. These officially printed cards were plain vehicles for short messages. From 1894, privately printed cards featuring pictures and other decoration could be posted at the halfpenny rate – the Edinburgh firm of George Stewart began publishing view postcards in that year, soon followed by James Valentine and Sons of Dundee – but British firms were for some years prevented from competing effectively in the production of postcards by a regulation limiting the size of card allowed. This did not change until 1899 when the standard was enlarged to 5½-by-3½ inches. The result was greater scope for illustration, a process extended further in 1902 by the adoption of the idea of dividing the back of the card into two parts (one for the message, the other for the address), which left one entire side free for illustration. Meanwhile, Germany had achieved virtually a European monopoly in the production of picture postcards, so much so that early greetings cards are known to collectors as *Grüss Aus* ('Greetings From') cards. For many years, most British publishers of picture postcards continued to order their cards from Saxony or Bavaria; and those who printed in the United Kingdom not uncommonly employed German craftsmen.[11]

Clogher Valley Railway train in the village street at Caledon, County Armagh, *c.* 1905, postcard by an unknown photographer.

BY KIND PERMISSION OF DESMOND QUAIL

The railway ran between Tynan, County Armagh, and Maguiresbridge, County Fermanagh – a distance of thirty-seven miles – from 1887 to 1942.

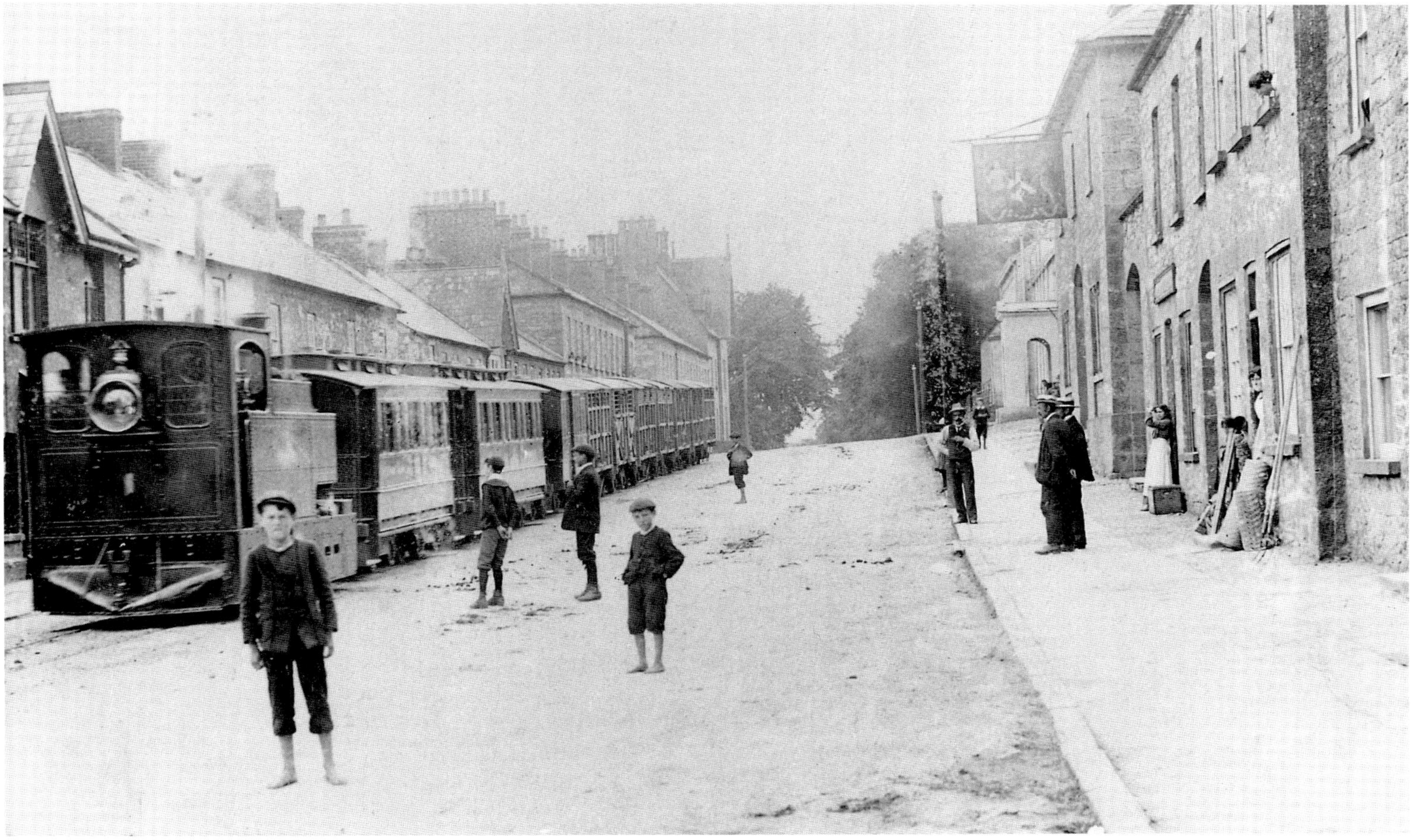

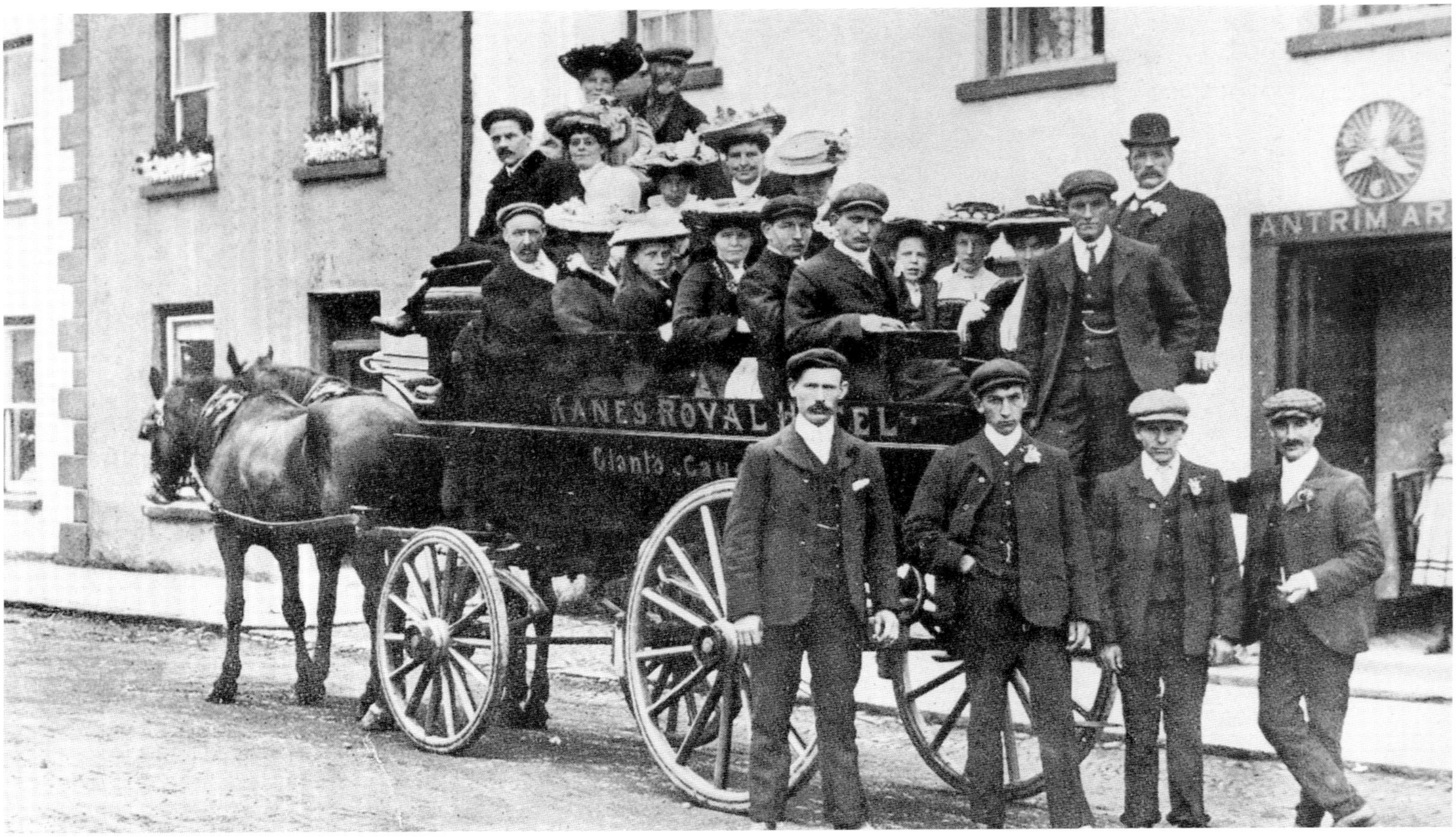

Dunseverick Choir on an outing to the Giant's Causeway from Bushmills, County Antrim, c. 1910, postcard by R.J. Malone.
BY KIND PERMISSION OF DESMOND QUAIL

Malone's main studio was in Ballymoney. Like Lee of Portrush, and others, he also operated seasonally at the Causeway.

Like carte-de-visite photographs in the 1860s, picture postcards became the subject of an extraordinary craze for collecting. Even the aged Queen Victoria succumbed to the new cartomania (or cartophilia as its victims preferred to call it). Special albums were produced to cater for them. Some of the cards, especially the coloured ones, used illustrations other than photographs, though many lithographs were taken from photographs coloured by hand. A great many, however, were halftone reproductions or, later, real photographic prints.

First in the field in Ireland was William Lawrence of Dublin, whose 'Irish Views' began to appear in postcard form in the early 1900s. Many Lawrence views of the north of Ireland were included. The Belfast photographer Hogg, on honeymoon in Killybegs in 1907, sent a Lawrence postcard to a cousin back home to say that he was 'busy taking views for postcards' of his own.[12] Mention has been made earlier of A.D. Coon as a noted publisher of his own postcard views, the earliest of which date from the same period. Later, W.A. Green with his 'Wagtail' series produced some fine work. Later still, in the 1930s, Stephen Butler began to publish a series of small-town views, similar to Coon's, from his base at Carndonagh, County Donegal. Like the collections of larger-format views published earlier in the name of local shopkeepers, numerous groups of local postcard views appeared. Photographers in tourist areas, Lee in Portrush for example, were open to competition not only from other Irish photographers or publishers such as Lawrence and

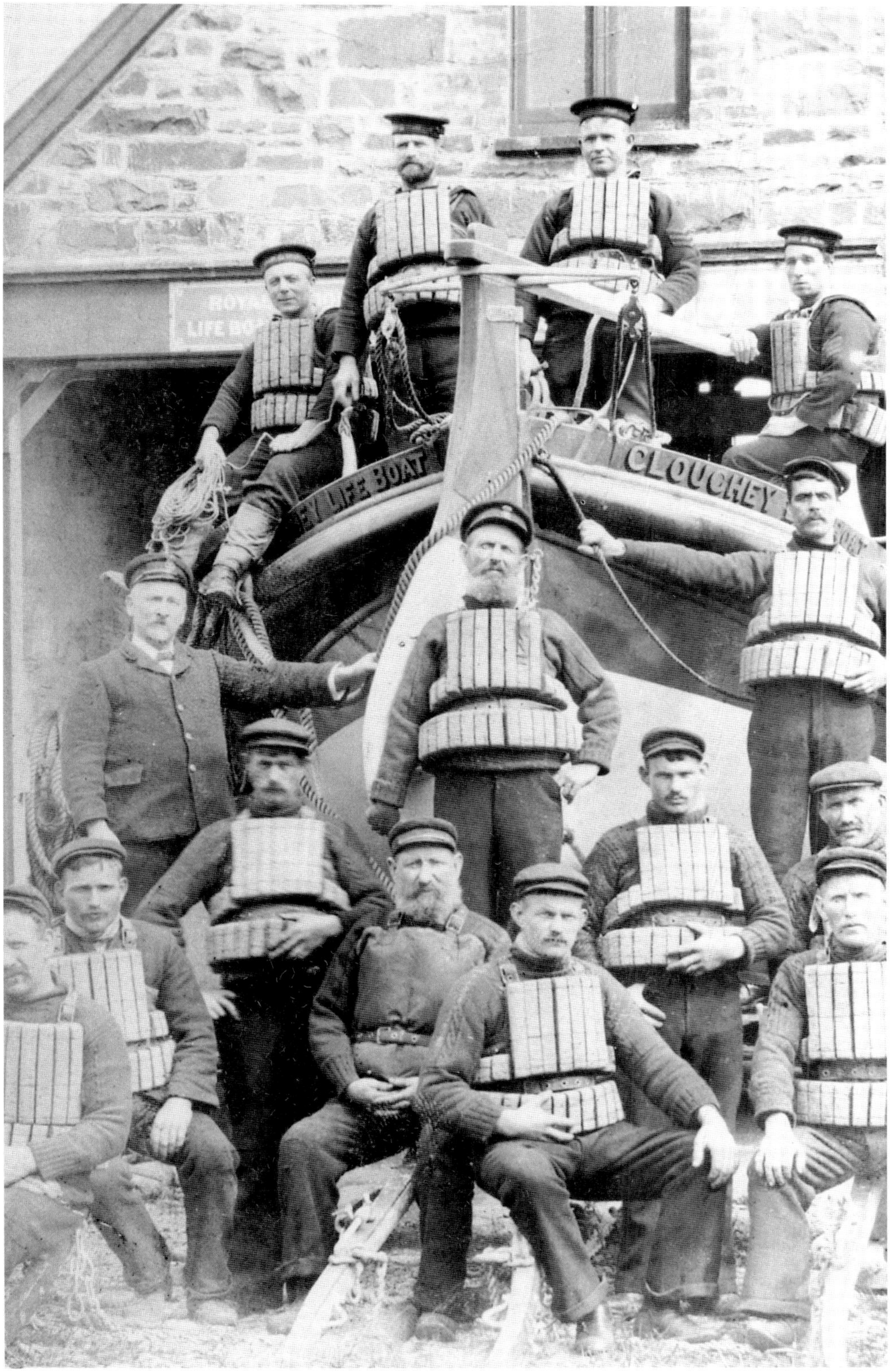

Lifeboat crew, Cloughey, County Down, *c*. 1910, postcard by an unknown photographer.
BY KIND PERMISSION OF DESMOND QUAILL

Eason's (Signal series) but also from the big cross-channel firms such as Valentine's of Dundee or Ritchie's (WR & S) of Edinburgh though, as we have noted, these sometimes purchased the work of local studios rather than go to the expense of sending their own photographers.

During the period 1880–1914, when the halfpenny postage rate applied, the total number of cards posted in the United Kingdom rose from 122.9 million in the year 1880–1 to 926.5 million in 1913–14.[13] A large part of this increase occurred during the last fourteen years of the period, in other words after the picture postcard had been freed from restrictions and when the use of photographic reproductions as illustrations had become more and more common. There are no separate figures available for Ireland, and of course a good many postcards did not feature photographs, but the sheer quantity of surviving examples reinforces the conclusion one can draw from common experience and observation, namely that the picture postcard was a godsend to many Irish photographers.

Two developments in the photographic profession itself in the north of Ireland between the wars are worth mentioning. The socially emancipated atmosphere of

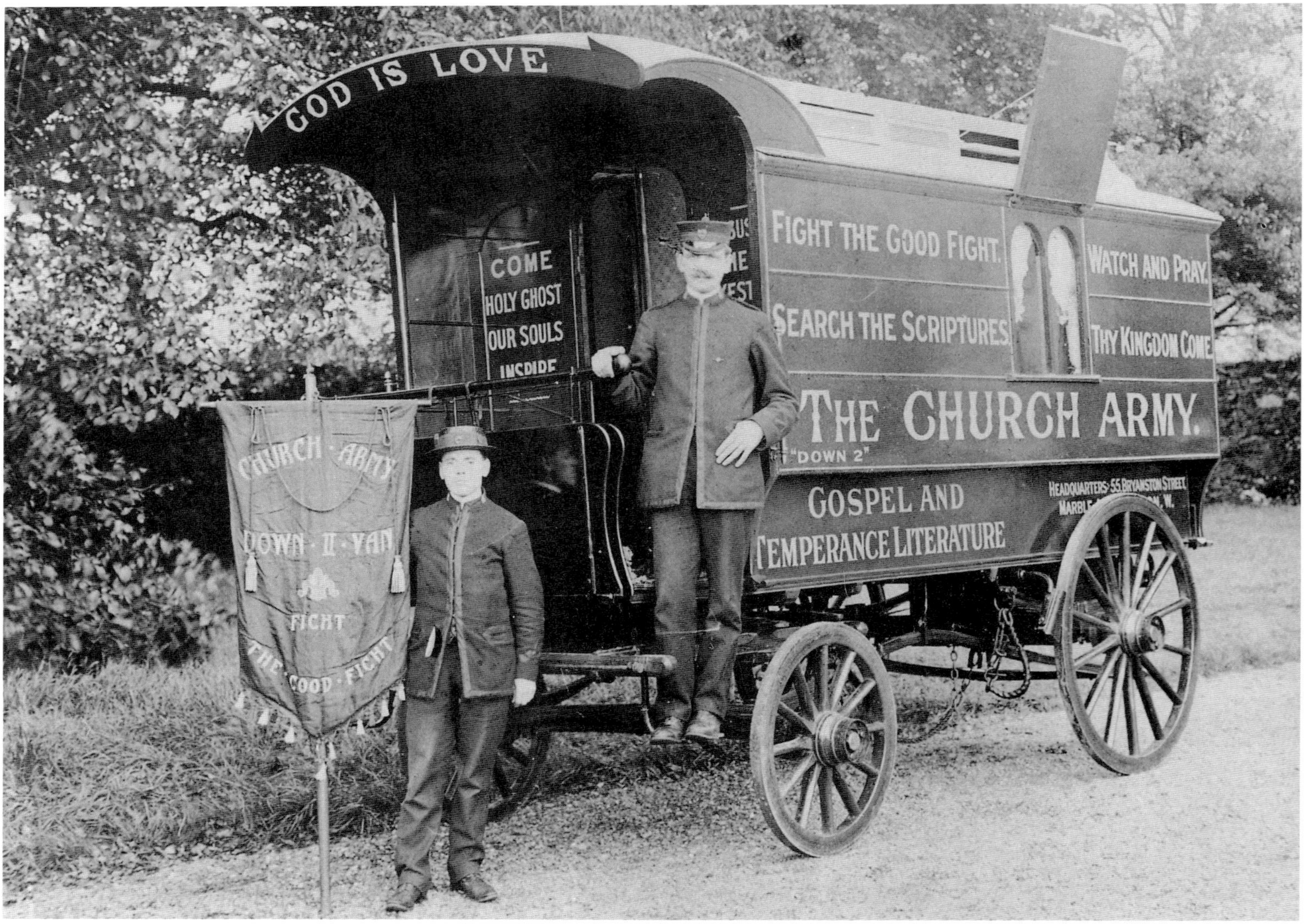

Church Army caravan, postcard by William Beattie, Newtownards, c. 1910.
BY KIND PERMISSION OF DESMOND QUAIL

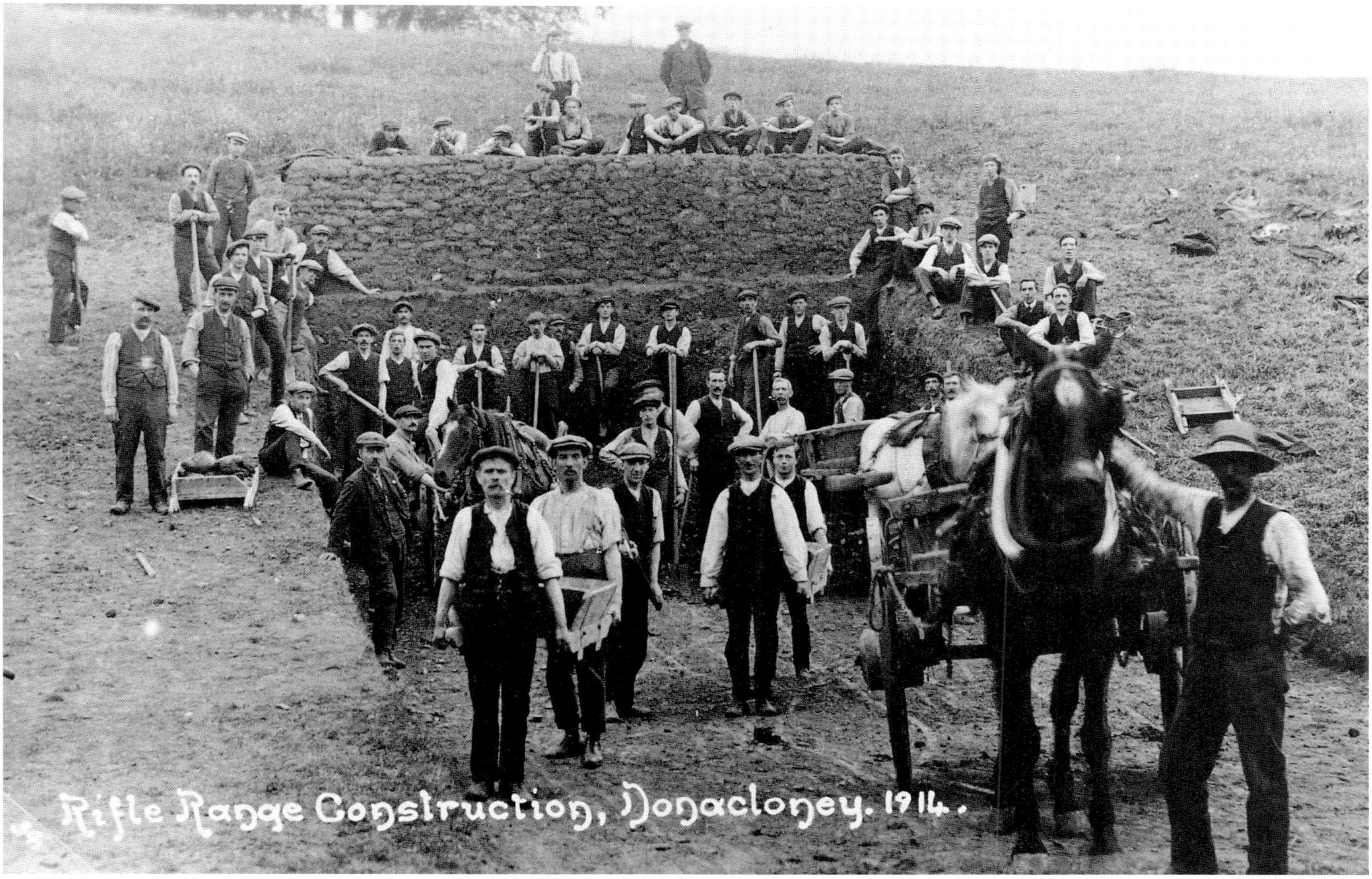

the 1920s encouraged more women to set up their own businesses. Whereas only four studios run by women are listed in the Belfast directories in the sixty-four years between 1850 and 1914, by the early 1930s the city had five, all recently established.

'Rifle Range Construction, Donacloney, 1914', postcard by an unknown photographer.

BY KIND PERMISSION OF DESMOND QUAIL

Given the date, these men were almost certainly members and supporters of the local Ulster Volunteer Force preparing to resist Home Rule.

This development coincided with the establishment of an Ulster branch of the Professional Photographers' Association. Alex Hogg, who had been a personal member of the organisation since at least 1918, took the lead in setting up a local branch, along with Francis Neill, in 1925. Neill, who had trained with Abernethy, had started his own business almost five years earlier. Hogg served on the national council in the 1930s. Other prominent figures in the early days were the veterans William Abernethy (president) and Robert Welch (vice-president). For many years Hogg took the group photograph of members on their annual outing. It is hard to know what practical effect, if any, these efforts to encourage professional solidarity may have had. The essential problem remained that anyone who wished could set up in business as a photographer, and professionals were in competition not only with each other but also with gifted amateurs and semi-professionals such as Arthur Campbell.

A further threat to those dependant for their living on the portrait trade was the appearance in the 1930s of polyfoto, which in Belfast operated in the basement of Robinson and Cleaver's department store. The polyfoto process produced in short order a sheet of multiple small prints from which to choose enlargements. It was particularly successful for photographing restless children. A much greater threat to photographers in general loomed at the end of the decade, when the outbreak of the Second World War immediately restricted photographic activity and supplies of materials became hard to get. Arthur Campbell recalled that when news of the start of the war broke he went down to a shop in High Street and bought all the 3 x 4 centimetre film they had in stock.[14]

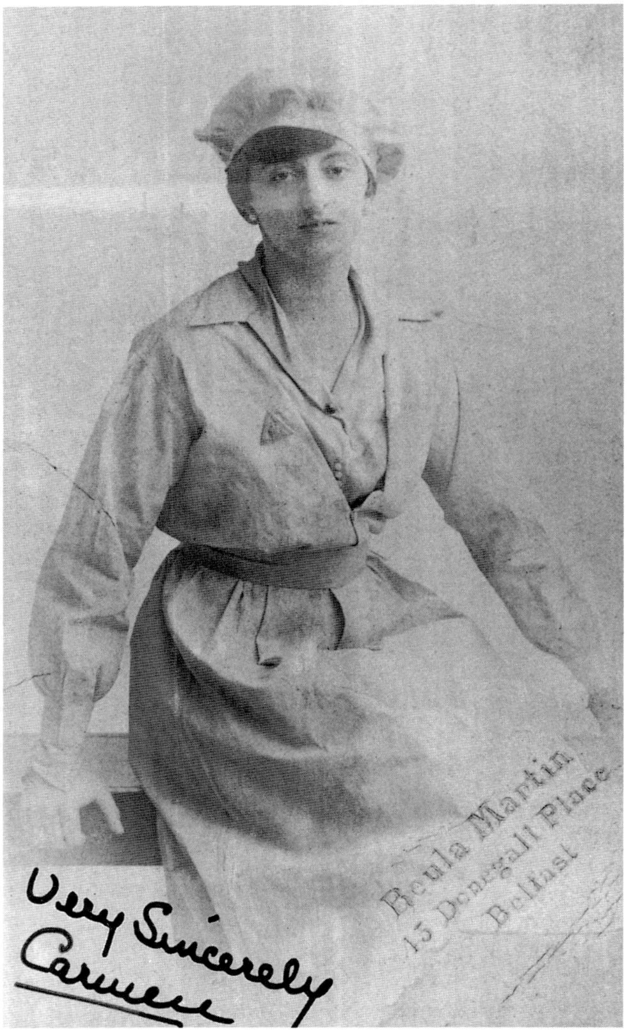

Portrait of 'Carmen', 1925 by Beula Martin.
MAGNI / UM

The photographer was one of the several women, proprietors of their own studios, who set up in business in Belfast between the wars. The portrait was printed in postcard form.

The most significant development in professional equipment in the inter-war period was the invention of the first commercially successful small lightweight camera. The German Leica, introduced in 1925 (though based on an earlier model), used 35 mm roll film with fast film advance, instantaneous exposure and a high level of image definition, so that good results could be obtained under a variety of lighting conditions. The electric flashbulb, which rendered obsolete all other means of artificial illumination, was also invented in Germany, in 1928.

Finally, the period between the world wars saw the development of modern-style aerial photography. Its origins went back to the balloon era, before flying machines. It seems not unlikely that some of the bird's-eye-view pictures of the expanding city of Belfast produced in the latter part of the nineteenth century were based upon photographs taken from stationary balloons, though there is no documentary proof of it. Balloon ascents from the Botanic Gardens were a popular feature of public festivals throughout the period (the last was at Easter 1894) and after the adoption of the dry plate in the 1880s it would have been feasible to attempt photography from the air. A lithograph entitled 'A Bird's Eye View of Belfast', dated 1890, seen from a vantage point just behind the Methodist College on the Malone Road – very close to the gardens – is the best candidate. Such a view could have been made up from several photographs, like the panoramic view from the tower of the new fire station

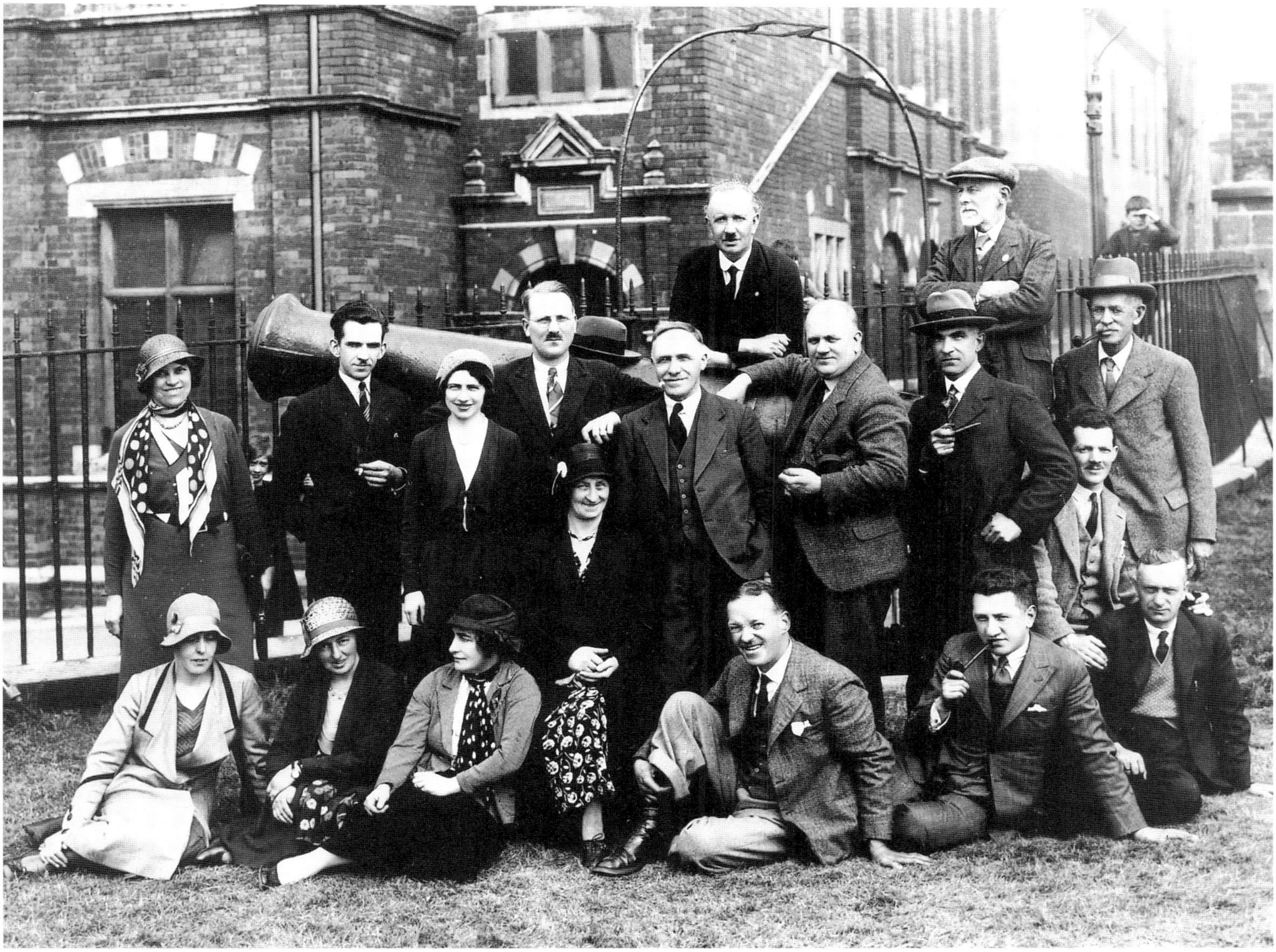

taken a few years later and published in *Sights and Scenes in Ireland*.

Aerial photography from aeroplanes appeared first on the western front during the First World War, developing rapidly to meet the demands of military necessity. By the 1920s it was well established. The Ulster Folk and Transport Museum has a collection of aerial views of Northern Ireland between the wars, many of them dated, some (as war loomed again in the 1930s) marked 'Passed by Censor'. The main public collection, however, is in the care of the Environment and Heritage Service of the Department of the Environment for Northern Ireland.

Most aerial photography at this stage was undertaken by the Royal Air Force and closely associated with military or strategic considerations. One interesting exception was the survey of Lyles Hill in County Antrim carried out by Wing Commander Wright, then commandant of the RAF station at Aldergrove, in 1927. Wright's diagonal view of the hill, looking west, struck him as interesting and he

Members of the Northern Ireland branch of the Professional Photographers' Association on an outing to Londonderry, 10 June 1932. Photo by A.R. Hogg.
MAGNI / UM (HOGG COLLECTION)

The two figures at the back are Hogg (left) and Welch.

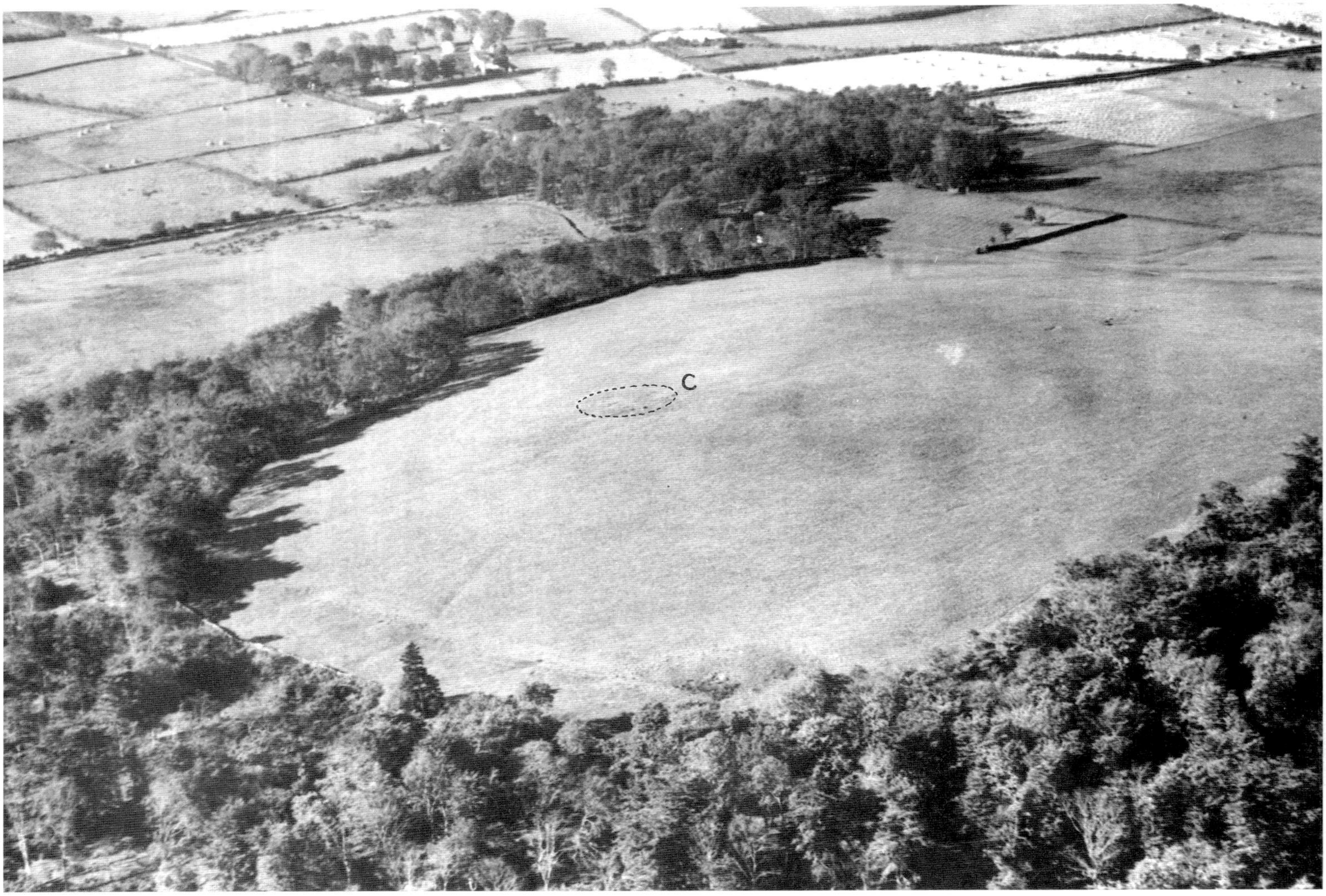

Aerial photograph of Lyles Hill, County Antrim, taken by Wing Commander Wright in 1927.

ENVIRONMENT AND HERITAGE SERVICE, DEPARTMENT OF THE ENVIRONMENT FOR NORTHERN IRELAND. © CROWN COPYRIGHT REPRODUCED WITH THE PERMISSION OF THE CONTROLLER OF HMSO.

C marks the suggested site of the neolithic cairn revealed by this historic photograph

drew the attention of the recently formed Ancient Monuments Committee to the earthwork and mound on the top. What had hitherto been taken to be the result of modern mining turned out, when excavation began some years later, to be an enormously important neolithic site. As Professor Estyn Evans put it in his eventual report, this discovery was 'perhaps the most notable contribution yet made by aerial photography to prehistoric archaeology in Ireland'.[15]

A much more sinister bird's-eye-view may serve as postscript. In the summer of 1940 Luftwaffe Heinkels and Dorniers, equipped with superb Zeiss cameras, secretly reconnoitred the coastal areas of Northern Ireland. The resulting photographs of Belfast's most important industrial and strategic sites – Short and Harland's (*das Flugzeuwerk*), Harland and Wolff's (*die Schiffwerft*), Victoria Barracks (*die* Victoria *Kaserne*) and so on – were used to prepare the maps that guided the German bombing crews in the Blitz of 1941.[16] In fact, the collection of photographs for military purposes predated the outbreak of war in 1939. We know this because after war began the German High Command produced, for official eyes only, a booklet summarising such information about Ireland. The area covered by aerial survey ran

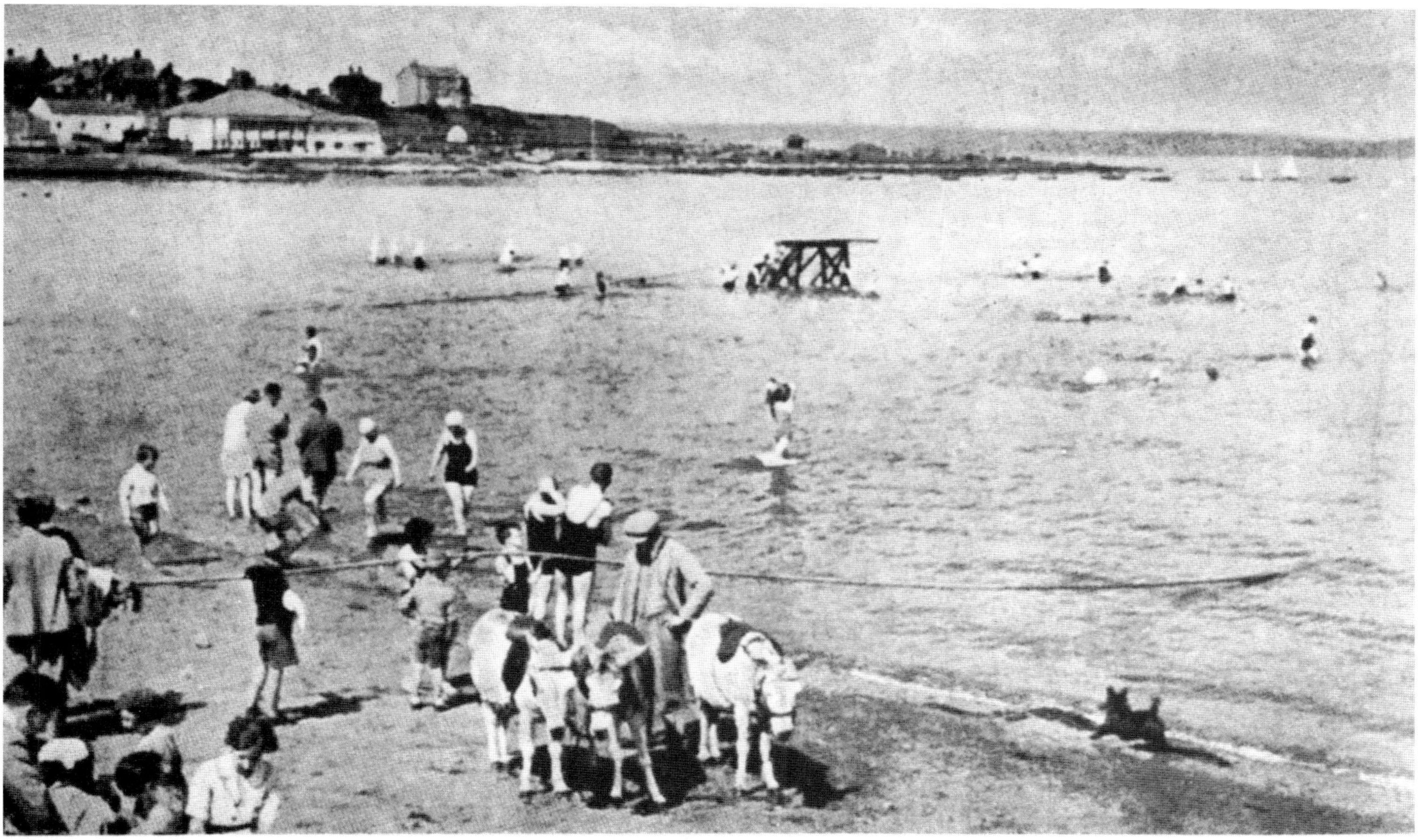

115. Strand bei Ballyholme.

from Mizen Head in Cork to Malin Head in Donegal – the entire coast of the island except for the west. The booklet juxtaposed prints of aerial reconnaissance with photographs, often postcard views, of the same locations on the ground. The contrast between the camera in the sky, with its sinister preparations for war, and that of the photographer below recording the innocent children and beach donkeys of a summer day at the seaside, could scarcely be more striking.[17]

Two views of Bangor, County Down, c. 1940, from *Militärgeographische Angaben über Irland* (Berlin, 1941).
MAGNI / UM

Ballyholme Beach, a postcard view. The Germans noted that with nine metres of deep water and shelter from prevailing winds this was a good anchorage.

In broad outline, the development of photography in the north of Ireland inevitably bears a close resemblance to what happened in other regions during the same period. Once invented, photography rapidly became a universal phenomenon. Successive improvements and refinements in all aspects of the technology and equipment associated with it were quickly adopted everywhere it was practised. Like the Industrial Revolution, it was the same in its essential aspects wherever it was encountered. Aptly enough Richard Beard, who in 1841 opened the first professional studio in the British Isles, displayed on his trade card this quotation from an essay in the *Edinburgh Review*: 'The art of photography is as great a step in the

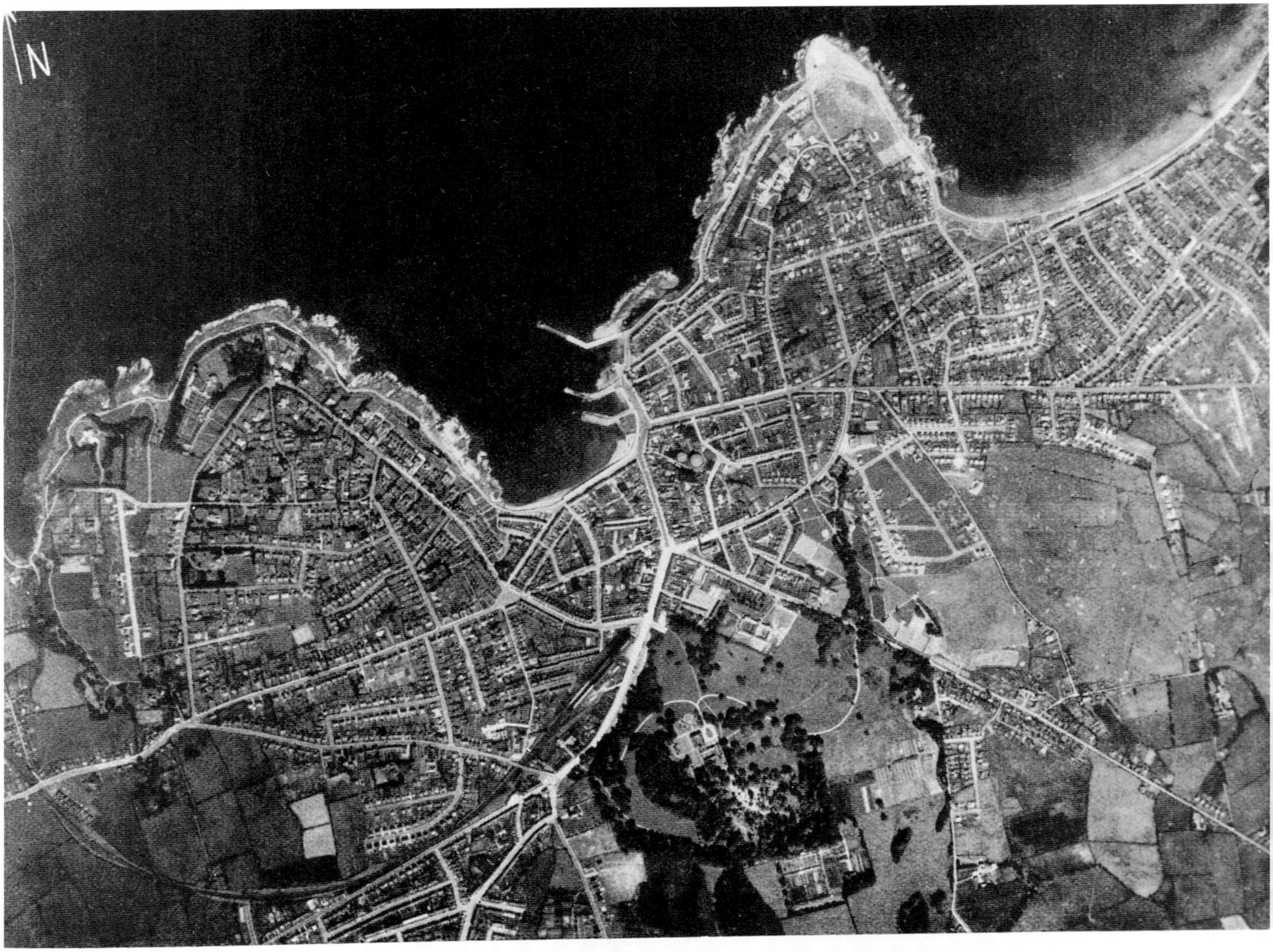

116. Bangor (13 320 Einw.).

Bangor from the air. Apart from its situation on Belfast Lough, the caption mentions the harbour and the terminal of the Belfast–Bangor railway. In September 1940, a passing Luftwaffe bomber on its way home dropped twenty incendiary bombs on Main Street, missing both of these potential targets. Later, during the great blitz on Belfast in 1941, Bangor too was bombed; five people were killed and thirty-five injured.

fine arts as the steam engine was in the mechanical arts.'[18]

Growing demand, created by economic and social change, in Europe (and in the colonies of Europe throughout the world) and North America, fuelled a continuous process of innovation and improvement – a process which still goes on apace. One index of the scale of the change brought about by technical advance may suffice by way of illustration. Of all the improvements in material and equipment made between the invention of photography and recent times, perhaps the greatest has been the remarkable increase in the light-sensitivity of film emulsion. It has been estimated that 'from the daguerreotype of 1839 to the new materials of the late 1970s the sensitivity of film in full sunlight has increased 24 million times'.[19] By 1939 that process had already gone a long way.

Yet, while technical change was a constant factor in the history of photography throughout the period, and governed to a considerable extent what photographers were able to achieve at a particular time, its role should not be emphasised to the exclusion of human considerations. Sheer manipulative skill was essential to success of any kind in the early decades and even, in dealing with volatile chemicals, to physical survival. Artistic ability, however defined, was no less desirable in the upper reaches of the profession. At any rate, the chief impression one gains from any extensive study of original photographs is of a remarkably high level of competence among professional photographers. Regardless of the equipment and facilities available to them, most did a good job, and the best were very good indeed.

Photographic histories have naturally tended to focus on metropolitan areas such as London or, in the case of Ireland, Dublin, where studios were established earliest and in greatest numbers, and where new ideas and improvements usually first made their appearance. It is true that the north of Ireland produced no second pioneer photographer of the stature of Francis Beatty, but then neither did Dublin itself or anywhere else in Ireland. The North's portrait photographers were on the whole just as good, or as mediocre, as those of the metropolis. Fewer of their sitters, however, were glamorous in some way or possessed more than local significance. In contrast, in the matter of 'Irish Views' and mixed-subject photography, practitioners such as Ayton, Welch, Hogg and Green could stand comparison with the best anywhere.

This volume celebrates the achievements of these people, resurrects other, forgotten figures and puts all of them – famous or forgotten – into the context of their time and place.

Professional photographers and studios in the north of Ireland
1839–1939

This list has been compiled mainly from the published directories covering the nine northern counties – Antrim, Armagh, Cavan, Donegal, Down, Fermanagh, Londonderry, Monaghan and Tyrone – that made up the traditional province of Ulster for most of the period under consideration. However, since directory listings are not always accurate or comprehensive a particular photographer may have operated earlier or later (or elsewhere) than indicated by the entry given here. Where no mention is made of directories, information has come from other sources, such as newspapers and photographs.

The list is intended mainly to provide a convenient tool for dating and locating photographs. The knowledge of local historians and collectors will no doubt be able to add much detail to it, and to correct its inevitable shortcomings. I am grateful to all the people who have already contributed information, whilst absolving them of blame. Much of the basic work of searching directories was carried out by Janet McConaghy when she was employed as a research assistant in the Department of Local History at the Ulster Museum in 1987. More recently, the preparatory sorting and processing of the material was done by Pauline Dickson.

The existence and whereabouts, if available to the public, of major photographers' collections are also indicated. In that connection, MAGNI means the Museums and Galleries of Northern Ireland, at either the Ulster Museum, Belfast or the Ulster Folk and Transport Museum, Holywood; PRONI means the Public Record Office of Northern Ireland, Belfast. Lastly, any student of the subject must consult the collections of the National Museum of Ireland in Dublin, above all the Lawrence Collection – a major source of professional photographs of the North of Ireland over the period 1860–1914.

ABERNETHY, HAROLD (1894–1939)	Son of William; co-manager of studio 1930–39
ABERNETHY, VICTOR (1896–1966)	Son of William; co-manager of studio 1930–*c.* 1938
ABERNETHY, WILLIAM (d. 23 February, 1930)	Directories 1887–1939; 29 High St, Belfast, *c.* 1886–1939 and branches: Rembrandt Studio, Belfast (1906); Prince's Studio, Belfast 1911; Dundalk; Bangor 1907–19; Newry 1906–17; Albertbridge Rd, Belfast and 19 High St, Belfast 1915–25. Finishing works at Bloomfield, Belfast Died at Bangor, County Down; portrait by Harry Douglas
ABERNETHY, WILLIAM G. (d. 1924)	Son of William; assistant photographer to his father
A. AND C. PHOTOGRAPHY	[Artistic and Commercial] Directories from 1935; 14 Howard St, Belfast
ACADEMY STUDIO	Belfast (no address) From a late carte de visite (1890s or early 1900s)
ADAIR, HUGH	From *c.* 1893, directories 1896–1900 8a Donegall Pl., Belfast Proprietor, not a photographer; *see* Mavius and Vivash
ADAMS AND DOWLING	*c.* 1865 Donegall Pl., Belfast
AGNEW, DAVID	Directories 1896 Carlisle Rd, Londonderry
ALBION STUDIO	Belfast (no address) Proprietor D. Ritchie; known by a carte-de-visite portrait of *c.* 1870s
ALEXANDER AND CO.	Directories 1892 79 Royal Ave, Belfast
ALLEN, ERNEST	Directories 1935–39 Lisanelly, Omagh, County Tyrone; 40 Market St, Omagh (1929)
ALLIANCE ART CO.	Directories 1907–10 63a York St (1907) and 63a North St (1909–10 and on some photographs), Belfast; Carlisle Rd, Londonderry (1909)
ALLISON, EILEEN (Mrs Kennedy)	Daughter of Herbert Allison senior. Ran the Newry studio, which closed in 1932
ALLISON, HERBERT THACKWRAY (1854–1947)	Directories *c.* 1905–39; Scotch St, Armagh; Dundalk, Newry and Warrenpoint COLLECTION: PRONI
ALLISON, HERBERT JR (1880–1957)	Ran the Armagh studio for his father from 1903, inheriting the business in 1947

ALLISON, MRS W.L. Widow of W.L. Allison; ran the studio through a manager, 1923–35

ALLISON, WILLIAM L. (d. 1923) Cousin of H.T. Allison
Directories 1905–23;
13 Donegall Sq. North, Belfast

ALLISON, WILLIAM AND HERBERT ALLISON Directories *c.* 1882–*c.* 1905;
13 Donegall Sq. North and 14 Queen's Arcade, Belfast (from 1892), Armagh (from 1900), Newry and Dundalk
see Allison H., Allison W.L. and Vienna Photo Art Co.

AMERICAN PHOTO ARTISTS Directories 1901–9
19 Gresham St (1901) and 24 Gresham St, Belfast
Manager Thomas Barnes

ANDERSON, JOSEPH AND SONS Directories 1935–39
Cookstown, County Tyrone

ANNESLEY STUDIO Directories 1930–32
7 Ann St, Belfast

AVENUE PHOTO CO. Directories 1906–09
85 Royal Ave, Belfast
Same as 'The Avenue Studios, 83 Royal Avenue' (from an early 1900s photograph)

AYTON, ALEXANDER (1829–1900) Directories 1865–1901
Kennedy Pl., Londonderry 1865–94 and Shipquay St, Londonderry 1890–1901

AYTON, ALEXANDER JR (d.1894) Campsie, Omagh, County Tyrone – thereafter Edinburgh

AYTON, GEORGE Son of Alexander senior
Directories 1897–1909
Carlisle Rd, Londonderry

BAINBRIDGE, J.R., M.SC. Directories 1928–39
597 Upper Newtownards Rd, Belfast

BAKER BROS Directories 1902–5
35 High St, Belfast

BALDWIN, C. Directories 1865–66
3 Corn Market, Belfast

BALDWIN AND FERRIS Directories 1868–70
Hammond's Court, Belfast

BARNES, THOMAS Directories 1909
24 Gresham St, Belfast
see American Photo Artists

BARR BROS Directories 1909
109 Donegall St, Belfast

BATES, JAMES Directories 1921–25
Keady, County Armagh

BEATTIE, WILLIAM Directories 1910–39
William St, Newtownards, County Down

BEATTY, FRANCIS S. Directories 1842
20 Castle St, Belfast

BEAUFORT'S PHOTOGRAPHIC GALLERY Directories 1857
11 Donegall Pl., Belfast

BEDFORD STUDIO Bridge St, Belfast

BELL, GEORGE Directories 1863–77
1 Bank Lane, Belfast (1878)

BELL, MATTHEW R. Directories 1865–68
Russell St, Armagh

BELL, ROBERT Directories 1912–22
Rathfriland, County Down

BELL'S PHOTOGRAPHIC STUDIO Directories 1894–1920
North St, Carrickfergus, County Antrim

BELLSMITH, L.C. Directories 1902–6
Union St, Lurgan, County Armagh (1902–6) and 35 High St, Belfast (1906)

BENSON, J. Directories 1910–15
Donegal

BENSON, R.J. Directories 1916–39
Scotch St, (1906–22), Market Sq. (1923–24), Milltown (1925–27), Park Rd (1926–39), Dungannon, County Tyrone

BENSON, WILLIAM (d. 1933) Directories 1892–1901
22 Lombard St (1892–98), 30 Great Victoria St (1896), 48 Arthur St (1898) and 15 High St (1901), Belfast

BEST, E. 20 High St, Lurgan, early 1900s

BEVIS, PERCY Directories 1899
High St, Omagh, County Tyrone

BINGHAM, S. Directories 1913
15 Holywood Rd, Belfast

BIRNEY, D. O'C Directories 1933–34
Dungannon, County Tyrone

BIRNEY, HUGH Directories 1894–1932
Ann St and Irish St, Dungannon, County Tyrone
see Burney

BIRNIE, A.D. Directories 1878
68 Donegall St, Belfast. Same as Alex?

BIRNIE, ALEX Directories 1870–78
33 Donegall St (1870) and 21 Church St (1878), Belfast

BIRNIE, EDWARD — Directories 1856–80
50 Fountain St (1856–59), Hercules Pl. (1863–66) and 21 Church St (1877–80), Belfast
Listed as Burney in 1865–66 directory

BIRRELL BROS — Directories 1865–66
33 High St, Belfast

BLACK, A. — Directories 1905–8
109a Donegall St (1905) and 22 Lombard St (1906–8), Belfast

BLACK, JOHN — Directories 1894
Armagh

BLACK, JOHN — Ballycastle, County Antrim (1892–95)

BLAIR, HUGH — Directories 1856–59
34 High St (1856) and 10 (or 12) Bridge St (1858–59), Belfast

BLAIR, R.J. — Directories 1892–1901
45 Donegall Pl., Belfast

BOOTH, MISS ANNIE (1858–1934) — Directories 1909–34
Booth and Milner, Main St, Randalstown (1913), County Antrim

BOWNES, A. — Directories 1898–99
Market Sq., Lisburn, County Antrim

BOYD, JAMES — Directories 1894–1901
Main St, Larne, County Antrim

BOYD, MRS JAMES — Directories 1902–04
Main St, Larne, County Antrim

BRADLEY, P.C. — Directories 1928–39
Hilltown, County Down

BROWN, SAMUEL — Directories 1877
71 Joseph St, Belfast

BROWN, WILLIAM — Directories 1870
31 High St, Belfast

BROWN BROS — Directories 1868
33 High St, Belfast

BUCHANAN, ALEX — Directories 1894–1914
15a Donegall Pl. (1894–96), 83 Royal Ave (1895–98), 44a Dublin Rd (1907) and 33 Bridge St (1908–14), Belfast

BUCHANAN, GEORGE — Directories 1870
Donaghmore, Dungannon, County Tyrone

BURNEY, HUGH — Directories 1916–19
Ann St, Dungannon
'tailor and photographer' 1898
see Birney

BURROWS, J.W. — Directories 1902–13
Railway Rd, Strabane, County Tyrone
see Cooper

BUTLER, STEPHEN R. — Directories 1920–39
Carndonagh, County Donegal
'publican, photographer and cycle agent'

CALWAY, A.G. — Directories 1904–7
23 Cornmarket, Belfast

CAMLIN, JAMES — Directories 1907
15 Wellington St, Ballymena, County Antrim

CASSIDY, J.D. — Directories 1913
Ardara, County Donegal

CASTLE STUDIO — Castle Pl., Belfast

CAUGHEY, S.M. — Newcastle, County Down, early 1900s

CHAPERO, E.C. — Directories 1905–7
154 Crumlin Rd, Belfast

CHARLES, ANDREW — Directories 1894–1924
56 James St, Cookstown, County Tyrone, also at Maghera and Magherafelt, County Londonderry

CHARLES, F. — Directories 1881–
45 Donegall Pl. and 14 Queen's Arcade, Belfast
see Vienna Photo Art

CHARLES AND RUSSELL — Directories 1898–1922
51 Ann St and 10 Royal Ave, Belfast

CHERRY — Donegall Place Buildings, Belfast (1845)

CHRISTOPHER, C. — Directories 1907–13
Carlisle Rd, Londonderry

CHRISTOPHER, C. — Directories 1907–10
112 Royal Ave, Belfast. Same as above?

CHURCH, EDMUND T. — Directories 1869–90
55 (53) Donegall Pl., Belfast

CHURCH, WILLIAM — Directories 1877–78
25 Castle Pl., Belfast

CINNAMOND, M. AND E. — Directories 1881
45 Donegall Pl., Belfast

CINNAMOND, MISS — Directories 1856–59
Arthur St, Belfast

CITY STUDIO — Directories 1925
6 Donegall St, Belfast

CLARKE BROS — Directories 1908
30 Woodstock Rd, Belfast

CLASSICAL STUDIO — Directories 1928
7 Ann St, Belfast

CLUB STUDIO — Portadown, County Armagh *see* Simmons

COBAIN, JOHN — Directories 1881
Fivemiletown, County Tyrone

COCHRANE, R.H. — Directories 1916
5 High St, Belfast

COGHLAN, FRANCIS (FRANK)	Directories 1896–1920 31 Carlisle Rd, Londonderry
COGHLAN, J.	Directories 1911–27 Ballycastle, County Antrim
COLEMAN, JAMES A. (d. 1946)	Main St, Bailieborough, County Cavan (1904–46)
CONN, WILLIAM J.	Directories 1909–30 Newcastle, County Down
CONNOLLY, JAMES	Directories 1894–1905 Main St, Ballymoney, County Antrim
CONNOP, J.H.	Directories 1863 5½ Donegall St, Belfast
COON, ALLEN DANIEL (1867–1938)	Active 1902–38 Londonderry; Letterkenny, County Donegal and Moira, County Down
COOPER, HERBERT FREDERICK THOMAS (1874–1960)	Directories 1914–39 Strabane, County Tyrone COLLECTION: PRONI (Includes work of J.W. Burrows)
COPELAND, J.	Directories 1877–80 29 High St and 7 Donegall St, Belfast
COPELAND, WILLIAM	Directories 1865–68 Orr's Entry and 30 High St, Belfast
CORRY, SAMUEL	Directories 1870–78 Ballyclare, County Antrim
CORSCADDEN, MISS M.	Directories 1925–28 18 Howard St, Belfast
CRAIG, C.A.	Directories 1928–37 High St, Portadown, County Armagh
CRAWFORD, ROBERT	Directories 1920s–1940s Glasslough St, Monaghan
CROWDER, GEORGE F.	Directories 1867–1922 Willoughby Pl., Enniskillen, County Fermanagh (1867–68), thereafter 26 Townhall St, Enniskillen; also 10 Brighton Terrace, Bundoran, County Donegal
CROZIER, JAMES	Dublin St, Monaghan from 1874 Watchmaker, employed a photographer
CUMINE, JAMES A.	Directories 1858–80 Joy's Entry, 29 High St, 48 Arthur St and 55 Upper Arthur St, Belfast
CUMING, J.T.	Directories 1865–66 Marcus Sq., Newry, County Down
CUNNINGHAM, JOHN	Directories 1910–35 Ballyclare, County Antrim
DAGUERREOTYPE PORTRAIT ROOMS	Belfast, 1842
DALLAS, GEORGE	Directories 1889–1912 Kilrea (1899–99), Maghera (1890–94), Coleraine (Bankhead Terr. 1892–1902; Railway Rd 1903–12), County Londonderry
DATCHER, THOMAS	Directories 1917–20 Needham St, Newry, County Down
DAVIES, W.	Directories 1896–1902 Trillick, County Tyrone
DAWSON AND CO.	Directories 1901–2 39 Dublin Rd, Belfast
DE GLEICHEN	5 Donegall St, Belfast (1858)
DE VOTO	Directories 1894–95 13 Fleetwood St, Belfast
DEREK'S STUDIOS	Directories 1932 19 High St, Belfast
DEVLIN, R.	Directories 1910–17 Donegal, County Donegal
DILLON, ROBERT	Directories 1904–7 44a Dublin Rd, Belfast
DIXON, J. AND J.R.	Directories 1892 Rainey St, Magherafelt, County Londonderry
DOHERTY, JAMES	Carlisle Rd, Londonderry, (1890s)
DONNELLY, JAMES	Directories 1933–37 William St, Cookstown, County Tyrone
DONNELLY, S.	Directories 1910–25 William St, Cookstown
DOUGLAS, HARRY R.	Directories 1895–96 35 Royal Ave, Belfast
DUFFNER BROS	Directories 1935–39 Hill St, Newry, County Down
DUNCAN, R.	Directories 1870–77 The Mall, Armagh
EGAN, MATTHEW	Directories 1895–96 41 Little May St, Belfast
ELECTRO ART STUDIO	Directories 1902 117 Donegall St, Belfast
ERLY, PATRICK	Directories 1894–1931 Newry, County Down (Mary St, 1894–1904; Hill St, 1905–8; Queen St, 1909–31)
ERWIN, T.	22 High St, Newtownards, County Down (carte-de-visite portrait of c. 1880)
ERWIN, THOMAS	Directories 1884–92 Church St, Ballymena, County Antrim

FAULKNER, WILLIAM Directories 1899, 1913
Main St, Castlederg, County Tyrone

FERRIS, W.R. Directories 1888
Bachelor's Walk, Lisburn, County Antrim

FINLAY, JOHN Directories 1902–30
Castle St, Antrim, County Antrim

FINNEGAN, J. Early 1900s – known only by a postcard view of Ahoghill, County Antrim

FRANCIS, M. Directories 1909
Bushmills, County Antrim
see Merten and Francis

FRENEY Directories 1921–22
Newry Rd, Armagh

FROST AND KELLY Directories 1905–13
3 High St (1905–8) and 22 Lombard St (1909–13), Belfast

FULLERTON, JOHN Directories 1888
Ahoghill, County Antrim

GALBRAITH, ROBERT Directories 1868–70
9 High St (1868) and 3 High St (1870), Belfast; owner of a hairdressing establishment, employed a photographer.

GALBRAITH, JENNINGS AND CO. High St, Belfast *c.* 1869.
see Jennings

GALWAY, JAMES Directories 1880–81
Fermanagh St, Clones, County Monaghan

GALWAY, KATHLEEN Directories 1890–1930s; Fermanagh St and Erne Sq., Clones, County Monaghan

GASS, MISS E. Directories 1905
Shaftesbury Sq., Belfast

GIBSON, JOHN Directories 1858–70
20 Castle Lane, Belfast

GILLESPIE, J.J. Directories 1939
Killybegs, County Donegal

GLASS, JAMES (1847–1931) Directories 1870–1939
65 Carlisle Rd, Londonderry; Strabane (1899).
see Young and Glass

GLASS, THE MISSES Directories 1934–39
65 Carlisle Rd, Londonderry

GLEDHILL, R. Directories 1916–24
63a North St and 94 Bridge End, Belfast (1916–22); Mill St, Ballymena, County Antrim (1921–24)

GLEN, HENRY G. Directories 1870–78
81 High St, Belfast

GLENDINNING, ROBERT Directories 1914
63a North St, Belfast

GLOBE STUDIO Lisburn.
see McGeown

GLYDE, SAMUEL Directories 1856–59
12 Bridge St and 3 Donegall Pl., Belfast

GORDON, W.R. Directories 1911–22
17 Bridge St, Belfast

GOULD, DAVID Directories 1901–10
20 Rosemary St, Belfast

GRAHAM, G.H. Directories 1865–66
James St, Cookstown, County Tyrone

GRAHAM, JOSEPH M. Directories 1868–70
Hill St, Monaghan

GRAY AND CAMPBELL Directories 1925–28
19 High St, Belfast

GREEN, WILLIAM ALFRED (1870–1958) Directories 1920s
4 Salisbury Villas, Belfast and Antrim
COLLECTION: MAGNI (Ulster Folk and Transport Museum)

GREER, J. SCOTT Directories 1902–94
109a Donegall St, Belfast

GUY, WILLIAM Directories 1908–10
Fintona, County Tyrone

HAIG, CHARLES Directories 1908–40
134 North St (1908–20) and 112 Royal Ave (1920–40), Belfast

HALE, HAMILTON Directories 1870
Belfast

HALLIDAY, A. Directories 1892
15 Fairview Terr., Belfast

HALLIDAY, CHARLES H. Directories 1914–39
14 Queen's Arcade, Belfast

HAMEL, E. AND CO. Directories 1908
122 North St, Belfast

HAMILL, JOSEPH Directories 1863–78
The Castle and 10 Sandy Row (1878), Belfast

HAMILL AND HUGHES Directories 1858–61
The Castle, Belfast

HARDING, F.J. Directories 1909
Main St, Ballymoney, County Antrim

HARDING, J. Directories 1918–28
Railway Rd, Coleraine, County Londonderry

HARDING, R. Directories 1914–16
Bann Terr., Banbridge, County Down

HARKEN, F. Directories 1892
Donegal, County Donegal

HARRIES, MRS	Directories 1939 Bishop St, Londonderry
HARRIS, ERNEST G.	Directories 1904–39 Bishop St, Londonderry
HARRISON, PERCY	Directories 1916 112 Royal Ave, Belfast
HARVESTON, THOMAS	Directories 1888–1911 Wellington St, Ballymena, County Antrim (1888); Hill St (1898–1904) and Windsor Ave (1905–11), Lurgan, County Armagh
HATCH, J. AND H.	Directories 1925 10 Donegall Sq. East, Belfast
HEFFERNON, J.	Directories 1925 45 Queen's Sq., Belfast
HEMBRY, H.R.	Directories 1897–1919 15a Donegall Pl., Belfast
HENFREY, CLAUDE (1890–1955)	Holywood, County Down (1920s)
HENRI, SOLOMON	Directories 1939 53 Donegall Pl. and 13 Donegall Sq. North, Belfast
HEWITT, J.	Directories 1931–33 Fintona, County Tyrone
HEZLITT, MRS	Directories 1889 Brook St, Coleraine, County Londonderry
HICKS, JOHN WALKER (1863–1938)	Cinematographer 1897–c. 1908 College Sq. North, Belfast
HIGGINS, HARRIET	Directories 1907–16 153 Divis St, Belfast
HIGGINS, MESSRS	Directories 1910–16 79 Royal Ave and 153 Divis St, Belfast
HIGGINS, THOMAS	Directories 1913 9 Mill St, Belfast
HIGGINS, THOMAS A.	Directories 1895–1909 79 Royal Ave and 153 Divis St (1898–1909), Belfast
HOGAN, WILLIAM J.	Directories 1907 232 Woodstock Rd, Belfast
HOGG, ALEXANDER ROBERT (1870–1939)	13 Trinity St (1901–21), 81 High St (1922–34) and 67 Gt Victoria St (1934–39), Belfast COLLECTION: MAGNI (Ulster Museum, Belfast)
HOLYWOOD, W.	Directories 1932–35 216 Albertbridge Rd, Belfast
HOPPER, W.	Aughnacloy, County Tyrone c. 1865
HOROBIN, A. J.	Directories 1939 Letterkenny, County Donegal
HOWARD AND CO.	Directories 1917–22 4 Windsor Ave, Lurgan, County Armagh; 53 Donegall Pl. Buildings, Belfast (1920s)
HOWARD'S STUDIO	Directories 1925–28 53 Donegall Pl. Buildings, Belfast
HOWELL, CHARLES	Directories 1912–39 112 Royal Ave (1912) and 44 North St (1937–39), Belfast
HUDSON, WILLIAM (d. 1959)	Directories c. 1913–39 Belmore St and from c. 1922 Darling St, Enniskillen, County Fermanagh
HUDSON AND BENSON	Directories 1911 Ballybofey, County Donegal; Newtownstewart, County Tyrone (1913)
HUEY, JAMES	Directories 1865–66 James St, Cookstown, County Tyrone
HUGHES, JOSEPH	Directories 1863–64 30 High St, Belfast
HUNTER, MRS	Directories 1890–99 Scotch St, Armagh
HUNTER, W.J. AND CO.	Directories 1878–99 Scotch St, Armagh and Monaghan (1890–94)
HUTHER, EDMUND	Directories 1865–78 Foyle St and 18 Carlisle Rd, Londonderry
HUTHER, MRS	Directories 1880–82 18 Carlisle Rd, Londonderry; Letterkenny, County Donegal (1880)
IMPERIAL ART CO.	Directories 1910–11 5 Cromac Sq,. Belfast
IMPERIAL PHOTO ART CO.	Directories 1895–96 4 Fountain Lane, Belfast
IMPERIAL PHOTO ART STUDIO	119 York St, Belfast
INGLEBY, B.	Directories 1909 72 Cliftonville Rd, Belfast
INGRAM, JAMES W.	Directories 1863–64 4 Fountain St, Belfast
IRENE'S STUDIO	Directories 1939 16 Donegall Pl., Belfast
IRISH PHOTO CO.	Directories 1912–14 6 Cromac St, Belfast
JAMISON, W.	Directories 1920–39 Regent St, Newtownards, County Down

JENNINGS, JOHN PAYNE (1843–1926)	Directories 1868 6 High St, Belfast *see* Galbraith
JEROME LTD	Directories 1939 23 High St, Belfast
JOHNSTON, J.	Directories 1912–32 24 William St South, Belfast
JOHNSTON, JOHN	Directories 1878 36 Hercules St, Belfast
JOHNSTON, ROBERT	Campsie Pl., Omagh, County Tyrone 1870s?
JONES, A.E.	Directories 1896–1902 High St, Portadown, County Armagh
KALTON, G. AND SON	Directories 1937–39 64 York St, Belfast
KEENAN, JAMES	Directories 1918–34 Castlederg, County Tyrone
KEITH, R.	Directories 1928 1a Canning Pl., Belfast
KELLY, EMILY	Directories 1919–22 153 Divis St, Belfast
KELLY, MISS	Directories 1939 Ballyshannon, County Donegal
KENNEDY, G.	Directories 1928 74 Limestone Rd, Belfast
KENNEDY, GEORGE	Directories 1907–20 Royal Ave and 50 York St, Belfast
KENNEDY, JOHN	Directories 1865–1907 20 Castle Lane (1865–66), 115 York St (1868) and 119/121 York St (1870–1907), Belfast; photographer and umbrella maker (1881)
KENRICK, WILLIAM E.	Directories 1901–06 Larne, County Antrim
KERR, H. & SON	Directories 1897–1909 Carlisle Rd, Londonderry
KERR, HUGH	Directories 1870–97 Market St (1870) and Carlisle Rd, Londonderry
KERR, JAMES	Directories 1877–98 High St, Holywood, County Down or (1890s) Kinnegar, Holywood; sometimes listed as 'artist'; in 1890, listed as proprietor of a fancy goods shop in High St
KERR, JAMES	Directories 1894–1918, though James Kerr died 1907. North Rd, Monaghan; son of Hugh Kerr, Londonderry
KERR, M. & SON	Directories 1910–13 Carlisle Rd, Londonderry
KERR, MISS	Directories 1914–24 Carlisle Rd, Londonderry (1914–24) and North Rd, Monaghan (1919–22)
KERR, MRS	Directories 1890 Brook St, Coleraine, County Londonderry
KERR, THOMAS	Directories 1865–68 Market St, Londonderry
KILLINY, JOHN	Directories 1877 79 Belvoir Pl., Belfast
KILPATRICK, WILLIAM J.	Directories 1892–1905 53 Donegall Pl. and 22 Castle Pl., Belfast
KIRK, CHARLES H.	Monaghan 1863
KNOX, DAVID	Directories 1870 Dunfanaghy, County Donegal
LAFAYETTE	Directories 1900–28 8a Donegall Pl., Belfast
LAIDLAW, GEORGE	Directories 1868–92 Lifford, County Donegal (1868); Strabane, County Tyrone (1868–92)
LAIDLAW, J.A.	Directories 1885–86 Stranorlar, County Donegal
LAMB, RICHARD	Directories 1917 Richhill, County Armagh
LANCASTER STUDIO	Directories 1909 50 York St, Belfast
LANNIGAN, JOHN	Directories 1901–37 McKeown St (1901), Antrim St (1902–20), Antrim Rd (1921–27)and Castle St (1928–37), Lisburn, County Antrim
LAVERY, MRS H.	Directories 1919–20 94 Royal Ave, Belfast
LAWLESS, MRS	Directories 1939 Rathmullan, County Donegal
LEE, ALEXANDER	Directories 1910–33 Bath Terr. (1910–23) and Main St (1924–33), Portrush, County Antrim; Gt James St (1927–39), Londonderry and Eglinton, County Londonderry (1934–35)
LEE, ROBERT	Directories 1894–1939 Causeway View (1894) and Main St (1924–39), Portrush, County Antrim
LEE, ROBERT AND SON	Directories 1886–1901 Causeway View and Lansdowne Terr. (1899), Portrush, County Antrim

LEE AND CO.	Directories 1905–39; Railway Rd, Coleraine (1899, 1905–39), Lansdowne Crescent (1903–11) and Main St (1909), Portrush, County Antrim
LEECH, H.	Directories 1913 Main St, Portrush, County Antrim
LEECH, MRS	Directories 1921–23 Main St, Portrush, County Antrim
LEITCH, ALFRED H.	Directories 1939 33 Castle Lane, Belfast
LEONARD, G.	Directories 1937–39 High St, Omagh, County Tyrone
LEONARD, J.	Directories 1928–39 Abbey St and Union St (1934), Coleraine, County Londonderry
LEVY, H. AND CO.	79 Royal Ave, Belfast, (1890)
LEWIS, J.F.	Directories 1898–99 13 Pakenham St, Belfast
LITTLE, R.C.	Directories 1920–25 2 Gray's Hill, Bangor, County Down
LITTLE AND CHARLES	Directories 1884 Conway Sq., Newtownards, County Down
LITTLE GEM	Directories 1907 38 Mill St, Belfast
LOMBARD STUDIO	Directories 1900 22 Lombard St, Belfast
LONDON AND NEW YORK STUDIO	Directories 1907 55 York St, Belfast
LONDON AND PARIS PHOTOGRAPHIC ART STUDIO	Directories 1896–1902 22 Castle Pl., Belfast
LOUDAN, B.M. AND CO.	Directories 1888 English St, Armagh and Portadown, County Armagh
LYTTLE, ROBERT OR R. CLEMENTS	'10 years with Abernethy'; Directories 1911–32 44 Dublin Rd (1911–22), 12 High St (1921–37) and 27a Donegall Pl., Belfast. Also Gt James St, Londonderry (directories 1916–20) and Newtownards
McALISTER AND McILHATTAN	Directories 1925 7 College St, Belfast
McBRIDE, JAMES	Directories 1909 Market Sq., Lisburn, County Antrim
McBRIDE AND CO.	Directories 1894–1939 3 High St, Belfast (1894–1901) and Market Sq., Lisburn, County Antrim (1897–1939)
McCAFFREY, WILLIAM	Directories 1909 Fivemiletown, County Tyrone
McCANN,	Directories 1930–31 Bellaghy, County Londonderry
McCAUGHEY, S.	Directories 1920–32 Newcastle, County Down
McCLEERY, GEORGE	Directories 1916–23 Main St, Larne, County Antrim
McCLELLAND, THOMAS	Directories 1865–66 Scotch St, Armagh
McCLURE, R.J.	Directories 1923–24 Aughnacloy and Warrenpoint, County Down
McCLURE BROS	Directories 1918–22 Aughnacloy, County Tyrone
McCOMB, M.	Directories 1912–39 Castledawson, County Londonderry; 'clerk and photographer'
McCONNELL, THOMAS	Directories 1890 Ramelton, County Donegal
McCOSKER, EDWARD	Directories 1892–1906 Raphoe, County Donegal
McCOSKER, P.	Directories 1910–20 Raphoe, County Donegal
McCOSKER BROS	Directories 1907–9 Raphoe, County Donegal
McCULLOUGH, A.M.	Directories 1937 327 Newtownards Rd, Belfast
McCULLOUGH, ALEXANDER	Directories 1907–9 William St, Newtownards, County Down
McCULLOUGH, MRS	Directories 1925 2 Hill St, Belfast
McCUTCHEON	Downpatrick, County Down
McDONAGH, E.	Directories 1910 60 Grosvenor Rd, Belfast
McFARLAND OR MACFARLAND BROS	Directories 1890–92 The Royal Ulster Fine Art Studio, 35 High St, Belfast
McFARLANE, A.J.	Directories 1930–39 High St, Omagh, County Tyrone
McFARLANE OR MACFARLANE, WILLIAM	Directories 1899, 1904–28 Campsie (1899) and High St, Omagh, County Tyrone

McGAHEY OR MEGAHY, RICHARD	Lurgan, County Armagh, (1870s and 1880s)
McGAHEY, S.	Directories 1909 Newcastle, County Down
McGAHEY, T.	Directories 1898–1918 Newcastle, Co Down
McGAW, JOHN	Directories 1907–20 79c Divis St and 121 Shankill Rd, Belfast
McGEE, J. AND R.	Directories 1928–39 Irvinestown, County Fermanagh
McGEOWN, WILLIAM	Directories 1890–97 The Globe Studio, Market Sq., Lisburn, County Antrim
McGOWAN , E.	Directories 1898–1903 High St, Omagh, County Tyrone
McGUIGAN, JAMES	Directories 1911–20 17 Albertbridge Rd (1911) and 56 Albertbridge Rd (1912–20), Belfast
McGUIRE, FRANCIS	Directories 1926–30 Ballygawley, County Tyrone
McGURK, JOHN	Directories 1907 134 North St, Belfast
McGURK, T.	Directories 1894–1907 William St and Coagh St, Cookstown, County Tyrone
McKEOWN, JOHN	Directories 1899–1902 Bridge St, Portadown, County Armagh
McKENDRY, JOHN	Directories 1868 Belturbet, County Cavan.
McKEY/McKAY, THOMAS AND CO.	Directories 1865–1903 Abbey St, Armagh (1865–66); Lurgan and Bainbridge ('late of Armagh'); 70 Hill St, Newry (1880–1903), County Down
McLAUGHLIN OR McLOUGHLIN, J.	Directories 1911–22 Bundoran, County Donegal
McLEAN, JAMES	Directories 1932 19 High St, Belfast
McMAHON, WILLIAM J.	Directories 1935 Earlsmount, Castlereagh, County Down
McMILLAN, AENEAS [ENEAS]	Directories 1870 17 and 45 Donegall Pl., Belfast
McMILLAN, E. and J.	Directories 1863–66 5 Donegall St, Belfast and 48 Donegall St
McMULLAN, JAMES	Directories 1916–19 Church St, Coleraine, County Londonderry
McMULLAN, JOSEPH	Directories 1913–32 Church St, Captain St (1913–14), Coleraine, County Londonderry
McWATTERS, J. JUN.	Armagh, (1880s)
MACK, ARTHUR	Directories 1912–17 Railway Rd, Coleraine, County Londonderry
MACK, E.W.	Directories 1894–1937 Charles St, Ballymoney (1894–98) and Main St, Larne (1902–37), County Antrim
MACK, J.	Directories 1890 Hibernia St, Holywood, County Down
MACK, J.H.	Directories 1877 Railway Pl., Coleraine, County Londonderry
MACK, JOHN	Directories 1870–80 Brook St N., Coleraine (1870) County Antrim; Kinnegar, Holywood, County Down (1880); 84 York St, Belfast (1877–80); Limavady 1880s (?), County Londonderry
MACK, JOHN	Directories 1894–1909 Kingsgate St (1894–99), Railway St (1901–8), Coleraine, County Londonderry
MACK, WILLIAM	Directories 1880–90 Brook St N. (1880–90) and New Row (1886–90), Coleraine, County Londonderry
MACK AND SONS	Directories 1884–90 22 Castle Pl., Belfast
MAGAHEY, WILLIAM	Directories 1863 High St, Lurgan, County Armagh
MAGDALA STUDIO	St James St, Belfast 1898 *see* Owens, J.
MAGILL, JAMES	Directories 1863–92 7 Castle Buildings (1863–68), 6 Castle Buildings (1865–66), 2 Castle Buildings (1880) and 2 Donegall Pl. (1865–92), Belfast
MAGUIRE, JOSEPH	Directories 1930–35 Ballygawley, County Tyrone; 'Photo agent'
MALLON, CHARLES	Directories 1868 7 Omar St, Belfast

MALONE, R.J.	Directories 1912–19 Main St, Ballymoney and Bushmills, County Antrim
MANN	Bangor, County Down (postcard 1906)
MARKS, JAMES	Directories 1877 Maghera, County Londonderry
MARTIN, BEULA	Directories 1919–33 45 Donegall Pl., Belfast
MARTIN (MERTEN?), R.	Directories 1912–15 Ferryquay St, Londonderry
MARTIN, R.C.	Directories 1898 83 Royal Ave, Belfast
MARTIN [MERTEN] AND FRANCIS	Directories 1907–11 Bushmills, County Antrim *see* Merten
MASSEY, A.G.	Directories 1884 35 High St, Belfast
MASSEY, ARTHUR	Directories 1877 Abbey St, Armagh; Arthur G., Abbey St, Armagh and 32 Market St, Lurgan, County Armagh
MASSEY, JOSEPH	Directories 1865–66 110 High St, Belfast
MASSEY, OSWALD M.	Directories 1895–97 168 Agnes St, Belfast
MASSEY, WARD AND CO.	Directories 1895–97 168 Agnes St, Belfast
MAVIUS AND VIVASH	Directories 1890–92 51 Ann St, Belfast
MAXWELL, J.	Directories 1898–1905 Church St, Banbridge, County Down
MAYER, RUDOLPH AND CO.	Directories 1870 13 Castle Pl., Belfast
MAYNE, ALEXANDER S.	Directories 1865–66, 1899 1–3 Donegall Sq. East, Belfast
MEGARRY AND JOHNSTON	Directories 1925–30 33 Bridge St, Belfast
MERCER, THOMAS A.	Directories 1881–1929 28 High St, Enniskillen, County Fermanagh
MERCER BROS	Directories 1906–22 51 Ann St and 22 Castle Pl. (1909–13), Belfast
METHVEN, RONALD	Directories 1939 Victoria Pl., Newcastle, County Down
MICKLETHWAITE, W.B.	Directories 1897–1903 Hill St and Corry Sq., Newry and Newcastle, County Down
MILLER, MISS E.	The Studio, Mall, Ballyshannon, County Donegal
MILLER, W.	Directories 1913 Main St, Ballyshannon, County Donegal
MODEL STUDIO	Divis St, Belfast
MOFFETT AND CO.	Directories 1901–39 Bridge St, Portadown (1901–39) County Armagh; Windsor Ave, Lurgan (1905–30) County Armagh; 12 High St (1905–8) and 53 Donegall Pl. (1909–22), Belfast
MOORE, JOHN	Directories 1916–18 Greencastle St, Kilkeel, County Down
MORRISON, JACK	Directories 1939 Ballytromery, Crumlin, County Antrim
MORRISON, LOUIS	Directories 1928–39 83 Royal Ave, Belfast
MORRISON, MISS	Directories 1909 Albert Rd, Carrickfergus, County Antrim
MORTON, H.S.	Directories 1900 22 Lombard St, Belfast
MORTON, J.	Directories 1898–1900 323 Albertbridge Rd, Belfast
MUIR, J.	Directories 1896–97 323 Albertbridge Rd, Belfast
MULHERN, LEO W.	Directories 1913 William St, Raphoe, County Donegal
MURDOCH, ROBERT	Directories 1904–15 Gt James St, Londonderry
MURRAY, J.	Directories 1888 Woodhouse St, Portadown, County Armagh
NAPIER, WILLIAM JOHN (*c.* 1870–1919)	Scarva, County Down
NEILL, F.M.	Directories 1935–39 24 Bradbury Pl., Belfast
NEILSON, AUGUST	Directories 1894–96 51 Ann St, Belfast
NEILSON AND CO.	Directories 1896–97 51 Ann St, Belfast
NELSON, ALEXANDER	Directories 1865–70 Church St, Dungannon, County Tyrone
NELSON, ROBERT	Directories 1865–70 High St, Omagh, County Tyrone
NEW YORK MINIATURE CO.	Directories 1906–7 112 Royal Ave, Belfast
NICHOLL, WILLIAM	Directories 1880 68 Donegall St, Belfast
NIMMOCKS, JOHN	Directories 1868–80 Castlerock, Coleraine, County Londonderry

NORTH BRITISH PORTRAIT CO.	Directories 1910–13 121 Shankill Rd, Belfast
O'CONNOR, J. W.	Directories 1884 3 York St, Belfast
ODEN, W.	Directories 1910–12 Newcastle, County Down
O'LOAN, JAMES	Directories 1880 29 High St, Belfast
O'NEILL, MISS S.	Directories 1928–32 60 Ann St, Belfast
ORANGE, EMILE	2 Castle Buildings and 22 York St, Belfast (1850–52)
ORD, WILLIAM	Directories 1870 Hibernia Pl., Holywood, County Down
ORDE, D. AND CO.	Directories 1860–61 7 Donegall Pl. Buildings, Belfast
ORDE AND WAITE	Castle St, Belfast (1860)
ORR, ANDREW	Directories 1886–89 Ramelton, County Donegal; Bennett St, Londonderry (1889)
ORR, MISS ELEANOR	Directories 1916–19 33 Bridge St, Belfast
OWENS, JOHN	Directories 1892–1903 Henry Pl. Belfast and Magdala Studio, Saint James St, Belfast, 1898.
PALACE STUDIO	Directories 1910–22 83 Royal Ave (1910–12) and 94 Royal Ave (1919–22), Belfast
PANOGRAPH PHOTOGRAPHIC STUDIO	Directories 1925–28 61 Waring St, Belfast
PANORAMIC PHOTO CO.	Directories 1932–39 565 Lisburn Rd, Belfast
PARKES, WILLIAM SCOTT	Directories 1870 7 Donegall Pl., Belfast
PARKES AND GEDGE	Directories 1870 Donegall Pl., Belfast
PARKS, F.W.	Directories 1916–17 Main St, Larne, County Antrim
PATTERSON, J.	Directories 1890–98 Belturbet, County Cavan
PATTERSON, JAMES	Directories 1865–70 High St, Omagh, County Tyrone
PATTERSON, JOHN	Directories 1880–84 68 Woodhouse St (1880) and High St (1884), Portadown; Market St, Lurgan, County Armagh
PATTERSON, MRS J.	Directories 1876 Omagh, County Tyrone
PATTERSON, R.A.	Directories 1909–17 The Parade, Donaghadee, County Down
PERY, JAMES	Directories 1870 Main St, Ballymoney, County Antrim
PETER PAN STUDIOS	Directories 1935–39 19 High St (1935–37) and 25 High St (1939), Belfast
PHILLIPS, J.	Directories 1914–16 Mill St, Ballymena, County Antrim
PHILLIPS, JOHN	Directories 1877–1916 7 Donegall St (1877), 79 Donegall St (1880–84), 143 Royal Ave (1887–1903), 173a York St (1902–3) and 45 Donegall Pl. (1904–16), Belfast
PICCIONE, FELIX	Directories 1861–78 Hammond's Court (1861), 22 Castle St (1877) and 71 Corporation St (1877–78), Belfast
PICCIONE AND BIRNIE	Directories 1861 Hammond's Court, Belfast
PIDDUCK, G.H.	Directories 1916–39 107 Donegall St (1916–22) and 19 High St (1928), Belfast; Queen's Parade, Bangor, County Down (1925–29)
PIDDUCK AND ARCHER	Directories 1906–14 5 High St (1906–13) and 109 Donegall St (1911–14), Belfast
PIPER, MISS	Directories 1894–95 22 Castle Pl., Belfast
PLIMMER, T.H.	Directories 1870–87 19 High St, Belfast
PLIMMER, T.H. AND T.S.	Directories 1863–66 10 Bridge St (1863–64) and 21 High St (1865–66), Belfast
PLIMMER, T.S.	Directories 1878–98 19 High St, Belfast
POLLOCK, J.A.	Directories 1905 47 Donegall Pl., Belfast
POLYFOTO	Directories 1939 At Robinson and Cleaver, 56 Donegall Pl., Belfast
PORTLAND STUDIO	Directories 1909 109 Donegall St, Belfast
PRATT, JAMES	Directories 1870 Letterkenny, County Donegal
PREDY, THOMAS	Directories 1877–1939 Limavady, County Londonderry
PRETORIA FINE ART CO.	Directories 1905–7 154 Crumlin Rd, Belfast

PRINCE(S) STUDIO	Directories 1904–13 19 High St, Belfast
PRIVATE PORTRAIT STUDIO	Newtownlimavady, County Londonderry 'C.D.H.C.'. 1880s?
PYPER, ARCHIBALD	Directories 1908–10 325 Newtownards Rd (1908) and 12 High St (1910), Belfast
PYPER, D.	Directories 1911–28 234 Newtownards Rd (1911–16) and 238 Newtownards Rd (1916–28), Belfast
PYPER, J.	Directories 1911–12 244 Newtownards Rd, Belfast
QUEEN ANN STUDIO	Directories 1910–11 39 Ann St, Belfast
QUEEN'S PHOTO ART CO.	Directories 1887–1905 Queen's Buildings, Royal Ave, Belfast (1886–92)
QUINN, WILLIAM H.	Directories 1865–80 5 Donegall St (1865–66), 42 Donegall St (1870–81), Belfast; 'rifle range, 1 John St', 1881
RAINEY, S.	Directories 1939 175 Agnes St, Belfast
RANSOM AND HALL	43 High St, Belfast (1854), 'just arrived from America'
RAPHAEL FINE ART CO.	Directories 1910–12 7 Queens Sq., Belfast
RAPIDE STUDIO PHOTOGRAPHS	Directories 1939 107 North St, Belfast
REGENT STUDIOS	Directories 1898–99 43a High St, Belfast
REID, GEORGE, J.	Directories 1921–22 63a North St, Belfast
REID, S.	Directories 1902 117 Donegall St, Belfast
REID BROS	Directories 1880–1932 81 High St (1880–1921), 114 Royal Ave (1921–28) and 231 Shankill Rd (1921–32), Belfast
REILLY, THOMAS HENRY	Directories 1865–66 61 High St, Belfast
REMBRANDT STUDIO	Directories 1904–7 53 Donegall Pl., Belfast
REVLIN	Directories 1910–15 Donegal, County Donegal
REW, HENRY	Directories 1903–5 5 Bridge End, Belfast
RIPLEY, JOHN	Directories 1912–39 William St, Lurgan, County Armagh
RITCHIE, D.	The Albion Studio, Belfast
RITCHIE, WILLIAM	Directories 1904–39 Garden St, Magherafelt, County Londonderry
ROBIN, H.O.	Directories 1921–24 Gt James St, Londonderry
ROBINSON, JOHN	Directories 1863–64 63 York St and Queen's Island, Belfast
ROBINSON, T.A.	Directories 1910–22 Donegal, County Donegal
ROSBOTTOM, T.A.	Directories 1898–1900 120 Dublin Rd, Belfast
ROSS, R.M.	Directories 1932 410 Beersbridge Rd, Belfast
ROYAL PHOTO ART CO./ ROYAL STUDIO	Directories 1895–1919 79 Royal Ave (1895–1916) and 153 Divis St (1898–1919), Belfast
ROYAL ULSTER FINE ART STUDIO	*see* McFarland/MacFarland Bros
ST GEORGE'S STUDIO	Directories 1908 35 High St, Belfast
SARONY, OLIVIER FRANÇOIS XAVIER (1820–79)	Directories 1861 12 or 12½ Bridge St, Belfast
SAUNDERS, H.R.	Directories 1932 21 Bridge St, Belfast
SEGGONS, ROBERT	Directories 1877–87 13 Castle Pl., Belfast
SEMPLE, W.S.	Directories 1899 Manorcunningham, County Donegal
SEWELL, J.	Directories 1895 323 Albertbridge Rd, Belfast
SHANNON, STANLEY	Directories 1921–25 Gt James St, Londonderry
SHIMMONS, DAVID	Directories 1903–04 33 Bridge St, Belfast
SHORTHOUSE, CHARLES DAVID	Directories 1922–39 Cushendall, County Antrim (1922–35) and 362 Ravenhill Rd, Belfast (1925–39)
SILO AND SON	Directories 1856–59 Donegall Pl. (1856) and Upper Arthur St (1858–59), Belfast
SIMMONS, R.G.	Directories 1881 Letterkenny, County Donegal

SIMMONDS [SIMMONS], G.V.	Directories 1894–99 The Club Studio, 59 Bridge St, Portadown, County Armagh
SMYTH, PATRICK	Directories 1868 East Port, Ballyshannon, County Donegal
SOLOMON, HENRY (OR HENRI)	Directories 1925–39 22 Lombard St (1925–32) and 53 Donegall Pl. (1932–39), Belfast
STANDARD CAMERA CO.	Directories 1932 109a Donegall St, Belfast
STANSFIELD, L.	Directories 1939 Darling St, Enniskillen, County Fermanagh
STANTON, J.S.	22 Castle St, Belfast, 1850
STAUNTON, THOMAS	Directories 1870 19 Gt James St, Londonderry
STEEN, JOSEPH	Directories 1919–39 79 Royal Ave, Belfast
STEVENSON, J.	Directories 1921–32 Burn Rd, Cookstown, County Tyrone
STEWART, JAMES SCOTT	Directories 1856 Castle Buildings, Castle Pl., Belfast
'STICKY BACKS' STUDIO	146 Upper North St, Belfast
STITT, WILLIAM	Directories 1885–90 26 Hillman St, Belfast
STUART, T.	Directories 1888 Randalstown, County Antrim
STUART, THOMAS	Directories 1895–1909 Main St, Larne, County Antrim
STUDIO CECIL	Directories 1925–39 51 Ann St, Belfast
TAIT, JOHN	Directories 1899, 1907–11 Newtownstewart, County Tyrone
TALBOT, ABRAHAM J.	Directories 1863–64 12 Bridge St, Belfast
TAYLOR, WILLIAM	Directories 1902–3 22 Castle Pl., Belfast
TAYLOR, WILLIAM HENRY	Directories 1868 48 Mill St, Belfast
THOMPSON, ALEXANDER	Directories, 1870 65 Donegall St, Belfast
THOMPSON, ARTHUR	Directories 1865–70 55 Donegall St (1865–66) and 60 Cavour St (1870), Belfast
THOMPSON, E.	Directories 1935 44 Dublin Rd, Belfast
THOMPSON, F.	Directories 1911–16 Bundoran, County Donegal
THOMPSON, J.	Directories 1896–1902 7 Donegall St (1896) and 35 High St (1897–1902), Belfast
THOMPSON, J.A.	Directories 1918–35 Carlisle Rd, Londonderry
THOMPSON, J.J.	Directories 1894–97 High St, Omagh, County Tyrone
THOMPSON, JAMES	Directories 1906–33 26 Crane's Buildings, Wellington Pl. (1906–12), 1 Grosvenor House, Wellington Pl. (1913–18) and Prudential Chambers, Wellington Pl. (1918–33), Belfast
THOMPSON, JOHN	Directories 1872–77 Omagh, County Tyrone
THOMPSON AND WOODS	Directories 1921–22 13 Donegall Sq. West, Belfast
THOMPSON'S PHOTO STUDIO	Directories 1930–39 Bryan St, Ballymena, County Antrim
THOMPSON'S STUDIO	Directories 1937–39 Carlisle Rd, Londonderry
TIERNEY BROS	Directories 1913–35 Fivemiletown, County Tyrone
TRIMBLE, WILLIAM J.	Directories 1890–39 Church St, Dungannon, County Tyrone; Banbridge, County Down; Lurgan and Portadown, County Armagh (1894)
TULLOCH, A.	22 York St, Belfast (1850)
TURNBULL, JOSEPH M.	9 Gosford St, Belfast
TURNBULL AND SONS	Directories 1884–1930 23 Garfield St (1884–1900), 7 Garfield St (1901), 9 Garfield St (1905–22) and 11a Garfield St (1928–32), Belfast
TUTTY AND CO.	Directories 1932 61 Waring St, Belfast
ULSTER PHOTOGRAPHIC STUDIO	Directories 1884 Carlisle Rd, Londonderry
ULSTER PORTRAIT CO.	Directories 1908 45 York St, Belfast
UNSWORTH, J.C.	Directories 1895–97 High St, Ballynahinch
UNSWORTH, JOHN OR JONATHON	Directories 1880–1926 Railway St, Ballynahinch, County Down
VARVISH, W.	Directories 1868 7 College St South, Belfast

VIENNA PHOTO ART CO.	Directories 1887–96 14 Queen's Arcade, Belfast; also Portrush (1892–96) and Larne, County Antrim
VIVASH	*see* Mavius and Vivash
WAIDE, HUGH	Directories 1865–94 Coagh St (1865–66) and Rock Cottage, (1880–94), Cookstown, County Tyrone
WALSH, WILLIAM	Directories 1887 31 Cranburn St, Belfast
WALSH (OR WELSH) BROS	Directories 1892 22 Castle Pl., Belfast
WARD, MARCUS AND CO.	Directories 1868–80 Donegall Pl., 110 High St (1868) and Dublin Rd (1877–80), Belfast
WARD, RICHARD AND CO.	65 Donegall St and 98 High St, Belfast
WATKIN, CHARLES	Directories 1890 Mill St, Ballymena, County Antrim
WATSON, WILLIAM	Directories 1877–1939 Donegal, Coounty Donegal
WEBB, GEORGE F.	Directories 1925–32 63a North St (1925–28) and 12 Lombard St (1932), Belfast
WEBSTER, J.	Belfast, 1930 (?)
WEINER, B.	Directories 1914 7 Glenravel St, Belfast
WEIR, WILLIAM	Directories 1887 17 My Lady's Rd, Belfast
WELCH, DAVID (d. 1875)	Directories 1863–70 Enniskillen, County Fermanagh (1863–68) and Newry, County Down (1870)
WELCH, ROBERT JOHN (1859–1936)	Directories c. 1880–1936 49 Lonsdale St, Belfast COLLECTIONS: MAGNI – Ulster Museum (Welch Collection); Ulster Folk and Transport Museum (Harland and Wolff Collection)
WELSH (OR WALSH?), W.	Directories 1890 Queen's Photo Art Co., Royal Ave, Belfast
WEST, JOHN	Directories 1863 10 Trinity St, Belfast
WILLIAMS, FRED	Directories 1937–39 Fivemiletown, County Tyrone
WILLIAMS, SYDNEY	Directories 1905–27 Fivemiletown and Clogher (1909)
WILLIAMS, THOMAS AND CO.	Directories 1880–82 25 Castle Pl., Belfast
WILSON, BENJAMIN	Directories 1863 Wall, Londonderry
WILSON, GEORGE	Directories 1865–66 Mill St, Newry, County Down
WILSON, I.B. AND CO.	Directories 1939 Castlederg, County Tyrone
WILSON, W.	Directories 1861–62 Church St, Banbridge, County Down
WILSON, WILLIAM	Directories 1896 Fintona, County Tyrone
WITCOMBE, E. LAWRENCE	Directories 1910 10 Donegall St, Belfast
WOODS, D.C.	Directories 1898 Church St, Coleraine, County Londonderry, and Portrush, County Antrim
WOODS, MISS	Directories 1897–1909 Church St, Coleraine (1899–1909) and Main St, Portrush (1897–1907)
YOUNG, J. BRUCE	Directories 1909–20 Wellington St, Ballymena, County Antrim
YOUNG, JOHN	Directories 1878 24 Argyle St, Belfast
YOUNG AND GLASS	Directories 1878 Carlisle Rd, Londonderry

Notes

Early days 1839–c. 1860

1 For an authoritative and exceptionally well-illustrated survey of early photography, see Helmut Gernsheim, *The Origins of Photography* (London, 1982); for the wider scene, see Naomi Rosenblum, *A World History of Photography* (New York, 1984).

2 Michael McCaughan, 'The first Irish photographer – Francis Beatty of Belfast', in *Ulster Folk and Transport Museum Year Book, 1981–85* (Belfast, 1985) and 'Shadows fixed forever: the daguerreotype and portraiture 1839–42', in papers from a symposium entitled *The History of Technology, Science and Society 1750–1914* (Belfast, 1989). See also Edward Chandler, 'Early Irish pioneers, 1839–1850', in *Photo Historian*, No. 92 (Spring 1991).

3 J. Moffat in *John Moffat: 1819–1894* (Eastbourne, 1989), p. 13, notes that in Scotland a significant number of early photographers – like Beatty in Belfast – came into the new profession from engraving.

4 [F.S. Beatty], *Dublin Journal*, 6 February 1858, the second of a series of six articles entitled 'The science of photography', printed between 30 January and 6 March 1858.

5 *Belfast News-Letter* and *Northern Whig*, 6 August 1840.

6 F.S. Beatty, 'Some historical recollections of photography', in *Photographic News*, 8 August 1879.

7 F.S. Beatty, 'Some historical recollections of the application of photography to portraiture', in *Year Book of Photography and Photographic News Almanac, 1884.*

8 [F.S. Beatty], 'The history of photography', in *Belfast Penny Journal*, Vol. 1, No. 3, 31 May 1845 (the third of five instalments). I am indebted to John Killen (Linen Hall Library) for this reference. Samuel Hawksett (1801–59) was a Belfast portrait painter.

9 Belfastiensis [Isaac Ward], 'The Donegall family and Ormeau', in *Belfast Municipal Art Gallery and Museum Quarterly Notes*, No. 31 (June 1912), p. 6. See also W.A. Maguire, *Living like a Lord: The Second Marquis of Donegall, 1769–1844* (Belfast, 1984).

10 *Banner of Ulster*, 27 and 30 May, 3 June, 1845.

11 Peadar Slattery, 'The Uses of Photography in Ireland, 1839–1900', University of Dublin, 3 Vols., 1991, Vol. 1, p. 8 (Ph.D. thesis).

12 *Belfast News-Letter*, 17 March 1854.

13 Stewart offered to use 'the new process of oil portrait by photography', claiming that 'the truthfulness of the photography' was retained in the painted portrait (Slattery, 'Uses of Photography', Vol. 1, pp. 13–14).

14 Slattery, 'Uses of Photography', Vol. 1, p. 13.

15 [Beatty], 'The science of photography', in *Dublin Journal*, 17 February 1858.

16 Slattery, 'Uses of Photography', Vol. 1, pp. 61–2.

Cartes and wet collodion: c. 1860–c. 1880

1 Slattery, 'Uses of Photography', Vol. 2, Appendix A.

2 W.A. Maguire, *Caught in Time: The Photographs of Alex Hogg of Belfast, 1870–1939* (Belfast, 1986), p. xix.

3 Slattery, 'Uses of Photography', Vol. 2, Appendix B.

4 *Industries of Ireland. Part 1. Belfast and the Towns of the North* (London, 1891); reprinted as part of *Industries of the North One Hundred Years Ago* (Belfast, 1986).

5 I am obliged to Jack Johnston for information about Hopper, and to Dr Brian Turner for information about Gribben.

6 See Oliver Matthews, *The Album of Carte-de-Visite and Cabinet Portrait Photographs, 1854–1914* (London, 1974).

7 Slattery, 'Uses of Photography', Vol. 2, p. 111; A. McClelland, *William Johnston of Ballykilbeg* (Lurgan, 1990).

8 Slattery, Vol. 2, pp. 139–42; for Jennings's Norfolk views see C.S. Middleton, *The Broadland Photographers* (Norwich, 1978). Selections of his work were published as tipped-in prints in *Photographs of Norfolk Broads and Rivers* (Norwich, 1890); in 1891 as autogravures of one hundred views entitled *Sun Pictures of the Norfolk Broads* (the volume was republished twice, on the last occasion by Jennings himself); and in 1895 in *Summer Holidays in North East England.* In 1911 he also published views of Surrey and Sussex.

9 *Belfast News-Letter*, 7 April 1859.

10 *Industries of the North*, p. 138.

11 Brian M. Walker and Hugh Dixon, *In Belfast Town, 1864–1880: Early Photographs from the Lawrence Collection* (Belfast, 1984).

12 See J. Sproule (ed.), *The Resources and Manufacturing Industry of Ireland, as Illustrated by the Exhibition of 1853* (Dublin [1853]).

13 *Belfast Working Men's Institute and Temperance Hall Exhibition Catalogue* (Belfast, 1872).

14 *Industries of the North*, p. 120. E.T. Church was possibly related to J.F. Church, 'Camp Photographic Gallery, Curragh Camp, Kildare' as he describes himself on a carte of *c.* 1875.

15 Welch Collection, Ulster Museum.

16 *Londonderry Sentinel*, 19 April 1864. I am indebted to Fred Logan for this reference.

17 Slattery, 'Uses of Photography', Vol. 1, p. 14.

18 Slattery, 'Uses of Photography', Vol. 2, Appendix M, pp. 162–3.

19 In addition to those in the Ulster Museum album, David Welch was almost certainly responsible for the views of Tempo Manor and village, taken about 1865, some of which were published in W.A. Maguire, *Heydays, Fair-days and Not-so-good Old Days: A Fermanagh Estate and Village in the Photographs of the Langham Family, 1890–1918* (Belfast, 1986).

20 *Armagh Guardian*, 24 March 1876. I am indebted to Desmond Fitzgerald for this reference.

21 See Frances Dimond and Roger Taylor, *Crown and Camera: The Royal Family and Photography, 1842–1910* (London, 1987), p. 218.

22 Slattery, 'Uses of Photography', Vol. 2, Appendix G; *Belfast News-Letter*, 18 May 1870.

Developing in all directions: 1880–1914

1 Slattery, 'Uses of Photography', Vol. 1, pp. 89 and 92.

2 Kate Newmann (comp.), *Dictionary of Ulster Biography* (Belfast, 1993), p. 15; Roger Dixon, 'Francis Joseph Bigger: Belfast's cultural Don Quixote', in *Ulster Folklife*, Vol. 32 (1997), pp. 40–7; Ulster Museum notes on the Bigger Collection, courtesy of Dr Vivienne Pollock.

3 Brian M. Walker, *Sentry Hill: An Ulster Farm and Family* (Belfast, 1981).

4 See Maguire, *Heydays, Fair-days and Not-so-good Old Days.*

5 Helen Lanigan Wood, *Enniskillen: Historic Images of an Island Town* (Belfast, 1990), p. 94.

6 Brian M. Walker, *Shadows on Glass: A Portfolio of Early Ulster Photography* (Belfast, 1976), pp. 8–19.

7 Walker, *Shadows on Glass*, pp. 56–65; Ulster Folk and Transport Museum note on the Rose Shaw Collection; Jack Johnston, *In the Days of the Clogher Valley: Photographs of the Clogher Valley and its Railway* (Belfast, 1987), p. ix.

8 Walker, *Shadows on Glass*, pp. 126–38.

9 *Industries of the North*, p. 128; information from Abernethy's grand-daughter, Mrs Johnston, 1987 and from his great grand-daughter Mrs J. Clarke.

10 *Industries of the North*, p. 156; information on the Glass family from Mrs Kyleen Clarke; Prionnsais Ó Gallachobhair, *History of Landlordism in Donegal* (Ballyshannon, 1962), p. 156; H.W. Massingham, *The Gweedore Hunt: A Story of English Justice in Ireland* (London, 1889). A police sergeant named Pratt had earlier taken scene-of-crime photographs at Gweedore (Slattery, 'Uses of Photography', Vol. 2, pp. 14–15).

11 Information about William Allison is taken mainly from his son's recollections of his father, courtesy of Professor Brian Walker; correspondence between Allison and the principal of the Technical College, Ulster Museum photographic archive, with acknowledgement to Dr Charles Ludlow.

12 Desmond Fitzgerald and Roger Weatherup, *The Way We Were: Historic Photographic from the Allison Collection* (Belfast, 1993), p. vi.

13 Recollections of James G. Little (1880–1970), courtesy of his son James M. Little, in the Ulster Museum photographic archive; obituary of James Little, *Belfast News-Letter*, 31 August, 1970.

14 *Illustrated Belfast* (Belfast, 1899), a guidebook produced for the British Christian Endeavour Conference, which met in the city that year.

15 Advertisement in Thomas Gaffikin, *Belfast Fifty Years Ago* (Belfast, 1894 reprint).

16 Information from Mrs Sheelagh Bell, a granddaughter of the artist. Theo Snoddy, *Dictionary of Irish Artists: Twentieth Century* (Dublin, 1996) quotes a *Belfast Telegraph* article by John Hewitt describing Douglas: 'A full-time professional [artist], a stoutish little man in knickerbockers with a red face and a snow-white moustache. His attitude to his craft was thoroughly Victorian; he set out to beat the camera.' No reference is made to his career as a photographer. His large portrait of the photographer William Abernethy is in fact a photograph over-painted in oils.

17 Walker, *Shadows on Glass*, pp. 76–87; and *Faces of the Past: A Photographic and Literary Record of Ulster, 1880–1915* (Belfast, 1974), pp. 11, 20, 24–5, 29, 31, 79, 84–5, 87, 92 and 100–1.

18 Recollections of the Lee family by Group Captain P.A. Lee, 1987, with observations by Dr D.B. McNeill. I am obliged to Dr McNeill for providing me with this material.

19 I am indebted to David Speers, Bushmills, for information about Merten and Francis; and to Dr Eileen Black for information about Bruno.

20 *Before I Forget . . .* , Journal of Poyntzpass and District Local History Society, No. VII (1994).

21 I am grateful to Jim Rankin of Randalstown for allowing me to use the fruits of his research into the career of Annie Booth. See Chapter 6 for further details about the effect of picture postcard publication.

22 I am obliged to Desmond Quail for bringing Henfrey to my attention and letting me see examples of his work, and to Tony Merrick for information about him.

Professional amateurs: Hogg, Welch and Green

1 A.R. Hogg, 'R.J. Welch – photographer', part of a composite article entitled 'Obituaries of R.J. Welch', in *Irish Naturalists' Journal*, Vol. 6 (1936–7), pp. 131–40. The other contributors were R. Ll. Praeger, A.W. Stelfox and J.W. Jackson. See E. Estyn Evans and Brian Turner, *Ireland's Eye: The Photographs of Robert John Welch* (Belfast, 1977), pp. 1–18.

2 Evans and Turner, *Ireland's Eye*, p. 1.

3 Evans and Turner, *Ireland's Eye*, p. 7. Welch's last commission from the Congested Districts Board was in June 1914. These prints, annotated by himself, are in the National Library of Ireland. See Noel Kissane (ed.), *Ex Camera, 1860–1960: Photographs from the Collections of the National Library of Ireland* (Dublin, 1990), pp. 25–6.

4 Dimond and Taylor, *Crown and Camera*, p. 213.

5 'Excursions Diary', Welch Collection archive, Ulster Museum.

6 John Scarry, *Monuments in the Past* (Dublin, 1991).

7 Evans and Turner, *Ireland's Eye*, p. 6.

8 Evans and Turner, *Ireland's Eye*, p. 6.

9 Praeger and Stelfox, in *Irish Naturalists' Journal*, Vol. 6, p. 136. Perfection was achieved at a price: Welch later blamed the recurrent rheumatism that plagued him on 'that 2 day work in the damp cloud Plant views & the 2 hours lying on wet ground to get the general view of the cliff & peak (free of cloud at top)' on Clare Island. Welch to Standen, 21 February 1922 (Welch archive, Ulster Museum).

10 Evans and Turner, *Ireland's Eye*, p. 18.

11 Stelfox, in *Irish Naturalists' Journal*, Vol. 6, p. 136.

12 Welch to Standen, 25 February 1922 (Welch archive, Ulster Museum).

13 Welch to Standen, 4 April 1922.

14 'Diary', Welch archive, Ulster Museum.

15 See W.A. Maguire, *Caught in Time*, for Hogg's career.

16 Maguire, *Caught in Time*, p. ix.

17 Maguire, *Caught in Time*, p. xx.

18 Maguire, *Caught in Time*, p. 126.

19 Maguire, *Caught in Time*, pp. 110–14.

20 The best published account of Green's career is T.K. Anderson, 'William Alfred Green FRSAI: the man and his photographs', in *Ulster Local Studies*, Vol. 13, No. 2 (1991), pp. 18–29. See also Walker, *Shadows on Glass*, pp 30–9.

21 Ulster Museum photographic archive.

22 Anderson, 'W.A. Green', pp. 25–6; Jane Crosbie, *A Tour of North Down, 1895–1925: Historic Photographs from the W.A. Green Collection* (Belfast, 1989) and *A Tour of the Ardes: 1910–1935: Historic Photographs of the Ards and North-east Down* (Belfast, 1990).

23 Anderson, 'W.A. Green', p. 22.

24 Information from school records, 1995, courtesy of the headmaster.

25 Oral information from Mr L. Symes, 1986.

Movers and shakers

1 Ulster Museum, Hogg archive.

2 The Lumière show had been presented in Dublin a few months earlier, on 20 April 1896 at the Star of Erin Variety Theatre (the Olympia).

3 James Doherty and Tom Thompson, *Standing Room Only: Memories of Belfast Cinemas* (Belfast, 1997), pp. 9–11.

4 I am indebted to John McCabe for his help in tracing the genealogy of the Hicks family, and to Tom Thompson for identifying essential sources for Hicks's cinematographic career.

5 Report of an interview entitled 'A Belfast cinematographer: Professor Kineto talks about himself and the Biorama', in *Ireland's Saturday Night*, 17 March 1900.

6 Liam O'Leary archive, National Library of Ireland, Dublin, with thanks to Bob Monks.

7 Kineto's book of press cuttings covers the years 1897–1909, with a few miscellaneous items of later date (including a photograph of him as an elderly man with a boy, presumably a grandson). I am greatly indebted to John Martin for letting me see and use this essential source material.

8 *Ireland's Saturday Night*, 21 September 1929.

9 I wish to acknowledge the help given by A.D. Coon's descendants, in particular his grandson Allen Coon. For a short published account of Coon's career, see John Foy, 'Allen Daniel Coon,

1867–1938: photographer and showman extraordinary', in *Picture Post Card Monthly*, No. 124 (August 1989), pp. 32–33.

10 Article by diarist 'Craig Brack' in the *Donegal Democrat*, 8 October 1976, prompted by a letter from Mrs Gladys Coon McCartney, the photographer's daughter.

11 Doherty and Thompson, *Standing Room Only*, p. 37.

12 Foy, 'A.D. Coon', p. 33.

13 Foy, 'A.D. Coon', p. 33.

Other developments: 1890–1939

1 See Rosenblum, *World History of Photography*, p. 280.

2 Edward Chandler, *Photography in Dublin During the Victorian Era* (Dublin [no date]), p. 18. Rosenblum illustrates a Joly process print dated 1898 (*World History of Photography*, p. 341).

3 See Bernard E. Jones (ed.), *The Encyclopaedia of Early Photography* (London, 1911, reprinted 1981) for a contemporary technical description.

4 *Irlande 1913: Clichés en couleur pris pour Monsieur Kahn par Mesdemoiselles Mespoulet et Mignon* (Paris, 1992). The Kahn collection is housed in the Museé Albert-Kahn (Départment des Hauts-de-Seine), 14 Rue du Port, 92100 Boulogne, Paris. I am indebted to J.C. Nolan for bringing this source to my attention.

5 Rosenblum, *World History of Photography*, pp. 612–15.

6 Chandler, *Photography in Dublin*, p. 19.

7 See Denise Webster, *A Whiff of Ulster from Old Cigarette Cards* (Belfast, 1975).

8 David Bigger and Terence McDonald, *In Sunshine or in Shadow: Photographs from the Derry Standard 1928–1939* (Belfast, 1990), p. v.

9 Malcom Brodie, *The Tele: A History of the Belfast Telegraph* (Belfast, 1995), p. 22.

10 Arthur Campbell, *Belfast and Beyond, Return Journey: 1936–1939* (Belfast, 1987).

11 See Frank Staff, *The Picture Postcard and its Origins* (London, 1966; revised edition 1979); and William Düval with Valerie Monahan, *Collecting Postcards in Colour, 1894–1914* (Poole, 1978).

12 Maguire, *Caught in Time*, p. xx.

13 M.J. Daunton, *The Post Office since 1840* (London, 1985), p. 80. These figures are taken from the Annual Reports of the Postmaster General.

14 Arthur Campbell, introduction, *Looking Back: 1939–60* (Belfast, 1989).

15 E. Estyn Evans, *Lyles Hill: A Late Neolithic Site in County Antrim* (Belfast, 1953), p. vii.

16 Brian Barton, *The Blitz: Belfast in the War Years* (Belfast, 1989), pp. 76–7.

17 *Militärgeographische Angaben über Irland, Süd-und Ostküste* (Berlin, 1941).

18 See John Hannavy, *The Victorian Professional Photographer* (Aylesbury, 1980), p. 5.

19 Rosenblum, *World History of Photography*, pp. 607 and 609–10.

Select bibliography

ANDERSON, T.K., 'William Alfred Green FRSAI: the man and his photographs', in *Ulster Local Studies*, Vol. 13, No. 2 (1991)

BIGGER, DAVID AND TERENCE MCDONALD, *In Sunshine or in Shadow: Photographs from the Derry Standard, 1928–1939* (Belfast, 1990)

CHANDLER, EDWARD, *Photography in Dublin during the Victorian Era* (Dublin, no date given, *c.* 1980)

CORCORAN, DOREEN, *A Tour of East Antrim: Historic Photographs from the W.A. Green Collection in the Ulster Folk and Transport Museum*(Belfast, 1990)

CROSBIE, JANE, *A Tour of North Down, 1895–1925: Historic Photographs from the W.A. Green Collection at the Ulster Folk and Transport Museum* (Belfast, 1989)

— *A Tour of the Ardes, 1910–1935: Historic Photographs of the Ards and North-east Down from the W.A. Green Collection at the Ulster Folk and Transport Museum* (Belfast, 1990)

DOHERTY, JAMES AND TOM THOMPSON, *Standing Room Only: Memories of Belfast Cinemas* (Belfast, 1997)

EVANS, E. ESTYN AND BRIAN TURNER, *Ireland's Eye:The Photographs of Robert John Welch* (Belfast, 1977)

FITZGERALD, DESMOND AND ROGER WEATHERUP, *The Way We Were: Historic Armagh Photographs from the Allison Collection* (Belfast, 1993)

FOY, JOHN, 'Allen Daniel Coon, 1867–1938: photographer and showman extraordinary', in *Picture Post Card Monthly*, No. 124, August 1989

GERNSHEIM, HELMUT, *The Origins of Photography* (London, 1982)

GERNSHEIM, HELMUT AND ALISON, *The History of Photography from the Earliest Use of the Camera Obscura in the Eleventh Century up to 1914* (Oxford, 1955; 2nd ed., London, 1969)

HANNAVY, JOHN, *The Victorian Professional Photographer* (Aylesbury, 1980)

HICKEY, KIERAN, *The Light of Other Days: Irish Life at the Turn of the Century in the Photographs of Robert French* (London, 1973)

HILL, MYRTLE AND VIVIENNE POLLOCK, *Women of Ireland: Image and Experience, c. 1880–1920* (Belfast, 1993)

Irlande 1913: Clichés en couleur pris pour Monsieur Kahn par Mesdemoiselles Mespoulet et Mignon (Paris, 1992)

JOHNSTON, JACK, *In the Days of the Clogher Valley: Photographs of the Clogher Valley and its Railway* (Belfast, 1987)

KISSANE, NOEL (ed.), *Ex Camera 1860–1960: Photographs from the Collections of the National Library of Ireland* (Dublin, 1990)

McCAUGHAN, MICHAEL, 'The first Irish photographer – Francis Beatty of Belfast', in *Ulster Folk and Transport Museum Yearbook, 1981–85* (Belfast, 1985)
— *Steel Ships and Iron Men: Shipbuilding in Belfast 1894–1912. The Historic Photograph Collection at the Ulster Folk and Transport Museum* (Belfast, 1989)
—*The Birth of the Titanic* (Belfast, 1998)

McMAHON, THEO, *Old Monaghan, 1785–1995* (Monaghan, 1995)

MAGUIRE, W.A., *Caught in Time: The Photographs of Alexander Hogg of Belfast, 1870–1939* (Belfast, 1986)
— *Heydays, Fair-days and Not-so-good Old Days: A Fermanagh Estate and Village in the Photographs of the Langham Family, 1890–1918* (Belfast, 1986)

MATTHEWS, OLIVER, *The Album of Carte-de-Visite and Cabinet Portrait Photographs, 1854–1914* (London, 1974)

RANKIN, J. FRED, *Wish You Were Here* (Bushmills, 1995). Amateur Photographs of the 1930s by W.J. Rankin ARPS.

ROSENBLUM, NAOMI, *A World History of Photography* (New York, 1984)

STAFF, FRANK, *The Picture Postcard and its Origins* (London, 1966)

WALKER, BRIAN M., *Faces of the Past: A Photographic and Literary Record of Ulster, 1880–1915* (Belfast, 1974)
— *Shadows on Glass: A Portfolio of Early Ulster Photography* (Belfast, 1976)
— *Sentry Hill: An Ulster Farm and Family* (Belfast, 1981)

WALKER, BRIAN M and HUGH DIXON, *No Mean City: Belfast 1880–1904 in the Photographs of Robert French* (Belfast, 1983)
— *In Belfast Town, 1864–1880: Early Photographs from the Lawerence Collection* (Belfast, 1984)

WOOD, HELEN LANIGAN, *Enniskillen: Historic Images of an Island Town* (Belfast, 1990)

Index

Page numbers in italics refer to illustrations.